MASCULINITY LESSONS

A *Feminist Formations* Reader

Masculinity Lessons

Rethinking Men's and Women's Studies

EDITED BY **James V. Catano and Daniel A. Novak**

The Johns Hopkins University Press
Baltimore

The Johns Hopkins University Press
2715 North Charles Street
Baltimore, Maryland 21218-4363
www.press.jhu.edu

All chapters in this book were originally published in the *National Women's Studies Association Journal* in the following issues: chapter 1, Spring 1989; chapter 2, Summer 1995; chapter 3, Spring 1995; chapter 4, Spring 1998; chapter 5, Spring 2003; chapters 6 and 14, Summer 2008; chapter 7, Spring 2000; chapters 8 and 9, Fall 2000; chapters 10 and 17, Spring 2009; chapter 11, Fall 1996; chapter 12, Summer 2003; chapter 13, Fall 2003; chapter 15, Fall 2005; chapter 16, Fall 2006.

ISBN 13: 978-1-4214-0224-6 (hc)
ISBN 10: 1-4214-0224-6 (hc)
ISBN 13: 978-1-4214-0225-3 (pbk)
ISBN 10: 1-4214-0225-4 (pbk)

Library of Congress Control Number: 2011921879

Special discounts are available for bulk purchases of this book. For more information, please contact Special Sales at 410-516-6936 or specialsales@press.jhu.edu.

The Johns Hopkins University Press uses environmentally friendly book materials, including recycled text paper that is composed of at least 30 percent post-consumer waste, whenever possible.

To Michelle A. Massé and Daphne S. Cain

Contents

Acknowledgments

This project would not have been possible without the work of a support-ive and far-reaching community of gender scholars. On the most imme-diate level, we could not have started or conducted this work without the generous support of our extraordinary colleagues in the Women's and Gender Studies Program at Louisiana State University. Nor, obviously, would this volume exist without the scores of scholars and editors at the *National Women's Studies Association Journal* who produced the inno-vative research that fills the pages of the collection. Particular thanks go to Becky Ropers-Huilman, editor of *Feminist Formations*, for providing the initial impetus and inspiration for this volume. Special thanks also to Collette Morrow for her advice and guidance through the early and inter-esting life of this volume, and in particular for her help in considering the audience for this book. To that initial impetus must be added the ensuing support provided by Fred L. Gardaphé, Michael S. Kimmel, and Elaine Showalter. Suzanne Flinchbaugh, acquisitions editor at the Johns Hopkins University Press, has always been the best of advocates for this volume. We have also benefited from the excellent editorial support and advice of Jeremy Horsefield and Juliana McCarthy, as well as help on the index from Brigitte McCray and Megan Atwood. We also have the great pleasure of thanking Gerard Byrne and Viaduck Video for the wonderful photograph used on the book cover. The image provides its own visual accompaniment to the arguments made within. Finally, but never lastly, we would like to acknowledge Michelle A. Massé and Daphne S. Cain. Their support cannot be measured by the confines of this book.

MASCULINITY LESSONS

Introduction

JAMES V. CATANO AND DANIEL A. NOVAK

The history of Masculinity Studies has hardly been without controversy, not a little of it due to certain strands within the discipline, defined in its broadest sense. Certain ways of thinking about men, such as the Iron John movement, did little to foster connections between feminist theorizing and the study of masculinity. In light of such reactionary attitudes, a common response both within and without gender-focused studies was, "Where (some shortened the question simply to) *does* the study of masculinity belong" in Gender Studies in general and Women's Studies in particular? For those reading the 1988/89 inaugural volume of the *National Women's Studies Association Journal* (*NWSAJ*), the answer was—and is—very clear. From the beginning, the study of masculinity has been integral both to the mission of the *NWSAJ* and to its role in shaping the development of Women's and Gender Studies.

In that inaugural volume, *NWSAJ* published the review that opens this collection: Margaret O'Brien's "The Making of Masculinities" (1989). This and the other reviews collected here demonstrate that the conversations and negotiations outlined in their discussions are ongoing and fluid, as Judith Gardiner again makes clear in 2003 with her *NWSAJ* review of masculinity texts and their place in Women's Studies. We are, to paraphrase the title of yet a third review not included here, continually in the midst of "shifting disciplines in Women's Studies" (Elizabeth Birmingham, 2007), and one important part of that activity is the regular discussion of masculinity.

Certainly, academic conversations about men and masculinity had not just begun when *NWSAJ* published O'Brien in 1989. As Women's Studies has always known and argued (against), masculinity—or at least men—has always been assumed to be the norm and by default the focus of much professional and popular conversation.

But being the focus of attention and being the subject of analysis, being the assumed content and being the object of interpretation are not the same thing. We need only remember that among too many men (and some women) some of the loudest reactions to Women's Studies are better described as backlash than as conversation. The situation went from men and their behavior being the unquestioned focus of attention to men claiming that they were having Women's Studies and feminist readings of masculinity "shoved down their throats."

Setting aside for the moment the obvious homophobia and misogyny of that still ubiquitous phrase, what O'Brien's review signals, in both its discussion and the three texts it treats, is an early attempt to create a useful conversation within Women's Studies about men and masculinity. That attempt to merge interests and approaches was already underway, of course, at the time her essay appeared. As O'Brien makes clear, texts such as Harry Brod's *The Making of Masculinities: The New Men's Studies* were already collecting essays (written primarily by academic scholars) interested in insights and methodologies that had been part of Women's Studies from the 1960s to the mid-1980s. The goal of these scholars was to adapt approaches to women's issues to the particular study of masculinity.

Thus, if the initial "first wave" of Masculinity Studies (to stretch the analogy a bit) gathered itself around a reactionary attempt to raise the gates and rattle the scepters of Iron Johns everywhere, the second wave attempted to delve more analytically into the question of men and masculinity. This second wave was never really essentialist, but an underlying concern with "balancing the books" remained, suggesting that studying masculinity was one way to give men their due.

This second methodological strain of what can legitimately be called Men's Studies still harbors an element of woundedness, of trying to find value in behaviors and attitudes that seem under attack. While hypermasculinity is no longer seen as an unquestionably positive form of behavior in this phase, there remains an ongoing attempt not only to understand society's "making of masculinities" but also to justify and value what masculinity should and "is known to" be from within the male experience.

There are admittedly problems within that lingering concern. Yet it needs to be stated that such second-wave approaches, in league with the best of consciousness-raising, scholarly analysis, and other related tools, have proved useful to the thoughtful study of masculinity—and to the pursuit of Women's and Gender Studies, Queer Theory, and Cultural Studies as well.

At the same time, there is now occurring what might be seen as a third wave in Masculinity Studies. Here the full import of gender is being brought to the fore, with the usefully paradoxical result that masculinity is itself no longer readily understood in the negative. Gardiner's review underscores the shift: as concerns in Women's Studies with identity and performance reach full development, and as masculinity sheds its essentialist alignment with sex and becomes a true gender concept, it is free to be considered—and even pursued—as part of a broad spectrum of behaviors and sexualities evidenced by men and women.

NWSAJ has proven itself once again if not prophetic then at least prescient regarding this ongoing movement within Women's, Gender, and Masculinity Studies. In reading the articles gathered here, we become aware that their importance lies not solely in what they tell us about historical developments in the study of masculinity but in their applicability to the contemporary social dynamic. From O'Brien's initial foray in 1989 to Fauzia Erfan Ahmed's 2008 discussion of masculinity in Bangladesh, a wide-ranging conversation about masculinity has been carried out in the pages of the *NWSAJ*—to the betterment of Women's, Gender, and Masculinity Studies and to the growth and development of forms of masculinity itself.

The sections into which we have divided this collection reflect our sense of *NWSAJ*'s contribution to this impressive variety of fields, as well as the integral role that the study of masculinity has played in Women's Studies in particular. We begin with a section entitled "Engaging the Issue: Masculinity in Women's and Gender Studies," focusing on the place of masculinity in Women's Studies as a discipline and as a pedagogical praxis. Margaret O'Brien's review of three texts published in 1987 demonstrates a variety of approaches applied to masculinity (from consciousness-raising to Marxism), growing interest in the study of men and masculinity, and awareness of the kinds of texts available for courses. Her comments on Harry Brod's anthology *The Making of Masculinities*, ranging as it does from biology and sociology to literature and history, are particularly suggestive of the wide disciplinary view already in the process of being established.

Of further note for our concerns here is the question with which O'Brien closes her review: "For readers of the *NWSA Journal* the[se] books raise many questions about the relative autonomy of women's studies and men's studies. Should each keep its separate identity, organizations, journals, and educational programs, or should some amalgamation take place?" While O'Brien expresses uncertainty about the answer ("No immediate answers are apparent"), her question both implies that separation between "men's studies" and "women's studies" is not necessary and prefigures a shift in and expansion of traditional Women's Studies to Women's *and* Gender Studies—a shift marked both in the scholarship traced in our volume and in the classroom.

In some cases, that approach may be literally modeled in pedagogical practice. Diane Suter and David Schweickart's essay "The Biology and Philosophy of Race and Sex: A Course" offers a practical guide to both team and interdisciplinary teaching in Gender Studies. Taught by a female biologist and a male philosophy professor, students in the course read texts such as Simon LeVay's *The Sexual Brain* alongside Simon de Beauvior's *The Second Sex*. The goal was to challenge students to think about the fluidity of gender categories not only in philosophy and critical theory but also in biology: "The point of this exercise was to convince students that, even biologically speaking, sexual identity is far more ambiguous than is commonly supposed" (p. 45). Despite the diverse disciplinary, racial, and gender backgrounds of their students, the authors report positive reactions and outcomes for a wide range of their students.

Focusing more on the (often defensive) reactions of men who encounter feminism in the classroom, Sue Cataldi's "Reflections on 'Male Bashing' " explores how teachers can (or should) address that sense of woundedness noted above—here couched in the perception that courses in Women's Studies are notable for their "chilly climate" for men. Countering that sense of personal attack, Cataldi "unabashedly" admits that "the work feminists do is destructive. We cannot create a new social order without destroying some of the old. . . . Resistance against us is formidable. I think we should *not* deceive ourselves into believing that what we are doing is not a fight, is not a struggle. But, personally, I do not think we have even *begun* to bash" (p. 22).

As Cataldi notes, the charge of "male bashing" perversely displaces literal violence *against* women into linguistic violence directed *by* women. For their part, Jayne E. Stake, Jeanne Sevelius, and Sarah Hanly's quantitative study, "Student Responsiveness to Women's and Gender Studies Classes: The Importance of Initial Student Attitudes and Classroom Relationships," notes success in changing student attitudes—a success that has "not been seen in non-WGS students even when researchers have controlled for relevant variables" (p. 74). While in the past students have expressed frustration with the Gender Studies curriculum and even demonstrated a "*decrease* in egalitarian attitudes," in this study the authors found that their "students reported more change in their awareness of sexism, more feelings of empowerment, and less anger and distress" (p. 89).

Moving out of particular academic practices in addressing masculinity, our second section, "Embodying Masculinity: Science and Society," is made up of essays that address the complex relationships gathered together within wider cultural ideologies of the body, gender, and sexuality. Because Queer Theory has historically engaged in a sustained critique of the normative standards of heterosexual masculinity, much of our focus here is on cultural readings of homosexuality and transgender identity. Yet this section, like the collection as a whole, is methodologically diverse—representative of the interdisciplinary nature of Women's Studies in general and the *NWSAJ* in particular.

Such interdisciplinarity, when matched with an expansiveness in what qualifies as a "proper" topic for Gender Studies, produces what Cressida Heyes's review essay refers to as "a new challenge to the inclusivity, scope, and terms of 'women's studies'" (p. 101). The impact and importance of such rethinking are evident in Celia Roberts's "Biological Behavior? Hormones, Psychology, and Sex," Bernice L. Hausman's "Do Boys Have to Be Boys? Gender, Narrativity, and the John/Joan Case," and Doris T. Chang's "Reading *Sex and Temperament* in Taiwan: Margaret Mead and Postwar Taiwanese Feminism." All these essays provide varied approaches to the question of masculinity, yet all are united by serious engagement with various forms of scientific research and the sexual politics of science. Chang, for example, explores Margaret Mead's anti-essentialism, while also critiquing her Westernized anthropological method and its ideological assumptions about gender roles in New Guinea during the first third of the twentieth century. In addition, Chang offers an informative summary of that thinking as it was reworked and represented to an Asian community in the late 1970s—and the direct impact of that thought on Taiwanese politics and policy in the latter part of the century.

Addressing masculinity from another angle, Celia Roberts attempts to chart a "middle way" between reductionist essentialism and a rejection of the role of biology in gender difference and sexuality. Following Spivak, Roberts argues for a shift away from simply critiquing essentialism and toward an analysis of the political dividends and uses of essentialism. Exploring similar territory, Bernice Hausman uses narrative theory to bridge the biological and the social in her study of intersexed individuals and a famous case of twin sex reassignment. She argues for the necessary and inevitable intermingling of bodies and stories: "gender can never just be an effect of biological processes, but is always part of a dialectical engagement of interpretation and story-making—that is, of narrativity—by specific subjects in concrete biosocial circumstances." For Hausman, "rereading the biological signifiers of sex can offer us the starting point for truly alternative stories of sexed identity" (p. 148).

The essays in the next two sections analyze enduring cultural narratives that refuse to die. Dividing masculine behaviors into the home or domestic sphere and the wider arena of public and institutional spaces, the essays in both "Performing Social Expectations" sections address stock figures and stereotypes from our cultural imaginary so as to challenge basic assumptions about the roles stereotypes play in representing masculinity.

Tiffany Joseph's essay addresses a common theme in the second half of the book and in masculinity as a whole: the role that violence and trauma play in gender expectations. One of the most common theaters for acting out and therefore representing such violence and trauma is, of course, the theater of war and its aftermath. As Joseph notes, "The time after any war, therefore, is often spent reorganizing domestic and economic spheres to conform to gender ideals" (p. 241), and her essay examines the fictional post–World War I setting of Fitzgerald's *Tender is the Night* as a source for discussing these motifs. Working with the novel's complex of characters, Joseph explores "the implications of gender performance from the context of war and postwar trauma in order to examine the intersections of gender and trauma" (p. 243).

Addressing a more contemporary setting and a different medium, Diana Shoos's "Representing Domestic Violence: Ambivalence and Difference in *What's Love Got to Do with It*" pursues concerns related to those of Joseph even as she echoes Cataldi's earlier point concerning masculinity's real versus imagined violence. Shoos explores the "invisibility" of abused women in contemporary culture through a reading of Brian Gibson's 1993 biopic about Tina and Ike Turner. Her complex analysis traces the causes of abuse to race, class, and the cultural construction of masculinity and desire: "the film's focus on a black man and woman whose musical success became their ticket out of poor, working-class families provides the opportunity for an analysis of the ways in which larger ambivalences about race and class become caught up with and support those that circulate within discursive formulations of abuse" (p. 225–26).

Cultural representations of race, class, and violence are also the focus of Linda Pershing's " 'His Wife Seized His Prize and Cut It to Size': Folk and Popular Commentary on Lorena Bobbitt." This essay explores how the media represented an act (for them *the* act) of violence by a woman against a man—Lorena Bobbitt's penile castration of her husband after years of abuse. Pershing focuses on two (among the many) effects produced by this event. The first was a highly visible identification of "male identity, power, and aggression" with the—here literally wounded—penis. As one writer noted, "John Wayne Bobbitt has become evangelical in the cause not only of *his* penis but of *the* penis." While general reaction to the Bobbitt case suggested the ongoing conflation of the penis/phallus, it paradoxically also served to clarify the role of the latter, making responses to and representations of Lorena Bobbitt (both mainstream and feminist) "emblematic of unresolved issues arising from current battles over identity politics" (p. 207).

If Pershing's essay suggests a certain intransigence of ideological constructs within masculinity, for her part Fauzia Erfan Ahmed argues for the possibility of changing these constructs in order to produce tangible economic effects in the developing world. Ahmed focuses on the Nobel Prize–winning Grameen Bank and its program for providing small loans to women in Bangladesh. Her essay points out the failure on the part of analysts to take into account the role of male relatives in limiting the economic opportunities of their wives. Arguing for the vital importance of "transforming men and masculinities," she suggests the use of "high-minded" men in workshops on masculinity to help alter the behavior of abusive husbands and foster both economic empowerment and social change. Ahmed makes clear that "the distinction between men and masculinity" is not merely an academic or theoretical concern; it carries real implications "important for practice [that can] lead to specific recommendations for practitioners and policymakers" (p. 289).

Such real-world implications of gender ideology, identity politics, and the stereotypes they often depend on are also the subject of the essays in the final section, "Performing Social Expectations: The Public Stage." Focused on the "case" of the Iraq war, these essays study the question of how stereotypes of masculinity are in play outside of the confines of the domestic sphere, portraying masculinity as quite literally a matter of national and international concern. In doing so, they demonstrate the continuing importance of Masculinity Studies for an increasingly diverse range of issues: global economics, technology, political negotiation, national interests, terrorism.

Discussing the United States' "domestic" as well as foreign policies, Carol Mason's "The Hillbilly Defense: Culturally Mediating U.S. Terror at Home and Abroad" demonstrates how newly created icons, Jessica Lynch, Lynndie England (of Abu Ghraib fame), and Eric Rudolph (the pro-life domestic terrorist), are represented as Appalachian "hillbillies" to perform ideological work in the public forum: "Defending America as a civilized nation by scapegoating Appalachians for 'uncivilized' behaviors or events [strategically redeploys familiar stereotypes] of Appalachian life, in which resistance to modern ways is alternately applauded and disdained" (p. 315). Whether the typing is used to morph domestic terrorist Rudolph into a folk hero or to transform aberrant masculinity at Abu Ghraib into "hillbilly" female sexuality run amok, Mason argues that "in the war on terror, such gendered stereotypes are called up again and again to steer the public away from thinking that any such transgressions or negotiations between civilized and uncivilized, humane and inhumane behavior are systemic" (p. 314).

Like Mason's essay, Mary Ann Tétreault's work suggests the contemporaneity and urgency of issues regarding masculinity—particularly questions of sadomasochistic dominance and violence. Working within a context of "orientalism" and its links to "the politics of the gaze" (p. 324), her essay also looks at Abu Ghraib, analyzing photographs and their place in construction of a masculinity that seems to come distressingly full circle in its enactment of degradation as a means of self-definition. While Tétreault focuses on violent performances of masculinity incited by the rhetoric and practices of the "war on terror," Stacey L. Mayhall's "Uncle Sam Wants You to Trade, Invest, and Shop! Relocating the Battlefield in the Gendered Discourses of the Pre- and Early Post-9/11 Period" explores the way in which the rhetoric of war, masculinity, and patriotism was applied to economic behavior after 9/11.

Drawing on Connell's work on masculinity and gender, Mayhall demonstrates that "[i]n the post-9/11 environment, the use of gender-coded images and language provided an important way for those individuals seeking to influence social, political, and economic responses to 9/11 to encourage desired behavior from men and women consistent with the dominant forms of masculinity and femininity" (p. 338–39). Efforts to induce such behavior were rarely subtle. Posters linked investors to first responders such as firemen and policemen. Images of Osama bin Laden sported captions that read, "He wants you to sell." Arguing that such imagery "at once powerfully located the dynamism of the American economy in the hands of masculinized, patriotic investors, while it relied on the image of the racialized other of Osama bin Laden to provide the impetus for that dynamism," Mayhall demonstrates just how central the rhetoric of gender and masculinity is to understanding contemporary geopolitical questions and issues.

As one of the most recent essays in this collection, Mayhall's contribution exemplifies the complexity and scope of contemporary work in Masculinity Studies—work that focuses less on men themselves and more on the gendered category of masculinity and its impact on men, women, and society in general. At the same time, all the essays in this collection also demonstrate how reading masculinity in relation to and from within Women's and Gender Studies provides particular insight about gender issues for the disciplines themselves. Throughout its history, the *NWSAJ* has been and remains central to these interrelated conversations. As these essays show, the journal has never been content to merely record or comment on developments; it has been a driving force for innovation in the field. This volume bears witness to that belief, and to the continued benefits to be gained from its pursuit.

PART I **Engaging the Issue: Masculinity and Women's and Gender Studies**

CHAPTER ONE

Making Masculinities
Book Reviews

MARGARET O'BRIEN

The Making of Masculinities: The New Men's Studies edited by
Harry Brod. Winchester, Massachusetts: Unwin Hyman, 1987,
346 pp., $39.95 hardcover, $14.95 paper.

*The Gender of Oppression: Men, Masculinity, and the Critique of
Marxism* by Jeff Hearn. New York: St. Martin's Press, 1987, 239 pp.,
$29.95 hardcover.

The Horned God: Feminism and Men as Wounding and Healing by
John Rowan. New York: Routledge, Chapman & Hall, 1987, 155 pp.,
$13.95 paper.

These three books, one American and two British, are indicative of the
growing academic inquiry into the position and experience of men. Since
the mid-1960s, in line with a heightened interest in sex and gender issues
in general, the number of social scientific articles published on male sex
roles has burgeoned. The books under review here seek to continue the
exercise of taking men into account while also offering reconceptualiza-
tions of pre-existing research. As Tim Carrigan, Robert W. Connell, and
John Lee in Harry Brod's collection, *The Making of Masculinities*, point
out: "Though most social science is indeed about men, good quality research that brings masculinity into focus is rare." The intention of the
books is to be proactive rather than reactive to feminist and women's studies agendas, although all are concerned that they not be perceived as
anti-feminist. Jeff Hearn, in *The Gender of Oppression*, and John Rowan,
in *The Horned God*, in particular, see their writing as being by men for
men—"a men's critique of ourselves"; however, it is noticeable that worry
about "the women's question" permeates all three books.

Although operating within very different theoretical frameworks, what
Jeff Hearn and John Rowan's books have in common is a personal account
of an encounter with feminism. Here lies their strength. Both provide
useful documentation, from an insider's perspective, of the early days
of the antisexist men's movement in the United Kingdom. Reading the
books in tandem is illuminating as Hearn's Marxist roots enable him to
describe the influence of leftist groups while Rowan's humanistic growth-
psychology orientation provides a complementary description of those
men interested in therapy. Rowan's account is especially engaging.

In the early 1970s, John Rowan's wife found feminism. Initially, he was
"baffled" by her involvement. He tried to listen but would find himself

"criticising her logic, her motives, her sense of balance." Eventually she persuaded him to join a men's group. This group was one of the early men's liberation groups in the U.K., and in 1972, the time Rowan joined, its members were arguing about a name: "Should it be 'Men Against Sexism,' 'Men's Liberation' or 'Unbecoming Men?' " The political disagreements and resulting fragmentation that so beset early feminism were also to be found in the men's movement. Rowan describes the pain of discovering his "patriarchal and oppressive consciousness" as "wounding" and argues that all men have to come to terms with this discovery in order to move toward less oppressive relationships. For Rowan the stage of "wounding" was then followed by a series of "healing" experiences. The conscious-raising activities of men's groups followed by "unconscious-raising" in therapy provided the contexts for the early phases of Rowan's healing process. He is candid about the impact of these experiences on his personal life; for example, in the early stage of his involvement in men's groups, Rowan was in effect an absent father to his four children. "It later seemed very sad . . . that I missed their childhood so much, that I took so little interest in them. At the time I was enjoying myself so much that it didn't seem to matter." Notwithstanding this refreshing honesty, the self-centeredness communicated by the aside is an underlying current in the whole book.

The later stages of Rowan's healing process are more problematic, at least for this reader. To help contest patriarchy at a deep symbolic level, Rowan finally turns to women-centered witchcraft in the name of the Great Goddess. One function of this (pagan) Goddess is to enable Rowan to "suck off Her . . . or to plug into Her," rather than drain the energy of individual females in the manner he perceives most men doing. She is joined, in Rowan's symbolic system, by a male subordinate—a sort of renaissance nonsexist male—the "Horned God" of the book's title. Rowan argues that the combination of these deities will allow contemporary men to learn about female power without losing male qualities and to move men and women toward a postpatriarchal world. The exact mechanism by which this process takes place is rather unclear, and towards the end Rowan's argument veers toward romantic idealism.

Hearn's dialectical materialist analysis of men and masculinity offers an opposing viewpoint but indeed can be criticized for leaving out the symbolic and unconscious areas Rowan so adventurously covers. In this collection of papers written over a ten-year period, Hearn attempts to critique "malestream" Marxism by exploring the gender of oppression. He contends that Marxism, like much social theorizing, tends to be more concerned with what people do, especially in the workplace, than with who people are.

> Social theory analyses what men do, particularly what work they do, and then equating all that with "economic relations," "economy," or "(economic) classes."

> Sometimes the equation is made, less satisfactorily still, with "humans" or "society". . . . Following such conflations it may or may not be pointed out that women sometimes do different things, that is, are "non-men." (p. 12)

Feminists and others have spent many years showing the poverty of such a blinkered approach to the study of women's experience, and in this book Hearn attempts the same exercise for men. He seeks to problematize the category man and introduce the domain of masculinity into social science, especially Marxist, discourse. The author covers a range of areas: men's professional roles in the management of people, men's studies, theories of patriarchy and reproduction, the position of men as fathers in families. A major part of the book is taken up with developing Mary O'Brien's ideas in *The Politics of Reproduction* (New York: Methuen, 1983) to take account of the specificity of male experience. A useful section concerns Hearn's analysis of the concept of patriarchy. He makes the distinction between "collective men," an oppressive gender class, and "individual men" who have a degree of agency and so may or may not be oppressive. According to Hearn, in order to contest patriarchy men should engage at both the individual and collective level; becoming "soft fathers, liberal professionals, or kind policemen" is not enough. Male participation in campaigns for better quality child care as well as sharing child care in the home, for Hearn, demonstrate more serious and legitimate antipatriarchal activity.

Most problematic about this book is the language used to describe and analyze interrelationships between men and women, men and children, indeed between humans in general. While offering a critique of production-based Marxism, Hearn himself utilizes an economistic work-speak in his account of subtle human relations. Child care becomes "child-work," masturbation becomes "self-sexual work," behavior becomes "practice." Indeed, the world of employment and the public sphere provide the root metaphor for most of the text. Labor-powers crop up everywhere—sexual labor-power, biological labor-power, generative labor-power, violent labor-power. Hearn finds it hard to throw off the mantle of reductionist Marxism.

The final text under consideration is Harry Brod's edited collection *The Making of Masculinities*. This is a wide-ranging interdisciplinary book with contributions from literature, sociology, psychology, biology, and history. Its purpose is to introduce the study of men to gender studies students, and as such it provides an excellent overview of contemporary American thinking on this topic. Brod argues a convincing case for the pursuit of men's studies.

> In inverse fashion to the struggle in women's studies to establish the objectivity of women's experiences and thereby validate the legitimacy of women's experiences as women, much of men's studies struggles to establish the

subjectivity of men's experiences and thereby validate the legitimacy of men's experiences as men. (p. 6)

He is very aware of the politically sensitive nature of men's studies and of some feminists' suspicion that the exercise is yet another male takeover bid. In the book Brod outlines a male- and a female-identified rationale for men's studies. The "male-identified" argument centers around the intrinsic physical and psychological hazards of current male roles. Demonstrating the personal cost of power, Brod suggests, can in some way enable men to ally with women against a patriarchal order. For those skeptical of such male altruism, Brod puts forward a "female-identified" rationale for men's studies. He suggests that knowledge is powerful and knowledge of "the enemy" is empowering.

The book is divided into five sections. The first part consists of state-of-the-art overviews. Joseph Pleck on the rise and fall of the concept of male sex-role identity, Harry Brod on men's studies, and an exploration of sociological work on masculinity from three Australian contributors, Carrigan, Connell, and Lee. The latter article offers a particularly interesting account of the changing nature of masculinities utilizing Gramscian theory. Like Pleck, they reject the moribund notion of one male sex role and invoke the concept of hegemonic masculinity, which enables a lucid analysis of the place of men in industrialized societies. The rest of the volume is organized around sections on history, work, social and biological bonding, and literature. The quality of the chapters is in the main good, although the balance of topics is rather uneven; for example, both biological aspects of masculinity and the loves of Byron are each given one chapter. Louis Crompton's study of Byron, however, does throw up useful insights on homosexuality in a hostile environment. The book is strong in its coverage of heterosexual male friendship with interesting chapters by Drury Sherrod on the problems and possibilities of close male relationships, a more critical stance on myths of male friendship by Dorothy Hammond and Alta Jablow, and a detailed case study of male attachment in nineteenth-century America. New ways of conceptualizing male friendship are emerging as the first fruits of men's studies.

All three books will be of great interest to students of gender relations. In distinctive ways and from diverse traditions, each documents the current range of men's studies. For readers of the *NWSA Journal* the books raise many questions about the relative autonomy of women's studies and men's studies. Should each keep its separate identity, organizations, journals, and educational programs, or should some amalgamation take place? No immediate answers are apparent.

CHAPTER TWO

Reflections on "Male Bashing"

SUE L. CATALDI

As a feminist philosopher and teacher of women's studies, I am both interested in and disturbed by the expression "male bashing." In analyzing this term and the uses to which it is put, this essay explores the following questions: What does "male bashing" mean? What, if anything, is wrong with it? Is it true that feminists and women's studies courses typically "bash men"? And if they don't, why have they acquired a reputation for doing so? Why do so many students—female and male—come into our courses wondering whether we will?

Is the surfacing of this expression part of the backlash against feminism? What can we learn from attempts to characterize the women's movement as a bashing of males? Finally, how, as feminists, should we respond to this criticism? Are there senses in which it is justified, and are there senses in which it is not?

To "bash" means to violently strike with a heavy, crushing blow. Colloquially, it connotes an indiscriminate (a random, confused) lashing out and also suggests that the staking of this blow is unfair, undeserved, or prejudiced. Sometimes the bashing is physical—as in "gay bashing"—when persons are violently attacked or mercilessly beaten because of their membership in a groups. Sometimes the word "bashing" indicates verbal abuse—a form of unjust criticism or condemnation, on the order of scapegoating—when one (convenient) group is made to bear the blame for the crimes, or the misfortunes, of others. Just a while ago "Japanese bashing" was in vogue. To bash the Japanese meant to unfairly blame them for the state of our economy, when we have only ourselves to blame. This second kind of bashing appears to involve unjustly denouncing the members of a group, who are really innocent victims.

As for the first, or physical, type of bashing, it is simply false that most or all feminists "bash men." While it is true that feminists are stereotyped as man-hating, aggressive females in a society that values the trait of aggression in males and devalues it in us, women do not, as a rule, tend to be violently assaultive, they are not traditionally bash*ers*. They are bash*ees*, so to speak, as we unfortunately know from the burgeoning numbers of women violently assaulted by men in our society. I find it interesting that these actual physical assaults on women are not, though they certainly can be, characterized as "female bashing."

Because it is false, generally, that women bash men (in the way that gays are bashed), the word "bashing" in the expression "male bashing" is evidently not supposed to be interpreted in its physical or literal sense. It is, however, important to realize that the use of such a loaded term can nevertheless avail itself of and hyperbolically exploit the ambiguities I have just discussed. By conjuring up images of abused men "bashed" by women and casting women in the role of bashers, it reverses what actually happens. This table turning can then operate, perniciously, as a form of victim blaming and as a means of exaggerating the seventy of any harm done to men who are, supposedly verbally, "bashed." Another shady reason for using this expression and co-opting its image of brutality is, I suspect, to lead us into thinking that the "male bashing" women supposedly do is relevantly similar or equivalent to—or perhaps (since "bash" seems to me to be a stronger word than "batter") even worse than—what men do to women. (Perhaps use of this term also means to suggest, through innuendo, as it does when we speak of Japanese bashing, that women have only themselves to blame for the state of their subordination.) Those who use the expression may also be attempting to siphon attention and support away from women who are physically harmed by men and, in a subtle slip from the first to the second sense of "bashing," to marshall the maximum amount of sympathy possible for "bashed" men—men who are really "innocent victims" and the target of unfair criticism.

But, of course, not all men batter or physically abuse women, and not all women bash or verbally abuse men. The charge of male bashing (and its companion charge, man hating) is specially reserved for feminists and the work they do—to hold them in derision and contempt. Feminists are accused, in writing about men, of overgeneralizing, of indiscriminately lumping all men together, of painting them all with the same villainous brush, so that all men are unjustly held responsible for the crimes of some. Complaints along these lines often appear in the media. I quote here from an editorial accusing women's groups of sexism (full article appended to this essay).

> Some of the problems:
> **Bashing all men simply for being men.** Women's groups have perpetuated a stereotype of men. Men are bad. All men.
> In most feminist writings, I am a monster—even if I've never raised a voice or fist or gun against a woman. The vast majority of feminist literature says "men" do this, and "men" do that. *I* don't [original emphasis]. Why am I being accused? What confounds me most is that this putting-down, this generalizing is *exactly* what troubled women, legitimately, for many years. Why prey upon me in the *same way* they were preyed upon?
> I am a powerful supporter of women's rights and women's equality. I am a good man, just as many of my man-friends are good men. (Vossler 1993, D5, emphasis added)

Bill Vossler, the author of this piece, recommends that feminists learn to qualify their statements (actually he dictates to us what we should say). If only we will do that (that is, "regularly say 'some men,' 'many men,' or 'a few men' commit the atrocities"), then good men like him will join our cause. (Aren't we lucky?) He asks why it is so "difficult for them [us feminists] to understand [ignoring his own slam and patronizing here—aren't feminists dumb?] not only that not all men are alike, nor all women, but that it hurts their [our] cause to falsely accuse those of us who are not criminals" (Vossler 1993, D5).

While feminism can sometimes be criticized for its generalizations, there are several problems with *this* sort of criticism, with blanket accusations of male bashing directed at feminists or women's groups.

For one thing, it is false, generally, that women's groups promote the idea that all men are bad. Moreover, unless the dehumanizing aspects of "manhood" are the topic of discussion,[1] it is also false, generally, that feminists are critical of men "simply for being men." The target of feminist critique is sexism in a male-dominated society. Through his failure to distinguish patriarchy bashing from male bashing, to distinguish between "attacking institutionalized, systematic oppression (the goal of any serious progressive movement) and attacking men as individuals." (Smith 117), the editorial writer subscribes to—is in fact publicizing—a common myth about feminism: that it is nothing but man hating. As Barbara Smith has written,

> This myth is one of the silliest and at the same time one of the most dangerous. Anti-feminists are incapable of making a distinction between being critically opposed to sexual oppression and simply hating men. Trying to educate and inform men about how their feet are planted on our necks doesn't translate into hatred either.
>
> The bodies of murdered women are strewn across the landscape of this country. Rape is a national pastime. . . . Battering and incest . . . are pandemic. . . . If you think that I exaggerate, please get today's newspaper and verify the facts.
>
> If anything is going down here it's woman-hatred, not man-hatred, a veritable war against women. . . . Wanting to end this war still doesn't equal man-hating. (1991, 117)

The most straightforward response to charges of male bashing is to differentiate it from criticism of sexism and simply to say that feminism is not "male bashing" or "man hating" but is a movement to end sexism—to end violence, oppression, exploitation, or unfair discrimination based on sex. One can be against sexism without hating men, just as one can be against racism without hating whites or against homophobia without hating heterosexuals.

Even if it were true that some feminists "bash men," an obvious problem with Bill Vossler's accusation that all feminists bash would still remain, for there is no way to level this criticism without committing the same mistake he is complaining about—that is, without bashing. Despite his stated concern with the importance of qualification, notice that *he* does not bother to diffentiate between women's groups or feminist

writings, rather, feminists and women's groups are all lumped together—
the "vast majority" of them painted with the same "male-bashing"
brush. According to his own logic then, the accusation on the part of this
(self-proclaimed) "powerful supporter" of women's rights—his claim that
feminists bash men "simply for being men"—is, pure and simple, feminist bashing.

A straw person is, of course, an easy target. It seems to me that criticisms of male bashing in feminism frequently boil down to setting up
"straw women" on the basis of reductive stereotypes of radical feminists.
Although radical feminism itself, like feminism generally, is heteroge-
neous and complicated, it is easily stereotyped as male bashing—the
"strong arm" of the movement—primarily since the word "radical" connotes "extremeness" and "militancy." In feminist usage, however, the term
has more to do with a concern with the "root" of social conditions. Radical feminism puts forth a radical critique of patriarchy, a radical critique
of masculinity, a radical gynocentrism. Of course, this radical critique is
disconcerting to men, it hurts their feelings, it seems to be unfair, it seems
to disregard their good intentions, it seems to generalize unfairly. But
whether or not one agrees with the radical feminist position, it is a complicated theoretical argument—and although it makes men feel uncomfortable, it does not follow that it is male bashing.

In my experience of women's groups (primarily through women's studies), they question the traditional subordination of women in society, see
it as unfair, and strive for liberation. The preferred paths in the feminist
struggle for social justice are nonviolent. The principal means include
consciousness raising, arguments, painstaking analyses and critical reflection, protest of injustices, and initiation of reforms. Feminists claim
the capacity to see and name social and political realities for ourselves,
as well as the ability to envision and create a better world. Reducing the
careful, valuable, insightful, intelligent, compassionate, and complex work
feminists do to the level of bashing is a gross, and malicious, distortion.
We need to understand why feminism gets distorted in this manner.

Characterizing feminism or feminists as male-bashing follows the old,
familiar pattern of devaluing women and the work that women do. It is also
an attempt to censure us/our work and to suppress, or erase, our expressions of anger.

In an article called "Anger and Insubordination," Elizabeth Spelman
has pointed out something that I think is relevant to a feminist analysis
of "male bashing." She says that while subordinate groups in a culture are
expected to be emotional, one emotion will not be tolerated, will be
eliminated from the dominant group's profile of them. That emotion is
anger (anger thought of as a "good" temper, in the sense of its being an
appropriate or justifiable response to injury, insult, or inequity and as a
middle ground between, say, irritation and rage). There is a pattern of men

responding to expressions of women's anger by either exaggerating it into hysteria or trivializing it as being "cute" (or, as several of my students remind me, attributable to PMS). In either case, expressions of the anger are stifled, silenced. Spelman believes that this censorship of anger is politically significant and an instrument of oppression. Since anger is our response to insult or injury, inequity or injustice, censoring anger is a way to censor judgments about wrongdoing, a way of silencing protest and repressing political speech (see Spelman 1989, 270–72).

In part, feminist critique is an expression of female anger over sexist injustice. These critiques are also exposés—with protest built into them. Disclosing and documenting sexist injustices is a way of saying that the sexist way things are need not, and should not, be. Of course, feminist disclosures are going to be found disagreeable or embarrassing to those involved. Of course, those we call to task would rather our voices not be heard, that we not be taken seriously. They stand to lose their unearned power, privileges, and benefits.

Characterizing feminist criticism as a "bash" against men seems to be an attempt to censure anger over sexist injustice and seems to follow the same pattern, and have the same purpose, as the other attempts to suppress female anger that Spelman has analyzed. That is, the characterization either trivializes and belittles the complicated work of feminist criticism as a confused, "slapdash" undertaking, or else it exaggerates the criticism by portraying it as unjustifiable "overkill," the product of irrational or indiscriminate hatred of men as individuals. Berating feminist criticism in this manner is an attempt to silence and censure our speech. It is a ploy on the part of those who would maintain the status quo to frighten us with a word, with a powerful word, with a word that no "nice woman," no "good man" wants to be associated with.

The use of this word is a scare tactic. It is intended to frighten people away from affiliating or associating with feminism. That this scare tactic has enjoyed considerable success is already evident from the numbers of young women and men who avoid taking, or skeptically enter, women's studies courses—already prejudiced against them, exhibiting and expressing fear that these classes simply bash men.

In a society where women's value depends on the approval of men, women (who are socialized never, under any circumstances, to hurt anyone) will not want to identify themselves as feminists—if feminists are "known" to be "male bashers."

Depicting feminism as a "male bash" also gives men a good excuse—a justification—for avoiding women's issues or studies and for failing to assume responsibility for opposing or resisting sexist injustice. Men need to learn about the oppression of women too. They need to learn to stop it. But men will not want to join with us in the experience of consciousness raising or in the struggle against sexism if they can be led to believe that feminism is just male bashing or that they will be bashed in women's groups simply for being there, simply for being men.

In short, if feminism and women's groups can be associated with male bashing in the public mind, then the result, of course, will be that fewer women and fewer men will be cooperatively participating, on personal and political levels, in the movement to end sexism.

Turning now to women's studies courses in particular, there is still an empirical question to be asked. It is the question of whether the media-fed assumption that women's studies courses are unfairly antagonistic toward men—hostile toward men qua men—is true.

While there is very little in the literature to either substantiate or refute the claim that women's studies classes are unfairly antagonistic toward men,[2] an article entitled "A Women's Studies Course: Its Impact on Women's Attitudes toward Men and Masculinity" by Dan Pence challenges this assumption. Pence believes, and I agree with him, that the popular perception that women's studies courses engage in male bashing is dangerous because it trivializes what takes place in them, contributes to their marginalization, and, perhaps most importantly, diverts the focus of attention from women to men (1992, 328).

Pence conducted a study (based on an admittedly small sample of three women's studies courses) to test his perception that women students "seem to have more understanding of men and their behavior *after* taking a course focused on women and gender than they had before" (323). What he found was that by providing an understanding of gender socialization, such a course actually improved female students' attitudes toward men as men; women were more supportive of nontraditional masculine behaviors after taking a women's studies course than they were at the outset. I quote his finding:

> Even though men were, at most, peripheral to the course content, by semester's end these students saw men as gendered beings whose roles and behaviors were also socially constructed. This provided a context for why men act the way they do. [They may still have been angry at specific men for specific actions], but the gendered framework also provided some understanding. (328)

Although Pence does not do so, I think it is important to point out that even if future surveys indicate that women's studies classes do result in more negative attitudes toward men—as I believe they sometimes might—such attitudes are not necessarily the consequence of male bashing or unfair criticism. Students' opinions of men may be lowered by these courses, but this may be because patriarchy has so inflated them. If sexual equity is the goal, then one cannot address the injustice of women's subordination without also addressing its companion, the injustice of men's supposed superiority, their superordination. John Stuart Mill, a (genuinely) powerful supporter of women's rights and a liberal feminist, argued quite eloquently, over one hundred years ago, that a positive consequence of women's achievement of equal rights would be the elimination of what he called male "arrogance" (1988, 88). So "knocking men down a peg"—from an assumed and illicit place of superiority—is not necessarily a "bash." If sexual equality is the goal, then sometimes it is only fair.

As mentioned earlier, feminism can sometimes be justly criticized for its generalizations (see Frye 1990, 178–80), for speaking of "all men" (or "all women" for that matter) *simpliciter*, for saying, for example, that "men oppress women" or that "all men benefit from sexism." Speaking in this manner covers over the fact that women with class and white-skin privilege can and do exploit and oppress other women and men, that women can and do play the role of oppressor and not just that of "innocent victim." Unqualified statements also often ignore the fact that all men do not share a common race and class status, nor do they benefit equally from sexism. It also tends to obscure the fact that men do not simply benefit but also suffer from and are harmed by sexism.

In their critique of white middle-class radical feminism, black feminist theorists like bell hooks have argued that the radical feminist notion that "men are the enemy" is the reason why many black feminists may feel alienated by and excluded from the women's movement. Although black women suffer from sexist oppression, they have also enjoyed the experience of political solidarity with men in their common struggle against racist oppression, hooks thinks that feminists need to elicit the support of men as "comrades in arms," that feminism needs "to develop new strategies for including men in the struggle against sexism" (1991, 491). She believes that fueling antagonism toward men is counterproductive to the movement, that male supremacy is more threatened by integration than by separatism, and that separatism encourages women to "ignore the negative impact of sexism on male personhood" (492). hooks advises us to realize that we can, as feminists, acknowledge and compassionately address the pain that men suffer as a result of sexist conditioning without "diminishing the seriousness of male abuse and oppression of women" and without negating their responsibility for exploitative actions (491).

hooks believes that the feminist agenda must begin to include ways for men to unlearn sexism, and she suggests that one way of drawing men in may be to spread the word that the feminist movement is not primarily "women's work," that making feminist revolution is not a sex role task.

I find hooks's insights and recommendations very valuable. I have learned a lot from her. But I sometimes get the impression that she, too, is operating on the assumption—though she does not use the word "bash" (indeed, no feminist I know does)—that most or many white middle-class feminists are male bashers and out of a fear that the (white) women's movement is socializing women to hate men rather than to hate the sexist injustices perpetuated by male-dominated society. This assumption is part of the problem.

I'd like to close these reflections on male bashing as topic and term by unabashedly saying that the work feminists do *is* destructive. We cannot create a new social order without destroying (some of) the old. There will be no liberation from sexist oppression without a social revolution. The oppression of women in male-dominated society is systematic and widespread. The systematic oppression of women is also linked to other systems of oppression. They are all unjust, and they need to be destroyed.

While I obviously do not think that feminism *is* male bashing, I do nevertheless believe that we ought to delight and revel in the blows we deliver to sexist injustices and institutions in the interest of putting an end to them. Perhaps because we have been socialized to abhor violence, we do not appreciate that some violence, some hatred, and some anger may be morally justifiable, may even be necessary in the process of social reform. Women (and men) do not press as hard or as often for reforms as we should. Resistance against us is formidable. I think we should *not* deceive ourselves into believing that what we are doing is not a fight, is not a struggle. But, personally, I do not think we have even *begun* to bash.

Appendix

Masquerade by Racists and Sexists*

Bill Vossler

In America we can criticize anybody except women's groups and minorities.

Well, technically we can criticize them. But the price to pay is a ghastly one. Far too often the initial words out of their mouths are, "You sexist!" "You racist!" In other words, don't deal with the issue, but fire up a smokescreen.

Some of the problems:

Bashing all men simply for being men. Women's groups have perpetuated a stereotype of men. Men are bad. All men.

In most feminist writings, I am a monster—even if I've never raised a voice or fist or gun against a woman. The vast majority of feminist literature says "men" do this, and "men" do that. *I* don't. Why am I being accused? What confounds me most is that this putting-down, this generalizing is exactly what troubled women, legitimately, for many years. Why prey upon me in the same way they were preyed upon?

---

*From the newspaper. *Fargo Forum* (Fargo, ND) 24 Jan 1993.

I am a powerful supporter of women's rights and women's equality. I am a good man, just as many of my man-friends are good men.

We decent men could be most powerful allies if the groups would regularly say "some men," "many men" or "a few men" men [*sic*] commit the atrocities, which just happens to be true.

And conversely, use "some women," "many women" or "a few women" instead of "women." Not all women feel the same as those in the feminist groups (only one-twentieth of 1 percent belong to NOW), so why are they being included? Why is it so difficult for them to understand not only that not all men are alike, nor all women, but that it hurts their cause to falsely accuse those of us who are not criminals?

Acknowledgments

I wish to take this opportunity to thank Sylvia Morgan, Nancy Gilliland, and Ted Gracyk at Moorhead State University and the editors at *NWSA Journal* for their help with this paper.

Notes

1. See, e.g., John Stoltenberg's *Refusing to Be a Man* (New York: Penguin, 1990).

2. See Pence, (1992, 321). My update of Pence's search for material pertaining to male bashing on the part of women's studies classes confirmed a lack of literature in this area.

References

Frye, Marilyn. "The Possibility of Feminist Theory." Ed. Deborah L. Rhodes. *Theoretical Perspectives on Sexual Difference.* New Haven: Yale UP, 1990. 174–84.

hooks, bell. "Men Comrades in Struggle." *The Sociology of Gender: A Text Reader.* Ed. Lau Kramer. New York: St. Martin's, 1991. 487–99.

Jaggar, Alison M. *Feminist Politics and Human Nature.* Totowa, NJ: Rowman and Allanheld, 1983.

Mill, John Stuart. *The Subjection of Women.* Ed. Susan Moller Okin. Indianapolis: Hackett, 1988.

Pence, Dan. "A Woman's Studies Course: Its Impact on Women's Attitudes toward Men and Masculinity." *NWSA Journal* 4, 3 (1992): 321–35.

Smith, Barbara. "Some Home Truths on the Contemporary Black Feminist Movement," *Changing Our Power: An Introduction to Women's Studies.* Ed. Jo Whitehorse Cochran, Donna Langston, and Carolyn Woodward. 2nd ed. Dubuque, IA: Kendall/Hunt, 1991. 117.

Spelman, Elizabeth. "Anger and Insubordination." *Women, Knowledge and Reality.* Ed. Ann Garry and Marilyn Pearsall. Boston: Unwin Hyman, 1989. 270–72.

Vossler, Bill. "Masquerade by Racists and Sexists." *Fargo Forum*, 24 Jan 1993, D5.

CHAPTER THREE

Feminist Intentions
Race, Gender, and Power in a High School Classroom

SHARON BERNSTEIN

> If guys say certain things that are wrong, I'll be saying something back to them.
> I know they'll have something good to say back. I can't even defend myself.
> > —Ann, a high school student, in an interview with the author

> And of course I am afraid, because the transformation of silence into language and
> action is an act of self-revelation, and that always seems fraught with danger.
> > —Audre Lorde, *Sister Outsider* (1984)

I met Ann, whom I have quoted above, when she was a student in a high school English class that was reading and discussing Tom Morrison's novel *The Bluest Eye* (1970). The novel explores the meaning of beauty, sexuality, love, violence, and survival in the lives of young African American girls making the transition to womanhood. It explores racism and sexism from the point of view of these young girls. When I first met Ann, I was interested in whether reading such a counterhegemonic novel in school would be liberating or "empowering" to her and other girls in the class and whether it would encourage them to speak out and challenge the boys during class discussions. What I found was that complex gender and race relations among the young people in the classroom served to regulate who could speak about what in class. Ultimately, the students created a discourse about sexuality in which female sexuality remained an object of disgust and disdain and male sexuality was expressed in a context of racial oppression of black men by white men. Even in this "feminist" classroom young people thus constructed race and gender relations that reproduced the status quo and served to subvert the feminist teacher's intentions.

I spent six weeks observing student interaction in Ann's class, a multiracial, middle-track, eleventh-grade English class at an urban California high school. It was composed of only about twenty students: two of them were white, three were Asian, two were Chicano, the remainder were African American. Slightly fewer than half of the students were girls. The class was part of the regular curriculum, it was not an elective, and therefore the students did not represent a self-selected group who came to the class particularly interested in studying literature by women of color. However, the teacher (whom I will call Ms. Martinez) chose to put some such literature into her curriculum, and she considered herself to be a feminist teacher.[1]

I read *The Bluest Eye* along with the young people in the class and observed their classroom conversations about the book. I paid close attention to how girls and boys talked together about this feminist novel and how the power relations between the boys and girls affected classroom dynamics. I noted who spoke in class and who did not, who spoke to whom about what kinds of issues, and who listened to whom in class. I wanted to understand how the different students participated in the classroom discourse and whose perspective that discourse represented.

After my first visit to Ann's class, I realized that my field notes were full of observations about the boys. For all my interest in girls' experiences in this classroom, I had paid attention mostly to the boys! I could already sense that in a classroom so dominated by boys it was easy to notice them and not to notice the girls. Even as a feminist woman researcher I felt the strength of the tendency to pay more attention to boys than to girls and saw how difficult it can be to truly study girls—from their perspective—in a coed classroom. I started sitting with the girls so that I could see them and hear the comments they made to the teacher and to each other. I also interviewed several of the girls in order to try to understand their perspectives on what happened in the classroom.

A few of the boys dominated the classroom both physically and verbally. They took up more physical space than did the girls. The boys would often get up from their desks and wander around the room when the teacher or other students were talking. A boy might get up from his seat and walk out of the room or go sit next to his friend on the other side of the room or go sharpen a pencil. The boys also often talked loudly to other boys who were sitting on the other side of the class, as if there were no other people in the room. They often just spoke out for everyone to hear. Most of their talk was in the form of jokes, usually sexist jokes about things such as how girls dress to come to school and how girls get upset if they mess up their hair. They would tell these jokes for the benefit of each other and at the expense of either the teacher or the girls in the class, although, as we will see later, the girls in the classroom often laughed at these jokes.

While most of the boys tended to move around the room, speak for a general listening audience, and crack jokes as a means of controlling the conversation, the Asian and Chicano boys were far more quiet than the African American ones. The two Asian boys, both graffiti artists, spent class time drawing and talking with each other. They rarely participated in class discussions. The extent to which these boys were not part of the dominant group illustrates that race intertwines with gender in determining the power structure within the classroom.

The girls in the class participated very differently than most of the boys. Physically they stayed in their seats and seldom got up or walked around the room. They would talk quietly with other students sitting near them or they would not talk at all. When the girls did participate in class discussions, they would usually face the teacher and speak directly to her. They did not usually speak loudly enough to be heard from other parts of the classroom. And other students often did not listen to what a girl had to say. While the boys made jokes to entertain each other and assert their authority, girls talked quietly to other girls sitting near them. They would whisper, lean close to each other, or pass notes. They created a small private space that did not include the boys.

Thus, one way that the girls participated in classroom relations was by creating a small space in which they could talk to each other without interference from the boys. Other times, however, they did speak up to the whole class and even directly challenged the boys' perspectives. In doing so, they posed a threat to the boys' control over classroom discourse. If one of the first things I had noticed about this class was that the boys were loud and the girls were quiet, I soon came to see that some boys never spoke at all and that two of the girls did speak up and often got into arguments with the boys. It was in these moments when the girls dared to speak as subjects (see hooks 1989; *Talking Back* Jordan 1981), and in the ways these moments were resolved, that I began to see an intricate webbing of gender, sexuality, and race informing how students spoke to each other during class conversations. I realized that the boys controlled classroom talk, but in more complicated ways than I first thought.

I found that these young people constructed discourses not only in relation to the teacher and curriculum but also in their relations to each other. Furthermore, these relations were complicated by race as much as by gender. This finding seemed to challenge the prevailing assumptions within critical educational research on speech and silence in schools, which has approached power relations as existing primarily between teachers and students but not among students themselves (see, e.g., Fine 1991; McNeil 1986). It also challenged most studies of gender and classroom talk, which do acknowledge power relations among students but which unfortunately have tended to emphasize an essentialized difference between female and male modes of communication (see, e.g., Belenky et al. 1985; Kramarae and Treichler 1990). In these studies women are typically seen as interpersonal, connected, and egalitarian communicators, while men are seen as more aggressive and competitive. This kind of analysis does not recognize the diversity or conflicted nature of girls' or boys' experiences in the classroom. It could not explain how race intertwined with gender in Ann's classroom.

Many critical educators have emphasized the liberating power of "student voice" or "dialogue," as if all the young people in a classroom, once allowed a voice, will form a united front opposing a racist and sexist world "out there."[2] This approach (mistakenly) assumes that all of the students in a classroom are equally dominated. Students in a classroom do *not* necessarily all share world views that are always in direct opposition to the controlling, silencing mechanisms of school and that can be unlocked through politically conscious kinds of pedagogy. Rather, some students will dominate others, and the different people in a classroom will often have confusing, conflicting, and intersecting interests.

In her article "Why Doesn't This Feel Empowering?" Elizabeth Ellsworth looks at these kinds of power struggles in a classroom in which she was the teacher. She notes that "no teacher is free of . . . learned and internalized oppressions. Nor are accounts of one group's suffering and struggle immune from reproducing narratives oppressive to another's—the racism of the Women's Movement in the United States is one example" (1989, 308). Thus, one oppressed group can create a narrative that effectively oppresses another group. The power relations among the students— their different and interacting race, gender, class, popularity, or beauty positions—affect how a narrative unfolds, who can speak, and, perhaps even more importantly, who will be heard.

In the class I studied, students actively participated in the process of marginalizing *each other*, a process that also contributed to the production of race, gender, and other categories. The young people in the class dominated, resisted, and struggled with each other as well as with the school or teacher. Four general themes emerged from my research, themes that connect and overlap to explain the dynamics among the young people in this class: (1) subject-object dualities based on gender, race, and sexuality; (2) the reduction of race to a black-white issue; (3) the articulation of gender issues as racial issues; and (4) a discourse of immaturity. I will now explore the connections among all of these themes by analyzing a few specific conversations that occurred in the classroom. Rather than analyze these themes one at a time, I will explore a few stories or events that illustrate, above all, their interconnectedness.

Why Was Shameka Embarrassed?

During a class conversation about sexual harassment, some of the boys did most of the talking. In the following interchange we can see that they looked at harassment from a point of view according to which male behavior was the natural result of girls' provocative behavior:

ED: Girls be settin' people up.
MICHAEL: Check this out. Look how they come [dressed] to school.
PATRICK: And then they say, "Stop staring."
MS. MARTINEZ: What makes you think that the way a girl is dressed gives you the right to say something?
DAVE: Law of nature.
MS. MARTINEZ: A woman is not an object.

DAVE: Sometimes.

BRAD: You don't see guys comin' to school in speedos. . . . Sometimes I think girls wear short skirts just to get a reaction. Some girls can't help it, though.

In this interchange, we can see the boys objectifying not just women but female sexuality. They talk about women as if they cannot control their own sexuality. It is a "law of nature" that the way a girl dresses gives a boy the right to stare at her or to say whatever he wants. The boys see these girls as objects for their own consumption, objects who "can't help" the way they dress or the fact that they invite male interest.

Given that the boys talk about female sexuality as an object for their own consumption, what happens when the girls assert a different perspective? One morning I observed just such a situation. Like (at least some of) the students, I came to class that morning having read pages 16 through 30 of the novel. In these pages the character Pecola starts menstruating for the first time and is scared because she does not understand what is happening to her. This scene tells the reader that Pecola is on the edge between childhood and womanhood, and places her developing sexuality at the center of her story. It also sets the stage for the tragedy about which Morrison has already warned the reader—Pecola's rape by her father, Cholly, and the death of her baby.

In class that morning Ms. Martinez asked the students a seemingly simple question: "How old is Pecola?" As I tried myself to answer the teacher's question, I realized I did not know how old Pecola was. I looked through the pages, and I noticed several students doing the same thing. All I knew about Pecola was that she had started menstruating for the first time and was scared, that she did not know what was happening to her—this could make her anywhere from ten to fifteen. The students talked, feeling frustrated and protesting the question, until Shameka, an African American girl, asserted resolutely, "She's eleven."

The talk stopped suddenly and attention focused on Shameka. Ms. Martinez asked her how she knew Pecola was eleven (I myself was wondering too). Shameka answered with confidence and certainty, "Because I was eleven when I started."

It seemed a simple enough statement. Yet as I pored over my field notes and rethought the meaning of Shameka's statement, I came to understand that what Shameka had done here was something that interrupted the normal tone and perspective of classroom discussions—she had asserted her sexuality as a source of knowledge and a subject for discussion.

The boys met her assertion with indignation. One retorted, "Oh, thank you. Tell us about it," making a show of his disgust and a point about the inappropriateness of Shameka's comment. There was an uproar of comment and talk among the boys. The girls were quiet. Shameka was left stranded.

This situation posed a problem for the teacher. With the boys in an uproar she seemed to have lost "control" of the classroom. She also clearly wanted to redirect the conversation so that the students would discuss and consider the female character's point of view and the author's intended messages. She took control from the boys and reasserted her authority by explaining that Pecola, in her ignorance of what was happening to her body, was left at the mercy of whatever might happen to her. She then asked the students, "What does this do to a girl?" With a tone of disgust, a boy named Patrick responded, "It's pitiful." Using the word "pitiful," Patrick signaled his discomfort with this discussion of a young girl's sexuality at the center of the novel. Other boys joined him, all talking at once and using words like "sick" and "weird" to describe the characters of the novel. Their words and laughter signified their dismissal of the story and of its specifically female perspective.

The boys were not necessarily alone in disliking this scene from *The Bluest Eye*. Some of the girls seemed to find the focus on a young girl's sexuality to be embarrassing and demeaning. And their critique was often—at least on the surface—cast in terms of race, not gender. For example, Shameka told me in an interview,

> It's embarrassing . . . it made me mad when it showed how this girl, when she started her cycle. Well, she . . . her parents didn't tell her that her body's gonna change, whatever, she just went through it, and it's like, why did they put this in the book? What does it have to do with the book? Is it showing that black people don't speak with their kids, growing up? I mean, that's what I got out of that part.

Something about this scene, and the book in general, made Shameka uncomfortable. She attributed her discomfort to the fact that the book made African Americans look weak instead of strong. (In direct contrast, Shameka told me that she really liked Richard Wright's *Black Boy*, because "not many people focus on the black race. . . . In *Black Boy*, he was able to overcome a lot of things that, you know, people say you're not goin' to be able to do this, and he was able to do it. That's what I liked about that book.")

What was so uncomfortable about this scene in which Pecola begins menstruating? Why did Shameka interpret it as demeaning to African Americans? And why were the boys so disgusted at Shameka's mention of her own sexuality ("I was eleven when I started") when they themselves talked about sex so often in class? For a long time I saw Shameka's feelings about this scene as being due either to her "misreading" of the novel or to the boys' relentless teasing and dismissal of the tale as just some "sob story." However, remembering a similar experience of my own helped me understand better the complexity of what I was seeing in the relations between these students.

That experience was seeing the movie *Rambling Rose*, in which a woman's sexuality is the subject of the story. The first time I saw this movie, I sat in the theater feeling very uncomfortable. I squirmed in my seat, sometimes I did not want to watch—I felt horrified by the main character, Rose, a young woman consumed by her sexuality. She comes to live with a southern family and take care of the children, immediately falls in love with and tries to seduce the family patriarch, then crawls into bed with his thirteen-year-old son. It disturbed me to watch this woman whose very sense of identity relied so completely on the sexual attentions of men.

Yet I say the movie made me uncomfortable—as opposed to angry. I did not dismiss *Rambling Rose* as yet another sexist instance in which a woman is reduced to a sex object, but I did not understand what about Rose separated her from all those other women in the movies. And at the same time, I still felt unsure of why the movie made me feel so uncomfortable. Something was unusual, and I did not know what.

Then I read an article in *Ms.* magazine that described *Rambling Rose* as a film in which a woman's sexuality is the subject, not the object, of the plot. I suddenly understood that this must have been the source of my discomfort and confusion about the movie. I am so conditioned to watching women as either sexual objects or asexual beings that I had not even recognized woman as sexual subject. I immediately rented the video and watched it again, this time understanding it as an exploration of a woman's sexuality as a complex element of her identity. Similarly, *The Bluest Eye* by Toni Morrison explores the sexuality and identity of several black women and young girls growing up in the small community of Lorain, Ohio. Like the movie *Rambling Rose*, this novel challenges stereotypes that objectify women's sexuality. It seeks instead to make black women and their sexuality the subject, not the object, of the narrative.

So—in a context in which the boys themselves often talked about sex—why did Shameka's comment that she was eleven when she started her cycle make everyone so uncomfortable? The difference was that when Shameka said she had started menstruating at age eleven, she asserted her own knowledge and her own sexuality.[3] Female sexuality as subject—as in *Rambling Rose*—made everyone in the class uncomfortable because female sexuality was usually the object of talk, scorn, jokes. It was not usually something one of the girls declared as the subject of her own knowledge and understanding. When the boys made jokes about sex, they objectified the girls and their female perspectives as a means of restoring or preserving the male point of view as the dominant one in the conversation. When the girls asserted their sexuality as subject, as Shameka did, it threatened the boys' control over classroom dynamics. The boys then acted disgusted as a means of embarrassing Shameka and deflecting the experience of female subjectivity from which she had tried to speak.

The conflict between the assertion of female sexuality as subject and the boys' desire to restore female sexuality to the position of object in the discourse became more obvious than usual during this class because of the nature of the novel the class was reading. Because *The Bluest Eye* explores the sexuality of its female characters, it often provoked class discussions in which girls spoke from their own experience, from their gendered or even sexual experience (sexuality as subject). The boys then expressed even more disgust or disdain than usual toward the girls in an effort to deflect the assertion of female sexuality (sexuality as object).

Furthermore, through this kind of joking pattern some of the boys managed to thwart the teacher's intentions and disrupt the conversation. At the same time, they monopolized the teacher's attention so that she could not continue to teach. One result of this dynamic in the classroom was that when a few of the boys successfully controlled the teacher's attention, she virtually ignored the rest of the students, especially the girls. Sometimes she would ask one of the girls a specific question and that girl would answer, speaking softly and directly to the teacher. Usually the boys did not pay attention to the girls' answers. The teacher would listen, but by the time the girl finished, the boys were again commanding her attention. Thus the power struggle between the female teacher and some of the male students served to further marginalize the girls in the class.

Not only did the boys deflect the girls' point of view about issues such as sexual harassment or menstruation, but the "sexiness" of the topics actually fueled their jokes. Discussing *The Bluest Eye* became not a stimulus for considering the effects of racism and sexism on African American women but a great opportunity to joke about sex. The boys did not look bored. They were lively, excited, and interested. The feminist novel *The Bluest Eye* thus ironically served to fuel their sexist jokes rather than challenge the sexism in their assumptions. The boys' control over classroom communication was reinforced, not undermined, during their discussions of *The Bluest Eye*.

"Why Doesn't He Beat Up an Asian?"

Another series of interchanges near the end of my fieldwork further complicated my understanding of the power relations among the young people participating in the classroom discourse. One Thursday morning Ms. Martinez began class by asking students to pull out their books and silently read a five-page section from *The Bluest Eye*, and then write down why they thought the character Cholly raped Pecola. Cholly is an African American man who is violent toward his wife, Pauline, and rapes his daughter, Pecola. The pages Ms. Martinez asked the class to read give some of Cholly's background: they tell of a time in Cholly's youth when two white men intruded into his first sexual experience with a young woman named Darlene and turned it into what Barbara Christian calls a "public pleasure show" (1980, 148). These white men pass a flashlight over the bodies of Cholly and Darlene, snickering, "Get on wid it, nigger" and "Come on, coon. Faster. You ain't doing nothing for her." When Cholly is able only to pretend, the men say, "Well, the coon ain't come yet . . . well, he have to come on his own time. Good luck, coon baby." Afterward, Cholly feels incredible anger, which he cultivates as hatred for Darlene.

After the students finished reading this section to themselves, Ms. Martinez asked them, "What are they doing to Cholly?" and different students responded "Harassing him," "Taunting him," "Provoking him," "Threatening him." Ms. Martinez wrote on the board "Humiliating." Then she asked, "What is missing in this scene?"

PATRICK: How they both felt. They explain how Cholly felt, not how the girl felt.
LISA: He just blamed the girl he was with.
MS: MARTINEZ Why?
ROB: Because she started feeling on him. Sticking her hand under his shirt.
LISA: That's not the point. . . . She was scared.
ROB: She started it and put him in that situation.
LISA: That's how he felt, but it wasn't her fault.
PATRICK: It made him feel better to blame it on her than to blame himself.
NAO: He was releasing anger.
PAUL: After all the years of oppression, they're used to blaming other people.
SHAMEKA: He felt weaker than the white men. . . . She was weaker than he was. . . . He felt he could take all his anger out on her.
MS. MARTINEZ: He couldn't turn on the white men . . . so who do you turn on?
LISA: The one who's weaker than you.
MS. MARTINEZ: How does this affect his relationship with his wife and daughter?
PATRICK: He feels he has to take a woman who's weaker than he is.
LISA: That's why he raped his daughter.
SHAMEKA: She might have been saying of the community, how they direct their anger toward each other.

While the boys initially seemed to resist this conversation, I noticed that they became very involved and interested. For a while, they discussed the character Cholly and his relationship to his anger and to the women in his life without joking about it or trivializing the feelings of anger and violence this character experienced.

However, this discussion of why black men might show violence toward black women then took a sudden turn toward more objectifying and violent explanations. In the following exchange we can see the boys explaining and even justifying violence against women:

MS. MARTINEZ: How do you change, when there's no one to help you?

BRAD: You gotta do it yourself.

PATRICIA: When you're a little kid, you don't know anything else other than what you learn from your parents.

ED: Me, I just learn how not to take things personally.

PATRICIA: But sometimes a man gets mad at his wife and she doesn't know what's wrong. She might think it's her fault. But she doesn't know why he's mad, if it's because she didn't clean the house or something.

At this juncture Michael interrupted Patricia, started swinging his arms as if he were beating someone, and exclaimed "But he will tell you as he's beating you! Clean the house! Clean the house!" He kept swinging his arms as though he were punching the person he was talking to: "Clean the house! Why was you outside in the streets?!" Most of the students in the classroom started laughing, and another boy joined in with Michael:

PATRICK. Why didn't you come home when I said?

MICHAEL. You don't just walk home and get popped in the head! *(Continues arm motions like he's beating someone.)* Clean the house!

Patricia had tried to articulate how the novel's female characters' lack of power over their own lives is closely intertwined with the unequal power relations between themselves and the men in their lives. Her attempt to enter into this conversation and to challenge the boys' ideology was met with a hostile and forceful response: Michael and Patrick acting out a scene in which they would control their wives by beating them. With this violent joke, Michael managed to turn the tables on Patricia, to effectively shut her down, and to regain control over the classroom conversation. It is not surprising that once the laughter died down, the boys went on to discuss rage (as opposed to how rage affects other people, specifically women) with no further participation from Patricia. Ultimately, this discussion only served the unfortunate purpose of explaining—possibly even justifying—the violence committed by Cholly, not the consequences of his rage for the women in his life.

Just moments later, another exchange illustrated that subjects and objects in this conversation were constituted along racial as well as gender lines. Students were still talking about rage, and Michael, an African American boy, asserted that "when you have rage and you can't do nuttin' about it, you gonna take it out on somebody you can. That's life." He looked at the teacher, nodded as if to reaffirm his point to her, and said again, "That's life." Another African American boy added, "He can't beat up a white person, he'll go to jail," to which Paul, one of the two Asian American boys in the class, responded, "Well, why doesn't he beat up an Asian?"

Paul was constantly drawing graffiti during class. While he often chatted with one friend who sat next to him, he rarely participated verbally in sanctioned classroom conversation. The above interchange was a notable exception. It was particularly notable because it was the *only time* during my fieldwork that anyone in the classroom mentioned race as anything but a black-white issue.

This reduction of race to a black-white issue was replicated in the curricular material for this class. Students read *Black Boy* and *The Bluest Eye*, both written by African Americans. Then they read *Huckleberry Finn*, written by a white man but focusing on black-white relations. They also took a field trip to see the newly released movie *Malcolm X*. Curricular material over the course of the semester focused entirely on the black-white experience or relations, as did class discussions.[4] Despite the many different racial identities of the students, race remained a black-white issue in the curriculum as well as in class discussions.

And a few of the African American students dominated those discussions. In this sense African American students could speak as subjects, asserting their perspective in the conversation. That perspective necessitated and legitimized a certain exclusion of other perspectives, such as the one Paul voiced when he said, "Well, why doesn't he beat up an Asian?" With this sarcastic comment, Paul pointed out that the position of powerlessness was not only inhabited by African Americans in relation to Anglo-Americans. He suggested that Asians are often the butt of much racism and violence.

This sarcastic, seemingly offhand comment was met with a rather confused response. For a moment, everybody was quiet. There was a kind of uncomfortable silence, as if someone had just told a joke that no one else thought was funny. Everyone looked around for a moment, one African American boy muttered, "Where did that come from?" and then with no further response to Paul, the conversation returned to a discussion of Cholly and the problems of violence and rage in the African American community. Paul had spoken from his own, neither black nor white perspective—and in a manner typical of the classroom dynamic, the African American perspective reasserted itself, suturing over this disruption and restoring itself as the guiding point of view.

As these exchanges highlight, the relations among students that allow some students and not others to speak as subjects involve more than male control of the conversation and total rejection of the female perspective. First, the Asian student's comment defying the black-white discourse on race relations was rejected or ignored by other students. The classroom discourse allowed the student to speak but did not allow anyone to hear him as an Asian subject.

I mentioned that in their discussion of Cholly's rage the boys initially seemed willing to address the subject of masculinity and male violence. They did not immediately dismiss the topic or reduce it to a series of jokes, as they had, for example, the topic of sexual harassment (although, as I have related, they did eventually turn it into a joke). It is interesting that the boys identified with this aspect of the novel, since the novel is definitely *exposing* masculinity in its weakness, not bolstering it. The boys' reaction suggests that their rejection of female sexuality as subject was more complicated than a mere rejection of anything feminine or of anything that challenged their masculinity.

The boys engaged masculinity as a *subject*; however, they engaged it only as a *subject of race*, racial oppression, and resultant black-on-black violence. They did not engage their masculinity as a *subject of gender* or as a *subject of sexuality*. Their discussion of masculinity was reduced to the relationship between black men and white men, not men of any other race and not women. Women become the object of masculine aggression, but their point of view did not figure into the discussion. Neither did Paul's Asian perspective.

While the concept of masculinity and violence that the boys discussed in class was very connected to their male sexuality, they did not address it as a matter of sexuality. While they could perceive and discuss masculinity as something they experience in terms of racial oppression, they did not approach it as something more connected to women and female sexuality. Instead they constructed their understanding of the male rage depicted in the novel as a logical response to racism.

In these class discussions we see how students centered violence and addressed it as primarily a black-white racial issue. The issue of violence as something that harms women was subsumed in the discourse about race. That is, the class discussed at length how Cholly was humiliated by the white men and yet *barely mentioned* the scene in which Cholly committed the violent act of raping his daughter! Even as students challenged the dominant construction of black men as violent and sexually aggressive, they reinforced the prevailing ideology that men should dominate women.

The Discourse of Immaturity

How did students themselves characterize the dynamics of the class? In my interviews with the teacher and the female students I was struck by the extent to which they all described the boys as immature, childish, silly, pigheaded, and refusing to "face the facts." The teacher and the girls in the class had created a discourse of immaturity in which they could explain and excuse the boys' behavior.

The girls I interviewed described the boys as immature and foolish. Tenisha said, "They want to act like little kids, so let 'em act like little kids. I'm gonna be a responsible student, you know." The girls felt frustrated with the way the boys acted—but their impatience stopped short of anger. In the following conversation Shameka discusses the way the boys had talked in class about sexual harassment:

> SHAMEKA: One thing I didn't like about it was the guys. All they say is if you're, you're wearing something that's tight, and you, say, show some thigh, what do you expect? Now I don't agree with that. . . . I like the discussion because I like to argue. That's what we're taught in criminal law, to argue the law, so I like that. Yeah, I like that subject. I didn't like what they were saying.
>
> SB: Did you feel like they listened to what you said?
>
> SHAMEKA: No! They say, I don't care what you say, I know this. . . . Majority of guys feel that way, though.

Thus, Shameka felt the unfairness of the boys' attitudes, but she explained it with the notion that "boys will be boys."

The discourse of immaturity served to explain and excuse the boys' behavior as much as it served as a way of describing frustration. This discourse, created by the marginalized female students and female teacher, became a means of understanding the very behaviors—such as joking, acting disgusted, and struggling with the teacher for power—through which certain boys controlled classroom talk and asserted their perspective over other students' points of view.

Furthermore, the African American girls described the boys' immaturity from a racial standpoint. Tenisha said that when the boys acted up, they made all minorities look bad. Several girls emphasized that the boys just did not want to face the facts of life. They seemed to see their immaturity as an avoidance of dealing with drugs, poverty, pregnancy—problems they understood as affecting them all as a race. They did not see these as particularly gendered problems. As Tenisha told me, "They're more into getting girls pregnant, sex. . . . Michael will be like, Hi, come on over here. You know, they're just rude . . . that was how they were brought up." When I asked how this made her feel, she responded,

> That makes me feel kind of low, because you know, I'm a black girl. He's a black boy. Okay, we're trying to work together. We're trying to go to class, do somethin'. I'm like, you want to talk about that, go outside, go someplace else. That makes all other minorities think, wow, we are low, we are trash. They just act the fool, that's all they do. Act the fool.

Even as these African American girls articulated their frustration with the boys' immaturity, they saw themselves as sharing a community bond with those boys and expressed mostly resignation toward their behavior. Tenisha framed her discussion about the boys' behavior in terms of race, and her irritation with the boys had as much to do with race as it did with gender. For the girls as well as the boys race was the dominant topic and gender issues were experienced within the discourse on race.

Conclusions

I began with the general observation that the girls in the classroom I observed were quiet and that the boys dominated classroom conversations. Closer analysis has shown, however, that the patterns of communication in class were far more complicated than that. Furthermore, I found that speaking in class can be liberating but is certainly not always so. In *Talking Back*, bell hooks emphasizes that

> moving from silence into speech is for the oppressed, the colonized, the exploited, and those who stand and struggle side by side a gesture of defiance that heals, that makes new life and new growth possible. It is that act of speech, of "talking back," that is no mere gesture of empty words, that is the expression of our movement from object to subject—the liberated voice. (1989, 9)

But what does it mean to move from object to subject? This is a critical point, for the ability to talk does not necessarily suggest the ability to affect a discourse, to alter its perspective. The epigraph to this chapter shows how Ann, a student in the class I observed, felt that even if she talked back to the boys in the class, they would "have something good to say back" and she could not defend herself. She could speak, but the prevailing discourse in the classroom would still reproduce the boys' perspective. I found that the students were engaged in a struggle to speak as subjects—that is, to speak and be heard, to speak in such a way as to influence the perspective of the overall discourse.

bell hooks uses the phrase "talking back" to mean the courageous act of speaking as an equal to someone in a position of authority. She reminds us that the effort to talk back, to speak as a subject, can be difficult and frightening because women often are not listened to when they do talk. Thus women who speak still have to fight to be heard. Similarly, the girls in the class I visited often fought to be heard, but the boys continually turned the tables on them: they turned the girls' fighting words into demeaning jokes, and they always seemed to manage to restore the dominance of their own perspective, no matter what the subject of conversation. Indeed, in interviews several girls alluded to the difficulty of trying to argue with the boys. Edna said that the boys made her mad, but that if she ever tried to challenge them, "they'd listen but they'd start arguing back, it gets you frustrated."

In a context in which the boys' "discourse of immaturity" prevailed, every time the girls tried to assert their knowledge about female sexuality, they risked having to endure the boys' scornful jokes. At the same time, however, they also indicated in interviews that they thought it was good to talk about these issues in class. For example, Tenisha told me that she had found the class discussion about sexual harassment that I mentioned earlier to be at least somewhat useful:

> SB: Did you like talking about sexual harassment?
> TENISHA: Yeah, I did. Because it did happen to me. At Urban High. It's very important to talk about it. Some girls might say, Oh, no big deal. But it happened to me. It's real important.
> SB: Do you think the class discussion helped?
> TENISHA: Yeah, it helped. Maybe the boys haven't been sexually harassed, but it's real important.
> SB: Do you think the boys listened to the girls?
> TENISHA: No. I think it just gives 'em another reason to take advantage of 'em.

Thus Tenisha expressed mixed feelings about the sexual harassment discussion. She knew that harassment was a very real problem. Yet she also knew that talking to the boys about it only gave them more reason to demean the girls. Her comments speak to the conflicted ways in which the girls experienced the opportunity to discuss issues like this one in class. They thought it was important to address the problem of harassment, which was very real for them, yet they also knew that the boys could, ironically, use the conversation to take further advantage of them.

Tenisha's comments highlight the importance of speaking about difficult issues of gender in class as well as the need to develop pedagogical strategies to interrupt the power relations that allow boys to harass girls. Furthermore, we need to remember that power relations in a classroom are complicated by race as well as gender: when Paul tried to suggest in class one day that Asian Americans experience racism in this country, the other students merely laughed nervously. Like the moment when Shameka asserted that she had started menstruating at age eleven, the moment when Paul asked, "Well, why doesn't he beat up an Asian?" made the classroom tense and uncomfortable.

We need to develop ways of dealing with these kinds of tensions in the classroom if we want to truly challenge young people to confront racism and sexism. In *Teaching to Transgress* bell hooks suggests that the multicultural classroom in which teachers and students address difficult issues of race, class, or gender oppression might not be a "safe" or harmonious classroom. It is common for teachers in potentially conflictual situations to want to retreat toward more "safe" ground. As hooks notes, "Many professors have conveyed to me the feeling that their classroom should be a 'safe' place, that usually translates to mean that the professor lectures to a group of quiet students who respond only when they are called on" (1994, 39). hooks writes here of the university classroom. I found in the high school classroom I studied that at uncomfortable moments teacher and students alike retreated. Unfortunately, this retreat colluded in silencing already marginalized individuals. Classroom strategies that focus on supporting marginalized students instead of seeking safety might increase the sense of conflict in the room but might go further toward interrupting the relations of domination in the classroom.

Reading *The Bluest Eye* in class did provide at least a small space for talking about issues that the dominant ideology does not acknowledge. However, young people can clearly construct unequal race and gender relations even as they discuss a feminist, antiracist novel. Thus we must make attention to classroom dynamics as much a part of our pedagogy as attention to curriculum. To do so would mean confronting the tensions that arise when someone like Shameka talks about menstruation or someone like Paul talks about violence against Asian Americans. We need to develop teaching strategies to address these kinds of tensions and interrupt the patterns of domination and exclusion that young people can perpetuate through their relations with each other.

Notes

1. For the purposes of this paper I will call the classroom I observed a "feminist" one, although after having done my research I no longer believe that *intent to expose* students to feminist ideas automatically constitutes a feminist classroom. As my fieldwork revealed, the complex dynamics among young people in a classroom can work to subvert a teacher's feminist intentions.

2. See, for example, Fine 1991, Freire 1971, McNeil 1986. Also see Ellsworth 1989 for a feminist critique of this work.

3. I am interpreting "sexuality" broadly to mean not just one's experience of sexual acts but one's experience of one's (sexual) body. Thus I suggest that menstruation is part of a woman's experience of her sexuality.

4. It is interesting to note that the teacher, Ms. Martinez, does not like to identify herself ethnically. Instead of positioning herself along racial or ethnic lines, Ms. Martinez positions herself as someone who has experienced political struggle and says that it is in the sense of shared struggle that students relate to her. Ms. Martinez spoke about race, however, only in terms of black and white. She told me that she teaches African American literature because it is relevant to the lives of her students. When I asked her about the Asian students, she said that the Asian kids do not really relate to the African American literature and often ask her why they do not read Asian literature. Ms. Martinez said she thought that her two Asian students, Paul and Nao, felt alienated but that their alienation was connected more to their feeling oppressed as graffiti artists than to racial tension. She did not see the Asian students' alienation as a racial issue and therefore did not seem to see

a contradiction between her reasons for choosing certain books (i.e., relevance to her students' lives) and the actual racial composition of students in her classroom.

References

Belenky, Mary Field, Blythe McVicker Clinchy, Nancy Rute Goldberger, and Jill Mattuck Tarule. "Connected Education for Women." *Journal of Education* 167, 3 28–45.

Christian, Barbara. *Black Women Novelists. The Development of a Tradition.* Westport, CT: Greenwood.

Ellsworth, Elizabeth. "Why Doesn't This Feel Empowering? Working Through the Repressive Myths of Critical Pedagogy." *Harvard Educational Review* 59, 3 297–324.

Fine, Michelle. *Framing Dropouts.* Albany: SUNY Press.

Freire, Paulo. *Pedagogy of the Oppressed.* New York: Herder and Herder.

hooks, bell. *Talking Back.* Boston: South End.

———. *Teaching to Transgress. Education as the Practice of Freedom.* New York: Routledge.

Jordan, June. *Civil Wars.* Boston: Beacon.

Kramarae, Cheris, and Paula Treichler. "Power Relationships in the Classroom." *Gender in the Classroom.* Ed. Susan Gabriel and Isaiah Smithson, Urbana U. of Illinois P.

Lorde, Audre. *Sister Outsider.* Freedom, CA: Crossing.

McNeil, Linda. *Contradictions of Control.* New York: Routledge.

Morrison, Toni. *The Bluest Eye.* New York: Washington Square.

CHAPTER FOUR

The Biology and Philosophy of Race and Sex

A Course

DIANE SUTER AND DAVID SCHWEICKART

> I learned so much useful stuff! My relationships have gotten better because I understand them more. I was able to relate what I learned to my other classes and to my life.
>
> Coming to class was like having an adventure, learning something exciting and new.
>
> The lectures, while sometimes they really pissed me off, were the best part of the course.
>
> This should be a required course for graduation. It's that good.
>
> Please offer this class every semester for other students. Wonderful—should be a required course to be an American.
>
> —Comments from Student Evaluations, Philosophy 276/Biology 395, Fall 1996

In the fall of 1996 we taught an unusual course, a three-credit-hour team-taught interdisciplinary course in which half of the students were enrolled for philosophy core credit and half for biology elective credit. Given the disciplinary, gender, and racial mix of the class, and the number of hot-button issues we had broached, we were more than a little apprehensive as we began looking over our evaluations. But apprehension evolved into elation as we proceeded. On a scale of 1–5, 5 being the highest, our forty students rated the course a 4.5. They rated us as instructors even higher. And they had offered such comments as those listed above.

It *was* a good course. We confronted many sensitive issues head on. We took risks. But the results, in our judgment, more than repaid efforts. Neither of us has ever taught a course that seemed to impact so directly and in so many ways on our students' lives.

This article aims to encourage other teachers to attempt something similar. As a result of our experience with this course, we have become strong advocates both of interdisciplinary teaching and of addressing in the classroom the controversies about gender, race, and sexual orientation that are the stuff of daily life for most of our students. Although it is not likely that our course would be duplicated in all its particulars by other teachers, we think that a presentation of our course in some detail might be of use to faculty who share our convictions and are willing to experiment.

Origins

The origins of our course date to the fall of 1993, when Diane Suter, Department of Biology, and David Schweickart, Department of Philosophy, submitted a proposal to a Loyola University Chicago Core Curriculum Committee to construct an interdisciplinary, team-taught course that would address the topics of race and gender from the points of view of science and philosophy. We were each awarded a summer grant, funded by the Mellon Foundation, to develop such a course.

The course evolved in stages. We worked together over the summer to come up with a tentative course syllabus. Dr. Suter then offered a trial version of the course as a Directed Reading to two students who were particularly interested in the subject matter. The two students, both women, one African American and one white, one heterosexual and one lesbian, responded well to most of the material, but they had important criticisms and suggestions, which were taken into account as we modified our syllabus for the first official offering of the course, Fall 1995. We further modified the course when we taught it again, Fall 1996. This most recent offering is the primary focus of this paper.

Course Structure

Early in our planning we decided to impose a modular construction on the course. The first third of the course would be devoted to gender, the second third to race, and the last third to sexual orientation. Given the vast amount of material available on each of these topics, we knew we would have to omit many relevant issues and neglect many relevant texts. We decided to aim for (relative) depth rather than breadth. We judged that it would be more effective to concentrate on a few authors and issues in some detail than to try to touch as many bases as possible.

We also decided early on to run the course in a true interdisciplinary fashion. Each of us would attend all the lectures. Each of us would read and grade all the assignments. The latter requirement meant that each of us would have to learn something of the other's discipline—not an effortless task but a rewarding one. It also entailed an extra step in the grading process. Each of us would grade each exam, keeping a record of how many points we assigned to each question. We would then meet and compare our results. In almost all cases we would simply average the two scores for each question. Where there was a wide discrepancy between our respective evaluations, we would sometimes reread the student's answer and negotiate a compromise. We strove to keep such negotiations to a minimum, however, for the sake of both time and nerves.

The first time we offered the course, one or the other of us would often teach several consecutive sessions in covering a particular topic. We modified this procedure the second time around, this time simply alternating philosophy and biology lectures. The new procedure made the disciplinary balance more secure—and removed a source of tension between us. (There was no longer the temptation for one of us to ask the other for an additional class day to cover material that had been planned but not covered.) Students, for whom the repeated switching of intellectual gears during an academic day is routine, had no trouble with this arrangement.

We gave three in-class examinations, one for each of the three modules. To alleviate student anxiety as to what to expect from so unusual a course— and to insure that they studied what we felt was most important—we gave out a list of study questions before each exam. We would typically list thirty or so technical terms to be identified and a dozen short-answer essay questions. The examinations were taken from these questions.

We also required some writing. In our Fall 1995 course we required that each student turn in a 5–7 page "reaction paper" for each of the three parts of the course. These were not graded, apart from an indication of satisfactory or unsatisfactory, but failure to do them resulted in a grade penalty. In the Fall 1996 course we substituted a journal requirement for the reaction papers. Students were expected to write roughly two pages per day, reflecting on the material covered. The journals were collected at the end of the semester and assigned a grade based on length, completeness, balance between science and philosophy, and quality of reflection. This grade accounted for 25% of the course grade.

In the Fall 1995 course we experimented with a concluding "group event," which substituted for a final examination. (Details of this event, a "Senate Hearing" on a gay rights ordinance, will be described in the next section.) We were compelled to drop this event from our Fall 1996 offering because of excessive enrollment. A registration misunderstanding resulted in forty-three students being admitted to the course, which was supposed to have been capped at thirty.

In Fall 1995 we had our students purchase Simone de Beauvoir's *The Second Sex* (1989), Simon LeVay's *The Sexual Brain* (1993), Stephen Jay Gould's *The Mismeasure of Man* (1981), W.E.B. Du Bois's *The Souls of Black Folks* (1961), Audre Lorde's *The Cancer Journals* (1980), and a course packet containing selections from *The Bell Curve* (Hermstein and Murray 1994) and from the writings of James Baldwin (1990), bell hooks (1981), Jonathan Kozol (1991), Richard Lewontin (1992), Michel Foucault (1990), and Adrienne Rich (1986). We revised our syllabus substantially for Fall 1996, particularly our module on race, dropping Gould, the *Bell Curve* material, Du Bois, Lorde, and Baldwin and adding Andrew Hacker's *Two Nations* (1992) and selections from Luigi Luca Cavalli-Sforza (1996), Harlan Dalton (1995), and Dean Hamer (1994). (Sec References for a full listing of the readings.)

The module on gender was carried over intact from Fall 1995 to Fall 1996. *The Second Sex*, with its emphasis on the (non-deterministic) importance of biology and its explicitly philosophical orientation, was a perfect text. Beauvoir begins straightaway with the fundamental question, "What is a woman?"—which, of course, also raises the question, "What is a man?" (1989, xix).

We read the first part of *The Second Sex* as an attempt to answer the historical question, Why patriarchy? We stressed the originality of her non-deterministic, existentialist hypothesis. We proceeded to Beauvoir's famous assertion. "One is not born but rather one becomes a woman." (267) and examined a portion of her phenomenological account of this becoming (her chapter on sexual initiation), and then her fierce moral critique of the institution of marriage. We concluded with her vision of a world without patriarchy.

Interwoven with Beauvoir's existentialist analyses were lectures on the scientific aspects of gender, which employed the opening chapters of *The Sexual Brain* as a framework. We began with a deceptively simple-sounding question: What is the difference between male and female? Our students discovered that, although they were pretty sure they could tell the difference between male and female humans, they were at a loss when it came to, say, seahorses or trees.

We then investigated the molecular mechanisms whereby a sexually indifferent human embryo develops male or female physical characteristics. We shook their confidence about human sexual identity by examining the phenomenon of intersexes—infants with ambiguous genitalia, individuals with male internal genitalia but female outward appearance, children whose outward appearance changes from female to male at puberty. The point of this exercise was to convince the students that, even biologically speaking, sexual identity is far more ambiguous than is commonly supposed.

Our race module began with a discussion of the reasons why we had chosen to emphasize black and white racial identities instead of being more inclusive. (We spoke of time constraints and also of our conviction that this particular racial dynamic is the most persistent and most virulent in our culture.) In Fall 1995 we adopted a historical approach in philosophy with Du Bois, Baldwin, and Kozol, while in science we focused on the *Bell Curve* controversy and its historical antecedents. We used selections from bell hooks for insights into the complex connections between racism and sexism.

While our Fall 1995 approach was not unsuccessful, we decided to confront current racial tensions more directly in Fall 1996. We kept bell

hooks but replaced our male writers with two recent works, one by a
white sociologist (Hacker) and one by a black law professor (Dalton). Both
are pessimistic about the immediate future, but both call for frank dialogue. Hacker supplies much statistical data and is rather brutal in his assessment of white attitudes. Dalton is equally frank, but his tone is more
hopeful. (Compare the book titles: *Racial Healing* as against *Two Nations:
Black and White, Separate, Hostile, Unequal.*)

The emphasis this time was to clarify racial perceptions, the differing
ways in which whites and blacks think about race. In the philosophical
segment we analyzed such concepts as racial identity, guilt and fear, and
the prejudice/racism distinction. We brought these concepts to bear on
an issue much in the news at the time: the referendum in California on
affirmative action.

For the scientific perspective on race, we used selections from Cavalli-
Sforza's recent work, *The Great Human Diasporas*, and a sample of Lewontin's masterful debunking of biological determinism from *Biology as
Ideology*. We dropped *The Mismeasure of Man* from the second iteration,
because the *Bell Curve* controversy had faded and because Gould's work
has a historical orientation more compatible with Du Bois and Baldwin
than with Hacker and Dalton.

Cavalli-Sforza's work makes three scientific points: first, available evidence points strongly to the conclusion that the human species was born
in Africa; second, although there is a gradual change in gene frequencies
as one moves across the continents, clean biological breaks that would
define races in a non-problematical fashion are non-existent; and third,
far more biological variation resides in the variation among individual
humans within a racial grouping than among racial groups themselves.

Although Cavalli-Sforza's book is accessible to the non-scientist, the
statistical concepts were somewhat difficult for our students to grasp. To
provide them with a memorable illustration using their own bodies, we
played "the genetics game," details of which will be given in the next
section.

Two recent works formed the scientific backdrop for our treatment of
sexual orientation, LeVay's *The Sexual Brain* and Hamer's *The Science of
Desire*. Both LeVay and Hamer argue that the evidence points to there being a genetic component to (at least male) homosexuality. Concurrently
we employed some selections from Foucault's dramatic reinterpretation
of "homosexuality" in ancient Greece to highlight some of the cultural
dimensions of sexual preference. (Foucault argues that the modern concept, "homosexual," has no application in classical Greece.)

Not surprisingly, many students were frustrated when they learned
that we could not give a definitive answer to the question of genetic disposition. At the same time, learning why we could not, which involved

looking closely at both the logic of the argument and the scientific procedures employed, was instructive. Both the ingenuity of the experiments and their limitations were underscored, and some general observations were made as to both the power and the pitfalls of deploying scientific methodology in arenas that are politically and morally charged.

With respect to lesbianism, it turns out that science has little to say at this point in time. When we were teaching our course in the fall of 1996, Hamer's research group had just published a genetic study on lesbians complementary to their work on gay men. No layperson's work had yet been written—and may never be written—so we recapped the results in lecture form: no genetic linkage between lesbian sisters like the one for which they had presented evidence in their study of gay brothers. We concluded our discussion of the scientific study of sexual orientation by observing that in fact there has been very little scientific study of lesbianism to date. Students were invited to speculate as to why.

For a philosophical perspective on lesbianism, we returned to Beauvoir, to her chapter. "The Lesbian," and followed that with Rich's brilliant, provocative "Compulsory Heterosexuality." (Interestingly, this article and *The Second Sex* were ranked by our students in their course evaluations as the two most significant works of the course.)

Special Features

The Senate Hearing

In the first iteration of our course we ran a Mock Senate Hearing on a fictitious bill extending several specific rights (to equal access to employment and housing, to serve in the Armed Forces, to legal marriage and adoption) to all persons regardless of sexual orientation. The event was well received by our students, so we decided to incorporate it into our Fall 1996 course as well. However, as noted above, over-enrollment forced us to abandon that plan. For a class of thirty or fewer, however, the event is popular and pedagogically useful. Here are some details:

Dr. Suter first started employing this role-playing device in a science class shortly after the televised Senate hearing on Clarence Thomas's Supreme Court nomination in which he faced Anita Hill's accusations of sexual harassment. Students at that time were reasonably familiar with the actual format of a Senate hearing. This situation no longer obtains, so it was necessary to specify to the students the basic structure: various expert witnesses for and against a proposed piece of legislation testify to a panel of Senators, who then question them. The hearing is moderated by the chair of the committee.

We invented some twenty roles, complete with a brief description of personalities—six members of the "Senate Committee on Human Rights," a number of "expert witnesses" in favor of the human rights ordinance, and a number of "expert witnesses" in opposition. Some of the roles came from the course readings—Simon LeVay, Simone de Beauvoir, Michel Foucault, and Adrienne Rich. (See Appendix I for the full project description.) We assigned students to roles, sometimes in pairs to accommodate the class size, after polling them for their preferences. (The one role to which careful consideration must he given in its assignment is that of the Senate Committee Chair, since that student moderates the entire hearing. The Chair must be strict in keeping the Senators and witnesses on topic and presentations on time.)

We allowed three hours for the event, one hour of in-class preparation on the last day of class and two hours—the time allotted for a final exam—for the Hearing itself. The last day of class was devoted to discussion within the three groups—the Committee, the witnesses in favor, and the witnesses against the bill—regarding what the important questions to be discussed should be, who should ask them, who should answer them, and what the answers might be. Individual students, or pairs of students (when they were sharing a role), were then expected to spend some time outside of class researching their roles and preparing their testimonies. The final exam period was devoted to the actual event, during which the witnesses provided testimony from their particular area of expertise, the Senators questioned the witnesses, and the instructors sat in the back corners of the room taking notes furiously, since each student's effort was graded. (We did not have this part of the course constitute a large percentage of the student's grade, only 10 percent. We thought it necessary to provide a grade incentive to insure serious effort, but we didn't want too much to turn on our evaluations.)

The Genetics Game

This "game," which is actually a laboratory exercise, proved to be an excellent instructional tool for showing that the concept of race is highly arbitrary from a biological point of view. Specifically, it demonstrates that genes that give rise to racial characteristics (skin color, hair texture, etc.) correlate very little, if at all, with other genetically determined traits.

First, the students were given a set of thirteen simple inherited traits and asked to determine which they had. (See Appendix II for a description of the traits.) Second, they were asked to make two lists of three names each: the three students in the class they think will have answers most like their own, and the three they think will be the most unlike. (We had our students stand under large name tags, which they made for themselves and taped to the wall, during this part of the process, since the students did not generally know more than a handful of their classmates' names.) Students were not required at any point to make their lists public, a policy designed to promote frankness.

The students turned in to us their answers to the genetics questions. These data were compiled and returned to the students at the beginning of the next science class. Students were then asked to determine which three students were in fact the most like themselves and which were in fact the most different and to compare these results with their guesses. Then we asked how many people had guessed right on all six names, on five names, etc. As is usually the case, no one had guessed right about more than two or three of their six names. It was pointed out that this would happen merely through random chance.

We then asked if anyone was willing to volunteer her rationale for choosing the names she did. No one was required to answer, but predictably, there were a few students willing to admit publicly that they chose along racial lines. The fallacy of this line of reasoning was discussed.

Extra Credit

During the Fall 1996 semester, there occurred no fewer than a dozen campus events (films, speakers, panel discussions) with direct relevance to the course material. Although we had not thought of doing so beforehand, we decided, when the first event came to our attention, to offer extra credit to students who attended such events. We decided to add one percentage point per event to the final grade of any student who attended an event announced to the class in advance, and who wrote up a one-page summary or reaction. Given such an incentive, most students attended at least one campus event that they would have otherwise skipped. (A few of our male students attended a talk by a gay, former professional women's basketball player, entitled "The Stronger Women Get, the More Men Love Football.") A couple of students attended as many as eight events. One of us also tried to attend each event to take attendance. This required more of a commitment than we had bargained for, since we had not anticipated that there would be so many relevant events on campus during a single semester, but it seemed necessary, given the potentially dramatic impact that this policy could have on student grades.

The end results seemed well worth the effort. Our students were pleased at having the opportunity to raise their grades. Sponsoring organizations (often Women's Studies or Black World Studies) were delighted to have the extra attendance at their events. Our students became more engaged than usual in the intellectual life of the campus. Many students commented on the valuable learning experience they had received outside of the classroom.

Closing Discussion

In lieu of the Mock Senate Hearing, we closed our Fall 1996 course with an Oprah Winfrey–style discussion. On the last day of class we called for an open critique of the course. We asked our students to share publicly whatever portion of their anonymous teacher-course evaluations (which they had just completed) they were willing to share. The instructors moderated the discussion by asking the students to answer specific questions. We started with non-threatening questions, like "What did you learn that surprised you?" then proceeded to a more provocative question, "What made you angry?" The discussion was both good-natured and serious (although not quite so candid as the anonymous evaluations). Our students seemed to enjoy this wrap-up immensely, apparently because it gave them an opportunity to learn more about their classmates, to reflect and synthesize, and to contribute to the ongoing development of what everyone agreed was a most important course.

Student Reactions

Students were overwhelmingly positive about our course. This is the large conclusion drawn from our student evaluations. Almost every evaluation was supplemented with high-praise written comments. (The analysis in this section, unless otherwise specified, refers to our most recent offering of the course, Fall 1996.)

Who were our students? Their interests and backgrounds were anything but homogeneous. Half of the students had signed up for the course as a biology elective; half had signed up for philosophy core credit. Most of the students were juniors or seniors, since they had enrollment priority, and the course closed very quickly. Three quarters of our students were women thirty of forty. A slight majority was white (twenty-three), with nine Asians, four African/Americans, three Hispanics, and one Native American composing the remainder.

The biology/philosophy mix was by design. Students were required to register for either Biology 395 or Philosophy 276, each of which was capped at twenty. As noted, the course closed almost instantly. There were far more students wanting to take the course than we were prepared to admit. One or more additional sections would easily have filled.

We are not certain as to why there were so many more women in the class than men. The Loyola undergraduate body is about 60 percent women, so it is not unusual to have a majority of women in a class, but the 75 percent figure is high. Presumably a course highlighting gender is more attractive (or less threatening) to women than to men. The racial mix of the class was also significantly greater than that of the general student body.

Ten percent of our students were African American, as compared to 2.5 percent of the Loyola student body (that latter figure, in the eyes of both of us, disgracefully low, especially for a Chicago university). Again we presume that advertised course content accounts for the greater racial diversity.

Although the course was evaluated highly by our students, not all parts were judged to be equally successful. Among the texts employed, Beauvoir and Rich were the most highly ranked, with Dalton, Cavalli-Sforza, hooks, and LeVay also getting high marks. (The question asked on the evaluation form was, Which of the following were the most significant? Least significant? Students could list as many authors as they wished in each category.) Both Hamer and Foucault were given more negative appraisals than positive. Students were split on Hacker. His overall appraisal was more positive than negative, but several of the negatives were vehement.

The element of the course most consistently criticized was the journal requirement. Some students liked doing the journal, but they were outnumbered by those who did not. Many thought the two-page per day requirement excessive. Many complained that too many people put off writing until the end and then tailored their writing to our guidelines.

The element most consistently offered as a "suggestion for improvement" was more discussion. Lack of sufficient discussion was a major complaint following our first offering of the course. We tried to incorporate more discussion this time, on a number of occasions having students break into small groups to discuss a given topic, then report back to the class. Students liked these discussions, but many still felt that we should have lectured less, discussed more.

Concluding Reflections: Interdisciplinary Teaching and Teaching Race

There are two aspects of the course that merit a more extended commentary than we have so far given: the interdisciplinary nature of the course and the particular difficulties we encountered, as well as strategies we devised for overcoming them, in teaching about race. Instead of a summary-conclusion, let us offer some reflections on these two topics.

In her Introduction to *The Second Sex* Beauvoir remarks on the ubiquity of the category "the other." Human beings are so quick to invoke a "we-they" distinction that it is sometimes enough for a group of people to share the same railway compartment to give rise to a sense of internal solidarity that is counterposed to "the others" (xxiii). All of us in the academy know how this category operates: *our* department, *our* discipline, etc., versus "the others." The category has particular force when it separates we (those) scientists from those (we) humanists. Our course has attempted to bridge these divides of department, discipline, and orientation, not only for our students but also for ourselves.

For the students, the first sense of interdisciplinarity derived from the faculty presence. They were surprised and impressed that we both attended every class. They learned that we each had knowledge of and opinions about the other's discipline. They particularly enjoyed witnessing our arguments with each other. This rudimentary sense of the possibility of seeing a thing through two different lenses came from our example.

The second level of interdisciplinarity, which was different for students of different majors, was an enhanced appreciation for the "other" way of knowing. Non-science majors, who are often confused and intimidated by science (often taught badly), became more engaged when science was brought to bear on issues of direct relevance to their everyday lives. Science majors, often apathetic about general education requirements, began to look at philosophy differently when they saw a scientist/role-model exhibiting a great interest in this other way of knowing.

A third level of interdisciplinarity, perhaps achieved by only a few students, was an awareness of the complementarity of two ways of knowing. Consider the first part of the first module. We began the course with Simon LeVay's modern-day review of how male and female bodies develop biologically. We immediately followed with Beauvoir's 1949 version of the same story (which, by the way, remains so much more current than any 1950s text written by any actual scientist that it takes a biologist's breath away). It is basically one and the same story, but the scientist's and the philosopher's ways of thinking about that story differ. Beauvoir surveys "the facts" so as to ascertain the biological constraints on human freedom. LeVay also sets out "the facts," but with a view to making comprehensible to the layperson the nature and significance of the research he has done, which has involved cutting and slicing as well as reading and writing. Both, however, are concerned to relate the facts of biology to interests that go beyond these facts: how human beings of differing genders and sexual orientations should comprehend and act out their lived situations.

For us as well as for the students the simple act of inviting another instructor into one's classroom on a regular basis constituted an important element of interdisciplinarity. We learned a lot from each other, both about the other's discipline and about our own. It was a refreshing surprise to have someone there to challenge one's assumptions. One is compelled to think more carefully about one's arguments when one knows that a colleague who is inclined to think of things from a different perspective is sitting among the students.

Partly by accident, partly by design we did something in our Fall 1995 class that went beyond the boundaries implicitly set in most interdisciplinary courses: we each ventured a lecture in the other's discipline. Midway into the semester Dr. Schweickart accepted a speaking engagement that required him to be out of town on the day he was to lecture on Adrienne Rich's "Compulsory Heterosexuality." Why couldn't a scientist present and discuss that essay? Dr. Suter agreed to do it. In recompense, Dr. Schweickart presented a technical section of *The Mismeasure of Man.* Why couldn't a philosopher master a small piece of statistical material? Both presentations were well received.

It occurred to us as we contemplated these adjustments to our syllabus that these boundary crossings were pedagogically desirable. Interdisciplinarity involves colleagues respecting the expertise involved in each other's discipline, but at the same time, an overemphasis on respect can reinforce the impression, common in our society, that only "experts" are qualified to comment on issues of scientific, moral, or political complexity. Our cross-disciplinary lectures demonstrated that neither biology nor philosophy is so esoteric that only a specialist in the field can speak about such matters with legitimate conviction.

Doubtless, the most difficult section of this course to teach was the module on race. We expected a sympathetic reception to our treatment of gender, since the class was overwhelmingly female. We were surprised at how little resistance we encountered in discussing sexual orientation, given that our university is a Jesuit institution with a heavily Roman Catholic student body. We were *not* surprised that our lectures and discussion about race were often tense.

White students are deeply ambivalent about race. None will think of themselves as racist. All will profess to believe in the basic equality of races. Yet many will have secret doubts: maybe there *is* a genetic component to black underachievement. (That is, after all, an easy and convenient explanation.)

Most white students will feel that racism is no longer a serious problem in our society. It once was, but it isn't anymore. At the same time, they all know that *something* is wrong. They know about crime and poverty. They know that many blacks are angry and resentful. They feel themselves unjustly targeted by this anger, so they are often resentful in return. They also know that many whites—friends, relatives, maybe even themselves—speak privately about racial matters in terms very different from what they would ever use in public.

What we tried to accomplish in this section of the course for our white students was to help them recognize and make sense of their conflicting attitudes and beliefs. We aimed at validating their basic belief that there is no *genetic* basis for racial inequality. We also wanted to get them to understand just how deep and how serious the racial divide remains, and to feel that it is *our* problem, our *collective* problem. The problem of race in America is not a "black" problem, a problem for blacks, a problem about blacks; above all, it is a *white* problem.

For our black students, we hoped to validate their own sense that racism is alive and well despite its having no biological basis, while at the same time helping them to understand the complicated and peculiar ways in which whites tend to think about race and racism.

Our students who are neither black nor white? We hoped they would learn something useful from the lectures and discussions. They are in the fortunate position of not being so deeply or personally implicated in the issues under scrutiny. We did anticipate that Asian students would tend to have views much closer to white students than to black students, and our sense here proved to be correct. Asians have become, or are in the process of becoming, in Andrew Hacker's unsettling phrase, "honorary whites."

The science lectures in this module were less fraught with tension than the philosophy lectures. These lectures confirmed what students really want to believe: that there is no scientific basis for racism. Students were supplied with facts and good arguments to counter assertions to the contrary when they encounter such views outside the classroom.

The pedagogical strategy underlying the philosophy lectures was twofold. Dr. Schweickart tried to signal to black students that he was on their side, and that he would do justice to their perceptions and feelings. At the same time he tried to signal to white students that he understands, from the inside, their own ambivalences.

White students resist lectures about race, because such lectures are perceived as being designed to make them feel guilty. To get at that problem, Dr. Schweickart began his first lecture, a historical overview of racism and anti-racism in America, with a quote from Richard Wright (from Max's speech at the trial of Bigger Thomas):

> Of all things men do not like to feel they are guilty of wrong, and if you try to make them feel guilty, they will justify it on any grounds; failing that, and seeing no immediate solution that will set things right without too much cost to their lives and property, they will kill that which evoked in them the condemning sense of guilt. And this is true of all men, whether they be black or white. (1966, 360)

We proceeded to discuss the difference between feeling guilty about something—and the destructive consequences of such feelings—and assuming a degree of personal responsibility for resolving a collective problem. Toward the end of that first session, students were asked to break into small groups and discuss two questions: What is your own racial identity? What does it mean today to be white in America? We had wondered ahead of time about whether to ask the black students to form their own group, or simply to let them mingle with the other students. The first option felt awkward; the second option meant that most black students would find themselves the only black voice in their group. On the strong advice of a black student whose opinion we consulted, we let the students choose their own groups. (They did not self-segregate along racial lines.)

This discussion proved to be fruitful. Students were given the occasion to reveal to one another something of themselves. White students were made aware that they do not normally think of themselves as having a racial identity—whereas black students certainly do. The question of being white in America generated some heat. One of our black students told us later that she thought she offended some of the white students in her group. Still, she thought the discussion was useful.

In addition to guilt we tried to address the issue of fear. Hacker writes about white fear of blacks and black fear of whites. During the discussion of Hacker's analysis, Dr. Schweickart raised another possibility: white fear of whites, that is to say, the fear and intimidation a white person often feels when confronted with an expression of white racism. A number of white students acknowledged this fear in their journals. One of our black students commented on black fear of blacks.

As it happened, the national debate was unfolding as we taught this class concerning the California "Civil Rights Initiative," which was to eliminate, among other things, all affirmative action considerations in granting admission to state universities and professional schools. We decided to devote a class period to this issue. (The first time we taught this course, the verdict of the O.J. Simpson criminal trial was handed down at precisely the time our class was meeting. We watched the verdict on a hastily recruited television monitor and discussed it during the remaining class time. It was a highly charged, emotional session.)

Dr. Schweickart began by explaining what the deceptively named "civil rights" initiative was about, and then tried to articulate how different most white perceptions of the issue were from most black perceptions. He then announced that he was going to argue for a position with which he presumed many in the class would disagree, namely, that to vote for the California Civil Rights Initiative was to commit a racist act.

The crux of his argument turned on the distinction between "racism," defined as actions or institutions chat tend to perpetuate the subordination of a racial group, and "prejudice," defined as the belief that most members of a racial group possess certain undesirable qualities. It is our view that this important distinction—a commonplace among black scholars and obvious to most black students—is quite difficult for white students to grasp. Schweickart proceeded to argue that although it was perfectly possible—indeed likely in many instances—that a person voting for the California Civil Rights Initiative was not prejudiced, nevertheless, such a person was guilty of racism.

Many of our students could not bring themselves to agree. The question was given to them to be discussed in their small groups. Although a majority reported that they would vote against the Initiative, a significant minority said they would vote for it. (The groups reported back their votes, but the identities of who voted which way were known only to the group members, not to the class at large.)

The students who supported the Initiative were doubtless unhappy with Dr. Schweickart's uncompromising position, just as some students were quite upset the year before when Dr. Suter argued that all whites have engaged in racist behavior at some time or another (again invoking the racism/prejudice distinction). But it seems to us important, for both moral and pedagogical reasons, for the good of our white students, as well as our black students, that we address certain issues squarely, without waffling.

It is our hope that our providing a detailed account of this course will inspire others to venture down a similar path. Although fraught with dangers and difficulties, there are few teaching experiences that can be so rewarding as addressing with a committed colleague immediate, important, highly charged social concerns. Scientists have long been in the business of changing the world. Since Marx, philosophers have been urged to do the same. Needless to say, no one course, however well designed and executed, will accomplish anything so grand, but we are convinced, as were many of our students, that such a course can accomplish something.

APPENDIX I: The Mock Senate Hearing

The following was distributed to our students. They were then asked to list in writing the roles they would most prefer to play and/or the ones they would least prefer. The next period we announced our assignment of the roles, then allowed the students the remainder of the class period to begin their preparation. The Hearing was conducted during the two-hour period allotted during Finals Week for a final examination.

FINAL GROUP EVENT
THE AMERICAN GAY RIGHTS BILL
SENATE HEARING

For the final group project in this class, we will hold a mock Senate hearing. In a Senate hearing, a particular Senate committee examines expert witnesses on specific facets of a political issue in order to gather information to help them vote knowledgeably on a bill before that committee.

For our group event, the Senate Committee on Civil Rights is considering the following bill, designated the American Gay Rights Bill: Residents of the United States are guaranteed equal rights regarding employment, legal marriage, adoption, housing, military service, and other civil matters, without regard to sexual orientation.

No such bill is currently pending in the U.S. Senate. Many local governments, however, have passed laws on both sides of this issue. The city of Chicago, for example, passed a Human Rights Ordinance in the mid-1980s that guarantees equal rights within the city without regard to sex, race, ethnic origin, age, or sexual orientation. On the other side of the issue, the state of Colorado passed a law several years ago that prohibited local governments from passing any local law barring discrimination based on sexual orientation.

The job of each student in the class will be to play the role of one person involved in the Senate hearing. The role of each Senator will be played by an individual student. The role of each expert witness will be played by a team of two students. Please note that most organizations mentioned below are fictitious, although they are similar to many organizations that do exist and work actively on issues regarding sexual orientation. The roles are as follows:

The Senators

1. The Chair of the Senate Committee on Human Rights. The Chair runs the hearings, recognizing each Senator in turn to examine the witnesses, and examines witnesses him/herself. The Chair must interrupt the proceedings if a Senator or a witness speaks too long, speaks out of turn, gets off the subject, or otherwise disrupts the flow of the Hearing. The Chair of any Senate Committee is a member of the majority party at the time. The Chair of our Senate Committee on Human Rights is a senior Republican who supports his/her party's public opposition to this bill, but who is duty-bound to run a fair and open hearing.

2. A second Republican Senator who is also opposed to the bill, and is up for reelection in 1996.

3. A third Republican Senator, a moderate elected from a moderate state, who supports the bill.

4. A fourth Republican Senator, a gay/lesbian whose sexual orientation is not publicly known. S/he personally supports the bill but has not made her/his position on the bill known before the hearing. S/he must struggle with the problem that her/his personal position is at odds with the announced position of the Republican Party.

5. A Democratic Senator, a liberal from a state with a large gay/lesbian constituency, who is in favor of the bill.

6. A second Democratic Senator, a moderate, who is also in favor of the bill.

Expert Witnesses Personally in Favor of the Bill

1. Dr. Simon LeVay, an acclaimed neurobiologist who published a famous study suggesting that the brains of gay men are structurally different from the brains of straight men.
2. Mr. Michel Foucault, a famous gay French philosopher, who views contemporary Western notions of homosexuality as being cultural constructions.
3. Ms. Simone de Beauvoir, another famous French philosopher, who takes a decidedly existentialist view of the question of sexual orientation.
4. Ms. Adrienne Rich, a poet and teacher, a lesbian, who has written extensively on sexual orientation, and particularly on lesbianism, from a feminist perspective.
5. The President of the Minnesota Parent. Teachers Association, a teacher who supports the right of gays and lesbians to choose education as a career and to teach at all levels.
6. A U.S. Army general who supports the admission of gays and lesbians into the military.
7. The President of Gay and Lesbian Catholics, an organization of Catholics in the United States who support the Catholic Church but disagree with its position that homosexual activity is sinful.

Expert Witnesses Personally Opposed to the Bill

1. The President of the North Carolina Parent-Teachers Association, who is opposed to the presence of gays or lesbians in the classroom because of concerns that they would influence the sexual orientation of their students.
2. The President of the Christian Coalition. This organization is a fundamentalist, politically ultraconservative organization. Its publicly stated position is in opposition to any recognition of equal rights for gays and lesbians, because it takes the view that homosexuality is a sinful, unnatural, and perverted way of life.
3. A U.S. Army general who supports the traditional military position of barring gays and lesbians from service in the U.S. military.
4. A spokesperson for the U.S. Catholic Bishops Conference. The Conference in general supports equal rights for gays and lesbians, even though the official teaching of the Catholic Church is that homosexual activity is sinful. The Conference is concerned and divided, however, on the issue of allowing gays and lesbians to teach at Catholic schools.
5. A prominent psychiatrist who supports a basically Freudian, non-genetic and non-biological view of the development of sexual orientation.

Rules and Suggestions

1. The witnesses have not been summoned by the Senate Committee to provide an opportunity to lobby. They have been invited because each one has expertise in a particular area of relevance, and the Senate Committee has need of their expertise. The witnesses would certainly try to support a particular position in the course of answering questions, but their most important job is to prepare and provide information in their area of expertise.

2. The job of the expert witnesses on the preparation day is to discuss how the area of expertise of each role is relevant to the Senators' decision-making process, and what questions the Senators are likely to ask of each person. The witnesses are encouraged to suggest to the Senators questions that they would find relevant. The expert witnesses should make sure that they prepare to answer potential questions from the point of view of the role they are playing, whether that point of view coincides with their own personal view or not. A good grade for the group event will depend upon your ability to make one or two careful arguments from the point of view of the role you are playing.

3. The role of the Senators is to consider the areas of expertise represented by the expert witnesses, consider how that expertise is relevant to the question of the bill at hand, and devise questions that will allow the expert witnesses to give testimony explaining what they know. The Senators are encouraged to discuss their questions with the witnesses in advance. The questions should not ask the witnesses for their opinions on the bill. Instead, they should ask the witnesses for their opinions in their areas of expertise that will assist the Senators in formulating their vote on the bill. Hint: Each Senator is most likely to ask questions of "friendly" witnesses that will elicit information favorable to his/her own opinion. The Senators may, however, ask questions that would force an expert witness to give testimony somewhat antagonistic to the witness's own personal position, as long as it is reasonably within the witness's area of expertise. For example, a Senator in favor of the bill may ask the psychiatrist to talk about "cure" rates, knowing full well that therapy is notoriously unsuccessful at changing a person's sexual orientation. The psychiatrist would then be compelled to provide accurate information, but would then want to give his/her own interpretation of that information. It is the job of the Senate Committee to be sure that all witnesses get approximately equal time, and equal opportunity to display their expertise. A good grade for a Senator will depend upon your ability to include all relevant lines of reasoning in the hearing.

APPENDIX II: Simple Inherited Human Traits

Copies of the following were distributed to our students in conjunction with the "genetics game." Each student did a self-evaluation during class, with assistance from classmates and instructors.

SIMPLE INHERITED HUMAN TRAITS

1. Attached ear lobes? In most people the ear lobes hang free, but in some the ear lobes are attached directly onto the side of the head.
2. Widow's peak? In some people the hairline drops downward and forms a distinct point in the center of the forehead.
3. Tongue rolling? Some people can roll the tongue into a distinct U-shape when the tongue is extended from the mouth. Others can do no more than produce a slight downward curve of the tongue when it is extended from the mouth.
4. Bent little finger? In some people, the last joint of the little finger bends inward toward the fourth finger. Lay both hands flat on the table and relax the muscles to look for this trait.
5. Hitch hiker's thumb? Certain persons can bend the last joint of the thumb back until there is almost a 90 degree angle between the last two bones. Use a protractor to check the angle that you can create, and enter a "yes" if it's close to 90 degrees.
6. Long palmar muscle? Some people have a long palmar muscle which can be detected by examination of the tendons that run over the inside of the wrists. Clench your fist tightly and flex your hand (that is, bend it forward). Now feel the tendons. If there are three, you have the long palmar muscle. If there are only two (the large middle one will be missing), you do not.
7. Pigmented iris? Some people have no pigment in the front part of the eyes, and a blue layer at the back of the iris shows through. Such people have blue eyes. Others have pigment deposited in the front layer of the iris, masking the blue to varying degrees, making the eyes appear violet, green, hazel, brown, or black.
8. Mid-digital hair? Some people have hair on the second joint of one or more of the fingers. Look carefully—sometimes the hair is very fine. Use a magnifying glass if one is available. Count yourself as a "yes" if you have hair on this joint on any finger.
9. Second finger shorter than the fourth? Put down a "yes" if your index finger is shorter than your ring finger.

10. Left-over-right in folded hand? Clasp your hands together with fingers interlocked. Which thumb is on top, the left or the right? Put down "yes" if your right thumb is on top.
11. Freckles?
12. Darwinian pinna? Some people have a small point on the outer rim of the ear, usually directed back toward the cup of the outer ear.
13. Color blindness? Look at the chart provided. [Such charts are readily available. Most introductory biology texts have them as will any geneticist.] If you can see the numbers "4" and "2" about equally well, you do not have color blindness. If you can see neither number, only one number, or one number much less well than the other, you have some degree of red-green color blindness.

References [Readings Used in Square Brackets]

Baldwin, James. 1990. *Notes of a Native Son.* Boston: Beacon. ["Notes of a Native Son"]

Beauvoir, Simone de. 1989. *The Second Sex,* New York: Vintage. ["Introduction," "Data of Biology" (3–9, 25–37), "Psychoanalytic Point of View," "Historical Materialism," "Nomads," "Sexual Initiation," "The Married Woman," "The Lesbian"]

Cavalli-Sforza, Luigi Luca. 1996. *The Great Human Diasporas: The History of Diversity and Evolution.* New York: Addison-Wesley. [62–70, and "How Different Are We?"]

Dalton, Harlan. 1995. *Racial Healing: Confronting the Fear between Blacks and Whites.* New York: Doubleday. [15–23, 27–31, 91–95, 105–13, 117–19, 150–57, 213–25]

Du Bois, W.E.B. 1961. *The Souls of Black Folk.* New York: Fawcett. [Chapters I, II, IX, XI]

Foucault, Michel. 1990. *The History of Sexuality, Vol II. The Uses of Pleasure.* New York: Random House. ["A Problematic Relationship," "A Boy's Honor," "The Object of Pleasure"]

Gould, Stephen Jay. 1981. *The Mismeasure of Man.* New York: Norton. [Chapters 1–3, 5 (146–58), 6, 7 ("Biology and human nature")]

Hacker, Andrew. 1992. *Two Nations: Black and White, Separate, Hostile, Unequal.* New York: Scribner's. [Chapters 1–4, 9, 14]

Hamer, Dean. 1994. *The Science of Desire: The Search for the Gay Gene and the Biology of Behavior.* New York: Simon and Schuster. ["Biological Mechanisms," "Psychological Mechanisms"]

Hermstein, Richard J., and Charles Murray. 1994. *The Bell Curve: Intelligence and Class Structure in American Life.* New York: Free Press. [1–7, 13–25, 295–311, 389–413]

hooks, bell. 1981. *Ain't I a Woman?* Boston: South End Press. ["The Imperialism of Patriarchy"]

Kozol, Jonathan. 1991. *Savage Inequalities: Children in America's Schools.* New York: Crown Publishers. ["Life on the Mississippi"]

LeVay, Simon. 1993. *The Sexual Brain.* Cambridge, MA: MIT Press. [Chapters 1–9, 12]

Lewontin, Richard. 1992. *Biology as Ideology: The Doctrine of DNA.* New York: HarperPerennial. ["All in the Genes?"]

Lorde, Audre. 1980. *The Cancer Journals.* San Francisco: Aunt Lute Books. [All]

Rich, Adrienne. 1986. *Blood, Bread and Poetry: Selected Prose, 1979–1985.* New York: Norton. 1986. ["Compulsory Heterosexuality"]

Wright, Richard. 1966. *Native Son.* New York: Harper and Row.

CHAPTER FIVE

Gender and Masculinity Texts
Consensus and Concerns for Feminist Classrooms

JUDITH KEGAN GARDINER

The Gendered Society by Michael S. Kimmel. New York: Oxford University Press, (1999) 2000, 336 pp., $30.00 hardcover, $25.95 paper.

Revisioning Gender edited by Myra Marx Ferree, Judith Lorber, and Beth B. Hess. Lanham, MD: AltaMira Press, 1998, 536 pp., $85.00 hardcover, $34.95 paper.

Men and Masculinity: A Text Reader edited by Theodore F. Cohen. Belmont, CA: Wadsworth Publishing, 2001, 512 pp., $42.95 paper.

The Gendered Society Reader edited by Michael S. Kimmel with Amy Aronson. New York: Oxford University Press, (1999) 2000, 416 pp., $50.00 hardcover, $24.95 paper.

Men's Lives edited by Michael S. Kimmel and Michael A. Messner. 5th ed. Boston: Allyn and Bacon, 2001, 557 pp., $42.00 paper.

Feminist Frontiers edited by Laurel Richardson, Verta Taylor, and Nancy Whittier. 5th ed. Boston: McGraw Hill, 2001, 592 pp., $43.44 paper.

As a feminist increasingly interested in masculinity studies, I've been thinking about how the turn to gender is shaping feminist scholarship and Women's Studies, looking at new gender textbooks that include more attention to masculinity, and considering how these texts advance or modify feminist interdisciplinary scholarship and agendas for social change. Several new books proclaim that they supersede earlier works of feminist scholarship by applying more complete and theoretically sophisticated understandings of the operations of gender in contemporary U.S. society. Here I discuss four new texts: Michael S. Kimmel's book *The Gendered Society*; the essay collection he edited with Amy Aronson, *The Gendered Society Reader*; a collection of essays entitled *Revisioning Gender*, edited by Myra Marx Ferree, Judith Lorber, and Beth B. Hess; and Theodore F. Cohen's edited *Men and Masculinity: A Text Reader*. I compare these new books with two textbook readers that have recently appeared in fifth editions, Kimmel and Michael A. Messner's *Men's Lives*, and *Feminist Frontiers*, edited by Laurel Richardson, Verta Taylor, and Nancy Whittier.[1] Altogether, the five anthologies include 214 essays, some repeated from volume to volume, most published in the past fifteen years, and many newly written.

I came to these texts with a number of questions. I wondered, for example, how congruent are the masculinity-based texts with Women's Studies approaches? How do they expand feminist approaches to gender inequality so that they include more discussion of men and masculinity, and how do they alter our understandings of gender difference, diversity, and hierarchy? How different are the agendas of even the most sympathetic men's studies texts from the approaches of Women's Studies? What happens to the feminist insistence on interdependencies among the categories of race, class, gender, and sexuality in these gender texts? What theoretical commitments and disciplinary allegiances underlie these approaches? What is lost or gained in the transition from Women's Studies to (masculinity-attentive) gender studies?

I discovered considerable consistency in all of these texts, which demonstrate a new consensus in gender studies based on feminist thought. They agree that gender is a hierarchical relationship that involves male dominance and female subordination in individuals, institutions, and ideological representations, rather than a set of complementary differences in individual personalities. Kimmel makes this case most forcefully: "I argue that gender difference—the assertion of two qualitatively different natures—is the result of gender inequality, not its cause. Gender inequality produces difference, and the differences produced are then used to justify gender inequality" (1999, xi). These books do not treat gender as symmetrical but point out that masculinity involves men's domination of both women and other men, and therefore masculinity and femininity are organized according to differing cultural logics. So Patricia Yancey Martin and David L. Collinson, in *Revisioning Gender*, note that in the contemporary U.S. workplace, "doing femininity" involves "doing heterosexuality," but "doing masculinity" means "doing dominance" (Ferree, Lorber, and Hess 1998, 300). All the texts define gender as relational, with masculinity governing relationships among men as well as between men and women, and the books' political perspectives are congruent. Concurrent with radical feminist theory in this regard, these books all highlight male violence as a serious problem and believe that gender inequality is a major cause: "virtually all the violence in the world today is committed by men," Kimmel states, and "from early childhood to old age, violence is the most obdurate, intractable behavioral gender difference" (1999, 243).

All the books under review agree that gender is not monolithic and static but internally divided, multiple, incoherent, and variable across cultures and historical periods. Favorite analogies are that gender is a process, project, or set of relationships rather than a thing in itself. R.W. Connell says that "gender is the domain of social practice organized in relation to a reproductive arena constituted by the materiality of the body," and "masculinity and femininity in the final analysis are gender projects" (Ferree, Lorber, and Hess 1998, 464–65). Furthermore, he notes that "the outcomes of human development, indeed, seem curiously nondichotomous" (457). According to these authors, conceptualizing gender in this way has political consequences. In *Men and Masculinity*, Cohen writes "because gender is a process, there is room not only for modification and variation by individuals and small groups but also for institutionalized change" (2001, 26).

These texts agree that gender is shaped by and helps to create other axes of social inequality. However, they do not all fully exemplify the "intersectionality" espoused by Patricia Hill Collins:

> The construct of intersectionality references two types of relationships: the interconnectedness of ideas and the social structures in which they occur, and the intersecting hierarchies of gender, race, economic class, sexuality, and ethnicity. Viewing gender within a logic of intersectionality redefines it as a constellation of ideas and social practices that are historically situated within and that mutually construct multiple systems of oppression. (Ferree, Lorber, and Hess 1998, 263)

Revisioning Gender, in which Collins's essay appears, is the most sophisticated of the texts in this respect, genuinely integrating race and class as well as gender and sexuality into the analytic frameworks of its essays, as in Evelyn Nakano Glenn's essay, which opens the collection, on "The Social Construction and Institutionalization of Gender and Race." In *The Gendered Society*, Kimmel adroitly illustrates the intertwined biases of earlier sex role theory by quoting a question from a 1936 survey in which affirmative answers indicate "femininity": "does: being lost; deep water; graveyards at night; Negroes [this is actually on the list!] make you AFRAID?" (1999, 71).

The text readers typically include a wide selection of essays by American people of color, and often these essays are personal rather than analytical. *The Gendered Society Reader*, which has the fewest essays, is least comprehensive in this respect, while *Men's Lives* and *Feminist Frontiers* emphasize their attention to global and domestic diversity.[2] For example, the six essays in *Men's Lives* on "Perspectives on Masculinity" include Manning Marable on black men, Maxine Baca Zinn on Chicano men, Yen Le Espiritu on Asian men, and Phillippe Bourgois on Puerto Rican men. *Feminist Frontiers* opens with a section on "Diversity and Difference" before a section on "Theoretical Perspectives." "Women everywhere live with a ubiquitous 'monotone' of male advantage. . . . Yet differences among women arise from factors like race, ethnicity, class, sexual orientation, age, geographic region, and religion," its editors tell us, adding that "just as gender varies for different groups of women, men also are not an undifferentiated group" (2001, 4–5). *Men and Masculinity*, too, has diverse contributors, with lead essays on homophobia and "macho," though unfortunately its first contribution by an African American author describes having participated in a gang rape. While all the readers consider gay perspectives, they include rather little contemporary queer theory. In fact, *Feminist Frontiers* says that although it added a selection by Judith Butler for "instructors who want to cover representation at a more theoretically sophisticated level," this excerpt "is easily omitted for lower-level courses" (vi).

All these texts are American based, though all include references to larger contexts. *Revisioning Gender* is the most thorough in incorporating globalism into its theoretical perspectives, while *Feminist Frontiers* includes a section on "Global Politics and the State." The general focus on the United States has multiple effects. The globalizing economy is particularly credited for changes in men's status, especially the erosion of breadwinner masculinity, but there is little attention to the American role and its results elsewhere, except in Connell's important essay on "Masculinities and Globalization" in *Men's Lives* and Valentine Moghadam's essay on "Gender and the Global Economy" in *Revisioning Gender*. Homogeneity of women tends to be implied in the gender and masculinity texts, even as a diversity of women is emphasized in women's studies readers, but a more thoroughly global perspective would further problematize diversities among both women and men.

The books agree in a general historical orientation informed by liberal political views. All see gendered meanings as altered by the splitting of household labor from waged work in the Industrial Revolution and believe that work, home, and hence gender are again being transformed by multinational capitalism. In this context, the texts question divisions between public and private, heterosexual and homosexual, masculine and feminine, and all other gendered binaries. All decry the poor scholarship of conservative appeals to a *traditional* family and gender structure, which they see as mystifications of white middle-class America for a brief period after World War II. Kimmel is scathing about conservative attempts to promote Victorian mores—which he calls an "unlikely (and thoroughly nasty) scenario"—and conservative appeals to family values— which he calls a "displaced quarrel with feminism" (112). All the texts appeal to government action and to independent social movements to rectify gender inequality. For example, Moghadam notes that internationally "the massive entry of women into the workforce around the world . . . has coincided with the political mobilization of women": "if there is a specter haunting the global economy, it may very well be that of its 'Other,' a global women's movement" (Ferree, Lorber, and Hess 1998, 150, 153).

These books follow a liberal, progressive, even triumphalist disciplinary narrative as well: earlier theorists shed some light on gender, but they were monolithic, ahistorical, and dependent on individual psychology in comparison to the current scholarship. The books under review share a disciplinary bias in favor of sociology, sometimes militantly so. To a humanist like myself, their dismissals of psychology, psychoanalysis, philosophy, poststructuralist theory, and literary analysis seem somewhat parochial. Media studies, however, are represented in the readers *Men's Lives* and *Men and Masculinity*, and Richardson, Taylor, and Whittier note that they expanded the coverage of culture and representation in the new edition of *Feminist Frontiers* with special attention to television, mass media, and representations of race, gender, and standards of beauty. Although all the texts argue eloquently for large social contexts over individualized psychology, the sociological methodologies of the anthologized text reader selections are often less grand: many of the essays are based on convenience samples and middle-class, mostly white, college students. The implication that sociology, but not other disciplines, can incorporate historical change seems similarly narrow, while these recent texts themselves historicize only fitfully. Kimmel remarks of a chart on nineteenth-century British criminality and gender, "things aren't very different today" (247), and *Men's Lives* caricatures the past in claiming that in seventeenth-century France, a "real man" wore "frilly white lace shirts" and "lots of rouge" (Kimmel and Messner xvi). The authors believe that individual and psychologized theories fail to account for all of gender's effects, and they persuasively argue the importance of gendered institutional contexts. A. Ayres Boswell and Joan Z. Spade, for instance, show that the same men behave differently in more egalitarian settings than in fraternities with a "collegiate rape culture" that objectifies women (Cohen 2001, 368; also Kimmel and Messner 2001, 167).

Another methodological similarity is that these volumes favor social constructionism and argue against biological and evolutionary gender determinism. The authors see their approaches to gender as more nuanced than earlier scholarship, especially than those that utilize socialization and sex role theory. Cohen articulates the common charges against socialization theory, arguing that "change can and does occur independent of the early socialization that would predict it" and that "institutionalized sexism is something that socialization alone could not end" (395). Kimmel and Messner in *Men's Lives* announce that "Men are not born; they are made. And men make themselves, actively constructing their masculinities within a social and historical context" (xv). Its editors apparently assume their students will hear the allusion to Simone de Beauvoir's famous dictum about women without a footnote. Excluding *Revisioning Gender*, which is organized from the macro-social to the personal, these texts tend to start with arguments about biology or sections on childhood socialization, then move to sections on relationships, sexualities, families, work, and health, to conclude with social movements and the future. This organization subordinates psychology as a developmental tale of gender acquisition, and the focus on relationships and sexuality suits the college context of the student readers. The books continue the life course up to adulthood but barely mention old age. Thus, age helps organize without being integrated into their theories of gender (Gardiner 2002, 90–118).[3]

One odd aspect of this methodological consensus is the insistence that only social constructionism can lead to social change, as against biological, evolutionary, or psychological explanations of gender, which are assumed ahistorical and so fixed, as in the claim that "because gender and sexuality are socially constructed by organizational practices, . . . they are potential sites of resistance and change" (Ferree, Lorber, and Hess 1998, xxix). However, we routinely modify biological facts, often with little controversy. My eyeglasses correct my hereditary nearsightedness, airplanes compensate for our inability to fly, and the evolutionary capacity of humans for murder does not prevent our efforts to form more peaceful societies. Perhaps this emphasis on social constructionism acts as a sort of political shorthand: if these writers do not tell us the future of gender, or if, indeed, the future should be genderless, they unite in excoriating conservative backlash and celebrating the sheer possibility of change.

Since the answers are political as well as disciplinary, this brings me back to my opening question, "What is lost or gained in the transition from Women's Studies to (masculinity-attentive) gender studies?" Despite a consensus around many issues, there are still differences between the Women's Studies, masculinity, and gender texts. Of course, these volumes are all aimed at specific audiences, students taking courses in Gender and Society or Men and Masculinity or Women's Studies, and their approaches and coverage vary accordingly. *Revisioning Gender* aims at scholars and upper-level students; the other texts are introductory, with the text readers including more personal essays and short entries than the other books. The male-authored books address their rhetoric more to male readers. In *Men and Masculinity*, Kimmel says, "this, then, is the great secret of American manhood: *We are afraid of other men*" (Cohen 2001, 35), while the editor of the book proselytizes for equality, assuming his students' male privilege: "some of you might trade longer lives for larger salaries, or deeper personal relationships for power and dominance, but some might prefer to think about that a little bit" (390).

The gender texts favor gender over feminist or masculinity studies, though incorporating both, with the result that much work focuses on gender itself as a theoretical tool and on studies of men and women in relationship. Kimmel is particularly acute at showing the complement to a gendered truism. Thus, for him the other side of the "feminization of poverty" is "the masculinization of irresponsibility," while the corollary to the "feminization of love" is the "masculinization of sex" for both genders (136, 221). All these texts gesture toward a more egalitarian future, and several provide positive examples, for instance, John Stoltenberg's report on "Why College Guys Are Confronting Sexual Violence" (Kimmel and Messner 2001, 202–8); Barbara J. Risman and Danette Johnson-Summerford's study of "postgender marriages" in which the couples share child care and housework (Cohen 2001, 219–38); and the profeminist "Statement of Principles" of the National Organization for Men Against Sexism (Kimmel and Messner 2001, 539).

The relational paradigms for patriarchy and dominant masculinity in these texts describe a systematic gender hierarchy that advantages all men with respect to women and some men with respect to other men. That is, as a theoretical matter, the current definitions of gender privilege discussions of men over women, whether as gay activists, fathers, each others' friends, co-workers, warriors, or rapists. Kimmel uses rape as his test case for comparing various gender theories in *The Gendered Society*. Cohen organizes his section introductions with sections labeled "Men versus Men" and "Men versus Women" (2001, 277–78). Women's relationships with other women tend to be downplayed in the male-authored texts. As in schools, where boys get more attention both for causing trouble and for doing well, men and masculinity get more attention in the masculinity and male-authored gender books but more theoretical attention in all of them. Masculinity is seen as compensatory, defensive, and needing explanation and modification, while femininity is virtually uninterrogated, apparently assumed to result uneventfully from daughters' identifications with their mothers and women's adaptations to male dominance. There also seems to be an assumption that feminists have been describing the problems of women for thirty years; now is the time to focus more on men and masculinity and on global economic and political forces.

Let me examine some of the implications of the move to gender, here focusing primarily on Kimmel, the major figure in three of these books, with selections in the others except *Revisioning Gender*. Moreover, his books attempt to integrate and stabilize the gender studies field. In an essay in *Men and Masculinity*, Kimmel tells "the story of the ways in which Marketplace Man becomes American Everyman" as "a tragic tale, a tale of striving to live up to impossible ideals of success leading to chronic terrors of emasculation, emotional emptiness, and a gendered rage" (Cohen 2001, 31). Tragic heroes are main actors in their stories. It is they who cause problems, they who must change, and they who may save their societies. A rhetorical and political issue that these texts face is how to persuade men that gender equality is in their interests. "A discussion about power invariably makes men, in particular, uncomfortable or defensive," Kimmel says in *The Gendered Society*; "most men, it seems, do not feel powerful. Here, in a sense, is where feminism has failed to resonate for many men" (1999, 92–93). Kimmel explains that feminism succeeded because many women felt powerless and they really were, but "that symmetry breaks down when we try to apply it to men. For although men may be *in* power everywhere one cares to look, individual men are not 'in power,' and they do not *feel* powerful" (93). In contrast, *Revisioning Gender* and *Feminist Frontiers* end with women's organizations and a much greater sense of women's agency to change societies toward gender justice. Even in the women's texts, however, there is little new theorizing on women's gender acquisitions and negotiations, or on female masculinity and transgender. Perhaps this is because currently perceived problems like rape, sexual harassment, or men's fears of losing their masculinity tend to get attention. In contrast, femininity is not considered a social problem now—with wide acceptance of women in the workplace and in some political roles—so long as women continue to nurture children, men, and other women.

On the other hand, the women writers are clearer in their conceptions of future goals than are the male writers in these textbooks. Kimmel says we are moving toward gender "convergence" now, a positive trend that he distinguishes from "androgyny" (265). Androgyny may be a negative term for students as well, in which case its repudiation seems largely a rhetorical ploy, since "convergence" here implies the blending of positive traits from both dichotomized genders and the reduction of gender salience for which many feminists call. If we eliminate gender inequality, Kimmel says, gender difference will have no foundation: "what will remain, I believe, is not some non-gendered androgynous gruel, in which differences between women and men are blended and everyone acts and thinks in exactly the same way" (4). "Being a man, everything I do expresses my masculinity," he claims, so his goal for the future is to "degender traits and behaviors without degendering people. We will still be women and men, equal yet capable of appreciating our differences" (266). This desire to hold on to men's masculinity as a positive grounding of identity is correlated with the insistence that men not become "feminized," though what this means is unclear: men can tend babies but will still wear mustaches and converse about basketball scores? Signing on to Nancy Chodorow's prescriptions for gender equality through dual parenting, he predicts, "when men and women fully share housework and the raising of children, gender inequality in the family will gradually decrease" and gender stereotypes dissolve: "a change in the private sphere will bring about dramatic changes in the public sphere," and then "love can abide" (149).

Kimmel asks that we "imagine a vision of equality based on respect for and embracing of difference"—but again without defining which differences will remain (265). He says that the more men and women converge in nurturance and competition, "the more likely that aggression will take other routes besides gendered violence" (246). But, will this reduce violence as a whole or reduce other inequalities? He claims, "as gender inequality decreases, the differences among people—differences grounded in race, class, ethnicity, age, sexuality, *as well as* gender—will emerge in a context in which each of us can be appreciated for our individual uniqueness as well as our commonality" (4). His distaste for the bland, coercive connotations he associates with androgynous sameness leads him back to a liberal individualism that his social constructionist perspective otherwise avoids. Thus, he concludes *The Gendered Society* by proposing that now the goal for all men and women can be a "protean self" that is "mutable and flexible in a rapidly changing world. Such a transformation does not require that men and women become more like each other, but, rather, more deeply and fully themselves" (268).

I've focused especially on *The Gendered Society* in these comments because it forcefully articulates the current consensus and promises to be a widely used text. It is well written, up to date, and designed to appeal to male as well as female students. It does tip the balance slightly toward men—assuming they need persuading to study gender and to become invested in changing the gender order—and this emphasis is reflected in a greater attention to fathers' roles over mothers', and gay men over lesbians. The book has a few annoying tics that will rapidly grow stale, like frequent rebuttals of the "interplanetary" theory that men and women are analogous to Martians and Venutians, and topical allusions to Newt Gingrich and the Clinton sex scandals (Kimmel 1999, 1). Race and sexuality are included but not always fully integrated, so that generalizations about undifferentiated men and women in families or friendship may be followed by information about gay people and people of color, and ethnic diversity is mostly represented in black and white.

The Gendered Society Reader includes some important essays, for example, Margaret Mead on cross-cultural gender diversity; Peggy Reeves Sanday on socio-cultural contexts for rape; Myra Sadker, David Sadker, Lynn Fox, and Melinda Salata on the gendered classroom; and Christine Williams on "The Glass Elevator" lifting men to success in "female" professions (Kimmel with Aronson 1999, 294). Premised on gender symmetry in its framing, the book's essays point out places where such symmetry breaks down or where stereotypes are reversed, so it treats of masculine gay men and nurturing fathers. An introductory feminist class using *The Gendered Society* as one text might well wish to replace *The Gendered Society Reader* with a women-focused reader more attentive to diversity, media representation, global politics, and feminist movements like *Feminist Frontiers*. For masculinity courses, the sustained arguments of *The Gendered Society* could complement an excellent men's studies reader like *Men's Lives*, which has wide representation by prominent feminist authors like Susan Bordo, Ann Fausto-Sterling, bell hooks, Lillian Rubin, and Gloria Steinem, as well by men's studies scholars. *Men and Masculinity* contains many fine essays but is overall less satisfactory as a text, less current in its theories, and sometimes unwise in its selections. With provocative and thoughtful essays by Joan Wallach Scott on gender and politics, Susan Starr Sered on women in religion, and Judith Lorber on gender and sexuality, among others, *Revisioning Gender* is a book that women's studies scholars will want to read themselves and assign to advanced classes.

Having surveyed these textbooks, I conclude that they clearly articulate feminist perspectives within gender and masculinity studies. My lingering questions concern gender studies as an academic discipline and a political force. While the sociological bias of these texts helps conceptualize institutional and global structures, the books may unduly slight the psychological, philosophical, and literary tools available to help students think about individuals' varying investments in and negotiations with their gender and sexuality. Feminists will find ample common cause toward gender justice in these new, classroom friendly and very useful masculinity-based gender texts, but the books still leave open the future of gender in a way that begs further analysis. I have noted here the very different investments that men, including masculinity scholars, appear to have in preserving masculinity as some intelligible and coherent grounding of identity in comparison to the skepticism and distance shown by feminists toward femininity. Thus, a paradoxical finding from looking at the masculinity-focused texts is that it may be time for feminists to return to theorizing femininity. We need to see whether or not, and how, this concept can now be of use. The very absence of a "crisis of femininity" in contemporary U.S. culture, compared to the anxiety, excitement, and increasing scholarship around "masculinity," may indicate some of the limits of "gender" as the catchall category for feminist theory, scholarship, and political mobilization.

Notes

1. To frame my sense of the field, I have also looked at Sheila Ruth's *Issues in Feminism: An Introduction to Women's Studies* (2001); Susan M. Shaw and Janet Lee's *Women's Voices, Feminist Visions: Classic and Contemporary Readings* (2001); Dina L. Anselmi and Anne L. Law's *Questions of Gender: Perspectives and Paradoxes* (1998); and Claire M. Renzetti and Daniel J. Curran's *Women, Men, and Society* (1999). But I don't attempt to survey introductory Women's Studies or other gender texts here.

2. To compare the readers, I tallied essays by and about men, by and about women, and by both and about both men and women or about gender, as well as essays focusing on racial or global issues. Since these are my judgments about content, and some of the authors' information was incomplete, these numbers are only approximate:

- *Men's Lives*: Total 54. By men 36, women 15, both 1, author gender unknown 2; about men 46, women 1, both 7; about racial or global issues 17.
- *Men and Masculinity*: Total 41. By men 31, women 10, both 0; about men 31, women 0, both 10; about racial or global issues 8.
- *The Gendered Society Reader*: Total 27. By men 8, women 13, both 6; about men 7, women 2, both 18; about cross-cultural issues 3, none specifically focused on race.
- *Revisioning Gender*: Total 16. By men 1, women 12, both 3; about men 0, women 1, both 15; about racial or global issues 4.
- *Feminist Frontiers*: Total 76. By men 8, women 66, both 2; about men 14, women 44, both 18; about racial or global issues 24.

3. I argue that age categories provide a promising alternative to male/female polarizations of gender in "Theorizing Age and Gender: Bly's Boys, Feminism, and Maturity Masculinity" (Gardiner 2002, 90–118).

References

Anselmi, Dina L., and Anne L. Law. 1998. *Questions of Gender: Perspectives and Paradoxes*. Boston: McGraw Hill.

Gardiner, Judith Kegan, ed. 2002. *Masculinity Studies and Feminist Theories: New Directions*. New York: Columbia University Press.

Renzetti, Claire M., and Daniel J. Curran, eds. 1999. *Women, Men, and Society*. 4th ed. Boston: Allyn and Bacon.

Ruth, Sheila, ed. 2001. *Issues in Feminism: An Introduction to Women's Studies*. 5th ed. Mountain View, CA: Mayfield Publishing.

Shaw, Susan M., and Janet Lee. 2001. *Women's Voices, Feminist Visions: Classic and Contemporary Readings*. Mountain View, CA: Mayfield Publishing.

CHAPTER SIX

Student Responsiveness to Women's and Gender Studies Classes

The Importance of Initial Student Attitudes and Classroom Relationships

JAYNE E. STAKE, JEANNE SEVELIUS, AND SARAH HANLY

The field of women's and gender studies (WGS) has enjoyed tremendous growth in the United States over the past three decades, with more than 600 undergraduate programs established on college campuses since the 1970s. In recent years, researchers have explored how students are affected by their experiences in WGS. This research has provided evidence that WGS students develop more awareness of and ability to critically analyze patriarchal societal patterns and that they develop more flexible, egalitarian attitudes about gendered roles and arrangements (Bryant 2003; Fellman and Winstead 1992; Finke et al. 1992; Katz, Swindell, and Farrow 2004; Malkin and Stake 2004; Stake and Hoffmann 2001; Stake et al. 1994). These attitude changes have been accompanied by an enhanced commitment to feminist activism (Hertz and Reverby 1992; Stake et al. 1994; Stake and Hoffmann 2001). Such student changes have not been seen in non-WGS students even when researchers have controlled for relevant variables such as class size, racial and gender composition of the class, academic level, social and political relevance of the class, and WGS teaching experience of the instructor (Stake and Hoffmann 2001). Furthermore, WGS students have reported more positive changes in their lives, including greater clarity in their career goals, as a direct result of their class experience than have comparison, non-WGS students (Stake et al. 1994; Stake and Hoffmann 2000). Thus, the extant research has provided evidence that the majority of WGS students are open to the knowledge offered in their classes and that they accept feminist interpretations of our gendered society, their place within it, and their role in working for social change.

Despite these very positive indicators of student responsiveness to WGS courses, when studies have included broad, representative samples of students and have used systematic, standardized measures, students have been found to vary greatly in their reactions to WGS. For example, Malkin and Stake (2004) reported in a large-scale study of over three hundred students in twenty-three WGS classes that, although student ratings of course experiences tended to be positive, ratings ranged from extremely positive to extremely negative. Dissatisfied students were not confined to one or a few classes but were found across the majority of classes. Further, although many students showed a positive change in egalitarian attitudes, one-third showed a *decrease* in egalitarian attitudes over the course of the semester. Thus, although the majority of WGS students have responded to their classes positively and have become more aware of sexism and more accepting of diversity in gender roles, some students have seen their WGS experiences as aversive and failed to show change toward more feminist attitudes (Stake and Malkin 2003).

WGS teachers have written about the challenges they face from those students who resist feminist teachings. As these writers have suggested, feminist theories and the information base of WGS may threaten students' internalized patriarchal beliefs that ignore systems of privilege and oppression and that characterize current societal systems as "natural" and "merit based" (Crawford and Suckle 1999; Orr 1993; Sanchez-Casal 2002). Students may resist WGS material by minimizing or discounting the existence of sexism in present-day society, noting exceptions to sexist practices, and denying personal advantage or disadvantage associated with sexism (Crawford and Suckle 1999; Hughes 2002). Students who feel that their own ideology is under attack may become angry and critical of the WGS teacher and course material or lapse into silence, refusing to participate in class discussions (Crawford and Suckle 1999; Orr 1993).

Now that some campuses require a diversity course for graduation and students sometimes enroll in WGS courses only to fulfill this requirement, WGS teachers have found that more students are entering their classes with negative attitudes and expectations about WGS (Crawford and Suckle 1999; Orr 1993). Given the growing number of resistant students coming to WGS, it is particularly important that we come to better understand individual differences in students' responsiveness to WGS and how students' initial attitudes on coming to class affect their reactions to WGS. These issues formed the central focus of the research presented here.

Pre-Class Student Attitudes and Responsiveness to WGS

Research on attitude change has shown that people are more likely to be influenced by information sources that they see as credible and with whom they share similar perspectives (e.g., Diamond and Cobb 1996). One might expect, then, that students who enter their WGS classes with a more egalitarian, feminist stance would be more likely to accept information presented in their classes and therefore shift their attitudes further in a feminist direction. Indeed, some WGS teachers have observed that students with more egalitarian attitudes and understanding of sexism at the start of class respond more openly and nondefensively to WGS readings and class discussions. For example, Rhoades (1999) observed that students who begin with more gender egalitarian attitudes are more willing to

move away from an individual responsibility model of sociopolitical issues and are less resistant to social construction analysis. Except for
anecdotal descriptions, there has been little standardized research to inform our understanding of how students' initial attitudinal orientations
affect their responsiveness to WGS. However, two large-scale studies that
employed standardized measures have provided some relevant findings.
Students with initially more egalitarian gender attitudes and more positive expectations for their WGS classes have given their classes more positive global ratings (Stake and Malkin 2003), and students with initially
positive expectations about their class have formed more positive relationships with their teachers and classmates and have shown greater change
in their openness to gender diversity by the end of their classes (Malkin and Stake 2004).

These findings notwithstanding, other evidence suggests that it is
those students with the most traditional gender views who show the most
change toward feminist attitudes. Studies have consistently found that
students' gender-related attitudes on entering their class are *negatively*
related to change in those same attitudes over the time period of the class
(Sevelius and Stake 2003; Stake and Hoffmann 2000; Thomsen, Basu, and
Reinitz 1995). For example, students entering with the least awareness of
sexism have gained the most in their awareness of sexism. These findings may be explained in terms of the amount of change in feminist attitudes that are possible for students who enter with conservative rather
than feminist views: Students who begin their classes with less egalitarian attitudes and less awareness of sexism have more room to change
toward feminist attitudes. Another reason for the negative relationship
found between initial attitudes and change may be that the index of
change used in previous studies has been the difference between pre-
class and post-class scores on the same measure. This method of measuring change is subject to "ceiling effects" because students with feminist
attitudes may make substantial changes that cannot be reflected in these
pre/post change scores. For example, students who initially endorse items
that show an awareness of sexism at or near the level of seven on a seven-
point scale cannot show significant change on the measure but may nonetheless grow in their understanding of sexism.

To understand better the relation between initial attitudes and attitude change, we designed the current study so as to circumvent this methodological problem in three ways. First, we asked students as their classes
were ending to report not only their present level of awareness of sexism but also the extent to which their awareness of sexism had changed
as a result of their WGS class. The latter measure, on which students
judged for themselves their amount of class-related attitude change, was
not subject to the ceiling effect of a pre/post measure. Because the negative relation between initial attitudes and change found in other studies

may be due to a ceiling effect, and in light of the evidence reviewed earlier of a positive relation between initial attitudes and class responsiveness, we expected that in the present study students who began their class with more feminist attitudes would report more change in awareness of sexism.

As a second means of circumventing the ceiling effect problem, we included measures of two types of gender attitudes that are distinct from one another but are both associated with a feminist perspective on gender issues: (a) awareness of sexism and the negative impact of gendered societal structures and (b) openness to and appreciation of diverse lifestyles and roles for women and men. These two types of gender attitudes have been discussed by feminist teachers (e.g., Rhoades 1999) and measured across several evaluations of WGS courses (e.g., Stake and Hoffmann 2001). Although these measures are related, students may score relatively low on one measure while scoring near the maximum on the other. By using two feminist attitude measures, it was possible to reduce the ceiling effect associated with pre/post comparisons by testing the relation between each feminist attitude at the beginning of class and change in the other attitude. We expected that students who had already recognized instances of sexism and the harmful effects of sexist practices by the time they began their WGS classes would have their perspectives validated in class and would be more open to expanding their acceptance and appreciation for alternate gendered roles and arrangements in response to knowledge learned in their classes. Similarly, we expected that students with more open, flexible gender attitudes would be more open generally to WGS course material and discussion about sexist practices and would therefore show more change toward awareness of sexism.

Our third means of assessing the relation between students' initial gender attitudes and responsiveness to WGS was to measure other aspects of class responsiveness in addition to attitude change. The other class responsiveness variables we measured were the quality of WGS relationships students developed and their emotional reactions to their class. We measured two types of relationships: Students' *alliances* with their teachers and *cohesion* with their fellow students. Alliance and cohesion are defined as relationships characterized by mutual trust, respect, and common purpose. We included three types of emotional reactions, based on teacher descriptions of student responses to WGS: enhanced feelings of empowerment, distress, and anger. We expected that students with more feminist attitudes at the start of class, who would likely share their worldview with their teacher and many classmates, would develop more positive WGS relationships and would experience greater feelings of empowerment and less anger and distress than students with more traditional views.

Classroom Relationships as a Medium for Student Change

As an additional goal of this study, we assessed WGS classroom relationships as a possible mediator of the relation between initial attitudes and
change—that is, a means by which change may come about in WGS.
Many educators have proposed that what students gain through their
education depends in large part on the quality of the relationships they
develop with their teachers and fellow students, and they have emphasized the value of collaborative, egalitarian relationships in the classroom (Shor and Freire 1987). Although there is little formal research on
the link between quality of classroom relationships and student attitude
change, large-scale studies of student change in higher education have
provided some indirect evidence of the link between personal relationships and student change during the undergraduate years. Pascarella and
Terenzini (1991) reported that greater informal contact with professors
was associated with changes toward more egalitarian social and political
attitudes, and Astin (1993) found that those students who spent time interacting with students from diverse ethnic groups increased in gender
egalitarianism.

Feminist teachers have particularly stressed the critical importance of
developing trusting, collaborative classroom relationships for the discussion of WGS topics (e.g., Orr 1993; Rinehart 1999, 2002). Rinehart has
argued that only in a positive, collaborative classroom environment
can highly charged sociopolitical issues be explored thoughtfully and in
depth. No previous empirical studies have tested the extent to which
classroom relationships may serve as a mediator between initial attitudes and responsiveness to WGS, but classroom relationships have
been found to mediate the relation between students' expectations for
WGS and both their attitude changes and ratings of their WGS experience (Malkin and Stake 2004; Stake and Malkin 2003). That is, students
with positive expectations about their classes tended to respond more
favorably; this relationship was accounted for by the positive ties that
students with positive expectations developed with their teacher and fellow students.

We may therefore think of the relationships students develop in their
WGS classrooms as not only a measure of their responsiveness to their
class but also as a medium through which students' experiences in the
class are shaped and defined. Whereas students with more feminist views
may be more inclined to develop positive relationships in the WGS classroom, students with more positive classroom relationships should, in
turn, experience their classroom environment as more supportive and
affirming and should therefore engage more openly with the course material and class discussions, leading to greater attitude change and more

positive affective reactions to their class. Thus, we predicted in the present study that, although students' initial attitudes would directly predict responsiveness to WGS, these relationships would be dependent, at least in part, on the development of a positive alliance with their teachers and cohesion with their fellow WGS students.

Summary of Study Goals and Hypotheses

Our goals in designing this study were to add to our understanding of how students' initial attitudes about gender issues influence their responsiveness to their WGS classes and to test for the first time the extent to which classroom relationships mediate the link between students' initial attitudes and their reactions to WGS. Based on the research and reasoning presented here, we expected that students who began their class with more feminist gender attitudes, in contrast to students with more conservative attitudes, would report more positive relationships with their teachers and classmates, show more change toward feminist attitudes when ceiling effects were minimized, and experience greater feelings of empowerment and less distress and anger. In contrast, as found in previous studies, students with more conservative attitudes were expected to show more change toward feminist attitudes in pre/post comparisons of the same measure. Further, we expected that the relation between students' initial attitudes and their responsiveness to WGS would depend on the quality of the relationships they developed in the WGS classroom. Differences between gender and ethnic groups were evaluated as well because differences in gender attitudes have been found previously among college undergraduates and had the potential to affect results (Bryant 2003).

Methods

Participants

WGS classes at six colleges and universities in a large Midwestern urban area were included in this study. Three of the institutions were public and three were private; all were moderate to moderately large in size. Students participated from forty-eight classes that were officially designated as WGS courses on their respective campuses. The classes took place over a fifteen-week semester. The classes represented a broad range of WGS topics, including introduction to women's studies (twelve classes), women and literature (four classes), women and the law (one class), women's health issues (six classes), psychology of women (four classes), gender issues in communication (nine classes), sociology (three classes), anthropology (three classes), and other topics in the social sciences (six classes). In regard to class size, twenty-eight classes had fifteen or fewer students, and twenty classes had more than fifteen students. Thus, some classes were conducive to a small seminar format and others to larger discussions and lectures.

Participating students were 519 women and 142 men. The majority of students identified themselves as Euro-American (74.1%); the remaining students identified themselves as African American (8.9%), Asian American (9.1%), Hispanic (1.8%), multiracial (2.3%), and other ethnic identity (3.8%). Most participants were between the ages of 18 and 22 years (77.6%). The college level of the participants was as follows: First year (5.7%), sophomore (26.0%), junior (32.3%), senior (30.7%), graduate (3.9%), nondegree student (1.4%). The social class of students, as measured by the highest education level attained by either parent, varied greatly from 14.6% with a high school education or less to 16.3% with a doctorate or other advanced degree. The average parent education level for private school students was a college degree plus additional education, whereas the average parent education level for public school students was a high school degree plus some college. Thus, students at the private schools tended to be of a higher social class as measured by parent education.

Procedure

We assessed students' gender attitudes during the first week of classes on a questionnaire that was distributed to students within the classroom setting. One of the three authors or eight research assistants administered the questionnaire. The researcher attended the class and explained to students that the goal of the study was to better understand students' experiences and attitudes and that their participation in the project was voluntary. All students agreed to participate. The researcher stressed that participants' responses would be held strictly confidential, that only the researchers would see their responses, and that participants should not put their names on their answer sheets. A code was used to match participants' responses at the beginning of class with their responses at the end of class. The researcher encouraged students to ask any questions they might have as they completed the questionnaire. The teacher either left the room or was seated away from the students during administration of the questionnaire so that students would not be influenced by the possibility that their teacher might observe their responses. During the last week of class, one of the researchers returned to the class to administer a second questionnaire by the same procedure described for the first questionnaire. This survey again assessed students' gender attitudes and, in addition, their perceptions of the extent to which they had become more aware of sexism as a result of the class, their emotional reactions to the class, and the quality of the relationships they had developed with their teacher and classmates.

Measures

Gender Attitudes. The measure of awareness of sexism selected for this study was the ten-item Discrimination and Subordination Subscale of the Liberal Feminist Attitude and Ideology Scale (LFAIS) developed by Morgan (1996). Items on the LFAIS were selected to represent contemporary gender issues. The LFAIS subscales have been shown to have good convergent, divergent, concurrent, and known-groups validity (Morgan 1996). The Discrimination and Subordination Subscale has been found to be reliable (alpha = .85) in college samples (Morgan, 1996), and it was equally reliable in the present study (alpha = .85). Sample items are "Even though some things have changed, women are still treated unfairly in today's society," and "People who complain that the media treat women like objects are overreacting." Respondents indicated the extent to which they agreed or disagreed with each statement on a seven-point scale that ranged from *disagree strongly* (0) to *agree strongly* (6). Participants' scores for this and all other measures were derived by first reverse scoring negative items and then calculating the average ratings across the scale items.

The measure of openness and appreciation for diverse gender roles comprised ten items. Six items were taken from the Gender Roles and Global Goals subscales of the LFAIS (Morgan 1996). Sample items are "Women should be considered as seriously as men as candidates for the Presidency of the United States" and "Men and women should be able to freely make choices about their lives without being restricted by their gender." Four additional items were selected for this measure to reflect openness to and appreciation of nontraditional roles and lifestyles for women and men (e.g., "It is wonderful to see all the different walks of life that women are entering today," and "I appreciate people who do not conform to traditional stereotypes of femininity and masculinity"). The reliability of this scale was satisfactory (alpha = .73) in a pilot sample of sixty WGS students and in the study sample (alpha = .80). As with the awareness of sexism scale, respondents rated the extent of their agreement with each statement on a seven-point scale. The correlation between the two gender attitude measures was +.53, which indicated that the two scales were measuring related but distinct aspects of gender attitudes.

Students' perceptions about how much their awareness of sexism had been affected by their WGS class were measured at the end of class with the items from the awareness of sexism scale described above. That is, after participants had rated their agreement or disagreement with each of the statements pertaining to awareness of sexism, they rated how much their opinion on the statement had changed due to the class. Students made their ratings on a seven-point scale that ranged from *not at all changed due to this class* (0) to *very much changed due to this class* (6). This scale was reliable in the pilot sample (alpha = .90) and in the study sample (alpha = .82). The correlation between this measure and the pre/post change in awareness of sexism scores was +.40. This moderate correlation means that, although students' perceptions about how much the class had changed their awareness of sexism were related to the amount of change we saw in their ratings of awareness over time, the two change measures provide distinct information about students' change in awareness of sexism.

Classroom Relationships. The quality of the relationships students developed with their WGS teacher was measured with an abbreviated version of the twenty-four-item Teacher Alliance Scale developed by Malkin and Stake (2004). The short form of the scale comprised twelve of the original items and correlated highly with the longer version of the scale (+.96). The scale assessed how students perceived their relationships with their teachers, including feelings of mutual liking, trust, respect, and agreement on class goals and tasks. Sample positive items are "I trust the teacher and the teachers' decisions" and "I feel the teacher and I agree upon what the goals for this class should be." Sample negative items are "I do not think this teacher appreciates having me in this class" and "I am frustrated by what the teacher asks me to do in this class." Students marked their agreement or disagreement on a seven-point scale that ranged from *disagree strongly* (0) to *agree strongly* (6). The reliability of the full-length scale was .95 (Malkin and Stake 2004); the reliability of the short form used in this study was .89.

The quality of relationships students experienced with their WGS classmates was measured with an abbreviated version of the twenty-four-item Student Cohesion Scale, which was also developed by Malkin and Stake (2004). The short form of the scale comprised twelve of the original items and correlated highly with the longer version of the scale (+.95). This scale assessed how students perceived their relationships with their fellow classmates, and these items were parallel to the items on the alliance scale. For example, positive items included "On the whole, I trust the other students and their decisions in this class" and "In general, I think the other students in this class share my own ideas about what the class should be like." Sample negative items were "I do not think the other students appreciate having me in this class" and "In general, I think the other students waste time in this class." Students again rated their agreement or disagreement on a seven-point scale. The reliability of the full-length version of the scale was .93; the reliability of the short form used in this study was .87. Validity information for the teacher alliance and class cohesion measures may be found in Stake and Malkin (2003) and Malkin and Stake (2004).

Emotional Reactions to Class. In the absence of previously established measures of affect suitable for this study, the authors developed three scales to assess students' feelings of empowerment, anger, and distress associated with their WGS classes. Thirty-six related feeling adjectives that appeared to relate to these constructs were selected for the original item pool from previously constructed scales (e.g., the Multiple Affect Adjective Checklist; Zuckerman et al. 1986). For the purpose of this study, it was important that students understand that they should describe how the class experience had made them feel rather than describe their emotions more generally. Thus, the phrase, "This class made me feel" was added to each item. A sample item is "This class made me feel inspired." Participants were asked to rate "how true each description is of how your experience in this class has made you feel" on a seven-point scale that ranged from *never or almost never true* (0) to *always or almost always true* (6).

Based on analyses of responses from the pilot sample, six items from the item pool were selected for the empowerment scale (assertive, strong, self-reliant, empowered, inspired, willing to take a stand), six for the anger scale (irritated, mad, angry, disgusted, outraged, offended), and six for the distress scale (overwhelmed, discouraged, hopeless, lost, nervous, shaky). In the pilot sample, the reliabilities of the empowerment, distress, and anger scales were .86, .82, and .83, respectively. All of the items selected improved the reliability of the scale to which it was assigned. The correlations between each item and the corresponding total score (item-total correlation) ranged from .52 to .73. In the study sample ($N = 662$), a factor analysis revealed a clear, simple factor structure in which each of the eighteen selected items loaded on one and only one of three factors. On-target loadings averaged .75 and off-target loadings averaged .14. All items loaded on their intended factor. The three factors together accounted for 63% of the total variance of the items. The reliability values for the empowerment, anger, and distress scales in the full study sample were .90, .87, and .84, respectively.

Findings .

Quality of Classroom Relationships, Emotional Reactions, and Attitude Change

As a group, the students responded positively to their WGS classes. The average teacher alliance rating of 4.61 and the average student cohesion rating of 4.41 were well above the neutral midpoint (3) of the six-point rating scale of relationship quality. Thus, students described their classroom relationships in positive terms. Further, students reported more frequent feelings of empowerment than feelings of anger or distress from their experience with the class. The average empowerment rating of 3.38 was between the scale anchor points of *occasionally true* (3) and *often true* (4), whereas the average ratings for anger and distress (1.81 and 1.18, respectively) were between the anchor points of *usually not true* (1) and *sometimes but infrequently true* (2).

To evaluate differences in the levels of the three emotions reported by students, a one-way analysis of variance was undertaken. The analysis revealed that differences between the three emotion ratings were highly statistically significant, $F(2, 1314) = 634.54$, $p < .0001$. (Statistical significance refers to the probability that one would obtain a result as large or larger than that found simply by chance. In this case, with $p < .0001$, the probability is less than 1 in 10,000.) Comparisons between each of the pairs of emotion ratings showed that students' feelings of empowerment were significantly greater than either their feelings of anger or distress ($p < .0001$). Feelings of anger were highly related to feelings of distress ($r = +.64$; see Table 4 for an explanation of r), but neither were related to feelings of empowerment. Thus, students reported minimal feelings of distress and anger, and neither of these types of emotions restricted students' sense of empowerment gained from the class.

The majority of students began their classes with gender attitudes that were at least somewhat consistent with the knowledge base and theoretical perspectives of WGS. The overall average student rating for awareness of sexism was 4.01 (close to the scale anchor point *agree slightly*), and the overall average for the openness to gender diversity items was 4.81 (close to the scale anchor point *agree*) as classes began. The average attitude scores at pretesting were very similar for students at the three public ($M = 4.45$) and three private ($M = 4.36$) institutions that students were attending, and attitudes were unrelated to social class as measured by parent education.

The attitude values at the end of class were 4.36 for awareness of sexism and 4.84 for openness to gender diversity. The small change in openness to gender diversity (+.03) was not significant, but the change for awareness of sexism (+.35) was significant by a *t*-test for correlated means, $t(659) = 12.08$, $p < .0001$. The size of the effect (d) was .39, which is considered a small to medium effect (Cohen 1992; see Table 2 for an explanation of d). In addition, the average student self-rating of change in awareness of sexism (2.72) was close to the scale midpoint anchor, *somewhat changed due to this class*. In sum, both the pre/post comparisons and the student ratings of change in awareness indicated that, overall, students showed an increase toward greater awareness of sexism but not toward greater openness to gender diversity.

Note, however, that students varied a great deal in the amount and direction of change they showed on the gender attitude measures. To evaluate individual differences in change, difference scores were calculated for each attitude measure by subtracting students' pre-scores from their post-scores. Across the entire sample of students, change scores for openness to gender diversity varied from −3.60 to +2.70, with a standard deviation of .70; change scores for awareness of sexism varied from −3.97 to +2.73, with a standard deviation of .75.

Students' Pre-Class Gender Attitudes as Predictors of Their Responsiveness to WGS Classes

Relations between students' pre-class gender attitudes and their responsiveness to WGS were analyzed in a series of simultaneous regression analyses in which the gender attitudes measured at the beginning of class were entered together as the predictor variables. Relations between each gender attitude and the outcome measures were therefore tested while controlling for the effect of the other attitude. The outcome variables were gender attitudes, classroom relationships, and emotional responses to the class. Table 1 displays the results of these analyses: The standardized regression coefficients (b) listed in the table indicate the degree of association between the predictor and outcome variables (see Table 1 for further explanation of b).

As presented in Table 1, pre-class gender attitude scores were highly related to post-class scores on the same attitude measure. Students who scored higher in awareness of sexism at the beginning of class did so at the end of class ($\beta = +.62$, $p < .0001$), and students who scored higher in openness to gender diversity at the beginning of class scored higher on the measure at the end of class ($\beta = +.54$, $p < .0001$). The high regression coefficients for these relationships show consistency in students' responses to the same measure over time. In addition, strong negative relationships were found as expected between pre-class gender attitudes and pre/post change in gender attitudes: Students who were less aware of sexism at the beginning of class showed more positive change on the same measure by the end of class ($\beta = -.50$, $p < .0001$), and students who were less open to gender diversity at the beginning of class changed more on the same measure ($\beta = -.51$, $p < .0001$). These comparisons between pre-class and post-class scores on the same measure are similar to results found in previous studies of gender attitudes in WGS.

Table 1 also provides information on the relation between each of the two gender attitudes measured at the beginning of class and the other gender attitude measure at the end of class. For both post-class scores and change scores, these relationships were positive and highly statistically significant. Most importantly, students who had a higher awareness of

Table 1   Relation of Pre-Class Gender Attitudes to Responses
to WGS Classes

	Pre-Class Gender Attitudes	
Responses to WGS Classes	Awareness of Sexism	Openness to Gender Diversity
Post-class gender attitudes		
Awareness of sexism	+.62***	+.13***
Openness to gender diversity	+.20***	+.54***
Pre/post change in gender attitudes		
Awareness of sexism	−.50***	+.15***
Openness to gender diversity	+.22***	−.51***
Self-reported change in awareness of sexism	+.15**	+.07
Classroom relationships		
Teacher alliance	+.24***	+.18***
Student cohesion	+.11*	+.16**
Emotional responses		
Empowerment	+.27***	+.16**
Anger	+.06	−.04
Distress	−.03	+.07

Note. Tabled values are standardized regression coefficients (β), which indicate the degree to which gender attitudes at the beginning of class predicted students' reactions to class (0 = no relationship, .30 = moderate relationship, .50 = strong relationship, 1.00 = perfect relationship).
$*p < .05.$ $**p < .001.$ $***p < .0001.$

sexism at the beginning of class showed greater gains in their openness to gender diversity ($\beta = +.22$, $p < .0001$), and students who were more open to gender diversity at the beginning of class showed greater gains in their awareness of sexism ($\beta = +.15$, $p < .0001$). Furthermore, students with a greater awareness of sexism prior to their class gave more positive self-reports of the change in awareness of sexism they recognized in themselves and attributed to their WGS class ($\beta = +.15$, $p < .0001$). Thus, when ceiling effects were minimized, we found that students who began their classes with more feminist attitudes showed more positive change in their awareness of sexism and openness to gender diversity by the end of their classes.

Pre-class gender attitudes also predicted the quality of classroom relationships. Students with more feminist attitudes at the start of class were more likely to describe their alliance with their teacher and cohesion with their fellow students in positive terms ($\beta s = +.11$ to $+.24$, $p < .05$). Pre-class attitudes also predicted feelings of empowerment attributed to the class (βs = +.27 and +.16, $p < .0001$) but were not significantly related to feelings of distress or anger. Thus, students with more feminist attitudes on beginning the class reported better classroom relationships and experienced more feelings of empowerment as a result of the class, but those with less feminist attitudes were not more often angered or distressed by the class.

Gender and Ethnic Identity Differences

Because gender and ethnic identity may have affected the relationships between attitudes and responsiveness to WGS, we assessed each of the study variables in relation to gender and ethnic identity. Table 2 displays the findings for gender differences. We performed a 2×2 (gender of student by time of testing [pre vs. post]) analysis of variance for both of the gender attitudes. By including pre and post-scores within the design of the analysis, we could evaluate both overall gender differences across time and gender differences in change from pre- to post-testing. As noted earlier, awareness of sexism scores were higher at the end of class than at

Table 2   Women's and Men's Pre-Class Gender Attitudes and Responsiveness to WGS Classes

Responses to WGS Classes	Women	Men	Gender Difference Effect Size (d)[a]
Pre-class gender attitudes			
Awareness of sexism	4.15	3.50	.65*
Openness to gender diversity	4.94	4.31	.77*
Post-class gender attitudes			
Awareness of sexism	4.53	3.75	.87*
Openness to gender diversity	4.98	4.36	.72*
Self-reported change in awareness of sexism	2.84	2.28	.39*
Classroom relationships			
Teacher alliance	4.68	4.36	.41*
Student cohesion	4.46	4.20	.28*
Emotional reactions			
Empowerment	3.59	2.62	.66*
Anger	1.84	1.73	ns
Distress	1.17	1.23	ns

Note. Tabled values are average scores on a 0 to 6 rating scale, based on 519 women and 142 men.
[a]d is the difference between groups in standard deviation units (small = .20, medium = .50, large = .80; Cohen 1992).
*$p < .0001$.

the beginning, $F (1,657) = 80.51$, $p < .0001$. In addition, the main effect of gender was significant,$F (1,657) = 90.86$, $p < .0001$, whereas the interaction of time and gender was not. These findings mean that women reported more awareness of sexism at both times, but women and men made similar gains in awareness over time.

In regard to openness to gender diversity, neither a main effect of time nor an interaction of time and gender was significant. However, we found a main effect of gender, $F (1,659) = 84.10$, $p < .0001$; women reported more openness to diversity in gender roles than did men at both times. Women also self-reported a greater change in awareness of sexism than did men, a stronger alliance with their teacher and cohesion with fellow students, and more feelings of empowerment attributable to the class. The effect sizes of these gender differences varied from small to large (.28 to .77), as shown in Table 2. There were no significant gender differences for feelings of anger or distress, which were very low for both women and men.

We examined ethnic identity differences for the three ethnic groups for which there were a sufficient number of participants to justify an analysis: African Americans ($n = 59$), Asian Americans ($n = 60$), and Euro-Americans ($n = 490$). There were not sufficient numbers of participants in the other ethnic identity categories (Latina/o and multiracial) to yield meaningful findings for these groups. See Table 3 for gender attitudes at the beginning and end of class for the three larger ethnic groups. We performed a 3×2 (ethnic identity group by time of testing) analysis of variance for both of the gender attitudes. For awareness of sexism, main effects for time, $F (1,604) = 52.56$, $p < .0001$, and ethnic identity, $F (2,604) = 6.19$, $p < .01$, were significant, and these were qualified by an interaction of ethnic identity by time, $F (2,604) = 6.11$, $p < .01$. This interaction indicated that the three groups showed different amounts of change over time. Follow-up analyses revealed that significant ethnic identity differences were present at the beginning of class ($p < .0001$), with African American students having a greater awareness of sexism than the other two groups. However, ethnic differences were no longer significant by the

Table 3   Gender Attitudes by Ethnic Identity Group

Ethnic Identity	Awareness of Sexism		Openness to Gender Diversity	
	Pre-class	Post-class	Pre-class	Post-class
African American	4.49	4.57	4.82	4.76
Asian American	3.77	4.33	4.54	4.52
Euro-American	3.97	4.34	4.86	4.91

Note. Tabled values are average scores on a 0 to 6 scale.

end of class because Asian American and Euro-American students significantly increased their awareness over time ($p < .0001$, effect sizes were .67 and .39, respectively) and African Americans did not.

We examined ethnic identity differences in openness to gender diversity with a 3×2 (ethnic identity by time) analysis of variance. Neither the main effect of time nor the interaction of ethnic identity by time were significant. However, the main effect of ethnic identity was significant, $F (2,604) = 6.07$, $p < .01$. Openness scores were somewhat lower for Asian Americans than for the other two ethnic groups at both the beginning and end of class, but change over time was not significantly different across the three groups. Further, there were no significant differences across ethnic identity groups for student self-reports of change in awareness of sexism, classroom relationships, or emotional responses to the class.

It was possible that the patterns of differences between women and men students might have varied across the three ethnic groups. We therefore tested the interaction effect of student gender and ethnic identity on the student response variables. No interactions were significant, which indicated that the gender differences reported earlier were similar across the three ethnic groups.

Because gender and ethnic differences were found for the pre-class gender attitudes and some of the class response variables, we again tested the relationships between pre-class gender attitudes and the class response variables while co-varying the effects of gender and ethnic identity. The results were virtually identical to the pattern of results described earlier. Thus, the relationships between initial attitudes and responsiveness to the class did not differ by the gender or ethnic identity of the students.

Classroom Relationships as Mediums for Change in WGS

To determine whether classroom relationships mediated the link between initial gender attitudes and responsiveness to WGS, we first correlated the quality of class relationships with both the attitude change and emotional reaction measures (see Table 4). We found that students who reported higher quality relationships with their teachers had changed more in the direction of greater awareness of sexism and more openness to diverse gender roles. Further, these students reported more change in their awareness of sexism, more feelings of empowerment, and less anger and distress. The correlations for student cohesion were similar except that students' self-reports of change in their awareness of sexism were not significantly correlated with their cohesion scores. Most salient in these findings were the strong associations between the quality of students' WGS relationships and their affective responses to the class.

We assessed the extent to which the quality of classroom relationships helped to explain (mediate) the link between pre-class gender attitudes and student responsiveness to their WGS class with a statistical test

Table 4   Correlations between Classroom Relationships
and Responses to WGS Classes

Responses to WGS Classes	Teacher Alliance	Cohesion with Classmates
Pre/post change in gender attitudes		
Awareness of sexism	+.11*	+.14**
Openness to gender diversity	+.14**	+.18**
Self-reported change in awareness of sexism	+.15**	+.08
Emotional responses		
Empowerment	+.48**	+.43**
Anger	−.24**	−.26**
Distress	−.40**	−.40**

**$p < .001$.

for mediation (Preacher and Leonardelli 2003). As pre-conditions for establishing mediation, it was necessary that the predictor variables (pre-class gender attitudes) were significantly related to the mediator variables (classroom relationships) and to the responsiveness variables (attitude change and emotions) and that the mediator variables were also related to the responsiveness variables. Tests for mediation were performed only in those cases in which all of the pre-conditions were met. The tests for mediation allowed us to determine the extent to which the significant relations found between pre-class attitudes and class responsiveness depended upon the quality of relationships developed with teachers and classmates.

In regard to the relation between pre-class awareness of sexism and change in openness to diverse gender roles, alliance and cohesion were both partial mediators (Sobel test statistics: alliance, 4.03, $p < .0001$; cohesion, 2.12, $p < .05$, respectively). That is, once class relationships were accounted for, the β value for awareness of sexism dropped from +.25 to +.20, which is still statistically significant. This amount of change is referred to as partial mediation because the quality of students' class relationships explained part but not all of the association between their pre-class awareness of sexism and change in openness to gender diversity. More specifically, students who began their class with greater awareness of sexism tended to develop better classroom relationships, and these relationships, in turn, led to more change in their openness to gender diversity; even so, students with higher awareness of sexism when they began their class were still significantly more likely to make positive changes in their openness to gender diversity regardless of the quality of the relationships they developed in their WGS class.

The relation between awareness of sexism and feelings of empowerment was also partially mediated by the quality of class relationships. The Sobel test statistic was 5.06 ($p < .0001$) for alliance and 2.17 ($p < .05$) for cohesion; once classroom relationships were controlled, the β value dropped from +.27 to +.17, which was still statistically significant. In addition, the relation between initial openness to gender diversity and change in awareness of sexism was partially mediated by alliance (3.17, $p < .01$) and cohesion (2.40, $p < .05$); the β value was reduced from .17 to .13, still a significant value, after controlling for classroom relationships. Finally, we found a full mediation effect for the relation between initial openness to diverse roles and feelings of empowerment: alliance, 3.69, $p < .001$; cohesion 3.22, $p < .01$; in this case, by controlling for classroom relationships, the β value dropped from +.16 to +.07, which is not statistically significant. Thus, initial openness to diverse gender roles was related to later feelings of empowerment only if positive classroom relationships were established. In sum, classroom relationships served as a medium through which students with more feminist gender attitudes came to respond to their class with greater attitude change and feelings of empowerment.

Discussion of Findings

Nature of the Study Sample

Before discussing the findings, the reader should note that the study sample was limited in some respects. First, the campuses on which the study took place were all located in one large Midwestern city, and one might question whether the attitudes of students in our sample are representative of students in other geographical areas of the United States. However, the private schools in this study draw students from across the country; the gender attitudes of these students did not differ significantly from those of students in the public schools, who were primarily local residents. Thus, it appears that the attitudes expressed by our sample were not unique to the Midwest but were more generally representative of U.S. students.

Another limitation of our sample is that Latinas/os were not represented in sufficient numbers to justify inclusion in the analysis. However, the samples of African Americans and Asian Americans were larger than in previous studies of this kind and did allow for an examination of differences across African American, Asian American, and Euro-American students. Moreover, students in the sample were from many types of WGS classes in private and public institutional settings, so the findings are not specific to a certain discipline, type of class content, instructor, class format (small seminar vs. larger discussion or lecture class), or campus environment. In addition, the social class backgrounds of the students differed greatly, and a sizable number of male students were included. Thus, the sample was in many ways broadly representative of students who are attending WGS classes in the United States today. Our sample is in marked contrast to the small samples and anecdotal findings that have been common in the study of students' reactions to WGS.

Student Responsiveness to WGS

Consistent with the findings from quantitative and qualitative studies of WGS reviewed earlier, and contrary to the claims of WGS critics, which are based on small, nonrepresentative samples (for a review, see Stake 2006), the students as a group described their WGS experiences in positive terms. Most students reported that they trusted and respected their teachers and classmates and that they were in agreement with the tasks and goals set for the class. Moreover, students emerged from their classes with greater feelings of empowerment and were not often distressed or angered by the content or process of the classes. The latter findings are particularly noteworthy because some critics have claimed that students become distressed by their exposure to WGS course material or feel angered and alienated by the nature of the perspectives they encounter in WGS classes (Stake 2006). Instead, it seems that the teachers included in our study were successful in presenting WGS material in a way that did not elicit strong negative reactions from students. Furthermore, African American, Asian American, and Euro-American students gave similar ratings of their WGS relationships and their emotional responses to class. Men did not evaluate the quality of their classroom relationships as positively as women, and they reported less feelings of empowerment; however, even the men's average relationship quality ratings were well within the positive end of the scale, and men reported more frequent feelings of empowerment than distress or anger.

Also consistent with previous studies was our finding that, overall, students gained in their awareness of sexist societal structures and practices. We found these changes regardless of whether change was evaluated directly by the students themselves or calculated by tracing attitudes over time. Further, although men began with a lower awareness of sexism, they showed about as much change in their awareness over time as women, and, although they themselves reported somewhat lower gains than women, they nonetheless saw in themselves some movement toward greater awareness.

Although students tended to respond favorably to the WGS classes, considerable variation in students' responsiveness was found, with some students showing large attitude changes toward a more feminist perspective and others showing the opposite effect. These changes were clearly influenced by the attitudes students' held as they began their classes. Students who came to their classes with greater awareness of sexism and more openness to diversity in gender roles reported more positive relationships with their teacher and fellow students and more feelings of empowerment as a result of their WGS experience. Further, students who were more aware of sexism initially changed more in the direction of greater openness to diverse gender roles. It seems that when the students began with a greater awareness of sexism and its negative impact, they were more willing to engage in the WGS material and to take on new perspectives, resulting in greater flexibility and acceptance of nontraditional gendered alternatives. Similarly, students with greater openness to diversity in gender roles at the beginning of class became more aware of sexism over time. A beginning stance of flexibility and willingness to entertain new ideas and information about gender allowed students to absorb and recognize the validity of information on the oppression of women.

In addition to initial gender attitudes, we found that responsiveness to WGS was related to the relationships students developed in their classes. Those who described strong alliances with their teachers and cohesion with their classmates changed more in their gender attitudes, felt more empowered by their classes, and were less angered and distressed. Moreover, the link between initial attitudes and class responsiveness depended in part on the development of class relationships. To interpret these findings, it is important to remember that students respond to WGS course materials within a social context that is made up of the network of relationships they develop with their teacher and classmates and that when students feel a mutual sense of trust, respect, and agreement with others in the class, they are more able to consider, absorb, and integrate the knowledge and theory they encounter in WGS, leading to more change in their gender attitudes and a greater sense of empowerment.

Ceiling Effects and the Measure of Change over Time

One of the main goals of this study was to assess whether previous findings of a negative relationship between initial attitudes and change in WGS classes were due to a ceiling effect. The findings generally support this conclusion. Whereas initial gender attitudes were negatively related to change on the same attitude measure, they were positively related to all other indices of change. Thus, when measures of change were less affected by ceiling effects, we found that students with more feminist leanings made greater gains than more conservative students toward greater awareness of sexism and flexibility and openness about gender issues.

Findings from the analysis of the three largest ethnic identity groups also suggest the presence of ceiling effects. Asian American and Euro-American students showed more change in the pre/post comparison scores;

however, when students were asked to describe how much the class had changed their attitudes, all three ethnic groups responded similarly, indicating a moderate degree of change. The African Americans had, as a group, already scored high in awareness at the beginning of class. For example, 88% of African Americans agreed or strongly agreed with the statement "Women have been treated unfairly on the basis of their gender throughout most of human history," whereas only 66% of Asian Americans and 75% of Euro-Americans agreed or agreed strongly with the statement. Thus, the African Americans had less room on the pre/post measure than the other ethnic groups to show change in their level of awareness, whereas they could directly report how much the class had changed them on the self-report change measure.

The problem of ceiling effects may also help to explain the lack of overall change in the openness-to-diversity scores. Students entering the WGS classes tended to endorse the statements pertaining to gender diversity more than those about sexism, and the average rating was already near the anchor point *agree* for the gender diversity scale. Thus, students had little room to show positive change in their openness to gender diversity. It seems likely that students would have reported some change on a self-report measure of change in openness, just as the African American students did on the self-report measure of awareness of sexism. In future research on change in gender attitudes over time, it will be best to include not only pre/post measures but also measures that allow students to describe directly how their class influenced them. Subjective measures of change should be interpreted cautiously, given that they may be influenced by factors other than veridical changes in attitudes (e.g., enthusiasm for the class and teacher), but they provide an alternate, supplemental perspective to add to our understanding of student change.

One might attempt to address the problem of ceiling effects by developing gender attitude measures that result in lower average scores. If most students did not score high on pre/post measures, they would have more room to show change toward more feminist perspectives, and their post-test scores would not be as affected by ceiling effects. Although it may be possible to develop such a scale, it should be noted that the gender attitude measures we employed in the current study were designed to reflect contemporary and controversial issues. The LFAIS was developed in the 1990s and was tested and validated with samples of college students. Even so, WGS classes tend to attract students who have feminist attitudes; therefore, regardless of the scale used, ceiling effects with pre/post measures are likely to occur.

Implications for Teaching

Given our findings that students' pre-class attitudes predicted their responsiveness to their classes, we recommend that teachers evaluate their students' gender attitudes as their WGS classes are beginning. By making this assessment, teachers can better understand and address their students' stances on gender issues, such as their assumption that sexist practices no longer exist in our society or that traditional gender roles are in everyone's best interest. Our findings suggest that by addressing these issues early in the class—helping students to recognize instances of sexism and reducing their resistance to considering alternate perspectives on gender—students will have a more rewarding WGS experience: stronger alliances with their teacher, greater cohesion with their fellow students, and greater feelings of empowerment.

Perhaps the most effective approach to enhancing students' awareness of sexism is to guide them to recognize their own social positionality as both the oppressed and the oppressor, emphasizing the crippling limitations of current gendered practices for men as well as women (see Orr 1993 for a description of this approach). Such early class discussions can provide the opportunity for students to draw from and re-examine their own fund of experiential knowledge of patriarchal structures and their effects, leading to greater awareness of previously unrecognized systems of privilege and oppression and opening up students' horizons to consider the value of alternate gendered arrangements.

Our findings on the effects of the teacher alliance and student cohesion provide evidence of the importance of establishing a learning environment in which students develop a sense of mutual trust, respect, and common purpose with their teacher and fellow students. These findings underscore the need, when addressing students' attitudes and resistance to feminist perspectives, to approach all students with openness, respect, and sensitivity so as to foster alliances with them. As discussed by several WGS writers (e.g., MacDonald 2002; May 1999; Rinehart 1999; Sanchez-Casal 2002), teachers can best develop a forum for honest and incisive analysis and debate by setting a tone of openness and affirmation of students. Thus, although teachers should expect students to seriously engage in the examination of course materials, teachers should not engage in "top-down" teaching approaches or expect students to agree with them but instead should welcome students' expressions of alternate points of view and the healthy debate of complex issues. Further, student cohesion should be encouraged by setting standards for students' behavior toward one another (Rinehart 1999). Students should be expected to treat one another with tact and empathy and to consider the contributions of other students as opportunities to enrich their own learning. By modeling an open, nondefensive stance toward alternate perspectives and by expecting the same from students—that is, by fostering alliances with students and cohesion among students—teachers can develop learning communities that can more effectively challenge patriarchal ideologies and encourage the empowerment of students.

Conclusions

Our findings provide much positive information about how students respond to the Women's and Gender Studies experience. As a group, students developed quality relationships with their teachers and classmates, experienced significantly more feelings of empowerment than distress or anger, and emerged from their classes with greater awareness of sexism. Students who held more feminist attitudes on beginning their classes appear to have benefited the most from WGS, and students' relationships with their teachers and fellow students mediated the relation between their initial gender attitudes and both change in attitudes and empowerment. Teachers may enhance students' awareness of sexism, openness toward and appreciation of gender diversity, and sense of empowerment by addressing students' opposing views early in their courses and by fostering collaborative alliances with and among their students.

Acknowledgments

The authors are grateful to Kevin Hoffman, Jenia Kincaid, Veronica Shead, Katie Mehner, Jennifer Seim, Estera Lucas, Debbie Royce, and Heather Eisele for their assistance in data collection.

References

Astin, Alexander W. 1993. *What Matters in College: Four Critical Years Revisited.* San Francisco: Jossey-Bass.
Bryant, Alyssa N. 2003. "Changes in Attitudes toward Women's Roles: Predicting Gender-Role Traditionalism Among College Students." *Sex Roles* 48(3/4):131–142.
Cohen, Jacob 1992. "A Power Primer." *Psychological Bulletin* 112(1):155–159.
Crawford, Mary, and Jessica A. Suckle. 1999. "Overcoming Resistance to Feminism in the Classroom." In *Coming into Her Own. Educational Success in Girls and Women,* ed. Sara S. Davis, Mary Crawford, and Jadwiga Sebrechts, 155–170. San Francisco: Jossey-Bass.
Diamond, Gregory A., and Michael D. Cobb. 1996. "The Candidate as Catastrophe: Latitude Theory and the Problem of Political Persuasion." In *Political Persuasion and Attitude Change,* ed. Diana C. Mutz, Paul M. Sniderman, and Richard A. Brody, 225–247. Ann Arbor, Michigan: University of Michigan Press.
Fellman, Anita C., and Barbara A. Winstead. 1992. "Old Dominion University: Making Connections in the Classroom." In *The Courage to Question:*

Women's Studies and Student Learning, ed. Caryn M. Musil, 83–108. Washington, DC: Association of American Colleges and National Women's Studies Association.

Finke, Laurie, Elaine Maveety, Carol Shaw, and Jean Ward. 1992. "Lewis and Clark: A Single Curriculum." In *The Courage to Question: Women's Studies and Student Learning*, ed. Caryn M. Musil, 43–81. Washington, DC: Association of American Colleges and National Women's Studies Association.

Hertz, Rosanna, and Susan Reverby. 1992. "Wellesley College: Counting the Meanings." In *The Courage to Question: Women's Studies and Student Learning*, ed. Caryn M. Musil, 109–131. Washington, DC: Association of American Colleges and National Women's Studies Association.

Hughes, Christina. 2002. "Pedagogies of, and for, Resistance." In *Gender, Teaching and Research in Higher Education. Challenges for the 21st Century*, ed. Gillian Howie and Ashley Tauchert, 99–110. New York: Ashgate.

Katz, Jennifer, Samantha Swindell, and Sherry Farrow. 2004. "Effects of Participation in a First Women's Studies Course on Collective Self-Esteem, Gender-Related Attitudes, and Emotional Well-Being." *Journal of Applied Social Psychology* 34(10):2179–2199.

MacDonald, Amie A. 2002. "Feminist Pedagogy and the Appeal to Epistemic Privilege." In *Twenty-First Century Feminist Classrooms. Pedagogies of Identity and Difference*, ed. Amie A. MacDonald and Susan Sanchez-Casal, 111–133. New York: Macmillan.

Malkin, Craig, and Jayne E. Stake. 2004. "Changes in Social Attitudes and Self-Confidence in the Women's and Gender Studies Classroom. The Role of Teacher Alliance and Student Cohesion." *Sex Roles* 50(7/8):455–468.

May, Vivian. 1999. "The Ideologue, the Pervert, and the Nurturer, or, Negotiating Student Perceptions in Teaching Introductory Women's Studies Courses." In *Teaching Introduction to Women's Studies*, ed. Barbara S. Winkler and Carolyn DiPalma, 21–35. Westport, CT: Bergin & Garvey.

Morgan, Betsy L. 1996. "Putting the Feminism into Feminism Scales: Introduction of a Liberal Feminist Attitude and Ideology Scale (LFAIS)." *Sex Roles* 34(5/6):359–390.

Orr, Deborah Jane. 1993. "Toward a Critical Rethinking of Feminist Pedagogical Praxis and Resistant Male Students." *Canadian Journal of Education* 18(3):239–254.

Pascarella, Ernest T., and P.T. Terenzini. 1991. *How College Affects Students*. San Francisco: Jossey-Bass.

Preacher, Kristopher J., and Geoffrey L. Leonardelli. 2003. "Calculation for the Sobel Test. An Interactive Calculation Tool for Mediation Tests." Retrieved February 1, 2007, from http://www.quantpsy.org.

Rhoades, Katherine Ann. 1999. "Border Zones: Identification, Resistance, and Transgressive Teaching in Introductory Women's Studies Courses." In *Teaching Introduction to Women's Studies*, ed. Barbara S. Winkler and Carolyn DiPalma, 21–35. Westport, CT: Bergin & Garvey.

Rinehart, Jane A. 1999. "When Things Fall Apart." In *Teaching Introduction to Women's Studies*, ed. Barbara S. Winkler and Carolyn DiPalma, 21–35. Westport, CT: Bergin & Garvey.

————. 2002. "Collaborative Learning, Subversive Teaching, and Activism." In *Teaching Feminist Activism*, ed. Nancy A. Naples & Karen Bojar, 22–35. New York: Routledge.

Sanchez-Casal, Susan 2002. "Unleashing the Demons of History. White Resistance in the U.S. Latino Studies Classroom." In *Twenty-first Century Feminist Classrooms. Pedagogies of Identity and Difference*, ed. Amie A. MacDonald and Susan Sanchez-Casal, 111–133. New York: Macmillan.

Sevelius, Jeanne M., and Jayne E. Stake. 2003. "Attitude Change in Women's Studies Students: The Effects of Prior Attitudes and Attitude Importance." *Journal of Applied Social Psychology* 33(11):2341–2353.

Shor, Ira, and Paulo Freire. 1987. *A Pedagogy for Liberation: Dialogues for Transforming Education*. London: Macmillan.

Stake, Jayne E. 2006. "Pedagogy and Student Change in the Women's Studies Classroom." *Gender and Education* 18:199–212.

Stake, Jayne E., and Frances L. Hoffmann. 2000. "Putting Feminist Pedagogy to the Test: The Experience of Women's Studies from Student and Teacher Perspectives." *Psychology of Women Quarterly* 24(1):30–38.

————. 2001. "Change in Student Attitudes, Social Activism, and Personal Confidence in Higher Education: The Role of Women's Studies." *American Educational Research Journal* 38(2):411–436.

Stake, Jayne E., and Craig Malkin. 2003. "Students' Quality of Experience and Perceptions of Intolerance and Bias in the Women's and Gender Studies Classroom." *Psychology of Women Quarterly* 27(2):174–185.

Stake, Jayne E., Laurie Roades, Suzanna Rose, Lisa Ellis, and Carolyn West. 1994. "The Women's Studies Experience: Impetus for Feminist Activism." *Psychology of Women Quarterly* 18(1):17–24.

Thomsen, Cynthia J., Andra M. Basu, and Mark T. Reinitz. 1995. "Effects of Women's Studies Courses on Gender-Related Attitudes of Women and Men." *Psychology of Women Quarterly* 19(3):419–426.

Zuckerman, Marvin, Bernard Lubin, Christine M. Rinck, and Stanley M. Soliday. 1986. "Discriminant Validity of the Multiple Affect Adjective Check List—Revised." *Journal of Psychopathology & Behavioral Assessment* 8(2):119–128.

PART II   **Embodying Masculinity: Science and Society**

CHAPTER SEVEN

Reading Transgender, Rethinking Women's Studies

CRESSIDA J. HEYES

Trans Liberation: Beyond Pink or Blue by Leslie Feinberg. Boston: Beacon Press, 1998, 147 pp., $20.00 hardcover, $13.00 paper.

Female Masculinity by Judith Halberstam, Durham, NC: Duke University Press, 1998, 329 pp., $49.95 hardcover, $17.95 paper.

Second Skins: The Body Narratives of Transsexuality by Jay Prosser. New York: Columbia University Press, 1998, 270 pp., $47.50 hardcover, $17.00 paper.

Representing the best popular and scholarly contributions to transgender/ sex studies, and with their mutual concern with female-to-male sex and gender crossing (among other topics), these three books mark an important shift in scholarship on gender and sexuality. Trans studies has reached a level of autonomy and sophistication that firmly establishes it as a field with its own theoretical and political questions. Of course, connections to feminist and queer theory are still very apparent in these texts, and all three authors are committed—to varying degrees—to reading trans identities against the backdrop of male dominance and heteronormativity. It's no longer enough, however, for feminist readers to dismiss the projects of trans theorists and activists as epiphenomenal to feminist discourses or even queer theory, or to view trans studies as an optional extra in discussions of sex and gender. These books represent the best arguments against this position and thus offer a new challenge to the inclusivity, scope, and terms of "women's studies."

"Transsexual" and "transgender" are essentially contested terms within and outside trans communities, and part of what is at stake in these texts is the relation between established sex, gender, and sexuality labels on the one hand and these emergent categories on the other. "Trans-" terms capture various kinds of sex and gender crossing and various levels of permanence to these transitions: from medical technologies that transform sexed bodies, to cross-dressing, to passing, to a certain kind of "life-plot," to being legible as one's birth sex but with a "contradictory" gender inflection. For some, the adjective "transsexed" captures the specific project of changing one's sexed body through surgery and hormones, while for others it more broadly describes a distinctive form of narrative. "Transgendered" might describe any project of gender crossing or blending that eschews medicalized interventions, or the term might be used

as a catch-all that includes anyone who disturbs established understandings of gender dichotomy or its mapping to sexual dimorphism. The authors of these books epitomize the complexity of trans identities: Judith
Halberstam identifies as a masculine woman, Jay Prosser as an FTM
(female to male) transsexual, and Leslie Feinberg as a trans person who
sometimes uses the shorthand "masculine female" but whose life and
work are actually not assimilable to any extant category. These authors
all seek to write their own experience as part of their intellectual projects.
They all build novel perspectives on what is erased, omitted, or glossed
over in existing scholarship and political activism, and all try to initiate
new theoretical paradigms and recast political movement. As I hope to
show here, there are also tensions within and among these three texts,
marking out a conceptual terrain where trans studies is established as a
diverse field of inquiry within which protagonists disagree about how
various identities should be understood and what political projects they
imply.

Leslie Feinberg: *Trans Liberation*

Feinberg's *Trans Liberation* is the popular book of the three. Clearly oriented toward a general audience, it is short, pithy, and represents diverse
trans voices in a pastiche of speeches and commentaries by Feinberg and
friends. The book's project is to present trans liberation as a political
movement "capable of fighting for justice" (1998, 5). This movement, in
Feinberg's account, includes "masculine females and feminine males,
cross-dressers, transsexual men and women, intersexuals born on the anatomical sweep between female and male, gender-blenders, many other
sex and gender-variant people, and our significant others" (5). Indeed, in
the short "portraits" by other contributors, an impressively wide range
of queer identities and stories inflected by class, race, and age are represented: from a male transvestite who became a full-time transgendered
woman talking with her wife about their relationship, to a drag queen recalling New York street life and Stonewall, to a gay transman on the significance of his Native heritage, to an intersexed activist discussing the
emergence of the intersex movement.

    This book has many strengths, including its insistence that sex, gen-
der, and sexual identities be understood narratively and in terms of relationship with others. Feinberg relentlessly connects different oppressions,
not shying away from acknowledging a debt to feminism and lesbian and
gay liberation in particular, but also resisting the reduction of trans history to these other struggles. It is refreshing to see the variety of radical
politics Feinberg supports. Too much popular writing on gender and sexuality is sustained and made palatable by very thin, liberal accounts of

freedom, justice, and equality, and by an emphasis on the hardships endured by relatively privileged and established social groups. It's remarkable that Feinberg is able to rouse support in hir written work and on hir speaking tours not only for "trans liberation" but also for radical class analysis and connections to anti-racism, anti-Semitism, and feminism.[1] This kind of multi-faceted political analysis too often appears only in abstruse academic form and goes against the grain of dominant political idioms, especially in the United States. Feinberg's rhetoric is therefore all the more impressive for its ability to capture the interconnection of oppressions and argue convincingly that we all have a stake in undermining them. Sections of the book would work well for undergraduate teaching in feminism or queer theory, especially at the introductory level where engaging and accessible radical texts are hard to find, although as a focal point for a course I would find it rather too theoretically insubstantial and polemical.

Despite this book's many virtues, there are interesting dissonances between Feinberg's analysis of trans oppression and hir reliance on political discourse that doesn't obviously work for this purpose. The language of choice, for example, appears throughout the book in terms of slogans such as "every person should have the right to choose between pink or blue tinted gender categories, as well as all the other hues of the palette" and "these ideas of what a 'real' woman or man should be straightjacket the freedom of individual self-expression" (4). But what is the self that lies beneath the "socialization" of gender and that is supposed to do the choosing here? Are all "choices" really normatively equal? While the point that compulsory gender deforms us all is well taken, Feinberg is too quick to jettison very diverse and supple constructionist accounts by reducing them to an implausible "social determinism": "I do not hold the view that gender is simply a social construct—one of two languages that we learn by rote from early age. To me, gender is the poetry each of us makes out of the language we are taught" (10). This disavowal leads hir to drift toward a kind of gender voluntarism that contradicts some of hir other arguments and has alarming political implications.

For example, the notions of choice and agency Feinberg deploys cause hir to move from an otherwise materially inflected and feminist account of gender to a curiously aesthetic and depoliticized version. The notion of gender freedom ze espouses is important in speaking against both the crushing weight of the dominant culture's gender discipline and some of feminism's more doctrinaire moments: "There are no rights or wrongs in the ways people express their own gender style. No one's lipstick or flattop is hurting us. . . . Each person has the right to express their gender in any way that feels most comfortable" (53). As ze seems to recognize elsewhere, however, the privilege of white bourgeois male masculinity is implicated in the cultural visibility of minority male masculinities, cultural disdain for femininity, and cultural intolerance and disgust directed against any gender "deviance." These social structures inform and support normative heterosexuality and white bourgeois patriarchy. Gender expression is thus not only an aesthetic choice about cosmetics or hairstyle, skirts, and suits. It's also implicated in politically fraught behaviors, economic marginalization and exploitation, and political consciousness. So even if the aesthetic choices of individuals aren't up for moral grabs (as I agree they shouldn't be), "gender expression" must surely (on Feinberg's own account) occupy a normative terrain. For example, many feminists have argued that misogynist violence is constitutive of certain kinds of masculinity, but it's hardly a form of gender expression that Feinberg can condone. Once when I heard Feinberg speak, I asked hir, with this problem in mind, "What's good about masculinity?" Ze seemed to miss the political import of the question, referring in hir answer instead to the diversity of masculinities across and within time and place, and again alluding to the freedom of individuals to express their gender without fear of reprisal.

This refusal to pass judgment on others' choices contributes to the appeal of Feinberg's rhetoric throughout hir work. But it also sometimes evades hard political questions about who is damaged and privileged by configurations of gender that themselves need to be transformed, sometimes from within the subject's own political consciousness. In other words, Feinberg's approach here elides a crucial aspect of progressive gender politics: the demand that we change ourselves. No doubt ze would resist such a demand on the reasonable grounds that trans people have too often been forced to conform to damaging gender norms, or been oppressively criticized for having the "wrong" sort of consciousness. But this response doesn't allow for important political distinctions between progressive transformations of consciousness initiated from within marginalized communities and disciplining moves that attempt only to reinforce established divisions.

Judith Halberstam: *Female Masculinity*

A possible solution to this problem can be found in Judith Halberstam's book *Female Masculinity*. This is a lively read and a wonderful academic contribution, offering the first comprehensive and theoretically developed account of the forms masculinity takes when performed or adopted by female-bodied people. Halberstam rejects the popular belief (implicit, as she persuasively argues, in a great deal of contemporary scholarship) that masculinity can be reduced to the male body and its effects. Instead, an investigation of the history and practices of female masculinities can reveal otherwise invisible ways in which male masculinities are constructed. If, as she maintains, "masculinity . . . becomes legible as masculinity where and when it leaves the white male middle-class body" (1998, 2), then minority and female masculinities are crucial sites for the exposure of the performativity of masculinity, and for the feminist and queer political projects that incorporate this recognition. Throughout Halberstam details the connections between lesbianism and female masculinity, as well as the complex dynamics of race and class that render some masculinities more visibly performative than others.

Halberstam uses a method she calls "perverse presentism" to outline and analyze case studies of female masculinity from the nineteenth and twentieth centuries. This method "avoids the trap of simply projecting contemporary understandings back in time . . . [while applying] insights from the present to conundrums of the past" (52–53). Uncertainty about the contemporary connection between females—especially lesbians—and masculinity, she argues, creates a concomitant uncertainty about the history of this connection. Resisting a method that conflates lesbianism and female masculinity, Halberstam aims not to deny the mutual implication of these terms in many contemporary contexts, but rather to hold open a conceptual space that will be able to account for the historical diversity of female masculinities. She pulls together primary sources and their contemporary interpreters (including a discussion of John Radclyffe Hall) to argue that the subject-positions of the tribade, the female husband, the invert, and the passing woman cannot be adequately understood through the lens of contemporary lesbian theory.

In a later chapter she again argues against dominant lesbian/queer readings of the "stone butch," challenging the "melancholic formulation of stone butch desire" as well as "the way in which we demand accountability from some sexual roles but not from others" (112). Resisting the claim that the stone butch is correctly read as "frigid, dysphoric, misogynist, repressed, or simply pretranssexual" (124), Halberstam offers instead an account of stone butchness as a problematic but nonetheless fully legible and satisfying form of female masculinity. I wanted to be convinced by this argument, but Halberstam is reading so much against the grain of the (auto)biographical, ethnographic, and theoretical literatures she examines that her method risks becoming more literally "perverse."

Halberstam thus tries to expand sexual discourse to account for "the myriad practices that fall beyond the purview of homo- and heteronormativity" (139). As an extension of this project, she also examines the conflicts between lesbian butches and female-to-male transsexuals. She returns to an earlier essay—"F2M: The Making of Female Masculinity" (Halberstam 1994)—and its FTM critics (who include Jay Prosser) to argue against the privileging of transsexuality in the border wars between butches and FTMs. She aims to "focus on certain categories of butch-ness without presuming that they represent early stages of transsexual identity within some progressive model of sexual trans-identity and with-out losing their specificity as masculine identifications within a female body" (152); "it is time to complicate on the one hand the transsexual models that assign gender deviance only to transsexual bodies and gender normativity to all other bodies, and on the other hand the hetero-normative models that see transsexuality as the solution to gender deviance and homosexuality as a pathological problem" (153–54). This is a fascinating chapter where the debates internal to trans studies are made most appar-ent: Halberstam lines up against other trans theorists, ending with a compelling critique of the politics of space (including colonialism) appar-ent in some transsexual accounts.

The book winds down with two chapters addressing filmic representa-tions of butch women and drag king performance, respectively. Both are clever and playful overviews of neglected cultural forms: in the former case Halberstam offers a survey and rough typology of butches in post-war movies (that would work well for teaching purposes in a film class). In the latter case she examines the aesthetics and politics of what she calls "kinging": drag humor associated with masculinity (238). In an insight-ful contrast with drag queen camp, Halberstam argues that dominant forms of masculinity are constructed through (and invested in) their own invisibility, such that drag kings face enormous challenges in mak-ing a performance out of nonperformativity. This chapter has wonderful photos and is enormously entertaining as Halberstam's pleasure in the club culture that has spawned drag king shows shines through. In a brief conclusion, Halberstam uses the image of the raging bull (dyke) and box-ing to consolidate her claim that masculinity has both a history and a future in its expression by women.

What's most valuable about this book is its novelty. There exists no other book-length treatment of female masculinity, and Halberstam has definitely set the terms of debate on this topic. The book's originality also contributes to the loose and speculative quality of many of the theoretical arguments. Halberstam is still finding her way on this theo-retical terrain, and this book should be read as an initial contribution to a conversation that will undoubtedly move on, rather than as the final word on this subject. It's nonetheless a smart, well-researched, and ambitious book that would be an excellent teaching text in upper-level courses on gender and sexuality, especially in cultural studies or Women's Studies. It's long and covers a lot of ground, so it taught as a whole it would need to be the centerpiece of the course, but with a little back-ground information on the project, students could also read individual chapters.

Jay Prosser: *Second Skins*

Finally, Jay Prosser's *Second Skins* is the most theoretically dense of the three books and is most obviously directed at an academic audience already immersed in the debates in which he engages. The two themes of the book are embodiment and narrative, which Prosser convincingly argues are central, under-explored modes of transition in transsexuality. I read this book first as an attempt to develop a politically sophisticated account of the dialectic relation between transsexual experience and the contradictory constructions of transsexed subjects by medical, literary, and academic discourses. Second, it attempts—with mixed success—to forge an intermediate path between a strain of poststructuralism that emphasizes language at the expense of the body and an approach to materiality that neglects the body's semiotic construction. The book includes a weighty chapter on Judith Butler's treatment of transgender, which argues that "queer studies has made the transgendered subject, the subject who crosses gender boundaries, a key queer trope" (1998, 5). Prosser criticizes a syllogism implicit in a number of queer theorists' work: transgender equates to gender performativity, which equates to "queer," and in turn, to "subversive," with the implicit counterpart: "nontransgender = gender constativity = straight = naturalizing" (33). These theoretical moves, Prosser argues, erase the nonperformativity of some transsexual trajectories. Transsexual subjectivity is too often deformed within the category "queer" by the latter's "poststructuralist problems with literality and referentiality" (58).

In an absorbing chapter on transsexual embodiment, Prosser takes up the important question "What does transsexuality, that fact that subjects do seek radically to change their sex, convey about sex, identity, and the flesh?" (63). Taking the concept of "skin ego" from psychoanalyst Didier Anzieu, Prosser analyzes the connection between self and soma, reading sex reassignment surgeries as the search for "a feeling of a coherent and integral body of one's own" (80). Prosser's theoretical insights into the "wrong body" tropes that dominate popular discourse about transsexuality are very welcome, and this is an important intervention into an extremely difficult set of questions in philosophy of the body. But there is something lacking here. The contention that "transsexuals continue to deploy the image of wrong embodiment because being trapped in the wrong body is simply what transsexuality feels like" (69) is unsatisfying. Prosser's claims here need to be further contextualized: many individuals experience related embodied dissonances (anorectics, for example), and we need a phenomenology of transsexual consciousness that does more than detail the significance of bodily transformation for psychic wholeness, and which more firmly situates that consciousness in historical and political context. Thus, while Prosser might resist causal accounts, the question "Why these experiences?" lurks in the background of many of these arguments.

The best chapter in the book asks, "What kind of autobiographical narrative is the transsexual?" (103). Cataloging the demands of clinicians and the conventions of the genre of autobiography, Prosser argues for an understanding of writing the transsexual life that places the trans subject as author of a nonetheless engineered narrative. Again, there is a tension here between Prosser's understandable desire to stress the authorial agency of transsexual subjects (as evidenced, for example, by his rejection of Bernice Hausman's argument that technology makes transsexuality possible, and his concomitant emphasis on the historical continuity of autobiographical tropes) and his meticulous elaboration of the over-determination of transsexual narrative. Had Prosser made this tension explicit, he might have addressed it more adequately. Like Feinberg, by insisting on trans agency and self-determination, Prosser risks an implicit reliance on a pre-social self that is at odds with his other theoretical insights.

In the same vein as Halberstam, Prosser reads *The Well of Loneliness* (Hall 1981) and *Stone Butch Blues* (Feinberg 1993) not merely as archetypal lesbian novels, but as texts with a commonly derogated trans subtext. In John Radclyffe Hall's case, the historical shift from sexological to psychoanalytic discourse, argues Prosser, impels the "discursive loss" of the invert in favor of the homosexual. By recuperating *The Well* as a transsexual novel, he argues again for the significance of inverts' self-understandings in generating the medical narrative of transsexuality and defends the historical continuity of transsexual identity. By examining the politics of home in the context of *Stone Butch Blues*, he relatedly examines the "emergence of transgender on the fault lines and tensions between transsexual and queer" (176). Controversially, Prosser reads Feinberg's life and work as evidence of "how uninhabitable is sexed dislocation," arguing: "that transgender as much as transsexual personal accounts continue to center on sexed crossings is, in my mind, a sure sign of the ongoing centrality of sexual difference in our world: a marker of the limits of its reconfigurability, and as a consequence of many subjects' yearning to locate in a stable position at least at some point in relation to this difference" (204).

Finally, in his epilogue, Prosser examines the paradox of transsexual representation through photographs in autobiographies: "photographs of transsexuals are situated on a tension between revealing and concealing transsexuality. Their primary function is to expose the transsexual body; yet how to achieve this when transsexuality on the body is that which by definition is to be concealed?" (209). Moving from simple portraits in older autobiographies to more self-consciously political images, Prosser details the ironies of representation, erasure, and gaze that construct these pictures.

This is an intelligent and original book that takes on difficult and much-neglected questions in trans theory, and it would be a great teaching text for more advanced undergraduate and graduate students in literature, Women's Studies, or queer theory. Halberstam and Prosser have written closely related books with overlapping content: both devote chapters to John Radclyffe Hall and the discourse of inversion, as well as *Stone Butch Blues*, and to representations of butches or transsexed subjects (in film and photography, respectively). Both authors are avowedly personally invested in their scholarly projects. Pragmatically, this makes these excellent companion books for teaching purposes; theoretically, it's a promising juxtaposition because the arguments are significantly different.

What is this contrast? Halberstam is concerned with identifying and making more inhabitable the spaces between genders, bodies, and sexualities. Her theoretical inclination is always to detach one identity label from another, to point to the erasure of experience and possibility that any reduction causes, most notably the reduction of masculinity to an effect of male bodies. Prosser, by contrast, emphasizes materiality, flesh, and complex kinds of authenticity. He seeks to bring transsexuality home, out of the theoretical spaces of queer theory where, he maintains, it has become a trope that celebrates an imagined possibility rather than a tangible, grounded experience: "in pushing past a transsexual narrative ('post'), in ceding our claims to sexed location, we relinquish what we do not yet have: the recognition of our sexed realness; acceptance as men and women; fundamentally, the right to gender homes" (204). Halberstam engages this aspect of Prosser's work at some length in her chapter on butch/FTM border wars, arguing: "The language that Prosser . . . use[s] to defend [his] particular transsexual project from queer appropriations runs the risk not only of essence and even colonialism, but . . . of using the loaded language of migration and homecoming to ratify new, distinctly unqueer models of manliness" (170). This particular criticism is well-taken. Of the three books, Prosser is least attentive to dynamics of race and class, and this omission is related to his investment in the realness of trans identity. This problem is in turn related to my criticisms of Feinberg, and it signals an impasse in transsexual studies: does any attempt to theorize transsexual authenticity necessarily mark an evasion of normative questions about gender expression? How can gender be simultaneously understood as a fundamental part of self and deconstructed, transformed, and criticized? These questions are, of course, also feminist questions, for non-trans women as much as for any trans subject, again illustrating the important connections and overlap between trans and Women's Studies.

Reading Transgender

Watching these arguments play out reveals that all three authors face a complicated political struggle: so much academic literature over-determines and erases the agency of the trans subject in favor of the grasp of technology, medical discourses, history qua regimes of power, or false consciousness. On the other hand, so much popular literature is clearly naively essentialist in its understanding of transsexual experience: tropes of wrong body, being "born that way," ontological necessity, and historical and cultural universality tend to be grossly under-theorized and easily feed into other essentializing discourses about sex and gender. Put these two trends together with the crucial insistence that trans subjects speak in their own voices and mobilize politically around less oppressive self-understandings, and writers in the area have an almost impossible task of navigation, negotiation, and representation.

These tensions notwithstanding, the field of transsex/gender studies has clearly reached a new stage of maturity. There is a complexity and political acumen to these books that should permanently foreclose the dismissal of trans studies by skeptics and render hopelessly dated the kind of radical feminist critique of transgender that has had currency in certain circles. There was a time when I sensed that trans studies was playing catch-up with feminism, trying to overcome the damaging legacy of Janice Raymond's work and related negative sentiment among non-trans feminists suspicious of transsexuals in particular. That time is truly past, and these books sit alongside the work of, for example, Kate Bornstein, Jason Cromwell, Jacob Hale, Henry Rubin, Sandy Stone, and Susan Stryker as evidence of the sophistication, complexity, and internal heterogeneity of this field of scholarship and activism.

Many questions need to be further explored: what account of subjectivity and agency will be adequate to the task of making sense of the experience of transsexuality? What ethnographic methods work best, and what are their pitfalls, when it comes to collecting information on trans subcultures and individuals? How can authors theorize their investments in particular constructions of identity without reducing theory to a justification of themselves? How are very different self-understandings and life projects among trans theorists to be negotiated or reconciled? How should non-trans feminists engage this literature, or conduct their own work on trans issues?[2] What normative demands can fairly be made of the various players in these debates, especially in terms of transforming themselves? Feminists of all stripes should pay close attention to emerging answers to these questions, not least because they have a lot to offer in rethinking the ever-shifting categories of "women's" studies.

Notes

1. Feinberg prefers to be described with the pronouns "hir" (in place of her/his) and "ze" (in place of he/she).

2. For a set of injunctions in answer to this question, see Jacob Hale, "Suggested Rules for Non-Transsexuals Writing about Transsexuals, Transsexuality, Transsexualism, or Trans ____," http://sandystone.com/hale.rules.html.

References

Feinberg, Leslie. 1993. *Stone Butch Blues*. Ithaca, NY: Firebrand Books.
Halberstam, Judith. 1994. "F2M: The Making of Female Masculinity." In *The Lesbian Postmodern*, ed. Laura Doan. New York: Columbia University Press.
Hall, Radclyffe. 1981. *The Well of Loneliness*. New York: Morrow/Avon.

CHAPTER EIGHT

Biological Behavior?
Hormones, Psychology, and Sex

CELIA ROBERTS

Since their "discovery" early this century, sex hormones have taken a strong role in the explanation of sex differences in human and other animal behaviors (Oudshoorn 1994). In recent times, for example, they have been held in popular scientific literature to indicate that women are better suited than men to child-rearing and to underlie women's incapacity for certain types of work (Moir and Jessel 1991). Within the sciences of psychology and behavioral endocrinology, sex hormones are attributed powers to produce sex differences in behaviors such as children's play and adult sexuality.

Given the political implications of such attributions, it is important that feminist responses to these sciences are complex and convincing. While critiques of biological reductionism in the explanation of sex differences in human and other animal behavior are well established within feminist thought (Bleier 1984; Fausto-Sterling 1992; Spanier 1995), I argue here that for two central reasons more specific attention needs to be paid to the positive theorization of the role of biology in the production of behavior. Firstly, on many occasions, scientists do attempt to account for the social in their work (that is, they do not provide accounts that are entirely reductionist in a biological sense); this work also needs feminist examination. Secondly, theoretical discussions within feminist thought demonstrate that it is difficult, if not impossible, to entirely dismiss the role of the biological in the production of sex differences. As I will argue, it remains inadequate (both theoretically and politically) for feminism simply to reject the biological. This paper, then, attempts to find a more complex "middle way" of approaching the biological in its powerful and historically specific instantiations (in this case as sex hormones), without being reductionist.

Part One: Hormones and "the Organ of Behavior"

How do scientific theories explain the connections between the brain, the biological body, and human behavior? What is the role of hormones in this understanding, insofar as it relates to sex differences?

The most simple view, and what biologist David Crews calls the classical view, is biologistic. It argues that "all somatic sexual dimorphisms, including brain, and hence behavior, result from gonadal hormone production that begins after morphological differentiation of the gonad" (1988,

332). In this view, brain and behavioral factors derive directly from sexed bodily differences. Thus, for example, studies are made of the sexuality of rats, whereby early androgen levels are manipulated and later changed patterns of sexual behavior noted. The theory is that androgen causes masculine behavior and its absence causes feminine behavior. As Bernard Donovan states, "This idea can be traced back to classical studies [in 1959] of the hormonal control of the differentiation of the genital tract, for when pregnant guinea-pigs were injected with androgen the genitalia of the female offspring were masculinized and they showed an increase in male-type mounting behavior and aggressiveness" (1988, 236). In later research, male rats were deprived of androgens by castration or by treatment with anti-androgenic drugs, which was seen to result in the "later manifestation of the female pattern of lordosis [the female position adopted during sexual intercourse, which is used as the yardstick of feminine sexual behavior in rats] after priming with oestrogen and progesterone" (236). Thus a simple causal chain was established between the sexual behavior of animals such as guinea-pigs and rats and their hormonally sexually differentiated bodies.

No matter how interesting the sexuality of rats and guinea-pigs may be to some, this research was important largely because of the leads it gave into compelling questions of human sexuality. In 1988, feminist theorists of science Ruth Doell and Helen Longino described the increasing attempts, since the early 1970s, to develop theories of human behavior based on extrapolation from these animal studies (1988, 56). Using the linear model applied in animal studies (the one-way causal model where chromosomes cause gonads, which cause hormones, which cause behaviors), human behavior is studied as an effect of prenatal hormonal input: "The human brain is treated largely as a black box with prenatal hormonal input and later behavioral output. The implication is that the effect of prenatal hormone exposure can be either quantitatively assessed as contributing a specific amount to the end result, or that it is, by itself, determinative of that result" (Doell and Longino 1988, 59). In this simplistic model, differences between humans and nonhuman animals are largely erased, and the influence of the social on behavior is reduced to little or nothing. Often cited examples of this type of work include that of psychologists John Money, Anke Ehrhardt, and Heino Meyer-Bahlburg, all of whom have studied the behavioral patterns of "special" human populations exposed to unusual levels of hormones in utero.

"Normal" human populations are also studied in this way. As it is not possible in these populations to know the levels of hormones to which infants were exposed in utero, measurements of current levels of hormones are taken. This is followed by measurement of whatever behavior is being observed, and the proposition of a causal link. Such a proposition, of course, extrapolates correlations to causes. Marianne Hassler, for

example, studies the "effect" of testosterone (T) on musical ability, finding "that an optimal T level may exist for the expression of creative musical behavior" (1992, 55). Many assumptions underlie this work: Hassler
admits to assuming that "current T levels can be looked at as a component of a relatively enduring biochemical system which has been organized
during prenatal and/or perinatal brain development under the influence
of androgens and/or estrogens" (66). She assumes, in other words, that the
brain is set up during the prenatal and/or perinatal period in a male or
female way, and levels of adult hormone can be used as an indicator of
this set-up. She rejects suggestions that the musical ability she finds may
have more to do with environmental influences than T levels by citing
examples of children from musical families where one child became a
musician and others did not (for example, Mendelssohn) (67). Hassler
considers this sufficient argument to establish the causal importance of
T levels and "male-type" or "female-type" brains and endocrine systems.
This view of what constitutes the social—i.e., that everyone in one family
has the same experience of "the social"—is extremely (in fact absurdly)
limited.

As Doell and Longino note, the linear model problematically figures
the brain as a passive biological entity. In much literature around human
and other animal behavior, however, some attention is given to the complexities of the brain and its relation to hormones and to the social.[1]
Doell and Longino argue that for many scientists this does not mean the
abandonment of the linear model of causation (1988, 60). As I will demonstrate, references to the importance of the social are often made and
then ignored. In cases where closer attention is paid, scientists acknowledge the brain as a meeting point between the endocrine system and "input" from the external world. Throughout this literature there are many
different frameworks of understanding this relation between the body,
brain, and the world, most of which involve a division of processes or
functions into those that are more biological (more directly caused by
hormones) and those that are more social. This process of division, I argue,
shows that these theories maintain a reliance on the social/biological
distinction.

The work of psychologists John Money and Anke Ehrhardt is a good
example of this. In 1955 Money suggested that there is a fundamental
difference between gender identity, or role (sense of self as male or female), and sex dimorphic behaviors. Gender identity, he found, was not
dependent on gonadal sex, but rather was determined by rearing. Thus a
child born with complete androgen insensitivity who was genetically
male but raised as a female had a female gender identity that was stable
and difficult to change, even when bodily changes in puberty made her
body seem male (Ehrhardt 1984, 42–44). Ehrhardt, a colleague of Money's,
follows this view in her work on sexed behaviors. She agrees that gender

identity may be socially caused, but argues on the other hand that sexed behaviors such as playing with dolls and rough-and-tumble play have a biological (prenatal hormonal) basis (Ehrhardt 1984; Ehrhardt and Meyer-Bahlburg 1981). Sexual orientation is further split off, as is cognitive behavior, such as performance on cognitive tests. The latter two are not seen by Ehrhardt to be hormonally caused, although she suggests that future evidence may prove that they are (Ehrhardt 1984; Ehrhardt and Meyer-Bahlburg 1981).[2]

Other theorists give more prominence to the role of the brain, conceptualizing behavior as a result of a complex brain/body interaction. June Macover Reinisch and colleagues, for example, acknowledge that much research has demonstrated the importance of the social in the production of human behavior. Thus they make a claim for "biological potentiality," rather than biological determinism. Reinisch and colleagues "have conceptualized the complex interaction between organismic and environmental factors in the development of sex differences in human behavior as the 'multiplier effect,'" where from birth to adulthood (prenatally) hormonally caused differences in the brain affect the sensations and perceptions received by the brain and the cognitions produced and establish "behavioral predispositions" that cause "slightly different" male or female behaviors (Reinisch, Ziemba-Davis, and Sanders 1991, 214). These "slightly different" behaviors, they argue, are then encouraged or discouraged by caretakers and others, which increases the influence of the social on behavior. As puberty is reached, differences are further "augmented," and during adult reproductive years the differences between men and women are at a maximum. "As humans age," they go on to argue, "perhaps because role expectations become less divergent, there appears to be a tendency for both sexes to become more androgynous and therefore more similar, resulting in the relative reduction of sex differences among older adults" (214).

Despite their adherence to this "multiplier effect" model, which takes into account the social via the insistence on brain differences between the sexes and the reinforcement of these through "social roles," Reinisch et al., in reviewing nineteen studies of the behavioral patterns of children and adults exposed to "prenatal hormone environments that were atypical for their sex," end up ignoring the effects of the social on human behavior (215). They position the role of the social as a possible confounding factor that can be separated surprisingly easily from a study of the role of biology (hormones):

> By studying the effects of prenatal exposure to these exogenous hormones, insight may be gained into the role of prenatal endogenous hormones in the development of behavioral differences both within and between the sexes. However, because the role of prenatal hormonal exposure in the development of human behavioral sex differences is potentially confounded by society's

differential treatment of male and female individuals, this review focuses on making comparisons within a given sex. The demonstration of within-sex behavioral differences attenuates the confound between prenatal hormonal contributions and environmental influences on the development of sexually dimorphic behavior. (215)

So by separating the sexes, everything becomes strangely simple. Remisch et al. erase the effect of culture through their acknowledgment of the differential treatment of boys and girls: yes, culture exists, they say, but it is relevant only insofar as it affects the sexes differentially. Thus, if we only compare males with males and females with females, the confound inflicted by the social will be "obviated." (271). The logic of this argument is clearly insupportable, as it assumes that the social treatment of all the members of one sex is identical.

In their review, Reimsch et al. examine studies of the behavior of adults or children who have been exposed in utero to atypical patterns of hormones. These people's behaviors are compared to others' who were not exposed to such "environments." Comparisons are made according to a scale of masculinity and femininity: with the help of the articles reviewed and with a group of four psychologists, Remisch et al. classify the sets of behaviors studied into masculine or feminine behaviors. They then indicate if the people exposed to atypical hormone levels are either masculinized, defeminized, feminized, or demasculinized, according to whether or not they exhibit behaviors nominated as either masculine or feminine. Masculinization and feminization are said to occur when the subject shows more of a clearly masculine or feminine behavior. Demasculinization or defeminization is said to occur when there is a decrease in a masculine or feminine behavior, but which is not necessarily seen to be a swing to its "opposite." Unsurprisingly, behaviors seen to be feminine include "interest in playing with dolls," "interest in appearance and hairstyles," and "interest in marriage and maternalism," while masculine behaviors included "rough-and-tumble play," "aggression," "interest in watching sports on TV," and "participation in sports." Homo- and heterosexuality are also figured here: for young male subjects, preferring to play with boys is rated as masculine, whereas playing with girls is rated as feminine. In late adolescence and adulthood, however, "this assumption was not made" (226). That these very categories reflect the social in historically specific ways is not examined by Reinisch et al. They simply note the hormonal influences on the infant, look at its later behavior, noting whether there has been a masculinization or feminization, etc., and then nominate this change as biological.

Logically, this process means that Reinisch et al. end up claiming either that there is some sort of biological force that produces "playing with dolls" and "interest in watching sports on TV," which is nonsensical, or that there is some (biological?) intermediary between the body/brain and these culturally influenced behaviors. This intermediary is presumably what they call "behavioral predispositions" (271), but as to what these actually are, we are given no information. We know there are hormones and there are social behaviors that can be socially rated as masculine or feminine, but there is still no explained connection between the two. In quoting Stephen Gould—"Humans are animals, and everything we do is constrained, in some sense, by our biology"—Reinisch et al. reveal their assumed position (qtd. in Reinisch, Ziemba-Davis, and Sanders 1991, 213–44). They prove nothing and yet claim to have demonstrated an important role for prenatal hormones in child and adult behavior. All they have shown is that people who were exposed to various hormones during fetal development occasionally show different scores on tests of stereotypical social behaviors. Nothing is demonstrated (but much is assumed) about the role of biology in the lives of their human subjects.

When science looks at the role of hormones in the establishment of sexually differentiated behaviors, questions of homo- and heterosexuality are never far behind. Cheryl McCormick, Sandra Witelson, and Edward Kingstone, for example, situate their study of the biological factors in the etiology of homosexuality within a growing search for such factors, which they claim is "partly due to results of experimental work of the last few decades which show that much of the sexual behavior of nonhuman animals is driven by sex hormones" (1990, 69). McCormick et al. argue that adult hormone levels will be unlikely to provide an explanation for sexual orientation, and so it would be more profitable to look to the brain, which they call "the organ of behavior" (69). They state that "to a certain extent, sexual differentiation of the brain is independent of the sexual differentiation of other parts of the body. . . . Thus, one may predict neural differences between homosexuals and heterosexuals without expecting other biological differences" (70). Their findings (which look at incidence of left-handedness in homo- and heterosexual men and women in order to indicate levels of brain hemispheric lateralization),[3] they argue, support the notion that prenatal neuroendocrine events are "a factor" in the development of human sexual orientation and that the mechanisms associated with sexual orientation differ between the sexes (69). In this work the brain is not a "black box" but more a neuroendocrine controller. Prenatal hormones are seen to affect the brain (and thus behavior) in a way that is separate to their effect on the body via gonads (measured in hormone levels in the blood).

This more complicated idea, that the brain itself is sexually differentiated by hormones in a separate process to the sexual differentiation of the gonads and thus the body in general, is taken up by many scientists. One year after this research on homosexuality, Witelson published a

review of studies of sex differences in human brain organization and behavior (1991). In this review she works through research concerning different neurological areas and finds evidence of sex differences in each.
These differences she attributes to prenatal and perinatal hormonal action. "Research has demonstrated," she asserts,

> that the brain is a sexually differentiated organ, that is, that fetal and perina-
> tal sex hormones have organizational effects on brain structure and also have
> subsequent activational effects on the brain. . . . Such results have led to hy-
> potheses of the role of sex-related biological factors leading to the variation in
> human brain function and behavior, *but the specific relationships and mech-
> anisms remain to be delineated.* (132; emphasis added)

In other words, she reports correlations between certain brain differences
and types of behaviors but can only assume causal relationships. Throughout the article Witelson states that sex differences in various parts of the
brain could affect particular behaviors, and so she ends up concluding that
there is a biological basis of behavioral and cognitive differences between the
sexes and between homo- and heterosexuals (148). The implications of this
finding do not disturb her, as she hands over responsibility to others: "The
challenge *to society,*" she asserts, "is to accept, respect, and effectively use
the neural diversity among human beings" (148, emphasis added).

In all of these theories, the claim to account for the role of the social
in the production of sexually differentiated behaviors is false. In each of
them, the social is reduced to simplistic ideas of what happens in families (the idea that everyone in the same family is treated equally), or in
society (that all members of the same sex are treated equally within a
society). Notions of racial, class, or cultural differences are ignored in
this research, as is the wealth of feminist and other work on the complexity of the social and its effects on human embodiment. As I have
shown, this simplistic understanding of the social allows these theorists
to strengthen their claims about the role of biological (hormones) in the
production of behaviors. They claim to have controlled for, or to have
examined, the social and then to have found that the biological is actually more important.

Part Two: Critiques of the Biological/Social Split

Is Biology Separate from the Social?

> Living processes are never static and this applies to the biological processes
> associated with sex differences. No matter what kind of sex difference has
> been measured, the difference can exist only at one point of time. The indi-
> viduals who have been tested . . . are constantly changing because they are in
> constant interaction with their environments. We actively select and change

our environments and, at the same time, we are actively selected and changed by them. Flexibility characterizes all levels of biology and behavior. (Rogers 1999, 118)

In the view of the scientists discussed in part one, biology can be separated from the social. The biological body is understood as established during development and is thought to remain quite stable throughout a life. The brain in particular is conceptualized as a relatively static entity. In contrast to this mainstream idea, other scientists stress the flexibility and responsiveness of the brain to the external world, arguing that the human brain is affected and changed by the external world, not just by prenatal endocrine events. Physiologist Lesley Rogers, for example, writes:

> The brain is able to learn and in so doing its biochemistry and cellular structure are changed. Thus environmental influences alter its storage and capacity to process information, and thus can affect the course of brain development. . . . This is often forgotten in discussions of brain structure and function. The brain is seen as a controller determining behavior, and often insufficient attention is paid to feedback of behavior and other environmental influences on brain development and function. Although it is possible that sex hormones can influence brain development, it is equally possible that environmental factors can do the same. (Rogers 1988, 49)

This means that there can be another interpretation of the correlations found between types of brains and certain behaviors discussed above: behaving in certain ways can change the brain. As Rogers argues, "the effect of testosterone on the brain does not occur in the absence of environmental influences and it cannot be considered in separation from these" (1988, 51). According to Rogers, the human brain remains plastic throughout life, and thus no correlation can be assumed to be caused by hormones or genes (1999, 111). The challenge to scientists, she states, is to design research that can investigate the simultaneous and perhaps inseparable effects of hormones and the environment on the development of brain and behavior.

There are many studies of nonhuman animals that show that brain development and production of sexed behaviors is dependent on social environment. Rogers' work describes the role of light on the outside of the egg for development of chicks' brains. Her studies demonstrate that, rather than being genetically or hormonally determined, lateralized brain development and subsequent sex differences in chicks' food-seeking behaviors are also influenced by this light (Bradshaw and Rogers 1993, 54–59; Rogers 1999, 111–15). Sex hormones interact with light stimulation to produce sex differences.

Psychologist Celia Moore comes to a similar conclusion in her extensive work with rats. In contrast to the classical studies discussed in part one, Moore demonstrates that hormonal development and adult sexual behavior in rats are partially dependent on maternal behavior when they were pups. In a series of studies, Moore and colleagues have shown that because of a scent they excrete, male pups receive more anogenital licking from their mothers than do female pups (Moore 1984; Moore and Power 1992; Moore and Dou 1996; Moore et al. 1997). When they do not receive this licking (for instance, when dams are prevented from smelling the pups or when they are stressed during pregnancy), rats do not display typical sexual behavior in adulthood (Moore 1984; Moore and Power 1986, 1992). Female rats who are treated with male hormones and receive more licking than others display atypical sexual behavior as adults. As Moore states, these pieces of evidence show that maternal behavior mediates the actions of sex hormones. Her studies "fail . . . to support generally accepted views that early hormones affect behavior through direct effects on brain differentiation. . . . Hormones coact and interact with other factors throughout development. . . . Hormone-based sources of sex differences may be located throughout the body and in the social surround" (Moore qtd. in Rogers 1988, 46).[4]

Other animal studies also show the essential role of the environment in producing so-called hormonally caused behavior: male cichlid fish have to have physical contact with other males in order to be hormonally able to reproduce (Francis, Soma, and Fernald 1993; Fox et al. 1997); in some birds sight of the male bird, or hearing his song, causes the female bird's ovaries to secrete hormones and accelerate egg growth (West and King 1987, 51–89); and female rhesus monkeys are unable to have sex or to care for their young if they are raised in isolation from other monkeys (Haraway 1989, 231–43). In humans, testosterone secretion in men can be suppressed under extreme stress and elevated through sport and sexual fantasy (Rogers 1999, 75–76).

Other research shows that the social and physical environment of certain animals can cause a complete change in sex and thus in sexed behavior. David Crews's work on reptiles, for example, demonstrates that in some species, gonadal differentiation is determined during embryogenesis as a consequence of environment (external temperature), rather than as a result of chromosomes (1988, 328–29). Other animals, including some types of fish, are hermaphroditic and change sex according to their social environment (for example, the disappearance of a dominant male or female) either only once or repeatedly (Crews 1994, 100–101). Still other animal species are not sexually differentiated at all (they are all females), but reproduce asexually in parthenogenesis (self-cloning). This does not mean that these animals (for example, species of whiptail lizards) do not engage in sexual behavior. They engage in behavior that is identical to the mating behavior of sexually differentiated species, but in which the females take turns to act male or female parts. This sexual interaction is believed to cause the females to lay more eggs than they would if they were alone (101).[5]

Crews uses this research to argue against the simplistic theory that chromosomes cause gonadal sex, which through hormones causes masculine or feminine characteristics and sexual behaviors. In particular, he argues against the notion, which goes along with this understanding, that males are the "organized" or differentiated sex, and females the "default" sex (that is, that the action of androgens causes males to develop, while females are produced in the absence of androgens).[6] Part of his argument here is evidence that both of the so-called female hormones—estrogen and progesterone—may play an active role in male sexuality. In some species, including humans and rats, testosterone is converted to estrogen in the brain and activates both male and female copulatory behaviors (Crews 1994, 103; Ehrhardt 1984, 40). As Rogers states,

> Males secrete the so-called "female" sex hormone, oestrogen, and females secrete the "male" sex hormone, testosterone. Indeed, some females have higher plasma levels of testosterone than do some males. In the brain, where sex hormones are meant to cause sex differences in behavior, the distinction between the sexes becomes even less distinct. There are no known sex differences in the binding of oestrogen in the hypothalamic area of the brain, let alone binding at higher levels of brain organisation; and testosterone must be converted to oestrogen intracellularly before it can act on neurones. (1988, 44)

As both Rogers and Crews point out then, animals do *not* form entirely male or female brains, and, in animals such as rats, female nerve circuits are not lost in males; hormone administration can cause them to be activated (Rogers 1988, 45; Crews 1994). It is the interacting roles of the social, environmental, and hormonal that cause any particular male or female behavior in animals.

These examples of the interaction of the social and the biological in nonhuman animals are useful challenges to the theories outlined in part one, because they demonstrate that even in supposedly "simple" animals such as rats and chicks (animals that are used as models in these sciences to argue for biological causality of behaviors), and lizards, birds, and fish, sexually differentiated behaviors are not caused by biology. Even though hormones are understood to play an important role in the production of these behaviors, this role cannot be theorized in isolation from the animal's physical environment and its interactions with other animals. If the behavior of "simple" animals is not caused biologically, then how can a legitimate claim be made in relation to humans, who are perceived within science as more complicated and complex than these other animals?

The Body as Lived

> Alterity is the very possibility and process of embodiment: it conditions but
> is also a product of the pliability or plasticity of bodies which makes them
> other than themselves, other than their "nature," their functions and identi-
> ties. (Grosz 1994, 209)

Contemporary feminist theories of the body provide tools for a critique
and rethinking of the biological/social distinction evident in psychology
and behavioral neuroendocrinology.[7] This section outlines this work,
with a particular focus on that of philosopher Elizabeth Grosz, in order
to develop a more complex notion of the interrelation of the social and
biological.

Grosz's book *Volatile Bodies* (1994) forms part of an important body of
feminist theory arising from the 1980s in the wake of poststructuralist analyses of psychoanalysis. This body of work, which includes Judith
Butler's *Gender Trouble* (1990) and *Bodies That Matter* (1993) and Moira
Gatens's *Imaginary Bodies* (1996), problematizes the distinction made in
earlier feminist thinking between sex and gender, in which sex was a biological substrate and gender an externally produced social interpretation.
Each of these writers theorizes the body as an entity that disrupts this
easy social-biological distinction and as active in the production of gender and sexual differences.

In opposition to the idea that the biological body exists independently
of representations of it (which can be objectively made by science), these
theorists argue that representations and understandings of the body participate in the very constitution of bodies. Grosz, for example, writes in
the introduction to *Volatile Bodies*, "I will deny that there is the 'real,'
material body on one hand and its various cultural and historical representations and cultural inscriptions on the other. It is my claim throughout this book that these representations and cultural inscriptions quite
literally constitute bodies and help produce them as such" (1994, x). Butler makes a similar claim about sexed bodies, arguing that these are
materialized through the repeated performative social practices that constitute gender.

Importantly, neither Grosz nor Butler suggests that bodies are utterly
constituted by language, or have no biological content. Butler clearly states
that there are "undeniable materialities" (including "hormonal and chem-
ical composition") pertaining to the body but suggests that there are no
clear boundaries that divide these materialities from cultural interpretations of them (Butler 1993, 66–67). This notion of the inseparability of
the biological and social in the production of sexed bodies is also espoused
by Grosz: "[T]he interimplication of the natural and the social or cultural
needs further investigation—the hole in nature that allows cultural

seepage or production must provide something like a natural condition for cultural production; but in turn the cultural too must be seen in its limitations, as a kind of insufficiency that requires natural supplementation" (1994, 21). Thus Grosz's suggestion is to attempt to problematize the strict division between nature and culture, or biology and society, and think of these terms instead as somehow mutually dependent, with each requiring the other for its existence. Biology is seen to be endlessly open to cultural intervention, but nevertheless to retain some existence: it is the body which then becomes "the threshold or borderline concept that hovers perilously and undecidably at the pivotal point of the binary pairs" (23).

This notion of the body as a threshold is further explicated in Grosz's understanding of sexual difference. Rejecting a social constructivist view of the body as a passive and neutral recipient of social inscription, and yet also refusing any simple biologistic view of "obvious" sexual differences, means that sexual difference must be rethought along the same lines as the body itself. Grosz writes:

> I am reluctant to claim that sexual difference is purely a matter of the inscription and codification of somehow uncoded, absolutely raw material, as if these materials exert no resistance or recalcitrance to the processes of cultural inscription. This is to deny a materiality or a material specificity and determinateness to bodies. It is to deny the postulate of a pure, that is, material difference. It is to make them infinitely pliable, malleable. On the other hand, the opposite extreme also seems untenable. Bodies are not fixed, inert, purely genetically or biologically programmed entities that function in their particular ways and in their determinate forms independent of their cultural milieu and value. (1994, 190)

Again Grosz argues that the problem here is the attempt to separate the biological and the social into two distinct categories. Instead she suggests that each side is necessary and limits the other in ways that can never be set in advance, but which nonetheless have significant effects. From this point of view, sexual difference, although always overwritten with cultural values, must contain some sort of biological dimension, a dimension that can be seen as a materiality that makes developments possible. Sexual difference is not a matter of pre-existing categories with set contents, but is an interval or gap—a radical difference—between the sexes' experiences and knowledges. It does not fit clearly into the dualism of nature and culture (Grosz 1994, 208–9).

In these theorists' deconstructive view of the nature/culture distinction, one side of the dualism always operates as a limit for the other side. Although it is argued that such limits are never knowable in advance, there is a tendency to emphasize the flexibility of the social in contrast to the fixity of the biological. Butler, for example, tends to place stronger emphasis on the flexibility of gender than the materialities of sex in her readings of discourses and events (Martin 1994, 110–12). As in the quote below, at times Grosz also positions the biological as more fixed than the social (the biological is theorized as a limit on the social, rather than the other way around). This emphasis allows an active/passive split to resurface as biology is positioned as a passive limitation on the social.

> The body is constrained by its biological limits—limits, incidently, whose framework or "stretchability" we cannot yet know, we cannot presume, even if we must presume *some* limits. The body is not open to all the whims, wishes, and hopes of the subject: the human body, for example, cannot fly in the air, it cannot breathe underwater unaided by prostheses, it requires a broad range of temperatures and environmental supports, without which it risks collapse and death. (1994, 187)

In a review article, Pheng Cheah argues that the radicality of Grosz's and Butler's theorizing about the body is undercut by the positioning of materiality as negative constraint (Cheah 1996). In Cheah's reading, Grosz's reliance on the Lacanian notion of "the natural lack in mankind" and Butler's focus on the performative role of language and signification mean that they focus only on *human* bodies as active and view nonhuman nature as passive. In relation to Grosz, for example, Cheah writes,

> [D]espite her astute observation that the body is indeterminably positioned between material weightiness and cultural variability so that either trait may be used depending on whether one opposes essentialism or social constructionism, the emphasis on strategic use favours variability as a higher level of strategic cognition. Often the weightiness of matter or nature in general is played down. Or inhuman nature carries an unfavourable connotation in comparison with human nature which is fluid and capable of retranscription. (1996, 127)

As I argued above, this view of nonhuman nature as completely biological (non-social) and unchanging is challenged by recent scientific work on the role of the social in the lives of many animal species.

Despite these criticisms, the theorization of the "interimplication" of nature and culture is of great value in its moving away from questioning whether "the body is social or biological" and more toward asking "how an examination of the body demonstrates the limitations of these categories." In relation to the sciences discussed in part one, this approach is extremely radical as it undermines the basic assumption that complex processes can be divided into entities that are either biologically or socially caused. The problematization of the biological/social distinction produced by feminist theories of the body means that questions about the causes of sexed behaviors must be completely reframed.

Part Three: A Feminist Response—Rejecting Essentialism?

I have argued that the sciences that describe the role of hormones in the
production of sexually differentiated behaviors tend toward biologistic
explanations. This is achieved through the devaluing and reduction of
social explanations, caused in part by adherence to a social/biological
dichotomy. Such biologistic explanations are commonly used to justify
and affirm oppressive situations, although they also have a long history of
being used to advocate tolerance of differences (Kenen 1997; Terry 1997).
They are always political. The status of science in Western culture is often used to bolster sexist and homophobic understandings of sexual and
sexuality differences, and often either through omission (thus race-
blindness) or admission to bolster racism (Harding 1993). The important
question for feminists then becomes, how can we most effectively critique such explanations?

One major feminist response to such biologistic explanations has been
to reject them as essentialist. Grosz defines essentialism as "the attribu-
tion of a fixed essence to women" and defines biologism as a subcategory
of essentialism: "a particular form of essentialism in which women's essence is defined in terms of their biological capacities" (1990, 334). The
problems of essentialist claims are listed by Grosz: "[T]hey are necessarily ahistorical; they confuse social relations with fixed attributes; they
see these fixed attributes as inherent limitations to social change; and
they refuse to take seriously the historical and geographical differences
between women—differences between women across different cultures
as well as within a single culture" (Grosz 1990, 335). Work such as that
produced by Reinisch et al. (described earlier) meets this definition.

However, the essentialism debates of the 1980s and 1990s have led
many feminists to question the value of critiques that stop at the accusation of essentialism. This questioning has centered around issues
concerning bodily differences between the sexes, asking: If we critique
biologistic explanations of sexual differences, what happens to the body,
or to bodily differences? Do we have to reject all descriptions of biology
in rejecting essentialism? Or can there be some other way of theorizing
biology that does not posit it as either primary or unchanging?

The idea that essentialism cannot be simply rejected was based on the
belief that feminism needs to retain some notion of "women" to survive
as a political movement. Many theorists have argued that feminism must
retain this word, even at the expense of opening itself up to the accusation of essentializing and thus not properly accounting for differences
between women, and/or claiming some sort of defining meaning of
"women" that does not exist. Rosi Braidotti puts it strongly: "[A] feminist woman theoretician who is interested in thinking about sexual

difference and the feminine today cannot afford not to be essentialist" (1989, 93).

When feminist theorists take this stand for what Gayatri Spivak names a "strategic" use of essentialism (1984, 11), however, they very rarely base their strategic use of the word "women" on a biological definition. Instead they tend to rely on some sort of shared cultural oppression, or lived and/ or psychical embodiment. In *Volatile Bodies*, for example, Grosz stresses a notion of sexual difference that is related to a shared experience of embodiment. She claims that some experiences of the cultural, political, signified, and signifying body are, in general if not in their specifics, shared by women: the experiences of menstruation and lactation. Grosz is quick to point out that

> this irreducible specificity in no way universalizes the particular ways in which women experience their bodies and bodily flows. But given the social significance of these bodily processes that are invested in and by the pro cesses of reproduction, all women's bodies are marked as different to men's (and inferior to them) particularly at those bodily regions where women's differences are most visibly manifest. (1994, 207)

Thus she relies on a notion of a certain commonality of women's bodily experiences while at the same time refusing to name this body "biological." In a footnote she explains further: "I am not advocating a naturalist or even a universalist attribute. Nonetheless, it is also true that all women, whatever the details of their physiology and fertility, are culturally understood in terms of these bodily flows" (Grosz 1994, 228).

The distinction between the biological and the morphological body is central to Grosz's argument. On the question of the relation of the biological body to essentialism, Spivak makes an important point in an interview with Ellen Rooney, who asks if our confusion about how to theorize the body is the root of the problem of essentialism. Interestingly, Rooney follows this question with a reference to a newspaper article that stated that women find it hard to find their cars during menstruation because of hormonal changes. Spivak interrupts and says, "Really? I didn't see that. It gives me an answer to the question" (1994, 176). By this, I presume that she means that the answer to Rooney's question about the central role of the biological body is "yes." Rooney then goes on to ask Spivak about her attempts to address bodies, and Spivak replies:

> I am against universalizing in that way. I mean I would look at why they're essentializing, rather than to say "this is bad" necessarily, because I think there is something, some biological remnant in the notion of gender, even in the good notion of gender. Biology doesn't just disappear, except it should not be offered as a ground of all explanations. So basically on that, you know, I'm a non foundationalist in that sense especially when grounds are found to jus-

tify bad politics. So it's almost as if I'm going at it the other way, a sort of deductive anti-essentialist, how is the essence being used? (1994, 176–77)

Spivak thus rejects an outright refusal of the notion of biology and focuses instead on an examination of how biology is used to make certain political claims. She stresses that there is no biology (or way of thinking about bodies and their functions) that is somehow pure, untainted by culture or the social: there is, for her, no "body as such" that can be thought outside of cultural systems of thought. In this her position seems to come close to that of Grosz. She states:

> But apart from that I would say that biology, a biology, is one way of thinking the systematicity of the body. The body, like all other things, cannot be thought as such. Like all other things I have never tried to approach the body as such. I do take the extreme ecological view that the body as such has no possible outline. . . . You know, if one really thinks of the body as such, there is no possible outline of the body as such. . . . There are thinkings of the systematicity of the body, there are value codings of the body. The body, as such, cannot be thought, and I certainly cannot approach it. (Spivak 1994, 177)

Spivak's position on essentialism and the body is useful here. For it avoids simplistic rejections of scientific arguments as essentialist (they are essentialist and *therefore* bad) and instead argues for an examination of the political uses of essentialist claims. Also, her position on biology avoids the reaffirmation of the biology/social distinction by refusing an absolute denial of the role of biology. We can assume that some sort of the biological exists, but it cannot be thought outside of discourse.

The danger to feminist criticisms of scientific positions such as those describing the role of hormones in producing sex differences is that if biology is simply rejected as essentialist, simplistic, or just plain unbearable, it is reinstated as unknowable and beyond the social, beyond feminism (see also Grosz 1999, 31–32; Wilson 1999). In turn, giving biology this status means that the social/biological distinction is affirmed, rather than deconstructed. Equally pertinent is the proposition that when scientific understandings of biology are examined, biology is not simply biological. I have shown above that even the behavior of supposedly "simple" animals as rats and chickens cannot be explained as simply biological (or non-social). Elsewhere I have shown that the more basic science of endocrinology is unable to sustain an argument that the sexed body itself is simply biological. Instead there are many complicated interactions and congruence that fluctuate and combine to produce any particular sexed body at any particular moment (Roberts 1998). Feminist theory, then, does itself a disfavor by presuming that biology is the opposite of the social, or that indeed the split between the social and the biological is anywhere clear or knowable. For it seems always that one is inside the other already: the social in the biological and, perhaps more perturbingly for feminist theory, the biological in the social. Neither can be understood in separation from the other. As Spivak says, "the body, like all other things, cannot be thought as such" (1994, 177).

Sex hormones play varied roles in the production of sex differences within different discourses. As has been demonstrated, these range from simple determination of differences via gonads, through the structuring of brains and mysterious "predispositions," to a more complex view of co-action with the social environment. While feminist theorists have successfully argued that the biological cannot be directly approached, we need effective ways of thinking through these historically powerful roles. To focus on the co-construction or "interimplication" of the biological and the social, rather than replicating their division, may prove fruitful.

Notes

1. While the articles discussed here represent important strands of research into sex hormones and brain development, this paper does not attempt a comprehensive appraisal of the field of neuropsychology Rather, the research is used as evidence of particular modes of understanding the social/biological distinction prominent within behavioral endocrinology and biological psychology. For a comprehensive feminist analysis of neuropsychology, see Wilson (1998).

2. Ehrhardt's work since the mid-1980s has focused on issues relating to HIV/ AIDS and sexuality, rather than sex differences.

3. A self-report, twelve-item questionnaire was used to ascertain the hand preference of thirty-two homosexual women and thirty-eight homosexual men. The levels of left-hand preference were compared to previously measured levels of handedness in a general population sample (N = 2322). The homosexual women were found to have higher prevalence of left-hand preference, a result which is used to argue for "atypical pattern of hemispheric lateralization in this group" (McCormick, Witclson, and Kingstone 1990, 2). Homosexual men did not differ from the general population sample. There are clearly numerous problems with this study: homosexual subjects were recruited from "a local homophile organization" and therefore may have had many social factors in common, and subject numbers are very low. The logic of the discussion is also odd: McCormick et al. argue that from their results, "one would expect" that 4 percent of left-hand-preferring women would be homosexual, and <1 percent of right-hand-preferring women to be homosexual. Ninety-six percent of left-handed-preferring women, then, would not be homosexual. As a causal explanation for female homosexuality then, brain hemispheric lateralization (as demonstrated by hand preferences) seems very weak indeed. For further critical evaluation of studies regarding hand preference and brain lateralization, see Rogers (1999, 103–18).

4. Rogers (1999, 109–11) also reports studies showing that handling of rat pups by humans after birth influences brain development when testosterone is also present (i.e., in males, or if females are injected with testosterone). These results also support the contention that the effects of hormones are combined with social interactions in the production of sex differences.

5. Crews's interpretation of these behaviors has been the subject of controversy within major scientific journals. For a discussion of this controversy and an analysis of Crews's diverse writing practices, see Myers (1990).

6. This view forms the basis of mainstream biological and physiological views of sexual development. It has been criticized by feminist theorists of science (see, for example, Fausto-Sterling 1995).

7. For a critical survey of contemporary theories of embodiment, including feminist theories, see Williams and Bendelow (1998).

References

Bleier, Ruth. 1984. *Science and Gender.* Elmsford, NY: Pergamon.

Bradshaw, John, and Lesley J. Rogers. 1993. *The Evolution of Lateral Asymmetries, Language, Tool Use and Intellect.* San Diego, CA: Academic Press Inc.

Braidotti, Rosi. 1989. "The Politics of Ontological Difference." In *Between Feminism and Psychoanalysis,* ed. Teresa Brennan, 89–105. London: Routledge.

Butler, Judith. 1990. *Gender Trouble Feminism and the Subversion of Identity.* New York and London: Routledge.

———. 1993. *Bodies That Matter. On the Discursive Limits of "Sex."* New York and London: Routledge.

Cheah, Pheng. 1996. "Mattering." *Diacritics* 26(1):108–39.

Crews, David. 1988. "The Problem with Gender." *Psychobiology* 16(4):321–34.

———. 1994. "Animal Sexuality." *Scientific American* 270(1):96–103.

Doell, Ruth G., and Helen E. Longino. 1988. "Sex Hormones and Human Behavior: A Critique of the Linear Model." *Journal of Homosexuality* 15(3/4):55–78.

Donovan, Bernard. 1988. *Humors, Hormones and the Mind. An Approach to the Understanding of Behavior.* New York: Stockton Press.

Ehrhardt, Anke A. 1984. "Gender Differences: A Biosocial Perspective." *Nebraska Symposium on Motivation* 33:37–57.

Ehrhardt, Anke A., and Heino F.L. Meyer-Bahlburg. 1981. "Effects of Prenatal Sex Hormones on Gender-Related Behavior." *Science* 211 (20 March):1312–18.

Fausto-Sterling, Anne. 1992. *Myths of Gender Biological Theories about Women and Men.* Revised edition. New York: Basic Books.

———. 1995. "How to Build a Man." In *Constructing Masculinity,* ed. Maurice Berger, Brian Wallis, and Simon Watson, 127–34. New York and London: Routledge.

Fox, Helen E., Stephanie A. White, Mimi H. Kao, and D. Fernald. 1997. "Stress and Dominance in a Social Fish." *Journal of Neuroscience* 17(16):6463–69.

Francis, Richard C., Kiran Soma, and Russell D. Fernald. 1993. "Social Regulation of the Brain-Pituitary-Gonadal Axis." *Proceedings of the National Academy of Science USA* 90 (August):7794–98.

Gatens, Moira. 1996. *Imaginary Bodies Ethics. Embodiment and Corporeality.* New York and London: Routledge.

Grosz, Elizabeth. 1990. "A Note on Essentialism and Difference." In *Feminist Knowledge: Critique and Construct,* ed. Sneja Gunew, 332–44. New York: Routledge.

———. 1994. *Volatile Bodies. Toward a Corporeal Feminism.* Sydney, AU: Allen and Unwin.

———. 1999. "Darwin and Feminism: Preliminary Investigations for a Possible Alliance." *Australian Feminist Studies* 14(29):31–45.

Haraway, Donna J. 1989. *Primate Visions: Gender, Race and Nature in the World of Modern Science.* New York and London: Routledge.

Harding, Sandra, ed. 1993. *The "Racial" Economy of Science. Toward a Democratic Future.* Bloomington: Indiana University Press.

Hassler, Marianne. 1992. "Creative Musical Behavior and Sex Hormones: Musical Talent and Spatial Ability in the Two Sexes." *Psychoneuroendocrinology* 17(1):55–70.

Kenen, Stephanie H. 1997. "Who Counts When You're Counting Homosexuals? Hormones and Homosexuality in Mid Twentieth Century America." In *Science and Homosexualities,* ed. Vernon A. Rosario, 197–218. New York: Routledge.

Martin, Biddy. 1994. "Sexualities without Genders and Other Queer Utopias." *Diacritics* 24(2–3):104–21.

McCormick, Cheryl M., Sandra F. Witelson, and Edward Kingstone. 1990. "Left-handedness in Homosexual Men and Women: Neuroendocrine Implications." *Psychoneuroendocrinology* 15(1):69–76.

Moir, Anne, and David Jessel. *Brain Sex: The Real Difference between Men and Women.* New York: Carol Pub Group.

Moore, Celia L. 1984. "Maternal Contributions to the Development of Masculine Sexual Behavior in Laboratory Rats." *Developmental Psychobiology* 17:347–56.

Moore, Celia L., and Hui Dou. 1996. "Number, Size, and Regional Distribution of Motor Neurons in the Dorsolateral and Retrodorsolateral Nuclei as a Function of Sex and Neonatal Stimulation," *Developmental Psychobiology* 29(4):303–13.

Moore, Celia L., and Karen L. Power. 1986. "Prenatal Stress Eliminates Differential Maternal Attention to Male Offspring in Norway Rats." *Developmental Psychobiology* 38(5):667–71.

———. 1992. "Variation in Maternal Care and Individual Differences in Play, Exploration, and Grooming of Juvenile Norway Rat Offspring." *Developmental Psychobiology* 25(3):165–82.

Moore, Celia L., Lisa Wong, Mary C. Daum, and Ojingwa U. Leclair. 1997. "Mother-Infant Interactions in Two Strains of Rats: Implication for Dissociating Mechanism and Function of a Maternal Pattern." *Developmental Psychobiology* 30(4):310–12.

Myers, Greg. 1990. *Writing Biology: Texts in the Social Construction of Scientific Knowledge.* Madison: University of Wisconsin Press.

Oudshoorn, Nelly. 1994. *Beyond the Natural Body: An Archeology of Sex Hormones.* New York and London: Routledge.

Reinisch, June Macover, Mary Ziemba-Davis, and Stephanie A. Sanders. 1991. "Hormonal Contributions to Sexually Dimorphic Behavioral Development in Humans." *Psychoneuroendocrinology* 16(1–3):213–78.

Roberts, Celia. 1998. "Messengers of Sex: Hormones, Science and Feminism." Ph.D. dissertation, University of Sydney.

Rogers, Lesley J. 1988. "Biology, the Popular Weapon: Sex Differences in Cognitive Function." In *Crossing Boundaries: Feminisms and the Critique of Knowledges,* ed. Barbara Caine, E.A. Grosz, and Marie deLepervanche, 43–51. Sydney, AU: Allen and Unwin.

———. 1999. *Sexing the Brain.* London: Weidenfield and Nicolson.

Spanier, Bonnie B. 1995. *Im/partial Science: Gender Ideology in Molecular Biology.* Bloomington: Indiana University Press.

Spivak, Gayatri Chakravorty, with Elizabeth Grosz. 1984. "Criticism, Feminism and the Institution." In *The Post Colonial Critic: Interviews, Strategies, Dialogues/Gayatri Chakravorty Spivak,* ed. Sarah Harasym, 1–16. New York: Routledge.

Spivak, Gayatri Chakravorty, with Ellen Rooney. 1994. "In a Word." Interview in *The Essential Difference,* ed. Naomi Schor and Elizabeth Weed, 151–84. Bloomington: Indiana University Press.

Terry, Jennifer. 1997. "The Seductive Power of Science in the Making of Deviant Subjectivity." In *Science and Homosexualities,* ed. Vernon A. Rosario, 271–95. New York: Routledge.

West, Meredith J., Andrew P. King, and David H. Eastzer. 1981. "The Cowbird: Reflections on Development from an Unlikely Source." *American Scientist* 69:56–66.

Williams, Simon J., and Gillian Bendelow. 1998. *The Lived Body: Sociological Themes, Embodied Issues.* New York and London: Routledge.

Wilson, Elizabeth. 1998. *Neural Geographies. Feminism and the Microstructure of Cognition.* New York: Routledge.

Wilson, Elizabeth A. 1999. "Introduction: Somatic Compliance—Feminism, Biology and Science." *Australian Feminist Studies* 14(29):7–18.

Witelson, Sandra F. 1991. "Neural Sexual Mosaicism: Sexual Differentiation of the Human Temporo-parietal Region for Functional Asymmetry." *Psychoneuroendocrinology* 16(1–3):131–53.

CHAPTER NINE

Do Boys Have to Be Boys?
Gender, Narrativity, and the John/Joan Case

BERNICE L. HAUSMAN

Preface

The other night, my four-and-half-year-old daughter was trying to convince my two-and-half-year-old son to eat a clementine (in her view, the only edible orange). Sam resisted, insisting that they were yucky, while Rachel said no, they were quite good. Suddenly, Sam said that later, when he became a girl, he would eat a clementine. Rachel commented that he couldn't change into a girl, whereupon he insisted that "yes he could." After a few more tense words back and forth, Rachel assented, a rare moment of acquiescence for an older sister. That's where we left it: when you are older and a girl, you eat clementines and enjoy them. Sam had apple slices with his dinner.

Introduction

Standard medical theory and practice for sex reassignment during childhood maintains that gender identity (the sense of oneself as one sex or the other) develops postnatally and is not established definitively until the child reaches about 2 years of age, that vaginas are more easily made than penises, that gender identity reflects sex assignment and rearing more than chromosomal and other physical factors, and that to be male without a penis is unthinkable in psychological or social terms. Thus, chromosomally (and often gonadally) male infants born with deformed or unspecific genitals are almost always reared as girls; throughout their childhood and adolescence, they are subject to medical and surgical treatments to bring their anatomy into conformity with typical female morphology.[1] This protocol was first initiated by John Money and colleagues in the 1950s at Johns Hopkins Hospital and then solidified as standard practice in the 1960s and 1970s (Dreger 1998; Fausto-Sterling 2000; Hausman 1995; Kessler 1990, 1998).[2]

According to Alice Dreger, 96 percent of intersex infants are "made into girls" (Dreger 1999). One in 1,500 infants are born with genitalia so unusual that sex assignment into the standard categories of male and female is difficult, although one in 200 or 300 infants are referred to surgery because of "somewhat problematic" genital configurations, such as hypospadias, a condition in which the urethra does not exit from the tip of the penis (Dreger 1999). One particularly interesting aspect of the treatment protocols for intersex infants, however, is that they are based on an "index case" where the initial sex assignment of the child was not in question. (An index case is one that establishes treatment for a particular condition.) In the late 1990s, the status and meaning of the outcomes of the index case for intersexuality came into question.

In the spring of 1997, a number of articles in the popular press announced that the medical community was now rethinking the standard treatment protocols concerning sex reassignment during childhood as the result of a follow-up study of an early, momentous case of identical twin boys, one of whose sex was reassigned following traumatic loss of his penis during his first year of life ("Medical Community Questions Theory on Sex Reassignment" 1997; "Can an Infant's Sex Be Changed?" 1997). The case became known as the "John/Joan" case, in reference to the pseudonyms used for the subject at different stages of his/her life, and in its original form was the recognized "index case" for treatment of intersexuality in infants. John Money was a principle figure in that original case, which was itself written up in *Time* magazine in the 1970s ("Biological Imperatives" 1973). In the recent medical account, published in *Archives of Pediatrics and Adolescent Medicine*, Milton Diamond and H. Keith Sigmundson revisit the case and show that the little boy whose sex was reassigned from male to female is now living as a man. In a lengthy discussion of the experiences of this "boy" reassigned as "girl," and then assigned again as a boy, Diamond and Sigmundson claim that "the evidence seems overwhelming that normal humans are not psychosexually neutral at birth but are, in keeping with their mammalian heritage, predisposed and biased to interact with environmental, familial, and social forces in either a male or female mode" (1997, 303). Thus the authors claim that this case, in its complete form, demonstrates that gender identity is not malleable before a specific age, as Money had originally asserted, but that it is innate and based on chromosomal and hormonal sex factors.

Diamond and Sigmundson's conclusion only makes sense, however, if one accepts the dichotomy that structures it: *either* gender identity is socially constructed through the individual's responses to environmental stimuli before the age of 2, or gender identity is innate and determined by genetics, prenatal hormones, or some other physiological force (or combination of forces) in fetal development. Yet while Money's original discussions of the case purport to demonstrate one theory, and Diamond and Sigmundson claim to show the other, the case in all its guises demonstrates that gender identity is the result of a process of self-naming that is embedded within the cultural milieu and influenced by its gender stories.

In this essay, I unsettle the "either/or" of the nature/nurture debate by interrogating the narrative features of each side and show that "gender identity" can be understood as an effect of narrative devices and expectations. Thus, I do not present a narrative analysis of the textual accounts but instead look at how certain elements of the medical case study that are regarded statically (i.e., with fixed meaning) can be understood dynamically by considering them in terms of narrativity. I also argue that elements of feminist theories of gender as a social construction can profitably be reworked in relation to narrative theory.

Gender and Narrativity

What does it mean to claim that gender (as identity, as positionality) is, at least in part, a product of narrativity? I want to suggest that even a basic consideration of the significance of story telling to the creation of identity and gender can reorient our thinking about what gender is and how a gender identity comes about.

Peter Brooks opens his book, *Reading for the Plot: Design and Intention in Narrative*, with the following description of narrative:

> Our lives are ceaselessly intertwined with narrative, with the stories that we tell and hear told, those we dream or imagine or would like to tell, all of which are reworked in that story of our own lives that we narrate to ourselves in an episodic, sometimes semi-conscious, but virtually uninterrupted monologue. We live immersed in narrative, recounting and reassessing the meaning of our past actions, anticipating the outcome of our future projects, situating ourselves at the intersection of several stories not yet completed. (1992, 3)

Later on, he claims that "narrative itself [is] a form of understanding and explanation" (10). Narrative, in these senses, is a particular organization of discourse, an ordered telling, whose logic, Brooks argues, is plot. Narratives suggest sequence and causality; they provide knowledge by being "a form of understanding and explanation." Narratives *convey*; they convey information, and, in a metaphorical sense, carry the subject from childhood into adulthood by providing a medium for self-representation. Finally, narratives make sense, literally by producing the patterns through which we learn to understand the world around us, patterns that become models for how "sense" is made.[3]

Disciplines produce typical narratives that match patterns previously established to account for evidence. This repetition of patterns is one way in which the sense of ideas as narratives (that is, as particular ordered tellings, as stories) is lost, and the information conveyed becomes instead a set of received ideas, facts without narrative history.

An interesting discussion of narratology by Mieke Bal divides narratives into three components: the *fabula*, events causally or logically related (the "real" of what happened); the *story*, aspects of the fabula presented in an organized fashion (in other words, the plot); and *text*, what has been written down ("finite structured whole composed of linguistic signs") (1985). This structural typology of narrative is helpful in discussing the narrativity of conflicting medical accounts, as it allows us to see precisely where the accounts differ—for example, at the level of "story/plot" or of "fabula/events"—and thus the points at which the medical interpretations of the case diverge.

Further, a narrative understanding of gender reorients what we think gender is, as well as what it does. The scientific accounts of the John/Joan case depend upon routine or systematic techniques of narration that can be typified with the categories just delineated. They also depend upon a static understanding of "gender," which is most often used to signify stereotypical social behavior. Considering "gender" in relation to the idea of narrative, it becomes a dynamic category of subjectivity, rather than a static referent of known contents. This analysis also makes it possible for us to see how the concept of gender is engaged to shore up the meanings of basic scientific and medical arguments about "sex."

While many scholars might think of gender as a social construction, many of those still adhere to a belief in gender as an ontology, a mode of being that is itself not questioned.[4] Even scholars writing specifically about intersexuality, scholars attempting to demonstrate how social ideas about gender are tied up with medicine's construction of sex categories, represent gender identity as an ontological necessity. For example, Alice Dreger, in her illuminating *Hermaphrodites and the Medical Invention of Sex*, writes,

> Whatever our physical make-up, none of us is fully a "boy" or a "girl" until that identity is made for us by our family and community and embraced by us. One's physical equipment is the signal, not the determinant, of gender identity. Indeed, all gender assignment must ultimately be recognized as preliminary; girls and boys born with the standard parts may grow up to create new and variant gender identities for themselves. So genitals should not be seen as the definitive arbiter of gender identity; in intersexed cases, gender can still be assigned. (1998, 199–200)

While it is clear that Dreger believes gender identity to be socially constructed, she argues that we shouldn't worry that intersexed individuals won't develop one.[5]

If "we have not seriously grappled with the fact that we afflict ourselves with a need to locate a bodily basis for assertions about gender," as Suzanne Kessler puts it in *Lessons from the Intersexed*, it may be because we have been concentrating on the wrong question (1998, 132). This question—whether gender identity is innate (and the result of biology) or nurtured (and thus socially constructed)—seems legitimate but it keeps us focused on the opposition between the categories, and thus the maintenance or destruction of that opposition. Nature *versus* nurture doesn't

work because both sides of the argument depend upon a loose, untheo-
rized, and highly stereotyped category of human behavior: gender. Once
we rethink gender in terms of narrativity, the important issue is how it
(gender) functions as a culturally salient category of experience. And then
all of the categories—gender, gender identity, and sex (etc.)—need to be
treated as ideas rather than as facts.[6] If it seems that we have left aside
the nature side of the debate and entered into culture, it is because typical discussions assume simplistic and undertheorized conceptions of
gender, all the while claiming to know its origins and its meanings.[7] To
subject both nature and nurture arguments to feminist and narrative
analysis will not explode or do away with the binary, but it will allow us
to consider how its very structure has limited our thinking on the topic.

Feminist scholars have argued that gender is less a natural fact of existence than a socially coded norm of behavior read back onto the body as
its origin (e.g., Butler 1990; Kessler 1998; Kessler and McKenna 1985;
Nicholson 1994). Sandra Bem argues that people become "gender natives"
through interaction with ideas about sex that are both explanatory and
productive, giving meaning to and producing sexed identity (1993). In
this fashion, discussions of gender development purporting to show its
innateness rely on unrecognized stories about gender, what I call "gender
narratives." These narratives, in turn, depend upon what Harold Garfin-
kel has called "the 'natural attitude' toward gender," which "encom-
passes a series of 'unquestionable' axioms about gender, including the
beliefs that there are two and only two genders; gender is invariant; genitals are the essential signs of gender; the male/female dichotomy is natural;
being masculine or feminine is natural and not a choice; all individuals
can (and must) be classified as masculine or feminine" (Hawkesworth
1997, 649).

For most people, stories about gender work as explanations; for Brooks,
of course, this is the function of narrative. People use the idea of gender
as a way to understand, categorize, and make meaningful connections
between the disparate experiences of being a sex; that is, people take the
events of the "fabula" that constitute their lives and produce stories—
gendered plots—out of them. "Boys like to throw things" is the one I hear
most frequently, as the mother of an active male toddler. Hawkesworth
writes that "the natural attitude postulates sex as the determinant of gender identity that flows naturally into a particular mode of heterosexuality and that mandates certain rational gender roles embraced happily by
individuals with uniformly positive gender-role identities" (1997, 657).
Thus, "boys like to throw things" demonstrates the speaker's acceptance
of this natural attitude, a happy congratulation that my son's behavior
verifies the idea of natural gender and that my son is in fact a natural
boy, that is, one whose boyness emanates from an innate disposition and
doesn't have to be enforced. (Lucky me.)

However, using gender as an analytic category, feminists and other scholars trace the cultural and historical contingencies of being a sex by noting changes in hegemonic social narratives about sex and identity (e.g., Riley 1987, 1988).[8] Hawkesworth suggests that using gender as an analytic category, "[f]eminist research designed to confound gender provides the analytic tools to loosen the strictures of the natural attitude and the oppressive social relations that the natural attitude legitimates" (1997, 653). Feminist researchers point out that the natural attitude depends upon or links up with other social discourses and they show that the ideas about gender salient in the natural attitude work in consonance with other ideas about the self, body, nature, and polity (Hausman 1995; see esp. Riley 1988). Revealing that gender has a history as a concept, feminist scholars expose scientific ideas that enforce the natural attitude about gender as being historically contingent themselves.

Another way to consider the difference between gender as explanation (that is, the natural attitude that uses gender to explain behavior) and gender as analysis (gender as a critical tool to undermine or unsettle what seems natural) is to think of the difference between ontology and epistemology. Gender ontologies take the form of narratives that justify or shore up a fundamental understanding of gender as a thing that acts as a force, generally an innate one. Epistemological approaches to gender, on the other hand, use gender as a mode of understanding, a way of interpreting gender ontologies. Epistemological approaches to gender interrogate and undermine gender ontologies. Gender ontologies narrate the status quo. Epistemological approaches to gender provide critiques, and through those critiques they offer deconstructive narratives that disseminate gender ontologies into irresolvability.

Current popularizations of feminist theory promote gender as an ontology; this feminist work on gender is thus about changing the *contents* of gender's concept, its fabula (e.g., Wolf 1993). An epistemological approach, as I see it, both refutes gender's fabula *and* promotes interrogations of it at the level of story and of text. Gender in this view is essentially *empty of content*, filled precisely for social needs. In the abstract, ontological and epistemological approaches to gender are oppositional, although in practice it is difficult to produce an epistemological theory of gender that refuses ontology completely.

Within the natural attitude toward gender, there is a general uncertainty about whether gender enculturation is simply an outgrowth of biological nature or an enhancement of biological proclivities. That is, if we look back at Hawkesworth's claim that "the natural attitude postulates sex as the determinant of gender identity that flows naturally into a particular mode of heterosexuality and that mandates certain rational gender roles embraced happily by individuals with uniformly positive gender-role identities," we see that while sex appears to be the origin of the resulting gender identity and gendered behavior, insofar as it "mandates" gender roles, the specific action of culture in relation to biology is not clear (1997, 657). Biology is the origin, but its force is uncertain, and thus gender enculturation must occur reliably in order to verify the natural attitude. This enculturation occurs, in large part, through specific narratives about gender that are articulated to explain and enforce appropriate behaviors, that is, as I suggested above, to produce the identity that they are said to describe. "Boys like to throw things" both describes my son's behavior *and* creates for him a gendered narrative to explain his behavior and ground his identity. Gender narratives are stories that organize life events into socially coherent plots about sex.

In the context of an epistemological approach to gender, one question that arises is whether researchers can put aside their beliefs in gender as an ontology to get at what we think of as biology at all. Investigating the twin sex reassignment case as a series of stories about gender shows that the theory of innate, biological sex identity put forth by Diamond and Sigmundson can be unsettled by attention to its own, unrecognized narrativity, and demonstrates that gendered identities are both process and product of elaborate attempts to make sense of the relationship between the body and experience (1997).[9] As such, gender can never be just an effect of biological processes but is always part of a dialectical engagement of interpretation and story-making—that is, of narrativity—by specific subjects in concrete biosocial circumstances.

John/Joan

Comparing accounts of the John/Joan case necessitates distinguishing the events of the fabula, some of which differ between the stories, as well as the plotted interpretations of these events, interpretations that produce the accounts we read as medical case studies. In Money's original discussions of the case, which appeared in two books, *Man and Woman, Boy and Girl* and *Sexual Signatures* (the first coauthored with Anke Ehrhardt, the second with Patricia Tucker), the case is presented with the kind of personal detail appropriate to books oriented toward lay audiences:[10] the parents of the twins are from farm backgrounds, with little education; the mother is very observant of gender appropriate behavior, the father less so (Money and Ehrhardt 1972, 123–31; Money and Tucker 1975, 91–98).[11] The routine report offered by Diamond and Sigmundson is very brief and lacks this level of detail concerning the family's background and ideas about gender (1997). It provides, however, other significant details, discussed below.[12]

In all of the recountings of the case, the story goes something like this: at seven months of age, identical twin boys were taken to a local hospital for an apparently routine circumcision.[13] The surgeon caused irreparable damage to the first twin's penis because he used excess electrical current in the cauterizing scalpel. The organ was completely ablated. The parents, understandably distraught, sought help and were eventually directed to the psychohormonal unit at Johns Hopkins Hospital, where the doctors encouraged the parents to raise the penisless twin as a girl, with appropriate medical and surgical intervention. The parents agreed, after some intervening months of indecision. When the twins were 17 months of age, the child without the penis underwent the first phase of surgical repair: orchiectomy (removal of the testes) and feminization of the external genitalia (shaping the empty scrotum to look like labia). After this, the child was dressed exclusively in girl's clothing, given a girl's name, and brought up with gender-specific behaviors and expectations. Yearly visits to the Johns Hopkins clinic monitored the development of both children.

In Money's original presentations of this case, the discussion always ends on a positive note, as if to suggest that "all's well that ends well."[14] However, Money's early presentations of the case were published while the children were still very young, about 9 years old. Diamond and Sigmundson's work suggests that Money's original conclusions were not only wrong, but inattentive. Their later interviews with the family (in 1994 and 1995) state that even before the age of 6 the little "girl" rejected her female role (Diamond and Sigmundson 1997, 299). Of course, these later interviews may have been influenced by hindsight, since by this time the subject was living as a male and wanting to demonstrate a consistent narrative history as a male subject.[15] Nevertheless, the story of the child's gender identity that Diamond and Sigmundson present is not of successful gender reassignment, which is the one Money told, but of the child's consistent resistance to feminization. In this organization of the fabula, at the age of 14 the child stopped living as a girl and succeeded in convincing a local team of physicians and psychiatrists (now in charge of the case) to be allowed to return to male status.

Diamond and Sigmundson's presentation and discussion of the case are illuminating, bringing out details that are embedded but somewhat obscure in the earlier publications. For example, they write that the Hopkins clinicians "enlisted male-to-female transsexuals to convince Joan [their pseudonym for the child as a girl] of the advantages of being female and having a vagina constructed" (Diamond and Sigmundson 1997, 300). This apparently bothered the child greatly, causing her to run away from the hospital on one occasion. This aspect of the treatment program is never mentioned in the original presentations of the case, although transsexuals do appear in a slightly different context. In *Sexual Signatures*, Money and Tucker write that the child's parents, originally reluctant to allow their child to be reassigned to the female sex, inadvertently saw a television program "about the work with transexuals [sic] at Johns Hopkins. On the screen was an adult male-to-female transexual who, they could see for themselves, looked and talked like a normal, attractive woman. After that they worked their way to the decision to reassign their son as a girl" (1975, 92).[16]

Diamond and Sigmundson add further elements of the fabula in their presentation of the story, however: "At their yearly visit to Johns Hopkins Hospital, the twins were made to stand naked for inspection by groups of clinicians and to inspect each other's genitalia. . . . John's brother, decades later, recalls the experience with tears" (1997, 301). In addition, as a teenager the reassigned child "rejected requests to look at pictures of nude females, which she was supposed to emulate" (301). These aspects of the case are confirmed and expanded in greater detail by Colapinto (1997).

Diamond and Sigmundson's account of the case sheds new light on the earlier, triumphant narrative of the social construction of gender identity (and hence the malleability of gender up to a certain age). Diamond and Sigmundson, of course, assert that their follow-up on the case shows that the child's *original* and *normal male* identity eventually won the day. They conclude with the following comment: "We suggest referring the parents and child to appropriate and periodic long-term counseling rather than to immediate surgery and sex reassignment, which seems a simple and immediate solution to a complicated problem. With this management, *a male's predisposition to act as a boy* and his actual behavior will be reinforced in daily interactions and on all sexual levels and his fertility will be preserved" (1997, 303; emphasis added). Diamond and Sigmundson assume that gender both precedes and follows from sex—the male's predisposition is to "act like a boy"—but it and the "actual behavior" of the boy need reinforcement "in daily interactions." In this use of gender-as-explanation, Diamond and Sigmundson maintain their claim about gender's innateness at the same time that they acknowledge gender as the result of social forces. This demonstrates their adherence to the natural attitude toward gender, which establishes gender as an ontology that is both origin and goal of development.

While one could hardly quibble with the preference for long-term counseling over the medical and surgical quick fix of sex reassignment, there are ways to interpret (and renarrativize) elements of the John/Joan fabula other than to conclude that males are necessarily predisposed to act as boys. My initial and continuing response to Diamond and Sigmundson's follow-up is that the child's return to a masculine identity was heavily influenced by the coercive attempts at feminization. That is, Joan resisted the heavy-handed plot to make her into a girl. In all of the accounts, appropriate behaviors (for the child) were clearly demarcated (by the adults) according to traditional gender codes: "At five, the little girl already preferred dresses to pants, enjoyed wearing her hair ribbons, bracelets and frilly blouses, and loved being her daddy's little sweetheart" (Money and Tucker 1975, 97). "Rehearsals of future roles can also be seen in girls' and boys' toy preferences. The girl in this case wanted and received for Christmas dolls, a doll house, and a doll carriage, clearly related to the maternal aspect of the female adult role, while the boy [the twin brother] wanted and obtained a garage with cars and gas pumps and tools, part of the rehearsal of the male role. His father, like many men, was very interested in cars and mechanical activities" (Money and Ehrhardt 1972, 127). "When the twins were 4 or 5 years old, they were watching their parents. Father was shaving and mother was applying makeup. Joan applied shaving cream and pretended to shave. *When Joan was corrected* and told to put on lipstick and makeup like mother, Joan said: 'No, I don't want no makeup, I want to shave' " (Diamond and Sigmundson 1997, 299; emphasis added).[17] Indeed, it was through such gender role training that the treatment protocol of reassignment was expected to succeed psychologically. Add to this rigid set of expectations the yearly clinical experience, where the child was made to display her body to the physicians at the hospital, submit to psychological testing, and agree to the desirability of vaginal construction (a proposal reinforced through conversations with transsexual women she did not know and had little understanding of), and we can begin to see this alternative narrative more clearly. Joan's desire to be John may simply have been a desire to be free of this coercive femininity, to be able to produce her own identity in opposition to the one that everyone else in her life seemed to want her to take on.[18]

She may also have been responding to unconscious tension in the family. In a long and well-developed article for *Rolling Stone*, John Colapinto does the best job of revealing the familial anxiety about Joan's gender identity, an important element that goes largely unexamined in all of the accounts (even his own, where its existence is palpable but not analyzed) (1997). Before deciding upon sex reassignment, the parents "sank into a state of mute depression" (58). By the time they decided on their course of action, "they had eradicated any doubts they might have had about the efficacy of the treatment," but when the mother first put a dress on Joan,

> "She was ripping at it, trying to tear it off" [the mother said] . . . "I remember thinking, 'Oh my God, she knows she's a boy and she doesn't want girls' clothing. She doesn't want to be a girl.' But then I thought, 'Well, maybe I can *teach* her to want to be a girl. Maybe I can train her so that she wants to be a girl.' " (64)

The twin brother recalled, as an adult, that " 'I recognized Joan as my sister . . . but she never, ever acted the part. She'd get a skipping rope for a gift, and the only thing we'd use *that* for was to tie people up, whip people with" (68). With every action and every thing in her life carrying such heavy associations, no wonder Joan had a desire to rebel, which for a girl often means acting like a boy. Colapinto writes that the parents

> were troubled by Joan's masculine behavior. But they had been told by Dr. Money that they must not entertain any doubts about their daughter, and they felt that to do so would only increase the problem. Instead, [they] seized on those moments when Joan's behavior *could* be construed as stereotypically feminine. "And she could be sort of feminine, sometimes," [the mother] says, "when she wanted to please me. She'd be less rough, keep herself clean and tidy, and help a little bit in the kitchen." (1997, 66)

In transsexuals' autobiographies, the problem of producing an identity in the face of coercive gender conditioning is a common theme.[19] For example, in his 1977 book, *Emergence*, female-to-male transsexual Mario Martino writes of feeling that no matter what he did (as Marie), he could not produce a convincing identity as a woman, which in his view included making baby Pablum in the right consistency without using up the whole box, and being in love with men, not women (Martino 1977). Martino's discussion of his inability to match conventional standards of femininity—rehearsal for motherhood, heterosexuality—is based on the "natural attitude" toward gender; in the context of this ontology, he understands his birth as a female to be a mistake. This same natural attitude toward gender is evident in the statements of John's family; for them, helping in the kitchen and staying clean is not only appropriate behavior for a girl, but evidence of an appropriately gendered identity within.

In most transsexual autobiographies from the 1960s through the 1980s, the inability to meet the hegemonic standards of masculinity or femininity that inhere in the natural attitude toward gender is attributed to some hidden physiological element of the other sex, not detectable by medical science, but existent and determining all the same (Hausman 1995). Thus, transsexuals, at least in their autobiographies, articulate an essentialized story of gender as biologically determined *at the same time* that they concur with Martino, that "my own destiny was not to be set by biological patterns" (Martino 1997, 144).[20] Here again is a compliance with a gender ontology seen as both origin and product of sex.

The transsexual autobiographies also demonstrate that becoming a man or a woman is a process of learning how to represent that identity publicly; in Judith Butler's terms, it means producing that identity through the repeated iterations of representing it as if it already existed (Butler 1990). If one can become a man by acting like one (as "Joan" was to become a girl at least in part by acting like one), then becoming a man can be understood as an antidote for coercive, enforced femininity. Becoming a man means establishing a definitive gender identity in the face of familial and medical uncertainty, as well as acquiring the cultural perks that go along with that privileged position: higher status, encouragement of active play, an allowance to get dirty while playing, greater sexual freedom, and toy trucks. Both Martino and "Joan" had brothers and thus could observe firsthand the comparative benefits of being a boy.[21]

Transsexualism—more precisely, sex change—works conceptually within current gender narratives because these narratives are set up within a clear either/or scenario of sexed being. Within this context, gender narratives can be manipulated to authorize new versions of the self as the other sex. Since the emergence of technological transsexualism in the 1950s, anatomical and hormonal "sex change" have become material possibilities,[22] and they are practices bolstered by traditional stories about gender as an irrevocable, binary ontology of the psyche (Hausman 1995). Thus, while transsexualism may seem to transgress what we think of as traditional gender rules, the practice of "sex change" relies on normative recountings of gender as an ontology.[23] We can interpret John's choice to be a man as an acceptance of our culture's basic gender ontology, that is, both a repudiation of the identity that others picked out for him ("I won't be a girl!") and, at a deeper level, an acceptance of the dichotomous system presented to him ("I must be a boy!"). Repudiating coercive femininity, he felt he had no choice but to be a man, or make himself into one.[24]

The "natural attitude" toward gender assumes heterosexuality, thus all those who are not heterosexual are suspected of being gender transgressors as well. This aspect of gender's ontology also works the other way: to be heterosexual is to guarantee other people's assumption that one has a "normal" (and thus socially appropriate, innate) gender identity. This is why Diamond and Sigmundson can be so secure in their claim that "John" has found his true "natural" gender as a man, because he is married and has adopted his wife's children. John's narrative has a happy and logical ending; the plot worked out the right way.[25]

In this narrative, "John's" response to his particular situation was to repudiate the identity picked out for him and go for the one his twin got. Thus, "after his return to male living he felt his attitudes, behaviors, and body were in concert in a way they had not been when living as a girl" (Diamond and Sigmundson 1997, 300). He ends up, then, as a completely "normal" man (his wife remarks that "there is no doubt who wears the pants in this family" [302]), which is understandable, of course, after the experiences of his childhood. As Colapinto writes,

> [John] speaks of his pride in his role as husband, father and sole breadwinner in the family that he never believed he would be lucky enough to have. "From what I've been taught by my father," he says, "what makes you a man is: You treat your wife well. You put a roof over your family's head. You're a good father. Things like that add up much more to being a man than just *bang bang bang*—sex." (1997, 97)

John's own words demonstrate that "being a man" is a completely *social* designation, given that what it takes to be one must be learned. Yet for Diamond and Sigmundson, John's status as male breadwinner, head of household, family disciplinarian, husband, and father, demonstrate that his original biological make up as a male made him the man he eventually became.

Money's original assertions were wrong, of course, but not necessarily wrong-headed, since they suggested the essential narrativity of gender. He claimed that, given the optimal window of opportunity, you can make any individual into a woman.[26] He argued that the stories about sex identity that one tells oneself and that are told to one are crucial to the development of identity. But this case might have taught him that gender narratives don't always work in the most expected ways, and that coercive narratives can incite creative, rebellious responses. (Publications of the Intersex Society of North America, such as the newsletter *Hermaphrodites with Attitude*, are bringing to visibility precisely such stories.) While the clinicians utilized gender narratives in their attempts to feminize the penisless twin, the child fought back with his/her own arsenal of stories. If a person's gender identity is a product of story-making, then what's to stop an individual from making him or herself up?

This begs the question, of course, of how coercive the imposition of gender is for those whose anatomy presents what are considered the normal signs of sex (what Alice Dreger [1999] calls "the standard parts"), and why most individuals do not seem to resist the rather forceful feminization and masculinization endemic to culture. One reason is that most people adhere to the natural attitude toward gender, they agree with and uphold culturally accepted gender ontologies (Kessler and McKenna [1978] 1985). For those subjects whose body does not seem to verify gender "naturally," or those who refuse the social requirements to make body and behavior match as binary gender coordinates, the coercive nature of its imposition is more salient, and thus subject to resistance in a more obvious way.[27]

The follow-up on the twin sex reassignment case does not demonstrate that gender identity is innate, as Diamond and Sigmundson claim. Their discussion, which curiously ignores the psychological impact of the early attempts to enforce "Joan's" femininity—except insofar as "John" feels angry at the attempted enforcement—demonstrates their inability to see outside of the nature versus nurture debate concerning the origins of gender identity. In their view, feeling uncomfortable with an enforced and exhibitionistic femininity is evidence of an innate masculinity, and not a sign that the imposition of such an identity can be a problem even for genetically female women. Opening up the John/Joan case to the multiple possibilities that understanding gender as a narrative allows—and interrogating the ontology implied by that narrative—suggests another reading, in which "John's" conviction of his innate masculinity and the authors' obvious acceptance of this conviction *as fact* show how readily some will believe that, after all, boys will be boys, especially if they won't be girls.[28]

Conclusion

Closer examination of the John/Joan case reveals deeply problematic connections between the biological and medical sciences, on the one hand, and cultural ideas about proper behaviors and sexual activities (i.e., gender narratives), on the other.[29] Indeed, investigations into scientific theories of gender identity and its development demonstrate the narrativity of biomedical discourses and ideas, as well as their dependence on language and its analogical resonances.

For example, as a putative discussion of Diamond and Sigmundson's findings, William Reiner's editorial "To Be Male or Female—That Is the Question" reveals the profound entanglement of our ideas about being a sex with traditional literary narratives (1997). Certainly the idea that there might be a question—or a choice—about being male or female is a culturally and historically bounded one, and thus not clearly a biological "either/or." Borrowing and bastardizing a line from Shakespeare demonstrates that the concepts we think with—those that allow us to name and narrate experience (even supposedly "objective" findings)—are deeply implicated with representations. In Shakespeare's period, to be a sex was different from what it is in our own, not the least because at that time the "one-sex" model of the body—with the female an inferior (and colder) version of the male—predominated in social and medical treatises (Laqueur 1990). Thus, any "choice" to "be male or female" in that context meant a slippage from one version of the same body to the other version (among other things), hardly the same as our current conception of making "the opposite" body.[30]

Reiner's use of this provocative line from *Hamlet* is meant, however, to elide any differences between these historical notions of sexed bodies, because he suggests that male and female behaviors depend on the "prenatal hormonally differentiated brain" rather than genital anatomy. In his view, the "choice" of being male or female is really about physicians accurately predicting the "brain's gender": "If the brain knows its gender independent of social-environmental influences, then we need to be able to predict what that gender is" (Reiner 1997, 225). Thus, Reiner calls Shakespeare in as a witness to the inevitable dichotomy of male and female as a function of brain chemistry, a theoretical position most certainly opposed to the dialectical interplay of behaviors represented in Shakespeare's dramatic work and thus a very bad interpretation of *Hamlet*, as well as an example of biomedical science's refusal to acknowledge that ideas about sexed behavior cannot exist outside of the circulation of narratives that give meaning both to the behavior and to the words used to describe it.[31]

But if we can criticize scientists' neglect of their own narrativity, their debt to stories that circulate in culture and help them make sense of their findings (and even structure the research that yields the findings), we can also recognize that we depend on certain forms of scientific knowledge in decisions about cases similar to the twin case. In cases of traumatic loss of penis, as well as cases of congenital intersexuality, physicians must first diagnose the condition, determining which organs are present and how well they function. Some conditions that lead to congenital intersexuality have potentially fatal complications that need immediate treatment. Apart from such necessary medical interventions, however, some intersexuals are currently organizing to end the early surgical and medical treatment of intersexuality. In a letter published in *Hermaphrodites with Attitude*, Virginia Slocum writes,

> I fear that . . . parents, in an attempt to give their children normal lives, will rob them of the chance to come to terms with their own difference. I suppose there is a great need to feel that the right thing has been done in choosing early surgical intervention. There might be a need to feel that everything has been fixed, or nearly fixed and that their child's acceptance of their difference will be as decisive as a surgery. Whether or not this type of surgery can ever be viewed as decisive is another critically serious topic. It would be nice if a young person didn't have to wrestle with puzzling terms like intersexed and did not have to contemplate what existed before surgery. But that is not the fate of those born like this. (1995, 7)

Like Diamond and Sigmundson, Slocum (an intersexual and a social worker) argues that a "lengthy course of therapy" is probably the most viable option for intersex children and their families. However, her plea for psychotherapeutic intervention is a call to allow intersexed individuals to consider (and narrate) their own experiences within the two-sex world, to encourage them to "wrestle with puzzling terms like intersexed," since this is what they will have to do anyway.[32] Diamond and Sigmundson, on the other hand, are concerned with "a male's predisposition to act as a boy," and the "reinforcement" of his "actual behavior"; in other words, they advocate psychological management of the intersexed male pseudohermaphrodite (or boy who undergoes traumatic loss of a penis at an early age) in order to encourage and enforce masculinity (1997). For the latter clinicians, the choice is only male or female, and counseling intersexed (or genitally damaged) patients manages the difficulties of such a choice for those whose bodies do not signify one or the other category appropriately.

The difference between these two perspectives shows how significantly intersexuality, were it to be recognized as a biological sexed position (or series of positions), would disrupt binary gender explanations (and thus the natural attitude toward gender), since the medical management of such a subject could no longer simply assume the straightforward enforcement of masculinity or femininity. Indeed, it is precisely because intersexuality unsettles the idea of gender as sex's precedent (a male's predisposition to act as a boy) that it must be made invisible as a legitimate social subjectivity.[33]

It very well might be the case that biology has some purchase on describing the seemingly distinct behaviors of the sexes, but we will never really know that for sure until we are able to identify and discuss how ideas about sex operate socially. The John/Joan case—with its outlandish sex stereotyping, its heavy-handed interpretive gender schema, its anguished parents and distraught children—will never prove that gender identity is the result of an innate biological force, be it prenatal hormones, genetic influence, or something else. All it can prove is that the attempt to make John into Joan didn't work, and that plausible social reasons why this was the case can be argued. The oppressive plot of female gender identity presented in all printed versions of this case is enough to make anyone run screaming from the room. We need to be asking why this narrative about gender's relation to the body is so readily accepted as a seeming antidote to the "horror" of the idea that gender is a social construct. And we ought to wonder about how such simplistic views of gender were allowed to proliferate (and still do) in discourses meant to study and treat complex human behavior.

The John/Joan case resembles, but is not identical to, the intersexual cases that currently receive treatment and sex reassignment soon after birth.[34] In both scenarios, there is a desire to "fix" the anatomical "error," as well as to "fix" the child into one sex or another. Diamond and Sigmundson recognize this when they comment that "[a]s parents will still want their children to be and look normal as soon after birth or injury as possible, physicians will have to provide the best advice and care consistent with current knowledge" (1997, 303). The current medical protocols for intersex infants certainly reveal a cultural discomfort with individuals whose bodily existence challenges categories we hold dear. These protocols also show that, at least in the realm of sexual behavior and identity, most of us suffer from a lack of imagination.[35] Instead of enabling the creation of new narratives, both to aid these individuals in developing their identities as sexed persons and to free other people's rigid identity constructions as well, medical theory and practice enforces upon all of us tired and oppressive stories about who wears the pants, who gets to shave, and who plays with dolls, because it assumes that these stories constitute the necessary foundation for a "normal" life. But if, as the intersex activists suggest, we can resist the either/or dichotomous opposition of current gender scenarios—if we can, in other words, "unfix" identity from its current mooring in traditional, bipolar gender narratives—rereading the biological signifiers of sex can offer us the starting point for truly alternative stories of sexed identity.[36]

The question then becomes, do there have to be boys (or girls, for that matter)?

Notes

1. Alice Dreger (1998, 182–84) provides an excellent discussion of why and how intersexed infants and children most often "become" female.

2. Suzanne Kessler's *Lessons from the Intersexed* (1998) and Alice Dreger's *Hermaphrodites and the Medical Invention of Sex* (1998) are the most recent book-length publications concerning intersexuality and its medical treatment. Both greatly add to the understanding of the phenomenon's history in relation to medicine. This essay is meant to expand on the ideas presented in these texts by examining the protocols for sex reassignment during childhood in order to question the idea that gender is either innate or socially constructed.

3. Gerald Prince (1994, 572) writes, "To explore the nature of all and only possible narratives, to account for the infinity of forms that they can take, to consider how it is that we construct them, paraphrase them, summarize them, or expand them, is to explore one of the fundamental ways, and a singularly human one at that, in which we *make* sense."

4. Here I am referring to scholars who uphold beliefs about the inevitability of certain masculine and feminine traits, even though they might agree that acquiring these traits is completely a result of "environment" or social nurture. See Tong's (1998) excellent discussion of "gender feminism."

5. Suzanne Kessler, noted feminist theorist, is more equivocal concerning gender as an ontology. In her concluding remarks to *Lessons from the Intersexed* (1998, 132), she writes, "By subverting genital primacy, gender will be removed from the biological body and placed in the social-interactional one. Even if there are still two genders, male and female, how you 'do' male or female, including how you 'do' genitals, would be open to interpretation. . . . Once we dispense with 'sex' and acknowledge gender as located in the social-interactional body, it will be easier to treat it as a work-in-progress." Thus while her final paragraph suggests that we actually "give up on gender" (132), how that will happen is less clear than her earlier sense that separating genitals from gender—giving up on sex as a determinant for gender—is a more plausible goal. This is a call, in a sense, for "doing gender" without reference to the body, not unlike Butler's (1990) call for a new performativity

of gender that treats all such performances as drag. The uncertain difference between "doing gender" differently and "giving up on gender" rests precisely on the distinction between a view that accepts a (radical) gender ontology and one that refuses gender ontologies altogether. Thus, while Kessler is clearly critical of intersex treatment protocols that depend on sexist and homophobic conceptions of society and the body (in other words, that depend on standard gender narratives), I am left at the end uncertain of her commitment to an epistemological approach. Does she consider doing away with gender ontologies unlikely or implausible?

6. This examination of gender as an idea has been a central focus of feminist theory, which has shown the *systematic* nature of gender imposition (e.g., Rubin 1975).

7. See Ruth Bloch (1996) for a critique of feminist approaches to gender that suggest that it is socially constructed but do not provide a complex view of "culture" and the place of gender within culture.

8. Hawkesworth (1997) provides an excellent, if brief, summary of the variety of feminist approaches to and uses of "gender" as an analytic category. Her critique, notwithstanding its polemical nature, demonstrates the value of broadly surveying current articulations of this concept.

9. Teresa de Lauretis (1987) provides an exhaustive examination of "gender" as process and product of representation.

10. Many of the sources that refer to these two texts identify Money and Tucker (1975) as the book for a lay audience, while Money and Ehrhardt (1972) is considered a scholarly text. Yet in the preface to the latter text, the authors write, "This book will be of interest especially to students of psychology, sociology, anthropology, ethology, genetics, neuroendocrinology, and medicine. In addition, it is a book for clinicians and, indeed, also for the general reader for whom especially the glossary of technical terms is provided" (xi). Originally published by Johns Hopkins University Press, the edition I am using for my research was issued by the New American Library (NAL) as a "Mentor Book" and is a slim paperback. What distinguishes between these two texts is really that *Sexual Signatures* was cowritten with a journalist, not a medical researcher. I think it is interestingly anomalous that this famous case was not published in a renowned scientific journal until 1975, although references to it were made in a longer discussion by John Money in the *Nebraska Symposium on Motivation* in 1973. In the 1975 essay (Money 1975), the story told is lifted almost word-for-word from *Man and Woman, Boy and Girl.*

11. Money (1973) also considers the case, although briefly. This is a particularly interesting source, in that Money claims to refuse the "nature versus nurture" dichotomy in favor of a more complex conception of the relationship of identity to environment and biology. See Hausman (1995, 102–8) and

Fausto-Sterling (1985, 134–41) for discussions of the genuineness and ramifi-cations of Money's attempts to refute the nature/culture dichotomy in dis-cussions of biological gender development. See Fausto-Sterling (2000, 66–71) for a more recent discussion of this case, published as this article was in press.

12. A fascinating account published by *Rolling Stone* (Colapinto 1997) offers more tantalizing details and *another* example of narrativity. This one, more complete than the others, uses its plethora of materials (gleaned from inter-views with the subject and biographical accounts of the medical researchers involved) to provide a riveting story, but one that demonstrates all the more how significant *telling* the story is to the believability of its medical theo-ries. In this long report, John Colapinto describes the cast of characters: John Money (who takes the role of sexually predatory villain, although he is in-terested in psychologically coercing, but not literally seducing, the victim), Milton ("Mickey") Diamond (the tireless and personally bland researcher, intent on demonstrating the errors of Money's theory, one of the heroes), H. Keith Sigmundson (psychiatrist for the adolescent Joan/John, a reluctant hero), the hapless parents and twin brother (the unwitting dupes who tried very hard to make Money's theory work but failed anyway), and John him-self (now an ordinary factory worker with a wife and three adopted children; in other words, a prototypical "guy"). Because of the publication venue, Co-lapinto can tell John's story with greater innuendo and more dramatic flair, but it is telling that both his narration and that of Diamond and Sigmund-son end on a similar note concerning the adult "normality" of John as hus-band and father.

13. In Colapinto (1997), the circumcision is noted at 8 months of age. The late-ness of the circumcision (a procedure usually conducted a day or two after the birth of a boy in the hospital, or eight days after birth for practicing Jews) is due to the fact that the parents didn't intend to circumcise their sons at all. However, the boys' foreskins began closing, making urination a problem (Colapinto 1997, 58). This is a condition known as phimosis, which is rou-tinely treated with circumcision.

14. Money also uses the term "differentiation" to refer to the child's develop-ment of gender identity, suggesting a continuation of the biological process of physical differentiation that occurs *in utero*. See Hausman (1995) for a more extensive discussion of the implications of Money's use of this term.

15. Colapinto suggests that Money deliberately ignored evidence available to him that implied an incomplete assumption of female gender identity (1997, 66).

16. This may have been the impetus for using transsexuals to convince the child as well; after all, it worked with the parents.

17. Colapinto (1997) also presents this last example, in much the same terms.

18. An earlier case from the medical literature may shed light on the story I am
trying to (re)construct here. In his landmark treatise, *Genital Abnormalities, Hermaphroditism, and Related Adrenal Disorders* (1937), urologist
Hugh Young relates the case of a young "male" orphan who, in 1925, at the
age of 7, was brought to Johns Hopkins Hospital with undescended testes
and a hypospadiac penis. Exploratory abdominal surgery revealed a uterus, a
fallopian tube, and what was thought to be an ovary. The surgeons did not
locate any testicular tissue on the right side. At this point, the child was assigned to a female orphanage and put into girl's clothing. After reassignment, "she" developed a habit of masturbation and was concerned about the
other children seeing her "clitoral appendage." Upon return to the hospital,
the doctor's noted that this appendage was "about the size of a ten-year-old
boy['s penis]"; they amputated it, in keeping with the subject's new status as
female. At 16, the subject returned to the hospital again, complaining of an
inguinal mass on the left side. Opening up "her" abdomen, the surgeons
found a testicle as well as some female reproductive organs. At this point,
the patient made it clear that "she" planned to live as a male when "she"
was able to leave the orphanage. The doctors elected to remove the testicle
anyway, since they had excised the penis earlier. This subject did go on to
live as a male—without penis and testes—to the astonishment of the doctors overseeing "her" case (Young 1937, 84–91).

Because this subject was a true hermaphrodite; with internal reproductive structures of both sexes, in this particular case it is more difficult to
claim gender identity as an innate predisposition to maleness or femaleness. In some ways, this case verifies Money's original thesis that gender
identity is formed irrevocably in the child's early years; this subject maintained the gender identity formed in "his" first seven years of life. However,
we can also tease out a narrative not unlike (although not quite identical
to) the one I have been developing in the twin sex reassignment case:
subjects whose sex is in doubt may choose a male gender identity as a
resistant response to enforced, coercive femininity. In Young's case, the
physicians interpreted physical signs of masculinity (masturbation, an
unusually large "clitoral appendage," a testicle and attending vas deferens)
as problematic for the child as a girl; in keeping with their understanding
of "her" as a girl, they removed those signs, regardless of the child's own
wishes. Faced with numerous hospitalizations during her childhood, each
of which focused on "her" status as a sex and most of which had as their
intent the maintenance of "her" in the category female, it is no wonder
that this subject chose to live as a male "although without penis or testicles and with the vagina still present." See Hausman (1995) for a discussion of female-to-male transsexuals' self-representations of resistance to
coerced feminization.

19. While Diamond and Sigmundson's (1997) article is not John's autobiography,
we can think of it as an "authorized" case study, since the authors write that
"John himself, while desiring to remain anonymous, strongly desires his
case history to be made available to the medical community to reduce the
likelihood of others suffering his psychic trauma" (1997, 299).

20. See Hausman (1995) for extended discussion of this point.

21. Indeed, the "draw" for John Money was that Joan was an identical twin, a circumstance that meant the case would have medical validity. Joan and her brother shared DNA, and in Money's eyes this would prove that gender identity had nothing to do with chromosomes or prenatal hormones (Colapinto 1997).

22. Although sex change is still imaginary, in the sense that plastic genital surgery recreates what Moira Gatens (1996) would call the imaginary body, as the reconfigured tissue simulates a certain socially codified perception of the body and its functions.

23. See Prosser (1998) for a different discussion of transsexualism in relation to narrative. Gender narratives can also be called on to affirm cosmetic surgical transformations into a more idealized version of the sex one already is (which is the case with routine, nongenital cosmetic surgery). Many, if not most, genetically female women construct identities to cohere with their "female" anatomy, and many, if not most, work to make their anatomy cohere with social expectations of femininity. We all enact this received story of gender; we are subject to its ontology. In this sense, the "gender work" that male-to-female transsexuals engage is not altogether different from that engaged by genetically female women. For transsexuals, however, the process is more blatant because their effort alters their original sexual physiology and anatomy, explicitly utilizing stories about gender to tranform physical sex rather than to enhance or exaggerate their existing sexual habitus. See Urla and Swedlund (1995, 305) for an interesting discussion of the differential impact of plastic transformation on those individuals located in diverse cultural situations.

24. But did he? I have heard one narrative of resistance to coercive femininity that has three endings. It goes something like this: "When I was growing up, I felt like a freak. I was smart, physically active, aggressive even, and I didn't like being submissive to boys. As I grew older, I knew I was (or would become) (a) a lesbian, (b) a feminist, (c) a man." (I have heard this narrative, in its varying forms, at a talk given by a lesbian scholar, by a lesbian scholar during a personal conversation, by transsexual men at a national convention for cross-dressers and transsexuals, and by feminist women in both personal and formal occasions. I have my own version of it myself.) This is not to say that this is the only narrative about identity development that lesbians, feminists, and transsexuals tell, although in autobiographies by transsexuals and medical treatises on transsexualism, this is the predominant (and officially recognized) story. Of course, lesbianism, feminism, and transsexualism are not *only* responses to the coercive enforcement of feminine gender identity in contemporary society. Indeed, feminism as a political identity represents less a gender identity than strategic positioning of the social self—that is, a repudiation of enforced gender *roles*—although such positioning obviously has an impact on identity formations. These identity

positions are also entangled with other ideological and enculturating discourses and experiences, such as those of a particular religion or class, for example. Traditional gender narratives suggest that these identities largely result from an inability to comply with conventional heterosexuality, understood as *the* measure defining the social and personal ways of being a sex. The opposing view argues that repudiating normative heterosexuality involves rethinking, remaking, and renarrating identity.

25. A discussion of this narrative context for the emergence and maintenance of gender identity is entirely absent from all of the write-ups of this case, even though all of the researchers involved understand the need for social approval and reinforcement of gender identity for it to "stick." "With this management, a male's predisposition to act as a boy and his actual behavior *will be reinforced in daily interactions* and on sexual levels and his fertility will be preserved" (Diamond and Sigmundson 1997, 303; emphasis added).

26. To be theoretically accurate, he argued that given the optimal window of opportunity, you can make any individual into a man or a woman, but the reality of phalloplasty means that the practical result of Money's theory is that most intersexes are brought up as female (Dreger 1998; Hausman 1995; Kessler 1990, 1998).

27. Sandra Bem (1993) provides a very clear discussion of how gender enculturation works in concert with theories of biological determinism to make "gender natives."

28. Stephanie Sanders (personal communication, January 1998) suggested to me that renewed attention to this case had radically split the sex research community along the predictable lines of nature versus nurture. Thus, revisiting this "index case" may eventually have a significant effect on treatment and theory of intersexuality, although the theoretical paradigm, nature versus nurture, remains the same and does not really change the terms in which gender is conceptualized.

29. Many feminist scientists and science critics have written about this complicitous relationship between supposedly objective science and cultural narratives of gender. See Bleier (1984), Fausto-Sterling (1985), Haraway (1989, 1991), Hubbard (1990), and Martin (1987).

30. Although current surgical procedures for male-to-female transsexuals invoke the older model, as the skin of the penis is used to line the newly formed vagina (Hausman 1995).

31. Consider the following discourse of Laertes, upon hearing of Ophelia's death, which suggests a nuanced and complex view of gender:

> Too much water hast thou, poor Ophelia,
> And therefore I forbid my tears. But yet

It is our trick; nature her custom holds,
Let shame say what it will. [*He weeps.*] When these are gone,
The woman will be out. Adieu my lord.
I have a speech of fire that fain would blaze,
But that this folly douts [drowns] it. (4.7.186–91)

32. Dreger (1998) notes that one significant problem is that current manage-
    ment protocols for intersexed infants make it impossible for them to provide
    a coherent narrative of their pasts to others, not only since some of the plot
    events are withheld from them by parents and physicians, but also because
    the story of intersexuality has been purposefully placed outside of legiti-
    mate narratives of sexed identity. Thus to say, for example, that one's sex at
    birth was uncertain, or that one spent one's first year as a boy before being
    changed to a girl, is impossible. Kessler (1990, 1998) provides lengthy discus-
    sions of the terms and discourses used by physicians treating intersex in-
    fants that avoid this difficulty by making it seem that the child's true or real
    sex was there all along but that the doctors needed to discover it.

33. Kessler (1998) suggests this.

34. Kessler (1998) mentions this as well. Dreger (1999) commented that using the
    John/Joan case as an index case for intersexual treatment was problematic
    from the beginning, given that the subject involved was not intersexual in
    medical terms.

35. Kessler (1998, 32) suggests a similar point.

36. Anne Fausto-Sterling (1993) has begun this process.

References

Bal, Mieke. 1985. *Narratology: Introduction to the Theory of Narrative*. Toronto:
    University of Toronto Press.
Bern, Sandra. 1993. *The Lenses of Gender*. New Haven, CT: Yale University Press.
    "Biological Imperatives." 1973. *Time*, 8 January, 34.
Bleier, Ruth. 1984. *Science and Gender: A Critique of Biology and Its Theories on
    Women*. Athene Series. New York: Pergamon Press.
Bloch, Ruth H. 1996. "A Culturalist Critique of Trends in Feminist Theory." In
    Debating Gender. Debating Sexuality, ed. Nikki R. Keddie, 73–100. New
    York: New York University Press.
Brooks, Peter. 1992. *Reading for the Plot: Design and Intention in Narrative*.
    Cambridge, MA: Harvard University Press.
Butler, Judith. 1990. *Gender Trouble. Feminism and the Subversion of Identity*.
    New York: Routledge.
"Can an Infant's Sex Be Changed?" 1997. *The Washington Post*, 18 March, Health
    Section, 7, 19.

Colapinto, John. 1997. "The True Story of John Joan." *Rolling Stone*, 11 December, 54–72, 92, 94–97.

de Lauretis, Teresa. 1987. *Technologies of Gender. Essays on Theory, Film, and Fiction.* Bloomington: Indiana University Press.

Diamond, Milton, and Keith Sigmundson. 1997. "Sex Reassignment at Birth: Long-Term Review and Clinical Implications." *Archives of Pediatrics and Adolescent Medicine* 151:298–304.

Dreger, Alice Domurat. 1998. *Hermaphrodites and the Medical Invention of Sex.* Cambridge, MA Harvard University Press.

———. 1999. "In Love with a Ruler: Phallometers and the Surgical 'Treatment' of Intersexuality." Paper presented at the annual meeting of the Society for Social Studies of Science, 29 October, San Diego, California.

Fausto-Sterling, Anne. 1985. *Myths of Gender: Biological Theories about Women and Men.* New York: Basic Books.

———. 1993. "The Five Sexes: Why Male and Female Are Not Enough." *The Sciences* (March/April):20–25.

———. 2000. *Sexing the Body: Gender Politics and the Construction of Sexuality.* New York: Basic Books.

Gatens, Moira. 1996. *Imaginary Bodies: Ethics, Power, Corporeality.* London, UK: Routledge.

Haraway, Donna. 1989. *Primate Visions.* New York: Routledge.

——— 1991. *Simians, Cyborgs, and Women.* New York: Routledge.

Hausman, Bernice L. 1995. *Changing Sex: Transsexualism, Technology, and the Idea of Gender.* Durham, NC: Duke University Press.

Hawkesworth, Mary. 1997. "Confounding Gender," *Signs* 22:649–85.

Hubbard, Ruth. 1990. *The Politics of Women's Biology.* New Brunswick, NJ: Rutgers University Press.

Kessler, Suzanne J. 1990. "The Medical Construction of Gender: Case Management of Intersexed Infants." *Signs* 16:3–26.

———. 1998. *Lessons from the Intersexed.* New Brunswick, NJ: Rutgers University Press.

Kessler, Suzanne J., and Wendy McKenna. (1978) 1985. *Gender: An Ethnomethodological Approach.* Reprint. Chicago: University of Chicago Press.

Laqueur, Thomas. 1990. *Making Sex: The Body and Gender from the Greeks to Freud.* Cambridge, MA: Harvard University Press.

Martin, Emily. 1987. *The Woman in the Body: A Cultural Analysis of Reproduction.* Boston: Beacon.

Martino, Mario. 1977. *Emergence.* New York: Crown.

"Medical Community Questions Theory on Sex Reassignment." 1997. *American Medical News*, 24–31 March, 48.

Money, John. 1973. "Prenatal Hormones and Postnatal Socialization in Gender Identity Differentiation." *Nebraska Symposium on Motivation*:221–95.

———. 1975. "Ablatio Penis: Normal Male Infant Sex-Reassigned as a Girl" *Archives of Sexual Behavior* 4(1):65–71.

Money, John, and Anke Ehrhardt. 1972. *Man and Woman, Boy and Girl.* New York: New American Library—Mentor.

Money, John, and Patricia Tucker. 1975. *Sexual Signatures: On Being a Man or a Woman.* Boston: Little, Brown.

Nicholson, Linda. 1994. "Interpreting Gender." *Signs* 20:79–105.

Prince, Gerald. 1994. "Narratology." In *The Johns Hopkins Guide to Literary Theory and Criticism*, ed. Michael Groden and Martin Kreiswirth, 524–28. Baltimore: Johns Hopkins University Press.

Prosser, Jay. 1998. *Second Skins: Body Narratives of Transsexuality.* New York: Columbia University Press.

Reiner, William. 1997. "To Be Male or Female—That Is the Question." *Archives of Pediatrics and Adolescent Medicine* 151:224–25.

Riley, Denise. 1987. "Does a Sex Have a History? 'Women' and Feminism." *New Formations* 1:35–45.

———. 1988. *Am I That Name?: Feminism and the Category of "Women" in History.* Minneapolis: University of Minnesota Press.

Rubin, Gayle. 1975. "The Traffic in Women: Notes on the 'Political Economy' of Sex." In *Toward an Anthropology of Women*, ed. Rayna R. Reiter, 157–210. New York: Monthly Review Press.

Slocum, Virginia. 1995. Letter. *Hermaphrodites with Attitude* (Summer):6–7.

Tong, Rosemarie. 1998. *Feminist Thought A More Comprehensive Introduction.* 2nd ed. Boulder, CO: Westview.

Urla, Jacqueline, and Alan Swedlund. 1995. "The Anthropometry of Barbie." In *Deviant Bodies*, ed. Jennifer Terry and Jacqueline Urla, 277–313. Bloomington: Indiana University Press.

Wolf, Naomi. 1993. *Fire with Fire: The New Female Power and How It Will Change the 21st Century.* New York: Random House.

Young, Hugh H. 1937. *Genital Abnormalities, Hermaphroditism, and Related Adrenal Diseases.* Baltimore: Williams and Wilkins.

CHAPTER TEN

Reading *Sex and Temperament* in Taiwan
Margaret Mead and Postwar Taiwanese Feminism

DORIS T. CHANG

In 1949, the Chinese Communists defeated the Chinese Nationalists in the civil war and the latter retreated to the island of Taiwan, imposing martial law on the Taiwanese population. In the early 1970s, within the context of the Chinese Nationalist government's greater tolerance for the freedom of intellectual expression, Yang Mei-hui, a translator, annotated and summarized in Chinese part 4 of Margaret Mead's *Sex and Temperament in Three Primitive Societies* (1935). In so doing, Yang served as a cultural intermediary who transmitted Mead's concept of cultural relativism on gender-role formation to her Chinese-speaking audience in Taiwan. Published in 1973, Yang's annotated summary serves as a case study of the ways in which a cultural intermediary's injections of her personal commentaries within a specific cross-cultural context can facilitate her audience's understanding of the arguments made in the original English text.

In this article, I will undertake a textual comparison of Yang's Chinese summary with the original English text in part 4 of Mead's *Sex and Temperament* in order to analyze the effectiveness of Yang's annotated summary in conveying Mead's arguments and research findings in New Guinea. In the 1970s, Yang's Chinese summary of Mead's *Sex and Temperament* was widely read by intellectuals and activists in Taiwan's nascent feminist community. The applicability of Mead's American social theory on gender-role formation in Taiwan's gender relationship during the 1970s could be attributed to the similarities in the gender-role expectations of males and females in both the Chinese society in Taiwan and Western societies. The relevance of Mead's argument in refuting the myth of biological determinism in shaping gender roles in both Chinese and Western societies played a crucial role in Taiwanese feminists' understanding of gender-role formation. As such, Mead's work posed a challenge to traditional assumptions about the innate gender differences between men and women in the Taiwanese society.

Among the notable feminist leaders who read the annotated summary was Lu Hsiu-lien (Hsiu-lien Annette Lu). In the 1970s, Lu was the pioneer feminist of the women's movement and a leader of the democracy movement in Taiwan. After Lu was court-martialed and imprisoned for her political activities in 1979, her feminist associate, Lee Yuan-chen, emerged as the feminist leader of the Taiwanese women's movement in the 1980s and thereafter.

Within the historical context of postwar Taiwan's authoritarian political culture and the island's democratization since the lifting of martial
law in 1987, Lee applied Mead's concepts of the malleability of gender
roles and an individual's pursuit of a career path based on one's aptitude
to the formulation of her indigenous feminism. Articulated in an essay a
year prior to the lifting of martial law in Taiwan, Lee's vision of democracy (minzhu) was not restricted to the narrow concepts of universal suf-
frage and individual rights to political participation and constitutional
protection. As a liberal feminist committed to women's self-determination,
her broadened definition of minzhu also encompassed an individual's
right to achieve the existential quest for self-realization (Lee 1986). Like
Mead, Lee's definition of self-realization encompassed an individual's freedom to choose her occupation and to strive for excellence in her professional
endeavor. In terms of a woman's personal life, self-realization consisted of
one's freedom to choose whether to remain single or to marry, and the
reproductive freedom to decide whether to have children (Lee 1988a, 71,
133; Li 1983, 42).

After Annette Lu was released from prison, the lifting of martial law
in 1987 ushered in the era of Taiwan's democratization. In 2000, Annette
Lu ran as a candidate of the opposition party and was elected the first
woman vice president of Taiwan (2000–2008). In fulfillment of her
party's campaign promise, the new government filled a quarter of the top
cabinet posts with notable women from political and academic communities (Lee 2000, 5). In 2002, Lee Yuan-chen, along with several other
feminist leaders, joined the Council for the Promotion of Women's Rights
in the Taiwan government. As council members, they offered advice to
the new government on policies pertaining to women.

In this essay, I will analyze the ways in which Yang Mei-hui's annotated summary of Mead's Sex and Temperament influenced both Lu's
and Lee's visions of gender equity and their critiques of socially imposed
gender roles in Taiwanese society. In order to situate Mead's research
findings in a broader context, I will briefly discuss the important impact
that her work has had on the American women's liberation movement and
the discipline of cultural anthropology, as well as the controversy over
her research findings in Samoa and New Guinea.

Controversy over Margaret Mead in Cultural Anthropology

In 1928, Margaret Mead published Coming of Age in Samoa based on her
fieldwork in Eastern Samoa in 1925. In the book, she argued that adolescent girls in Samoa enjoyed sexual freedom and did not experience
feelings of guilt and sexual anxiety as did their Western counterparts. In
the 1920s, most Americans assumed that adolescents' biological changes

were the main causes of their sexual anxiety and rebellious behaviors. Mead contended that the lack of sexual anxiety among Samoan adolescent girls attested to the primacy of cultural conditioning and social environment in shaping adolescents' temperaments and behaviors.

Whereas Mead's *Coming of Age in Samoa* was about Polynesians, her next book, *Sex and Temperament in Three Primitive Societies* (1935), was based on her fieldwork in three distinctive Melanesian societies of New Guinea. These societies were the mountain-dwelling Arapesh, the river-dwelling Mundugumor, and the lake-dwelling Tchambuli. These three societies were chosen as sites for Mead's field research because they were by and large isolated from the influences of Western culture in the 1930s. In *Sex and Temperament*, Mead took biological heredity and cultural conditioning into account in her assessment of the development of human personality. According to Mead, innate temperamental differences exist between individuals, and these innate temperamental traits are not sex-linked. To illustrate this point, Mead pointed out the differences in personalities among individuals in the Tchambuli society. But it was the Tchambuli women who were solely responsible for catching fish and selling them in the local markets. Mead then concluded that Tchambuli women were more economically independent and dominant than their male counterparts. This gender-role reversal in contrast to traditional Western societies demonstrated that gender-role differentiation was socially constructed rather than biologically predetermined (Mead 1935, 245–84).

In the early 1960s, Betty Friedan spearheaded the postwar American women's liberation movement with the publication of her book titled *The Feminine Mystique*. In this work, she summarized Mead's research findings on the three New Guinea societies in order to demonstrate the malleability of gender roles in different sociocultural contexts. Like Mead, Friedan urged every woman to choose her own career path based on an individual's innate gifts and freedom of choice rather than performing the socially imposed gender roles (Friedan 1963, 136–37). When the struggles for gender equality within the United States took on a new urgency, this transformational message made a profound impact on the women's liberation movement.

In her edited volume titled *Woman, Culture, and Society*, Michelle Rosaldo, a cultural anthropologist and feminist scholar, suggested that the participation of Arapesh males in child care and domestic life in Mead's *Sex and Temperament* should serve as a good example for American males to emulate. Based on Rosaldo's cross-cultural comparative study, she posited that gender inequality was the greatest in societies where there had been a rigid division of labor between the relatively low-status female-dominated domestic realm and the socially prestigious male-dominated public domain. To promote gender equality, Rosaldo encouraged men to participate in the socialization of children and other domestic responsibilities and urged women to fully engage in the political and economic life of the public sphere (Rosaldo 1974, 14, 41–42).

In addition to her profound influence on feminist scholarship, the women's liberation movement, and cultural anthropology, Mead was also the most well-known and influential popularizer of cultural anthropology in the twentieth century. An effective and prolific writer, both *Coming of Age in Samoa* and *Sex and Temperament* were written in plain and simple American English without academic jargons. This made Mead's works accessible to the American public. As a powerful speaker, Mead, on average, delivered a hundred lectures per year to share new research findings in cultural anthropology with both academics and the general public (Mitchell 1996, 122–30). With her creative use of all types of mass media, Mead's transformational message on the unique aptitude of each individual and the malleability of gender roles reached a wide international audience. Mead's popularity as an authority in cultural anthropology remained virtually uncontested until the 1980s.

In 1981, Deborah Gewertz, a cultural anthropologist, published her research findings to reassess Mead's assertion of female dominance in Tchambuli (Chambri) society. While Gewertz concurred with Mead's assessment of Tchambuli women's crucial role in providing economic subsistence for their families and society, Gewertz also pointed out that the exclusion of women from political decision making made them vulnerable and politically dependent on the decisions made by male members of their natal families and their husbands' families. Thus, Tchambuli women were political subordinates in a patrilineal society (Gewertz 1981, 94–104). In addition, Gewertz was critical of Mead's conceptualization of the Tchambuli as a static and nonchanging society whose members had a determined future. In contrast, Mead portrayed modern Western societies as dynamic and ever changing, with freedom of choices for individuals to shape their own destinies. Appropriating Edward Said's concept of Orientalism in her analysis of Mead's work, Gewertz contended that Mead was orientalizing the "other" in the non-West and thus failed to acknowledge the modern Westernized aspects of indigenous people's way of life in New Guinea. With Mead's simplistic contrast of the primitive other versus the modern "civilized" West, she failed to realize the cultural interactions between the indigenous peoples of New Guinea and Western societies in modern world history (Gewertz and Errington 1991, 80–87).

In addition to Gewertz's critique of Mead's research findings of New Guinean societies, some indigenous inhabitants of Manus Island at New Guinea were critical of Mead's explication of their society. In *Papua New Guinea: Anthropology on Trial* (1983), the inland inhabitants of Manus Island criticized Mead's lack of understanding of their customs

and her culturally biased depiction of inland inhabitants as less techno-
logically sophisticated than the people of Pere, a coastal fishing village
on Manus Island. Since most of Mead's informants were from Pere, they
transmitted to Mead their prejudices and negative stereotypes of inland
inhabitants. The latter traded the sago they extracted from palm trees in
exchange for fish from the people of Pere. Furthermore, some indigenes
of Manus Island contended that Mead's informants at Pere were her
source of knowledge about the culture. In contrast to traditional New
Guineans' reliance on oral tradition to transmit their knowledge, Western scholars with a written language possessed the power to record the
knowledge they collected from their indigenous informants. This unequal relationship enabled Mead to publish her research findings and
become famous by means of telling stories about indigenous people's
lives. In the early 1980s, several young indigenous scholars in New
Guinea wondered whether it is fair for outsiders from the West to explicate and interpret the meanings of New Guineans' way of life on behalf
of the indigenous population. Should not New Guineans themselves tell
the stories of their own people in their own voices?

The question of whether insiders of an indigenous society or outsiders
from the West should study and write about the indigenes' way of life remains an unresolved controversy in social theory today. As long as an anthropologist from the West would not use his or her cultural assumptions
and biases to observe and interpret the culture of a non-Western society, a
scholar from outside could actually bring new perspectives into his or her
interpretations of the indigenous culture that an insider might have taken
for granted or overlooked. On the other hand, it is equally important for
insiders of an indigenous culture to tell their own stories in their own
words. Whether the researcher is indigenous or from a Western society,
the controversy highlighted the importance for researchers to consult
with the informants on the accuracy of their written narratives.

In 1983, Derek Freeman, an anthropologist who posited the primacy of
innate biology in shaping human personality and behavior, published
Margaret Mead and Samoa based on his fieldwork in Western Samoa since
the 1940s. With the rise of sociobiology and the resurgence of the biogene-
tic explications concerning human differences in the development of
social sciences during the 1980s, Freeman labeled Mead a cultural determinist whose overemphasis on cultural conditioning was largely a reaction to the racism and biological determinism of the early twentieth
century. From Freeman's perspective, Mead went to New Guinea looking
for evidence of the malleability of gender roles and basically saw only
what she wanted to see. She overlooked the influences of heredity and
biology in determining Samoan adolescents' temperaments and behaviors. In contrast to Mead's assessment, Freeman's research findings demonstrated that adolescent girls in Western Samoa inhibited their sexual

activities in order to preserve their virginity within a highly stratified society with strict sexual mores. According to Freeman, Mead falsely depicted Samoa as an idyllic paradise populated by sexually promiscuous Pacific Islanders (Freeman 1983, 281–93).

Like Freeman, cultural anthropologist Martin Orans considered Mead a cultural determinist. Orans argued that Mead's inadequate data, unscientific research method, and vague overgeneralization about Samoan culture make Freeman's refutation of Mead's work about Samoan adolescents "not even wrong." The Mead/Freeman controversy over whether social-cultural conditioning or biological heredity was the main determinant of an individual's temperament underscored the importance for social theories to take both nature and nurture into account in assessing human development. Orans posited that the broader implication of the Mead/Freeman controversy for social theory today is that human personality and behavior ought to be a result of the complex interaction between biological heredity, cultural conditioning, and social environment (Orans 1996, 10–13).

Some anthropologists, such as Lowell Holmes, suggested that it was Mead's notoriety as a cultural anthropologist who questioned biological determinism's role in shaping human personality and behavior that set the precedent for Freeman's attack. In contrast to Freeman's and Orans's negative evaluations of Mead's work, Lowell Holmes, a cultural anthropologist, conducted a yearlong restudy in the same Samoan village in 1954 as Mead did in 1925 in order to test the validity and reliability of Mead's research methodology and findings. Holmes's restudy found that Mead's research results in 1925 had a high degree of accuracy. Like Mead, he found that most Samoan adolescents experienced easier transitions to adulthood than their American counterparts. Most Samoan adolescents had gentle temperaments and a healthy attitude toward their sexuality. Holmes, in *Samoan Village* (1992), questioned the validity of Freeman's criticism of Mead's conclusions. In the book, Holmes pointed out that Freeman did his fieldwork on an island in Western Samoa, whereas Mead conducted her fieldwork on a different island in Eastern Samoa. Holmes observed that most communities in Western Samoa were more Westernized than their counterparts in Eastern Samoa. Thus, it was not a fair comparison to equate adolescent girls' experiences in Eastern Samoa with their counterparts in Western Samoa. Holmes then refuted Freeman's contention that Mead, like her professor, Franz Boas, was a cultural determinist. Based on Holmes's perspective, both Boas and Mead took biological heredity and cultural conditioning into account in their assessment of the development of human personality (Holmes 1992, 139–52). In the 1970s, Mead's *Sex and Temperament* exerted a profound influence on Taiwan's nascent feminist community. Like Mead, Taiwanese feminists urged women to choose occupations based on their innate aptitude rather than their gender identity. They also considered gender roles a product of sociocultural conditioning. It was through Yang Mei-hui's Chinese annotated summary that Taiwanese feminist activists came to know Mead's *Sex and Temperament*.

Yang Mei-hui's Annotated Summary of *Sex and Temperament*

In the mid-1960s, Yang Mei-hui pursued graduate studies in sociology at Tufts University and obtained her Master's degree. During the American women's liberation movement, she became especially interested in and concerned about the problems and oppression that women experienced in both the United States and Taiwan. This awareness subsequently motivated her to write annotated summaries of excerpts from Western theoretical writings on women and gender inequality (Yang 1979, 325–28).

In the preface of Yang's Chinese text, she stated her decision not to translate Mead's *Sex and Temperament* verbatim. Rather, she summarized the main arguments and ideas in Mead's work (Yang 1973, 1–2). Since Yang's Chinese text is a concise summary of Mead's work rather than a literal translation of the original English text, I characterize the Chinese text as an annotated summary. Inasmuch as the Chinese-speaking audience of Yang's annotated summary in postwar Taiwan shared the Confucian cultural heritage with their counterparts in mainland China and Japan, Yang added several examples from the East Asian cultures of China and Japan not previously evident in Mead's original text. These additions served the purpose of facilitating her Chinese readers' understanding of the above-mentioned arguments in Mead's work. Through a textual comparison of the contents' main arguments in both Mead's original text and Yang's annotated summary, I endeavor to demonstrate that Yang was by and large accurate and comprehensive in her summary of Mead's research findings. She was also effective in adding cross-cultural examples previously not included in Mead's original text to demonstrate the universal applicability of Mead's concept of socially constructed gender roles in different cultures and at different times.

In Mead's English text, part 4 was titled "The Implications of These Results." It was in part 4 of *Sex and Temperament* that Mead summarized the results of her fieldwork in the three Melanesian societies. Mead also contemplated the implications of her research findings for the problems associated with the social construction of children's personalities along the lines of their gender identities in Western societies. It should be kept in mind that the gender roles in Western societies to which Mead referred in part 4 were the cultural norms in the 1930s and before.

Comparatively, Yang's annotated summary of part 4 of *Sex and Temperament* was entitled "*Yang gang he yin rou.*" Deriving the title from the traditional Chinese cosmology's assumptions about men's and women's innate temperamental differences, Yang's chapter title literally meant "the unyielding firmness of masculine yang and the yielding gentleness of feminine yin." For three thousand years, Confucian scholars have conceptualized the yin and the yang as two primal forces in the material universe whose constant interactions with each other have created all physical phenomena, living beings, and myriad things in the universe. Yin was conceptualized as a negative material force associated with the female, yielding, gentleness, weakness, receptiveness, earth, nourishment, turbidity, and the moon. By contrast, the yang was seen as a positive force associated with the male, firmness, strength, dominance, clarity, Heaven, and brightness of the sun. In the Confucian classics of Chinese antiquity, women were instructed to stay at home, whereas men were expected to participate in affairs outside the home. Although Confucian scholars conceptualized the masculine yang as dominant over the feminine yin, yin and yang were also seen as opposite and interdependent forces that complement each other to comprise the totality of the physical universe (de Bary, 1960, 191–92, 463–68; Lu 2004, 239–40).

As we shall see in this article, Yang Mei-hui, through her annotated summary, had the intention of exposing the fallacy of the Chinese cosmological assumption, which ascribed innate strength to the masculine yang and innate gentleness to the feminine yin. In "*Yang gang he yin rou,*" Yang summarized the entire text of part 4 except for the concluding chapter. In the following section of the article, I will first discuss portions of Yang's annotated summary that have conformed with and emphasized Mead's original arguments. Then I will explicate the examples in Yang's Chinese text that did not previously appear in Mead's original text. Finally, I will discuss the portion of Mead's original text that Yang omitted.

In her annotated summary, Yang was by and large attentive to Mead's main arguments in *Sex and Temperament*. Based on her narrative of Mead's empirical observation, Chinese readers would understand that most personality and behavioral traits, such as aggressiveness and passivity, are not sex-linked characteristics. In order to debunk the traditional assumptions about the biologically predetermined masculine aggressiveness and feminine passivity, Yang paraphrased Mead's contention that aggressiveness and passivity ought to be viewed as a continuing spectrum, with different individuals positioned on different points of the spectrum, regardless of sex. In other words, a female child could be born with more aggressive behavioral traits than a male child in any given society.

In the section where Yang dealt with the diverse gendered personality traits among the Mundugumor, the Tchambuli, and the Arapesh in Mead's

research findings, Yang stated that both male and female children of Arapesh were socialized to develop personality traits that were obedient,
cooperative, and gentle. As a result, the Arapesh men and women had personalities and behavioral patterns that were generally considered feminine and maternal by Western standards. Conversely, both male and
female children of Mundugumor were socialized to become cold and
emotionally detached, aggressive, and crude. Based on the Western standard, both the men and women of Mundugumor had masculine personalities and behavioral patterns. Hence, a Mundugumor individual born
with more aggressiveness than his peers would most likely be chosen as a
leader. Conversely, if a person with the same aggressive personality were to
live in the Arapesh society, he or she would be branded as a cultural deviant (Yang 1973, 42, 45).

In her annotated summary, Yang accurately conveyed Mead's characterization of Tchambuli personalities and behavioral patterns as different
along gender lines. That is, Tchambuli men's and women's gender roles
were the inversion of traditional gender roles in Western societies. Her
summary accurately depicts the process of Tchambuli boys' socialization
into gentle, emotional, and verbally expressive persons. By contrast, female children in Tchambuli society were socialized to develop personalities that were emotionally detached and dominant (Yang 1973, 42).

According to Yang's narrative of Mead's perspective, the so-called feminine qualities were absent in both men and women of the Mundugumor
society. On the other hand, Western societies by and large perpetuated
the idea that women's natural temperaments should consist of warmth,
gentleness, household management skills, and a love for the caring of children. These same traits were manifested mostly in males of the Tchambuli society. In the Arapesh society, the norms for both men's and women's
temperaments and behavioral patterns were analogous to the above-
mentioned feminine qualities in traditional Western societies. Thus,
Yang effectively conveyed Mead's contention that there is no direct correlation or natural relationship between differences in gender identities
and differences in genetically based temperaments (Yang 1973, 43).

Based on the relativity and diversity in the temperaments and behavioral patterns of men and women in the three societies, Yang effectively
conveyed Mead's perspective that a society could select specific temperamental traits common in most males and females to be socially reinforced
in the personality of one sex at the exclusion of the other sex. Every
culture exerts pressure on a child to accentuate socially acceptable personality traits and suppress socially disapproved traits. The child's
personality is thus molded into a personality that conformed to societal
expectations. If a society were to exert pressure on boys and girls to develop divergent personalities and behavioral patterns along the lines of
their gender identities, the children would learn to think and behave in

accordance with societal definitions of maleness and femaleness (Yang 1973, 43–44).

To illustrate this point, Yang presented Mead's example of the different patterns of male and female socialization in Western societies. When a Western society sanctions warfare as an exclusively male occupation, it is expecting all the men and boys to be brave and fearless. In other words, boys are taught to suppress their feelings of vulnerability. Conversely, girls are expected to be timid and emotionally expressive. Even though the feelings of fear, bravery, timidity, and vulnerability are innate in both boys and girls, Western societies selectively ascribe bravery to males and timidity and vulnerability to females. These gender-specific personality traits are then socially reinforced from childhood to adulthood. Inasmuch as these gender-specific personality traits are so deeply entrenched and pervasive in Western societies, one tends to assume that they are innately male or female (Yang 1973, 49–50).

Despite traditional Western assumptions about the innate differences in temperaments between males and females, Yang effectively conveyed Mead's contention that most boys and girls still experience some tensions between their innate dispositions and the socially sanctioned personalities for males and females. It is only through extensive cultural conditioning that boys and girls learn to conform to the socially approved personalities and behaviors of their respective genders (Yang 1973, 51–52).

In accord with Mead's text, Yang stated that a small minority of children are born with the innate temperaments that conform readily to the socially approved personalities for boys and girls in Western societies. These children require the least adjustment to the gender-specific personalities that the society expects of them. In societies where only males are socially expected to be aggressive, boys with innately aggressive temperaments experience positive reinforcement and validation from the society for presenting masculine manners. The boy is taught to believe that it is the man's place to dominate over woman in society. With his self-centered and haughty disposition, the aggressive male would use the same attitude toward women to interact with passive males (Yang 1973, 62–63).

Consistent with Mead's argument, Yang accurately stated that a dominant male who is well adjusted to his gender role would feel especially threatened by a woman whose strong character and male-oriented skills exceed his own. In fact, this would cause him to question his masculinity with considerable unease. Similarly, a passive and agreeable woman raised to be always attentive to men's demands would also be perturbed by self-doubt when encountering a dominant woman. When the dominant woman engages in a conversation with authoritarian overtones, the contrast in the two women's temperaments and behaviors would lead the passive woman to question her own tendency of making excessive concessions for the accommodation of others' needs and wants (Yang 1973, 63). Thus, Yang effectively summarized Mead's contention that the most well-adjusted individuals in a society that rigidly divides men's and women's social personalities into binary oppositions still experience moments of self-doubt and emotional unease.

Consistent with Mead's argument, Yang accurately stated that the daily lives of a minority of individuals who do not fit into the socially ascribed gender roles are even more difficult than the well-adjusted individuals who conform to a gender dichotomy. This minority of individuals are seen as eccentric deviants or immature neurotics. Inasmuch as the culture disapproves of their personalities and behaviors, these maladjusted persons experience considerable self-doubt and emotional anguish over their gender identities (Yang 1973, 58, 62).

Hence, Yang effectively narrated Mead's analysis of the troubling consequences for every individual member in a society that insists on gender dichotomy as a main determinant of shaping social personalities. No individual in this type of society can escape moments of self-doubt and emotional unease in regard to his or her gender identity, personality, and behavioral pattern. In a society where there is a rigid dichotomy between the social personalities of males and females, a girl who has shown a great deal of potential and interest in taking on socially ascribed male-oriented tasks could be blamed for making the wrong choices. She could also be chastised for having the personality of the opposite sex. In this and other similar cases, parents would sometimes threaten to socially disenfranchise the child from his or her gender identity. With adults' social disapproval, the child's inability to adjust would sometimes cause him or her to question his or her gender identity. This maladjustment could also contribute to low self-esteem and emotional anguish (Yang 1973, 51–63).

In her summary of Mead's argument, Yang stressed that any society that presumes a person's gender identity as a main determinant of his or her personality is bound to cause the cultural maladjustment of many individuals. Inasmuch as the vast majority of temperamental traits, such as aggressiveness and passivity, are not sex linked, the relative degrees of aggressiveness and passivity ought to be conceptualized as a continuum. In fact, most people's temperaments fall somewhere along this continuum. Yet, Western societies imposed a rigid dichotomy of male aggressiveness versus female passivity on each individual. Many people thus found it difficult to fit their temperaments into the socially defined personalities ascribed to their gender (Yang 1973, 45–62).

In accordance with Mead's argument, Yang stated that a girl who has the natural talents and interests in socially defined male-oriented activities often finds herself without any female role model to emulate. This situation is to be expected in a society that discourages women from engaging in male-oriented tasks and occupations. Hence, the girl would have no other alternative but to emulate the men who have had the same occupational interests and talents that she has. By emulating her male colleagues, she would consequently adopt more masculine personality traits and behavioral patterns. Obviously, the society does not encourage an individual to emulate and identify with the social personalities and behavioral patterns of one's opposite sex. Yet, the rigid dichotomy of distinguishing between male and female personalities is precisely what has compelled the girl with socially defined male-oriented talents and interests to emulate and identify with male colleagues (Yang 1973, 56).

Analogous to Mead's narrative, Yang stated that another unexpected consequence of socially separating male and female personalities into two binary opposites is the problem of cross-gender identification. In cases of cross-gender identification in Western societies, a boy whose temperament is gentle and agreeable would be classified as a male child who identifies with his mother's personality. The theory of cross-gender identification is based on the presumption that the boy's failure to imitate and identify with his father's personality during his character formation has resulted in his abnormal and girlish temperaments. If this feminine personality persists when the boy reaches adulthood, he is made to feel unworthy of the superior realm of male activities and occupations (Yang 1973, 56–61).

Consistent with Mead's argument, Yang stated that it is easier for a boy who shares a similar personality trait with his mother to imitate that particular aspect of his mother's personality. At the same time, there are other aspects of the boy's innate dispositions that resemble those of his father. In these instances, it is natural for the son to imitate his father's personality traits. Since every individual is born of both parents, a person will likely inherit temperamental traits from both parents. Thus, it is natural for each person to inherit some personality traits from the parent of the opposite sex. In other words, there is no reason to assume that a child who has either inherited more from or identified more with the parent of the opposite sex should be considered abnormal (Yang 1973, 57).

Yang then reported Mead's comment about the unwillingness of the American public and the scientific community to transcend their assumptions about innate gender distinctions and recognize the importance of social conditioning in selectively reinforcing certain hereditary traits in the making of individual personalities. Depending on societal needs and social structure, every society has its respective set of personality traits to which it expects individuals in the society to conform. The more highly developed a culture, the more complex and multifaceted is the combination of personality traits that the society expects an ideal individual to possess (Yang 1973, 45–46).

In her Chinese text, Yang conveyed Mead's assertion that some individuals are innately more inclined to excel in certain occupations than others. In other words, each individual is born with a unique set of gifts and non-sex-linked temperamental traits. Because Western societies presume that most temperamental traits are sex linked, parents and teachers often direct boys and girls toward different occupations based on their gender identities. In line with Mead's observation, Yang stated that a child's gender identity tends to obscure parents' and teachers' judgments of the individual child's genuine talents and occupational aspirations. In this way, the artificial division of temperaments and occupational categories along the lines of gender differences serves to distort and inhibit each individual's natural development and true potential (Yang 1973, 61–62).

Consistent with Mead's text, Yang stated that most married women in the United States had been financially dependent on their husbands in the past. Many had no choice but to acquiesce to their husbands' dominance and control. By the twentieth century, some American women had achieved greater financial autonomy, but the traditional social expectations of husband's and wife's roles in the familial context still persisted. This inconsistency had in turn caused confusion and tension in many households. As it was in the past, a man's capacity to make a living still served as the societal yardstick for measuring his worth. But once a man became unemployed, his emotional anguish was often exacerbated by his financial dependence on his wife (Yang 1973, 64).

In addition to conveying the negative consequences of American males' rigid gender-role expectations, Yang also effectively summarized Mead's explication of the three types of societies worldwide. Each of these societies has its respective social expectations for individuals. The first type of society concentrates most of its time, energy, and resources on the training of their young into individuals with certain extreme personality traits. It aims at the creation of a single personality type for all its members. Inasmuch as almost all the society's members are subjected to the same type of socialization and education, the majority of the people in every generation would thus possess the same extreme personality traits and strive to conform to the monistic ideal (Yang 1973, 46–47).

In contrast to the monistic and extreme personality traits of the above-mentioned first type of society, Yang stated Mead's contention that the second type of society selects moderate personality traits in socializing the young. In the second type of society, the standard and definition of ideal personality traits are not as clearly defined as the above-mentioned first type of society. Unlike Mead's original text, Yang added the toleration of diverse personality traits in her description of the second type of society. Based on Yang's own interpretation, the second type of society tends to accentuate children's moderate temperament and tolerate diversity and eclecticism of personality traits (Yang 1973, 47).

Consistent with Mead's narrative, Yang stated that the third type of society is not as variegated as the second type, nor is it as monistic as the first type. Rather, the third type of society ascribes specific personality traits and acceptable behavioral patterns to the members of each gender, age group, class, and profession. Figuratively, the society's social structure resembles the patterns of a mosaic. It is expected socially that an individual who belongs to a certain station or sector of society should exhibit certain distinct personality traits and behavioral patterns in the third type of society. In this highly stratified society, it is socially acceptable for members of the nobility to acquire a haughty disposition. Members of this class are also more prone to take offense at humiliations. Yet, these temperaments are seen as inappropriate for the commoners to acquire. In addition to class stratification, the third type of society could also be organized along occupational and religious lines. In this case, each occupational group and religious denomination would select, institutionalize, and reinforce certain temperaments and behavioral patterns among their members (Yang 1973, 48).

To facilitate her Chinese-speaking audience's understanding of Mead's arguments, Yang added numerous examples not included in the original English text of *Sex and Temperament*. To illustrate the tolerance for diversity in the above-mentioned second type of society, Yang added the example of contemporary American society. According to Yang, tolerance for diverse personalities and respect for the golden mean in the second type of society resemble the characteristics of modern American society. In the 1970s, Yang saw the new America as a salad bowl with a mélange of raw vegetables. In this new society, each vegetable retains its own distinctive quality (Yang 1973, 47). Conceivably, Yang added this example to enhance her Chinese audience's understanding of contemporary American society.

For the purpose of illustrating the third type of society to her Chinese-speaking audience, Yang chose to describe the social stratification of Japan during the age of the shoguns and the cultural distinctions in different regions of traditional China. Since peoples of China, Japan, and Taiwan shared the Confucian heritage in East Asia, Yang's Chinese-speaking audience had some familiarity with Japanese and Chinese history. According to Yang, there were ideal temperaments and behavioral patterns ascribed to the socialization and training of samurai warriors during the era of the shoguns. In the rigidly stratified society, samurai warriors, peasants, Buddhist monks and nuns, artisans, and merchants all had their respective temperaments and behavioral patterns that distinguished one group from the other (Yang 1973, 48–49). Unlike the temperaments and behavioral patterns of the traditional Japanese, which were organized along the lines of social stratification and occupational status, the temperaments and behavioral patterns of the traditional Chinese tended to be organized along the lines of different regions of the country. Comparatively, most Chinese south of the Yangtze (*Yangzi*) River tended to acquire gentler temperaments than their northern counterparts. These relatively gentle dispositions were evident in the ways that most southern Chinese interacted and conversed with each other (Yang 1973, 49). By using her own examples not previously included in Mead's text, Yang effectively demonstrated the predominant influence of socialization in shaping the distinctive temperaments and behavioral patterns of East Asian peoples along the lines of geography, class, and occupational affiliations.

To illustrate the possibility of gender-role reversal within the Chinese cultural context, Yang added two sections not included in Mead's original text. Drawing from Chinese literary tradition, Yang cited the fictional work entitled *Jing hua yuan* (Flowers in the Mirror), which was written in 1825 by Li Ju-chen (Li Ruzhen), a male scholar in the Qing dynasty. According to the novel, the imaginary kingdom of women socialized females to be leaders in the public domain. Conversely, men were expected to stay at home and perform household tasks. It was in vogue for men to wear cosmetics and earrings. Men were also expected to have their feet bound to look attractive to women. With this provocative novel, Li seriously questioned whether the rigid gender roles in early nineteenth-century China were truly heavenly ordained as the neo-Confucian ideology would like everyone to assume (Yang 1973, 43).

In addition to using *Jing hua yuan* as the example to debunk the traditional Chinese assumption about the innate differences between men's and women's gender roles, Yang added the Chinese legend of *Hua Mulan* in her text to illustrate to her Chinese readers that cross-gender identification is not a deviant behavior. As a young woman with an innate aptitude in military affairs, *Mulan* identified with her father's gender role and fought with valor and exemplary leadership on the battlefield in the place of her elderly and ailing father. In so doing, she fulfilled her duty as a filial daughter to her father (Yang 1973, 57).

For the purpose of illustrating the applicability and relevance of Mead's argument within the Chinese cultural context, Yang added a section not included in Mead's original text. Yang contended that the cultural assumption of gender-role differences as predestined and the dominant influence of gender-specific socialization in shaping one's behavioral patterns are also evident in traditional Chinese culture. To illustrate these points to her Chinese readers, Yang quoted several passages from classical Chinese texts. The first of these passages was written by Pan Chao (Ban Zhao), a notable female historian of Han imperial court. Trained in the Confucian classics in a family of court historians, Pan Chao was granted the status of imperial court historian after the deaths of her father and her brother. In the first century C.E., she wrote *Nü Jie* (Instruction for Women) for the socialization of girls in their gender roles. In order to facilitate girls' recitation of the precepts, *Nü Jie* presented eighty gender-

172 DORIS T. CHANG

specific admonitions written in five-character verses. Among these admonitions, there was a precept that admonished girls not to dress or behave like men. The second of these passages was written during the Song dynasty (960–1279 C.E.) by the Neo-Confucian literatus Ch'en Ch'un (Chen Chun). These passages were five-character poems for children to recite and internalize in their minds. In the text, he stated that it is ordained by heaven that men's rightful place is outside the home, whereas women's rightful place is inside the home (Yang 1973, 54).

For the purpose of brevity, Yang omitted the concluding chapter of Mead's book in her summary. In her introductory remarks to "Yang gang he yin rou," Yang did not indicate to her readership that the concluding chapter in part 4 was omitted from her annotated summary. Conceivably, the concluding chapter was left out of Yang's summary because it did not directly pertain to the result of Mead's fieldwork. As a consequence of Yang's omission, Mead's suggestions for Americans' socialization of children were not presented to the Chinese-speaking audience.

In the concluding chapter, Mead used the Arapesh as a prime example of a society's sacrifice of heterogeneity for the attainment of social homogeneity. Not only did Arapesh society lack the categories of rank and status, but the distinctions between the social personalities of men and women were also kept at a minimum. Inasmuch as almost all Arapesh children were socially expected to acquire passive, mild, and cooperative dispositions, individuals with active minds, intense temperaments, and great individual creativity would find a lack of emotional and intellectual outlets for expressing themselves in the society. Socially, those individuals who could not adjust their temperaments and behavioral patterns to the culture's one-sided emphasis were branded as cultural deviants. Thus, the Arapesh sacrificed individuals' innate temperaments and unique potential for the attainment of social homogeneity, simplicity, and harmony. In so doing, the culture also deprived its members of the various social experiences of a diverse and complex society (Mead 1935, 313–16).

Unlike the harmonious simplicity and lack of contradiction in the behavioral patterns of men and women in the Arapesh society, Mead contended that women's roles in American society were the most contradictory and ambiguous. Legally, a husband was still the head of household. But due to the increase in the number of American women entering the workforce and their progressive upbringings, it was not unusual for wives to be more assertive and dominant than their husbands. Inasmuch as American girls tended to model their personalities and behaviors after their assertive mothers and female schoolteachers, modern American society had reversed the tradition of European male dominance to a considerable extent. Based on the evidence in Mead's empirical observation, the ambiguity and contradiction between men's and women's actual power and legal status could also be found in the Tchambuli society.

Nominally, a Tchambuli man was still the head of his household. On the other hand, a Tchambuli woman's dominant, assertive, and secure disposition actually equipped her better for the leadership position than her male counterpart (Mead 1935, 310–11).

According to Mead in the concluding chapter of *Sex and Temperament*, the best solution for resolving the contradictions in the society and for minimizing suppression of one's talents and potential was to replace the molding of artificial personalities along the lines of gender, class, and race with the development of every individual's unique talents and innate temperament. In this way, no child's talent would be wasted owing to his or her class origin, gender identity, or racial background. In other words, every individual's natural talents and innate temperament would be respected and given the freedom to develop to the fullest potential. Collectively, the natural potential and diverse talents of different individuals in society could contribute to the advancement of all aspects of human endeavors. By replacing the artificial differences socially imposed on each class, race, and gender with the genuine differences between individuals, the society could be enriched by diversity and heterogeneity. At the same time, no individual's freedom to develop personal gifts and potential in his or her chosen occupation would be sacrificed.

In the final analysis, Mead presented her solution as the best alternative for developing the fullest potential of a society as well as its individual members. Inasmuch as Taiwan in the 1970s was a modernizing society experiencing its transition from an agricultural economy to a newly industrialized society where male dominance was still prevalent, Mead's proposed vision for the replacement of an artificial gender dichotomy with the genuine differences between individuals could have been seen as a valuable suggestion. The inclusion of Mead's concluding chapter in part 4 of *Sex and Temperament* in Yang's annotated summary would have strengthened Mead's argument in the Chinese text. Yang also failed to include Mead's empirical observations of Tchambuli women's tendencies to be possessive, practical, actively sexed, and willing to initiate sexual relationships. Within the context of Taiwan's socially conservative environment in the 1970s, it is conceivable that Yang avoided the discussion of sexuality in order to pass the party-state's censorship of her work.

Lu Hsiu-lien, Lee Yuan-chen, and Gender-Equity Legislation

Despite the omissions in Yang's Chinese summary of Mead's original text, Yang's annotated summary of Mead's *Sex and Temperament* enjoyed a positive reception in Taiwan during the 1970s and thereafter. Lu

Hsiu-lien (Hsiu-lien Annette Lu), the pioneer feminist of postwar Taiwan, was a notable cultural critic of Confucian patriarchy. In order to
promote women's participation in the public domain, Lu, a young government official who obtained her law degree in the United States, became a
self-styled liberal feminist who spearheaded postwar Taiwan's autonomous women's movement in 1972. With the financial support and voluntary effort of her feminist associates, Lu created telephone hotlines for female victims of sexual assault and domestic violence in the two largest
cities in Taiwan, Taipei, and Kaohsiung. She recruited many women vol-
unteers with professional expertise to offer legal counsel, psychological
counseling, and medical attention to the female victims. As a social activist who derived much of her inspiration from the liberal tradition of Western feminism, Lu organized highly publicized lectures and roundtable
discussions with legal experts about ways to revise gender-biased family
laws and civil codes. In order to publish her writings and disseminate her
feminist messages to the Taiwanese public, she, along with her feminist
associates, created *The Pioneer Press* (Lu 1994, 293–96).

In the 1970s, Taiwan's feminist community universally recognized Lu
Hsiu-lien's *New Feminism* (*Xin nüxing zhuyi*) as the main text of Taiwan's feminist discourse. Written in 1973, the content of *New Feminism*
was subsequently revised and republished in 1977 and 1986.[1] Based on Yang
Mei-hui's annotated summary of Mead's research findings, Lu criticized
the assumption that gender roles were biologically predetermined. In
New Feminism, Lu endorsed Mead's contention that socialization was the
predominant determinant, molding personality and behavioral patterns.
Lu argued that both male and female individuals were born with unique
temperaments and behavioral traits that were not sex linked. She stated
that Western and Chinese societies had suppressed socially ascribed female traits and accentuated the socially ascribed male traits in boys. The
same societies suppressed socially defined male traits and accentuated
the socially defined female traits in girls. To persuade her Taiwanese audience that sociocultural conditioning rather than biological difference
shaped men's and women's gender roles, Lu wrote a section in *New Feminism* to introduce the main arguments in Yang's annotated summary of
Mead's *Sex and Temperament* (Lu 1986, 120–26).

Among the three distinctive societies in New Guinea during the
1930s, Lu stated that both the males and females of the Arapesh society
had personalities, temperaments, and behavioral patterns that were considered feminine and passive by traditional Chinese and Western standards. Conversely, both males and females of the Mundugumor society
were socialized to acquire aggressive temperaments and behavioral patterns from childhood. Thus, both sexes had personalities considered masculine by Chinese and Western standards. Tchambuli males, however,

were socialized to be passive; women were socialized to acquire dominant personalities. The gender-role differentiation in Tchambuli society could be seen as an inversion of traditional gender roles in Chinese and Western societies. With this summary, Lu tried to undermine her readers' assumption that traditional gender roles were absolute and universal in different parts of the world over time. She suggested that the socially acceptable gender roles in Taiwan and Western societies might not be socially acceptable in other societies, like the three in New Guinea. The striking differences in the three New Guinean societies' conceptualization of gender also demonstrated the relativity of socially constructed gender in different cultural contexts (Lu 1986, 121; Yang 1973, 39–65).

In *New Feminism*, Lu's notion of individual variation based on a person's unique aptitudes and interests rather than gender distinction was derived from Mead's *Sex and Temperament*. Both Mead and Lu asserted that each woman's and man's unique talents and interests should be the main determinants of his or her roles and occupations in the public domain. In order to overcome occupational segregation along gender lines, Lu, like Mead, advocated that women should have the individual freedom to make occupational choices and participate in any work in the male-dominated public sphere (Lu 1986, 145–55; Mead 1935, 321–22).

In addition to Lu's vision of integrating women fully into the male-dominated society, she also played a leadership role in Taiwan's democracy movement and served as an editor of *Formosa: A Magazine of Taiwan's Democratic Movement*. Between 1979 and 1980, Lu was arrested and court-martialed on the charge of sedition after making a speech at a commemoration rally of the Universal Declaration of Human Rights in the city of Kaohsiung. In the aftermath of the Kaohsiung Incident, seven other leaders of the Democratic Opposition were also court-martialed and sentenced to long prison terms. While Lu was in prison, her mother became terminally ill. Although she petitioned the prison authority to grant her a short visit to see her mother, Lu was devastated when she found that her mother had died. In order to keep her mind active and focused, Lu wrote novels at night on toilet paper and stuffed it inside her comforter to evade confiscation by prison guards. Family members took the comforter with them after a visit with her at the prison (Liu 2006, 204–9). Meanwhile, Amnesty International in West Germany adopted Lu as a prisoner of conscience and secured her release on medical parole for treatment of thyroid cancer in 1985. In the same year, Lu published *These Three Women* (*Zhe sange nüren*), one of the novels she wrote in prison.

Prior to Lu's release, her feminist associate, Professor Lee Yuan-chen of Tamkang University, emerged as a leader of the autonomous women's movement in the 1980s. In order to circumvent martial law's proscription on the formation of nongovernmental organizations, Lee and a group of feminist intellectuals and activists created the *Awakening* Magazine Publishing House in 1982 to serve as an organizational base for the autonomous women's movement (Fan 2000, 19–33).

In the 1970s, Lee also read Yang's annotated summary of Mead's *Sex and Temperament*. Consequently, Mead's concept of cultural relativism in gender-role formation exerted significant influence on Lee's formulation of her feminism. Like Mead, Lee conceived of every individual's unique personality, talents, interests, and choices as the main determinants of his or her occupation and roles. No individual would be socially pressured to assume a role or an occupation based on his or her gender identity. Every man and woman could freely aspire to become a leader, an inventor, a secretarial clerk, or a caregiver. In other words, Lee envisioned men's and women's freedom to express their individuality without having to conform to the socially defined gender roles (Lee 1988a, 156).

In contrast to Lu Hsiu-lien's conception of motherhood solely within the context of marriage, Lee suggested that the single women who chose motherhood could consider adoption or artificial insemination. However, she cautioned that only the single women who were emotionally and financially ready should take on this long-term responsibility (Lu 1986, 163; Lee 1988a, 120). Just as Lee envisioned the possibility of single women's motherhood, she also contemplated the possibility of gender-role reversal. Like Mead and Michelle Rosaldo, Lee contended that the society should respect a couple's decision to let the husband be the primary caregiver of children at home, as his wife performs the role of the breadwinner of the family (Lee 1988a, 89; Lee 1989, 5; Li 1983, 41–42).

With the revocation of martial law in 1987, Awakening feminists saw a new window of opportunity to challenge the gender-biased curriculum of the national education system. A sociologist of Taiwan studies, Thomas Gold noted that the feminist movement both contributed to and was made possible by the development of a vibrant civil society during Taiwan's democratization in the 1980s and 1990s. With their strong conviction that children's social conditioning was the key to subverting traditional gender roles, Awakening feminists in 1988 conducted a comprehensive textual analysis and criticism of gender-role stereotyping in elementary and junior high textbooks (Awakening Foundation 1988, 2). By exposing the gender biases and authoritarian tendencies in the textbooks, Awakening feminists urged the Taiwanese public to join hands with the women's movement to exert pressure on the Ministry of Education to revise the textbooks' contents (Ch'ao 1988, 1–4).

In the same year, Lee Yuan-chen critiqued Taiwan's authoritarian educational system as a major hindrance to children's critical thinking and freedom of expression. Lee stated that Chinese culture had been authoritarian and ideologically monistic for most of its history. Within the Chinese cultural context, Taiwan's educational system emphasized ideological indoctrination and conformity with Confucian patriarchal social norms and state orthodoxy at the expense of sociopolitical tolerance, creative thinking, and diversity. These authoritarian and monistic tendencies were not conducive to educating the young to adapt to the social realities of a modern democratic society (Lee 1988b, 4–7).

As a cultural legacy of Confucianism's ascription of women's traditional roles as managers of the household and good mothers, wives, and daughters-in-law in the domestic realm, the textbooks anachronistically depicted men and women as conforming to these traditionally ascribed gender roles: Women were primarily depicted as good mothers and wives who handled all the household responsibilities, whereas men were the breadwinners and successful professionals outside the home. Similar to Mead's depiction of the tension between an American working wife and the traditional gender-role expectations of her husband in the 1930s, most male children in Taiwan during the 1980s were still socialized to expect their wives to do all the housework. This anachronistic expectation intensified many women's double burden during the time when one-third of the adult female population worked full-time outside the home in Taiwan's newly industrialized economy. In order to realize Lu Hsiu-lien's vision of cooperative home economics, Lee demanded that social studies textbooks emphasize the sharing of housework by the male and female members of a family. In this way, children of both genders would be taught from an early age to consider housework as men's and women's shared responsibility (Lee 1988b, 4–7).

Lee advocated that the textbooks' contents should include professional women's contributions to various occupational endeavors. In this way, male students could learn to respect their female colleagues and female students would have professional role models. Like Mead, Lee conceived of an educational experience that would foster the freedom of expressing one's individual personality rather than conforming to the socially imposed gender roles. To this end, Lee advocated that the Ministry of Education should offer seminars for both male and female teachers to transform their gender-bias attitudes and their traditional acceptance of authoritarian indoctrination (Lee 1988b, 4–7; Lee 2000, 9).

After nearly a decade of advocacy by a coalition of feminist activists, educational reformers, and parents' groups, the National Institute of Compilation and Translation in 1996 ended five decades of monopolizing the compilation and editing of elementary school textbooks. In the spirit of democratic pluralism, the Taiwanese government welcomed various commercial presses to compile and publish elementary school textbooks. In the following year, the Ministry of Education established the Council for Gender-Equity Education. The Council's mission was to promote gender egalitarian education in every level of the national education system. Revisions of textbooks to eliminate gender biases were underway. On the elementary school level, teachers were given greater autonomy to choose textbooks that promote gender equity in the family and the society. In the 1997 edition of middle school textbooks entitled *Renshi Taiwan* (Getting to know Taiwan), the book on society devoted a section to the discussion of postwar Taiwan's autonomous women's movement (Lee 2000, 8–9).

Based on the proposed draft bill of Taipei's feminist lawyers and educators, Taiwan's legislature passed the Gender-Equity Education Act in 2004. The law stipulated that a gender-equity curriculum should be integrated into students' learning experiences from kindergarten to the twelfth grade. Every university and college in Taiwan should offer courses in gender studies. The law prohibited discrimination against pregnant women and girls and any prejudicial treatment based on a person's sexual orientation in the school system. Also, the Act stipulated the creation of a Gender-Equity Education Committee in the Ministry of Education, in every city and county government and in every school and university in Taiwan, mandating that at least half of all members in each Committee would be women. The Gender-Equity Education Committee in every level of government and school is in charge of formulating and implementing gender-equity policies and coordinating gender-equity curriculum. The Committee in each school is also vested with the power and responsibility to investigate cases of sexual assault and sexual harassment on campus and to recommend appropriate punishment for offenders based on legal stipulations. In addition to the creation of the Gender-Equity Education Committee, the Act stipulated the establishment of a Faculty Evaluation Committee and a Grievance Review Committee in every school and university in Taiwan. Each of these committees have at least one-third of its members of either gender (http://law.moj.gov.tw/Eng/Fnews).

In order to promote gender equity in employment, several feminist lawyers from *Awakening* authored the first draft bill for gender equality in employment in 1989. After twelve years of ongoing dialogue between the feminist lawyers, government officials, and legislators, the final draft bill of the Gender Equality in Employment Act passed the Legislative Yuan in 2001. The law stipulates that a parent of either gender is eligible to apply for a leave of absence from work for no more than two years to care for a child three years of age or younger. In order to lighten the employers' financial burden, the government promises to absorb the cost of a parent's insurance policy during an employee's leave of absence from work to care for a child. Lastly, the Act obliges companies with more than 250 employees to establish child care facilities with the aid of government subsidies (*Min Sheng Daily* 2001; *Taipei Times* 2001).

In addition to the legislative achievement, Taiwanese women also made great strides in the political arena. In the presidential election of 2000, most feminists supported the nomination by the Democratic Progressive

READING _SEX AND TEMPERAMENT_ IN TAIWAN 179

Party (DPP) of Hsiu-lien Annette Lu as the vice presidential running mate of Ch'en Shui-bian, the former mayor of Taipei. The feminist community's support for Lu could be attributed to her stature as the pioneer feminist of postwar Taiwan and the DPP's concurrence with the feminists' demand for filling a quarter of all top cabinet posts with women. With the DPP's victory in the election of 2000, the opposition party replaced the Chinese Nationalists as the ruling party for the first time in fifty years. Lu also became Taiwan's first woman vice president (2000–2008).

In conclusion, Taiwan's nascent democracy provides a forum for feminist activists to advocate for women's rights and to translate their vision into gender-equity legislations. Despite the controversy over Mead's research findings in the English-speaking world, Yang Mei-hui's annotated summary made a profound impact on transmitting the main arguments in Mead's *Sex and Temperament* to the Chinese-speaking audience. From the Chinese summary of Mead's work, Taiwanese feminists realized that both men and women should choose their occupations based on their innate gifts and aptitudes, rather than settling for vocations and societal roles based on their gender identities. Thus, feminists in Taiwan applied Mead's concept of cultural relativism of socially constructed gender to subvert the rigid gender roles in Taiwanese society. In so doing, they facilitated Taiwanese women's self-determination in a nascent democratic society.

Acknowledgments

I would like to thank Dorothy Billings for introducing me to works in anthropology. Also, three important references pertaining to Taiwan's women's movement were consulted during the writing of this article: Farris (2004), Ku (1989), and Rubinstein (2004).

Note

1. Written in 1973, the first edition of *New Feminism* was published in 1974. According to Lu, the 1977 edition and the 1986 edition were identical in content. Since the 1977 and 1986 versions were more comprehensive in their coverage of Lu's ideas than the 1974 edition, I use the 1977 and 1986 versions.

References

Awakening Foundation. 1988. *"Dui jiaoyu gaige zhi yijian"* (Opinions on the educational reform). *Awakening*, 10 March, 2.

Ban, Zhao (ca. 49–120). 1988. *The Chinese Book of Etiquette and Conduct for Women and Girls: Instruction for Chinese Women and Girls (Nü Jie)*. Translated from Chinese by S. L. Baldwin. Brussels, Belgium: Editions Thanh-Long.

Ch'ao, Teng-mei. 1988. "*Xiaomennei de nanzun nübei: liangxing pingdeng jiaoyu zuotanhui*" (Respecting males and depraving females: a panel discussion on an education based on gender equity). *Awakening*, 10 April, 1–4.

de Bary, William Theodore, Wing-tsit Chan, and Chester Tan, eds. 1960. *Sources of Chinese Tradition*. Vol. 1. New York: Columbia University Press.

Fan, Yun. 2000. "From Politics without Parties to Politics with Parties: Women's Movement in Taiwan's Political Transformation, 1980–." In *Taiwan2000—Envisioning a Pluralistic Future: Proceedings of the Sixth Annual Conference of the North American Taiwan Studies Association, Harvard University, Cambridge, Mass., June 16–19*. Cambridge: North American Taiwan Studies Association.

Farris, Catherine. 2004. "Women's Liberation under 'East Asian Modernity' in China and Taiwan: Historical, Cultural, and Comparative Perspectives." In *Women in the New Taiwan*, ed. Catherine Farris, Anru Lee, and Murray Rubinstein, 325–76. Armonk, NY: M. E. Sharpe.

Freeman, Derek. 1983. *Margaret Mead and Samoa*. Cambridge, MA: Harvard University Press.

Friedan, Betty. 1963. *The Feminine Mystique*. New York: W. W. Norton & Co.

Gewertz, Deborah. 1981. "A Historical Reconsideration of Female Dominance among the Chambri of Papua New Guinea." *American Ethnologist* 8:94–106.

Gewertz, Deborah, and Frederick Errington. 1991. "We Think, Therefore We Are?" *Anthropological Quarterly* 64:80–89.

Gold, Thomas. 1996. "Taiwan at the Fin de Siecle." *China Quarterly* 148:1091–14.

Holmes, Lowell D. 1992. *Samoan Village: Then and Now*. 2nd ed. Fort Worth: Harcourt Brace Jovanovich.

Ku, Yen-lin. 1989. "The Feminist Movement in Taiwan, 1972–87." *Bulletin of Concerned Asian Scholars* 21:12–22.

Lee, Yuan-chen. 1986. "Liangxing dou xuyao Funü xinzhi" (Both genders need Awakening). *Awakening*, 10 April.

———. 1988a. *Funü kaibuzou* (Women's forward march). Taibei: Shenghuo wenhua.

———. 1988b. "Quanwei jiaoyu de bihai zhi yi" (One of the negative consequences of authoritarian education). *Awakening*, 10 March, 4–7.

———. 1989. "Liangxing kongjian de duoyuan mianmao" (The many faces of gendered spaces). *Awakening*, 1 July, 5.

———. 2000. "Taiwan fuyun ji qi zhengzhi yihan" (Taiwanese women's movement and its political significance). A Paper Supplied by Lee Yuan-chen to the Author. Department of Chinese Literature, Tamkang University, Taipei, Taiwan.

Li, Chu'ung-yueh. 1983. "Nannü ruhe huxiang xuexi" (How can men and women learn from each other). *Awakening*, 10 September, 40–43.

Li, Ju-chen (ca. 1763–1830). 2005. *Flowers in the Mirror (Jing hua yuan)*. Translated from Chinese by Lin Taiyi. Nanjing: Yi lin chu ban she.

Liu, Min-chu. 2006. *Shijie zhi nü: Lu Hsiu-lien* (Woman of the world: Lu Hsiu-lien). Translated from Korean to Chinese by Chin Hsuen-ch'en. Taibei: INK Publishing.

Lu, Hsiu-lien. (1977, 1986). *Xinnüxing zhuyi* (New feminism). Taibei: Dunli.

———. 1985. *Zhe sange nüren* (These three women). Taibei: Zi li wan bao she.

———. 1994. "Women's Liberation: The Taiwanese Experience." In *The Other Taiwan*, ed. Murray A. Rubinstein, 289–304. New York: M. E. Sharpe.

Lu, Hwei-syin. 2004. "Transcribing Feminism: Taiwanese Women's Experiences." In *Women in the New Taiwan*, ed. Catherine Farris, Anru Lee, and Murray Rubinstein, 223–43. Armonk, NY: M. E. Sharpe.

Mead, Margaret. 1928. *Coming of Age in Samoa*. New York: William Morrow.

———. 1935. *Sex and Temperament in Three Primitive Societies*. New York: William Morrow.

Min Sheng Daily. 2001. "New Law Will Boost Gender Equality at Work." *Min Sheng Daily*, 5 June.

Mitchell, William E. 1996. "Communicating Culture." In *Popularizing Anthropology*, ed. Jeremy MacClancy and Chris McDonaugh, 122–30. New York: Routledge.

Orans, Martin. 1996. *Not Even Wrong*. Novato, Calif.: Chandler and Sharp Publishers.

Papua New Guinea: Anthropology on Trial. Nova Series. Arlington, VA: Public Broadcasting Service, 1983. Videocassette.

Rosaldo, Michelle Zimbalist, and Louise Lamphere, eds. 1974. *Woman, Culture, and Society*. Stanford: Stanford University Press.

Rubinstein, Murray. 2004. "Lu Hsiu-lien and the Origins of Taiwanese Feminism." In *Women in the New Taiwan*, ed. Catherine Farris, Anru Lee, and Murray Rubinstein, 223–43. Armonk, NY: M. E. Sharpe.

Su, Yu-ling. 2002. *Development and Practice of Gender Equity Education in Taiwan*. Taipei: Nüshu.

Taipei Times. 2001. "Law Passed for Working Women." *Taipei Times*, 7 December.

Yang, Mei-hui. 1973. *Funü wenti xinlun yucong* (A collection of translated works on the new theories pertaining to the woman question). Taibei: Chenzhong chubanshe.

———. 1979. *Funü wenti xinlun* (The new theories on the woman question). Taibei: Lianjing chubanshe.

CHAPTER ELEVEN

"His Wife Seized His Prize and Cut It to Size"

Folk and Popular Commentary on Lorena Bobbitt

LINDA PERSHING

> John Bobbitt was never a loner.
> In fact, he was known as a roamer.
> His wife seized his prize
> And cut it to size.
> Now John is his own organ donor.
>
> —Limerick circulated in 1993–94

In January 1994, the trial of Lorena Bobbitt, who was charged with the "malicious wounding" of her husband, captured the attention of the public in the United States and abroad. The case received extensive media coverage, much more than had the earlier trial of John Wayne Bobbitt, who was accused and acquitted of the rape (marital sexual assault) of his wife. Lorena Bobbitt was in the limelight not because she broke the law but because she violated a cultural taboo: she cut off her husband's penis. The incident and subsequent media attention became the subject of intense national debate. It also sparked a flurry of jokes, limericks, urban legends, T-shirt slogans, and advertising gimmicks. Bobbitt-related discussions filtered into everyday conversations, office jokes, and electronic mail networks. Children circulated their own Bobbitt folklore.[1] For months, nationally known stand-up comedians and television talk show hosts performed extensive repertoires of Bobbitt jokes, while members of the general public created new lyrics to popular melodies (e.g., "The Ballad of the Bobbitt Hillbillies" sung to the *Beverly Hillbillies* theme song).

Folklore—which may be defined as informal or traditional communication that arises out of a shared aesthetic and is transmitted through dynamic processes of social interaction—often provides a socially acceptable way for people to communicate their thoughts, feelings, and responses to issues of the day. Because folklore emanates from people's everyday expressive behavior and is often spontaneous in nature, it offers a window to ideas, values, and concerns not always articulated in official or "high" culture. People use folklore to educate or enculturate one another about their sense of identity, social values, and views of the world, and the study of folk expression can contribute valuable insights about the political aspects of social and cultural life. This essay offers an analysis of Bobbitt-related folklore (or Bobbitt-lore, as I call it) and the cultural politics embedded in expressive responses to the Bobbitt cases. My goal is to discern the underlying messages conveyed by different types of Bobbitt-humor and to demonstrate how Bobbitt-lore provided diverse groups of people with a vehicle for commenting on identity politics and social relations as they are defined by ethnic, class, and gender differences.

First, some background information: On the evening of 23 June 1993, John Bobbitt came home to his apartment in Prince William, Virginia, after a night of barhopping.[2] His wife Lorena testified that he was drunk, insisted they have sex against her will, raped her, and then went to sleep. John's account differed. At various times, he said that they had not had sex that evening, that he could not recall if they had had sex, that Lorena had tried to initiate sex but he had been too tired, that they had had sex but he had slept through it, and that the sex had been consensual. Afterward, Lorena got out of bed and went to the kitchen for a glass of water. A knife that was lying by the sink caught her eye. She picked it up, stared at it awhile, and memories of past abuse raced through her head. She recalled, "I remember[ed] many things. I remember[ed] the first time he raped me. I remember[ed] the put-downs that he told me. . . . I remember[ed] the first time he forced me to have anal sex, the bad things he said. I remember[ed] the abortion. I remember[ed] everything." Lorena went back to the bedroom where John was sleeping, pulled down the sheets, and cut off his penis.

She then left the house, got into her car, and drove away. She said that while she was driving, she looked down and was horrified to see the severed penis still in her hand. She threw it out the car window into a nearby field. Soon afterward, she called police and told them where to find it. Surgeons managed to reattach John Bobbitt's penis in an operation that lasted nearly ten hours. If convicted of the class-three felony offense, Lorena Bobbitt faced a fine of up to $100,000 and a mandatory prison term of five to twenty years. Following nine days of testimony, the jury (seven women, five men) found Lorena Bobbitt not guilty by reason of temporary insanity. She was held in custody at a mental institution in order to undergo psychiatric observation. A month later, psychiatrists determined that she posed no threat to herself or others and recommended that she be released to receive ongoing outpatient treatment.[3]

The case became legendary almost overnight. As one observer put it, "not since Lizzie Borden have a woman and her cutlery received so much attention" (Shales 1994, G1). By late 1993 and early 1994, jokes and stories about the Bobbitts flourished. Did you hear the one about Lorena Bobbitt being released on her own recognizance while awaiting trial? The judge ruled that Lorena could go home for the Christmas holidays, but only on the condition that she didn't hang any balls on the Christmas tree. On Halloween 1993, near Washington, D.C., a group of women went trick-or-treating dressed up in Lorena look-alike wigs and carrying big wooden knives (Lowther 1993, 35). There were humorous claims that Lorena Bobbitt had signed advertising contracts with the makers of Ginsu knives and Weedwackers or that John Bobbitt had become a spokesperson for Peter-bilt Trucks and Snap-on Tools. At a take-out restaurant, a neighbor of mine overheard one man asking another whether he wanted a "Bobbitt" or a full-sized submarine sandwich. Meanwhile, a radio disc jockey offered Slice soda and cocktail wienies with ketchup from his on-site broadcasting booth near the Manassas, Virginia, courthouse, while vendors sold buttons that read "Lorena Bobbitt for Surgeon General" (Kaplan 1994, 52; Leiby 1994, B1).

Professional comedians were quick to add their own commentary. Bobbitt jokes made David Letterman's "Top Ten List" on several occasions.[4] The January 1994 "Comic Relief VI" television special on HBO became a virtual circus of Bobbitt satire. Comedian Robin Williams began with this promotion: "I know that many of you . . . paid forty dollars to see John Wayne Bobbitt's penis on television [on Howard Stern's 1993 New Year's Eve pay-per-view special], but for only thirty dollars you can get a Comic Relief T-shirt that has better stitching and won't shrink in cold water!" Meeting the challenge, Whoopi Goldberg and Billy Crystal—along with a dozen other celebrities—tried to outdo one another with Bobbitt-related comedy routines. In the end, Williams stole the show by enacting a bizarre scene in which a severed penis took on a life of its own, fell into a toxic waste dump, mutated to a height of fifty feet, and then tried to screw New York's Holland Tunnel.

Journalists immediately entered the fray, providing daily coverage of Bobbitt-related events as well as shaping and amplifying public perceptions of the case. *Vanity Fair*, the only magazine to get a personal interview with Lorena Bobbitt, called her a "national folk heroine" (Masters 1993, 168), while the 27 December issue of *People* magazine named Lorena Bobbitt one of the twenty-five most intriguing people of 1993. By January 1994, reporters had written approximately 1,300,000 column inches about the Bobbitts ("Unkindest Cut" 1994, 14). Lorena's trial made the front page of major newspapers like the *New York Times* and *Washington Post*, and there were televised news reports each evening on the NBC and ABC television networks (CBS executives decided not to cover Lorena's trial until it was over, summarizing it after the fact). The Court TV Network and CNN provided live coverage of the trial to millions of people across the country.[5] A poll conducted by *Newsweek* revealed that 60 percent of the U.S. population followed the case, "both men and women equally" (Kaplan 1994, 52). When, rather than Lorena Bobbitt's trial, CNN chose to air President Clinton's announcement of an agreement to destroy 1,800 nuclear warheads on Ukrainian soil, the station received hundreds of phone calls from viewers who objected to their decision ("Clinton" 1994, C4).

Simultaneously, Bobbitt language began appearing in everyday conversations. The humorous implications of the name itself (as if Bobbitt
weren't enough—did his given names *have* to be John Wayne?), morbid
fascination with the idea of a woman severing a man's penis, and popular
interpretation of Lorena's act as an assault on male authority all ignited
the public imagination and contributed to the proliferation of Bobbitt
language and wordplay. Some of it seemed fairly neutral: Virginia police
joked that the dog used to track down the wayward penis had been a
cocker spaniel (Leonard 1993, 617), and in Miami's Little Havana, cus-
tomers began ordering "Lorenas" instead of *cortaditos*, black coffee "cut"
with a bit of milk (Roman 1994, B1). Most Bobbitt wordplay had more of
an edge to it, however, denigrating either John or Lorena in some way, as
did this riddle: What's the difference between a used car salesman and
Lorena Bobbitt? Answer: A used car salesman is a slick pricer (electronic
mail from Chris Baldwin, 26 Jan. 1994). Journalists went wild creating
headlines for their articles, among them "Forrest Stump" (an interview
with John Bobbitt in *Gentleman's Quarterly*), "Phallus Interruptus" (*Nation*), "Severance Pay" (*People*), "The Unkindest Cut of All" (*U.S. News
and World Report*), and "Grin and Bobbitt" (*Village Voice*).[6] Predictably,
the name Bobbitt came to refer to a penis or to any object that had been
severed or separated, and men were warned about "Bobbittectomies" or
being "Bobbittized" (see Algeo and Algeo 1994, 295–96).[7]

As Bobbitt jokes became a national pastime, some people began to
wonder about the meaning of the phenomenon. In a January 1994 article
for *Maclean's* magazine, for example, Allan Fotheringham asked, "What's
going on here? Why is mutilation such a source of humor? The press and
late-night comedians have never had so much fun." Perhaps, he suggested, people responded to the Bobbitt cases with humor because "the
organ in question is so inherently goofy looking" (1994, 72). While amus-
ing, Fotheringham's analysis ignored some deeper issues. Although both
men and women circulated Bobbitt-lore, there was often a difference in
the messages they communicated. Some men told jokes that belittled
Lorena Bobbitt's testimony, as did the *Tonight Show* host Jay Leno in his
18 January 1994 opening monologue: "Lorena Bobbitt stated that she
couldn't remember the night she was raped. She couldn't remember! Hey,
and they get mad at us when we forget a wedding anniversary!" Women,
in turn, responded with their own gender commentary: What do you call
a guy who's lost 90 percent of his intelligence? Answer: John Wayne Bobbitt. The reactions of people who were deeply disturbed by the creation
and circulation of Bobbitt humor—particularly those who were personally offended by the idea of cutting off a man's penis and those who were
sensitive to the issue of violence against women—demonstrated that
Bobbitt-lore was seldom neutral or apolitical.[8]

During the last three decades, the study of humor has commanded the attention of feminist scholars from a range of disciplinary backgrounds. These studies indicate that people often use jokes to express ideas they are unable or unwilling to state more overtly. Humor can help maintain the status quo through the comic devaluation and satirization of alternate cultural identities, behaviors, or ways of thinking. It can also undermine the existing social order by calling it into question, thereby suggesting alternative social and political configurations. For many people, Lorena Bobbitt and John Bobbitt became cultural icons, symbolic of much more than their individual experiences. Through Bobbitt-related humor and folklore, people reified, explored, and criticized social relations between men and women as well as an array of other problems.

Issues of Ethnicity

Claims and counter-claims about ethnic relations and stereotypes were among the messages conveyed in Bobbitt-lore. Of the hundreds of jokes and stories I collected for this essay, none mentioned John Bobbitt's racial or ethnic heritage, thereby reinforcing the assumption that whiteness is the unspoken American norm. However, some Bobbitt commentary focused on Lorena's identity as a Latina and first-generation immigrant.

In some jokes Lorena, and by inference all Latinas, was portrayed as emotional, irrational, unpredictable, inept, or stupid. Camille Paglia called Lorena "a Latin firecracker" (1994, 42), while members of the general public satirized her linguistic heritage in jokes like this one, which offered a clumsy pun about Lorena's maiden name, Lorena Gallo: "Lorena's maiden name is 'Gallo,' which is Spanish for 'cock.' And in one of the Ecuadorian native tongues, the name 'Lorena' means 'young, dumb woman who will one day, after her husband rapes her, stumble into the kitchen, grab the first sharp object she finds, go back into the bedroom, and cut off her husband's'" (electronic mail from Chris Baldwin, 26 Jan. 1994). In the "Comic Relief VI" television special, stand-up comedian Paul Rodriguez warned the audience that Latinas are castrating Furies: "Remember that Lorena Bobbitt is a Latina. Latina women will sever your penis! They will!" Attempting to counter this stereotype by appealing to another—the image of the pious religious practitioner—Lorena's defense attorneys "packaged" her as a demure and devout Catholic, whose innocence and purity were symbolized by the white silk blouse and ever-visible crucifix on the necklace she wore in the courtroom (Goldstein 1994, 8).

Some Ecuadorians and other Latinas/os, however, rejected these dichotomous representations and offered counterreadings of the ethnic subtext of the Bobbitt cases. When a rally to support Lorena was suggested during a local Spanish-language radio talk show on Radio Borinquen (WILC 900 AM), calls flooded the station from people who wanted to get involved. Ninea Guiterrez, a thirty-year-old Virginia resident who immigrated from Mexico, told reporters that she joined a demonstration in Manassas because "I think it's important for Lorena to see that her people are supporting her, and that we understand what made her do that." According to Lorena, John repeatedly ridiculed her for being too small, too skinny, and too "Spanish-looking"; several of the Latinas at the courthouse said that they had similar stories to tell about their own abuse by lovers and husbands (Margolick, 1994, A7). Some mentioned that although they did not necessarily condone Lorena's actions, they understood her desperation and wanted to champion her cause because she was Latina (Sanchez 1994, B3). Cary de León, coordinator of services for battered women in Dade County, Florida, told a reporter for *El Nuevo Herald* that she hoped Lorena Bobbitt's acquittal would encourage women, especially Latinas, to speak up about their own experiences with domestic violence (Santana 1994, B1). For these women, Lorena became a signifier for Latinas in general and for the devaluation and gender-related abuse they experience as a result of their ethnicity, and for some Latinas, she became a liberating symbol of their desire to contest and reformulate Latina identity and gender relations within Latin American communities.

A group of feminists in Ecuador reacted dramatically. Interpreting Lorena's trial as an example of patriarchal denial of violence against women and, in a larger sense, imperialist U.S. policies (because Lorena faced deportation if found guilty), the National Feminist Association of Ecuador called several news organizations in Quito, threatening that they would castrate one hundred American men living in Ecuador if Lorena Bobbitt went to prison (Achenbach and Lieby 1994, D7). Ecuadorian journalist Maria Gómez traveled to Manassas to cover the trial. In sharing her reactions to the incident, she reportedly commented, "Sometimes women have to take the law into their own hands. What she did was brave" (Leiby 1994, 8). For these Latinas, Lorena's trial became not only an example of men's violence against women but also, in a broader sense, a "tale of marital colonialism" against the people of Latin America (Goldstein 1994, 8).

While some Latinos took Lorena's action and her acquittal as a direct affront to their masculinity (see "Lorena Bobbitt no es" 1994, 8; Martinez 1994, 21), there were also Latinos who demonstrated public support for Lorena Bobbitt, often emphasizing shared ethnicity over gender differences. A dozen Latino cabdrivers volunteered their services in transporting people to the site of her trial for free. In below-freezing weather, approximately two hundred people of Latin American descent, many of them men, kept a vigil outside the Manassas courtroom, cheering for

Lorena when she entered or left the courthouse and carrying Ecuadorian flags and signs with slogans like "Lorena, estámos contigo" (Lorena, we are with you; Miller and Tousignant 1994c, A12; Sanchez 1994, B3).

Class Commentary

Class issues also shaped both the lives of Lorena and John and the incident that made them famous. Lorena came to the United States aspiring to be the "model immigrant." When she was a child, her family moved from Ecuador to Venezuela in pursuit of greater prosperity. There her father worked as a dental technician (none of my sources say whether her mother worked outside the home), and the family lived what Lorena described as a lower-middle-class existence (Masters 1993, 172). In 1986, Lorena moved to the United States on a student visa. She was delighted with the accessibility of consumer goods and the affluence she saw around her. Her first impression of the United States was that "everything was just pink and beautiful. . . . [D]on't get me wrong," she continued, "[in Venezuela] we do have McDonalds. We do have Pizza Hut. We do have hotels and beautiful shopping malls. But for some reason this was my dream in the back of my head. I said to myself, 'Oh my God, this is the place I want to be'" (172). She enrolled in English-language classes and took a job as a nanny and later as a manicurist at the Nail Sculptor salon in Prince William, Virginia.

It did not take long for Lorena to become disillusioned with the American Dream. When John and Lorena got married in June 1989, they had very little money and lived in a studio apartment with minimal furniture. Eventually they moved into a two-bedroom apartment and then bought a house in 1990. According to Lorena, the house was more than they could afford, especially since John spent most of his income buying luxury items (a satellite dish, computer, and two cars) and barhopping with friends, often stealing money from her purse to cover his expenses. At the time of the incident, Lorena worked ten hours a day, six days a week; her pretax income was about $17,000 a year (Masters 1993, 209). After John got out of the Marines on 1 January 1991, he found and lost several different low-paying jobs (Lorena said nineteen, John's lawyers said six). One journalist noted that John Bobbitt's attitude toward money was much like his attitude toward sex: "getting and spending, filching and borrowing—was the dominant motif" (Berger 1994, 12).

The debts mounted, the bank foreclosed on their mortgage, they moved into an apartment, and Lorena and John argued constantly about their finances. When things got tight, Lorena embezzled money from her employer and shoplifted dresses from Nordstrom's department store (Masters

1993, 209). Mirroring the consumer culture in which they were immersed, John and Lorena tried to buy status and happiness through products and goods they could not afford. When Lorena left in a daze after slicing off John's penis, she took a Gameboy and a hundred dollars with her rather than her shoes (Berger 1994, 12).

It is noteworthy that class-related commentary about Lorena and John's financial situation was absent in the jokes and stories I heard, even though the particulars of the case (satellite dish, Gameboy, and all) offered ample opportunity for satire. I can only speculate that this omission occurred because class differences are so often avoided, naturalized, or otherwise rendered invisible in U.S. culture. The media focused much more attention on issues of gender and, secondarily, ethnicity but had little to say about the pressures that Lorena and John faced as working-class people who fought with one another about their limited financial resources, rather than questioning the larger economic system.

Nevertheless, class issues *did* affect the public reaction to Lorena's trial. Barbara Ehrenreich ("Feminism") and Katha Pollitt noted that while working-class women often supported Lorena, well-known feminist intellectuals and activists were more reluctant to do so. According to Pollitt, those who openly expressed their feelings of solidarity with Lorena were women who had to cope on a daily basis with "female-ghetto jobs, too much housework, too little respect, too many men like John Bobbitt" (1994, 147–48). She commented that among feminist acquaintances who were writers, academics, and lawyers, "the closest anyone would come to defending Lorena was to suggest that while, mind you, not condoning *in any way* slicing a male even as despicable as John Bobbitt . . . , you could sort of . . . maybe . . . see how she might have flipped out" (147).

In fact, nationally recognized, middle- and upper-class women rarely spoke out in Lorena's defense. For example, Susan Estrich (University of Southern California law professor and campaign manager for Michael Dukakis in 1988) commented.

> Lorena Bobbitt is a criminal, not a feminist heroine. Those feminists who have flocked to her defense have done a disservice not only to the cause of feminism, but more important, to the real victims of battered wives' syndrome—the millions of women who are beaten by their husbands and do not respond by assaults on their organs. They are the women who deserve sympathy and attention, and support from the criminal justice system—not Lorena Bobbitt. (1994, E3)

Rita J. Simon and Cathy Young, president and vice president of the Women's Freedom Network in Washington, D.C., wrote in a *New York Times* letter to the editor that

> not all women gloat because a woman mutilated the genitals of her sleeping husband and got away with it. We all sympathize with battered women. While

spouse abuse should be taken seriously, it should not be an excuse for legalized revenge. . . . If feminism means equal rights and equal responsibilities, Mrs. Bobbitt's acquittal is not a victory for feminism. The [jury's] decision trivializes female violence, infantilizes women and fuels hostility between the sexes. (1994, A22)

Naomi Wolf, who has been outspoken in her belief that feminists have too often glorified the victimization of women, cautioned against envisioning Lorena Bobbitt as a hero by noting, "Women are just as capable of mayhem and sadism and cruelty as men. But it's just not acceptable to support violence" (Gleick et al., 1993, 96).[9] Observing this trend, Pollitt suggests, and I agree, that

the current attack on "victim feminism" is partly a class phenomenon, a kind of status anxiety. It represents the wish of educated female professionals to distance themselves from stereotypes of women as passive, dependent, helpless, and irrational. From this point of view, women like Lorena, if not punished, taint all women. (1994, 148)

Those who took this position focused on Lorena's reactions rather than on John's violence, contending that all she had to do to stop the violence was leave the violent relationship. Within this debate, there was no discussion of the economic and class-related factors that make battered women feel desperate or prevent them from leaving their abusers. Little attention was given to John's power to affect Lorena's livelihood: her immigration status depended on him, and his habit of stealing her earnings and his extravagant spending put economic self-sufficiency beyond her reach.[10]

The Politics of Gender: Phallocentric Reactions and the Reassertion of Male Dominance

Gender issues were always in the foreground in Bobbitt-lore. Although even superficial survey data indicated otherwise, some authors claimed that reactions to the Bobbitt trials were bifurcated along gender lines: men sided with John and women with Lorena.[11] Writers for *People* magazine, for example, contrasted the Bobbitt cases to the earlier trials of Amy Fisher and Joey Buttafuoco, noting, "Also like the Amy and Joey affair, their conflict seems to have become a symbolic skirmish in the war between the sexes. Even the endless torrent of jokes affects men and women differently" (Gleick et al. 1993, 94). More insightful authors noted that in its own perverse way, public expression about the Bobbitts usually ended up objectifying the penis and reinforcing stereotypes about castrating females and emasculated males (see Goldstein 1994, 8). If nothing else, there was widespread recognition that casual discussion of sexual activity and saying the word "penis" in public settings became more permissible as a result of the incident.[12] Suddenly reporters and newscasters were writing and talking about penises, anal intercourse, and whether or not a woman is entitled to an orgasm. Journalist William Safire wrote that 13 July 1993 would "be remembered as the day the word penis appeared in 30-point type in the *New York Times*," noting that before the Bobbitt trials, the word "vagina" was acceptable for journalists, but "penis" had to be replaced by "male sex organ" (1994, F10). Comedian Whoopi Goldberg bemoaned the fact that in light of the Bobbitt, Buttafuoco, and Menendez trials, 1994 should have been named "the Year of the Dick."[13] *Newsweek* writer Cynthia Heimel observed that in making penis jokes about the Bobbitts, many male comedians seemed like a group of sniggering twelve-year-olds. Howard Stern's 1993 New Year's Eve television special typified this behavior by featuring John Bobbitt on stage with a ten-foot-tall rendition of a penis, surrounded by a group of virtually naked women (Heimel 1994, 59).

The increased public discussion of the penis had a dual effect. On the one hand, as Judy Mann observed, it signified a "big step in achieving a balance of power between men and women. The penis is no longer sacred, off-limits, spoken of only in hushed tones as it if were a religious icon. We can now talk about it openly" (1994, E3). This was a significant development given the fact, as Maxine Sheets-Johnstone noted, that the penis "is never made public, never put on the measuring line in the same way that female body parts are put on the measuring line. On the contrary, a penis remains shrouded in mystery. It is protected, hidden from sight" (1992, 69).[14]

However, public discussion of the penis in the aftermath of the Bobbitt case also reified men by once again fetishizing their sexual organs and linking them to male identity, power, and aggression. As one writer noted, "John Wayne Bobbitt has become evangelical in the cause not only of *his* penis but of *the* penis" (Junod 1995, 234). When John commented to his publicity manager Aaron Gordon that after the trials were over, he would be ready to fall in love again, Gordon retorted, "You are in love, John—with your penis," commenting under his breath, "his whole life revolves around his dick" (234). John's fascination and obsession with his own sexual organ resonated with other men. Dale Stephanos, a nationally syndicated political cartoonist, captured this idea in his depiction of a male broadcaster who gets a thrill from his news report: "And now, a Bobbitt update . . . penis penis penis penis, and furthermore, penis penis penis. . . ." Behind the television camera, the technician reacts: "I think he's starting to enjoy this!" (1994, 5).

Suddenly, promotion of the phallus and the centrality of the penis was not only allowable but also encouraged in popular culture. Not all men, however, celebrated this trend. Noting that the Bobbitt trials had provided the opportunity for some men to reclaim a notion of sexuality that objectifies both men and women, one man lamented,

> It is men who have cut ourselves off from our own penises by fetishizing them as phalluses, emblems of male power over women. We have severed our bodies from our minds and forfeited our emotional life by making sex a power game. . . . It is from the phallus, the power-symbol . . . that men must cut ourselves loose. ("International" 1994, 4)

According to anthropologist Mary Douglas (1966, 1970, symbols of group conflict frequently take forms that emphasize the human body. Body parts often become signifiers for whole bodies, and particular bodies become signifiers for groups. Within this conceptual framework, attacks on a single body part or individual may be perceived as an affront to a group that shares a sense of common identity. In the Bobbitt cases, Lorena's attack on John was read as women's attack on men more generally, and severing his penis became a symbolic gesture representing women's desire to disempower all men.[15] Less than a month after Lorena's acquittal, the cover story of *Time* magazine was "Are Men Really That Bad?"— illustrated by a large photo of a white pig wearing a business suit. The accompanying article by Lance Morrow complained about the rising popularity of "male-bashing," noting that "masculinity is in disrepute. Men have become the Germans of gender"; and "Bobbitt-lopping" has become the "feminist over-response to male violence against women" (1993, 54, 58). Within the larger social and historical context of power relations that are increasingly contested by women, lesbians and gays, people of color, and colonialized populations, men often reacted angrily to Lorena's acquittal, because they interpreted the verdict as one more assault on male primacy. Some objected that the verdict condoned Lorena's actions and, by inference, vilified all men. One man commented:

> I know that when I hear "expert" after "expert" doing convoluted rhetorical handstands to show why any violent act by any woman against any man is justifiable self-defense "under patriarchy," I get so angry and bitter that my ability to listen to, and empathize with, legitimate female victims of male violence becomes greatly impaired. I don't WANT to be insensitive in this manner, but I am only human, and when too many of my "buttons" are pushed at once, it just happens. The battered women's movement would make more progress in the long run if they gave higher priority to ending violence than to categorically blaming all males. The fact is, we men really AREN'T all two-dimensional, cardboard-cutout enemies who want to live in a society in which all women are beaten into submission, cowed and afraid. Many of us genuinely care and want to be supportive of battered women. But when we feel as if the issue is being used unfairly to demonize and bludgeon us, and that legitimate male victims are being ignored and/or blamed, we wind up becoming part of a backlash. (Electronic mail, 24 Jan. 1994)

One journalist speculated that during the Bobbitt trials, constant repetition of the word "penis" may actually have served as a talisman for men who somehow hoped that if they made jokes about John's loss and thereby shifted the focus to another man, what happened to John Bobbitt would never happen to them (Goldstein 1994, 8). Many Bobbitt jokes seemed laden with male anxiety: What did John Bobbitt say when he was propositioned by a hooker? Answer: Sorry, I'm a little short this week (electronic mail from Alan Hall, 3 Feb. 1994). Or, Why won't they be able to convict Lorena Bobbitt? Answer: There's no hard evidence, and the evidence they have won't stand up in court (electronic mail from Tom Rowe, 17 Jan. 1994). Puns like these suggested male insecurity about men's sexual prowess and performance, their status in the changing social order, and, particularly, the possibility of rejection or retribution by women. Why, we might ask, did so many journalists think it was important to describe the *length* of the knife (some said eight, others said twelve inches) Lorena used to sever John's penis, or the fact that it had a *red* handle (perhaps a metonymic image referring to blood)?

Susan Bordo suggests that despite the glorification of the male body as a symbol of strength, men's sense of insecurity may stem from the unpredictable and fluctuating character of the very organ they have fetishized. "Indeed, the penis—insofar as it is capable of being soft as well as hard, injured as well as injuring, helpless as well as proud, emotionally needy as well as cold with will, insofar as it is vulnerable, perishable body— haunts the phallus, threatens its undoing" (1993, 698–99). Similarly, journalist June Callwood asked whether men's insecurities may stem from the fact that their sexual organs hang outside their bodies, making them feel vulnerable to possible damage or harm (Fotheringham 1994, 72). This notion suggests an inversion of phallocentric cultural values, a recognition that contrary to the usual theorizing about the physical weaknesses or limitations of women, it is possible to postulate that men are vulnerable precisely because of the physiological characteristics of the organ frequently identified as a sign of male power.

But beyond their anxieties and concerns that all men are being blamed for the bigotry and oppression exercised by some men, male transmitters of Bobbitt-lore also expressed their discomfort over the loss of male and white-skin privilege signaled by the Lorena Bobbitt verdict. One man noted:

Here are some random thoughts from an embittered male. Personally, I feel that the verdict was a travesty. Like many straight white males I know, I feel like somewhat of an outcast. I find I must be substantially better than any visible minorities, women or aboriginal people when I am applying for a job. I feel that society's hatred towards straight white males was reflected in the verdict. . . . There is a double standard in our society that says if a man is abusive, he is an animal that must be caged, but if a woman is abusive, then men are only getting their just desserts. Part of the problem is exacerbated by what

I feel is an incredibly militant, left-wing women's movement that will mobilize at any opportunity to spread their own agenda, which is in itself harmful to the fabric of our society. (Electronic mail from Andrew Lapsley, 18 Feb. 1994)

Angry reactions like this one suggest a sense of anxiety about lost gender and racial privileges but little acknowledgment that men who are now feeling disenfranchised rarely protested cultural assumptions about gender roles and power imbalances when they benefited from them.[16] The backlash against feminism and other voices of resistance spurred the creation of a distinctive type of misogynistic Bobbitt-lore, the most popular and prevalent kind I encountered. In addition to other uses, the term "Bobbitt" became a slang expression for a woman who ignores or refuses to cater to men, a woman who "cuts off men as cruelly as Lorena did, with the scissors of her indifference" (J 1995, 81). Bobbitt-lore of this type conveys a pervasive concern about women who are assertive, cunning, and who step out of prescribed social roles by taking aggressive action against men. Around the time of Lorena's trial, one man quipped that his wife would not think of cutting off his penis, because she was too busy leading him around by it (electronic mail 7 Feb. 1994). Jokes about Lorena Bobbitt frequently compared her to other assertive women who were in the news during the time of her trial, particularly figure skater Tonya Harding and Hillary Rodham Clinton. In one joke, a man tells his friends: "I had a really strange dream last night. I dreamt that I went to bed with Hillary Clinton, Lorena Bobbitt, and Tonya Harding. When I woke up this morning, my knee was killing me, my manhood was gone, and I didn't have any health insurance!" (electronic mail from Joseph Goodwin, 2 Nov. 1994).[17] One of the most popular Bobbitt riddles meshed the three women into a single, terrifying personality: Who's the most feared woman in America? Answer: Tonya Rodham Bobbitt. Folklorist Elizabeth Kissling noted that these three women were lumped together because they were "known for speaking their minds, acting autonomously, and in their own self-interests—all dangerous behaviors for women, in a society where femininity means nurturance of others, passivity, and dependence" (5).

Expressions of male anxiety and vulnerability emerged repeatedly in patriarchal Bobbitt-lore. Was it incidental (or accidental) that a September 1994 television special about declining sperm counts in men and the evolution of hermaphroditic animal species was entitled "Assault on the Male," or did the program mirror a more pervasive concern?[18] Funny stories regarding male insecurity about even the *mention* of Lorena Bobbitt, and subsequent efforts to reassert male primacy through phallic imagery, sometimes emerged in unexpected places. Ann Risley Strawn recounted the following incident:

Our Cub Scout Pack was having a cook-out. I walked up to the serving table and noticed that my friend Betsy was holding a steak knife in one hand and an uncooked hot dog in the other, at which point I inquired if this was the Lorena Bobbitt Invitational Barbecue. The conversation continued as we conjured up the idea for a Bobbitt Wiener Toss and a Memory Skills Test (you have to remember where it landed, of course). We noticed that suddenly the men were all looking quite uncomfortable about these uncooked hot dogs and their proximity to the knife-wielding wives and mothers. The best moment was looking at the campfire and seeing fifteen men and boys peacefully roasting their "wienies" (the term used by the scouts)—but we noticed that they had placed the hot dogs the *long way* on the sticks, rather the standard cross-way mode. We thought it was a rather poignant ending to a humorous situation. (Electronic mail, 28 Jan. 1994)

Just the mention of Lorena Bobbitt made some men nervous. As one journalist commented, "It serves, first and most frighteningly, as a man's scariest fantasy of Feminine Revenge, worse than any plot of Lysistrata" ("Ballad" 1994, A20). Editorial cartoonist Mike Luckovich captured this feeling in his depiction of "Thanksgiving at the Bobbitts," in which a woman raises a carving knife in the air, and the men and boys hide under the table in terror. The woman in the cartoon is faceless, she is everywoman—neither young nor shapely, and she appears in a traditional domestic role. With this image in mind, people joked that after the Bobbitt incident, men were less likely to insist that women belong in the kitchen or quipped that millions of men had suddenly taken to sleeping on their stomachs. Columnist Art Buchwald similarly described the discomfort that he and other men experienced during a dinner party conversation about the Bobbitt cases:

> Mary Patterson declared: "Mrs. Bobbitt was sending her husband an important message and that's essential in a relationship. Unfortunately, John was watching football."
> It wasn't what Mary said that bothered the men at the table, it was the way she was cutting her steak as she said it.
> Chuck McDermott laughed nervously. "Mary, the beef is already dead. You don't have to slice it with such vengeance." (1994, B1)

The fear that other women would follow Lorena's example was a popular motif in Bobbitt-lore.[19] Jay Leno quipped, "I'll bet Bob Packwood is nervous now, eh? Today, up in Oregon, twenty-nine women just bought Ginsu knives, and they'll all be looking for him." This theme echoed across electronic-mail networks, as people joked that when volunteer firefighter Howard Perry found John Bobbitt's severed penis in the field, he proclaimed, "I don't know if it's the right one, but it fits the description" (electronic mail from Alan Hall, 3 Feb. 1994). One unnamed male author, who supported Lorena Bobbitt's acquittal and was critical of the responses he was hearing from other men, put it a bit more succinctly:

> The recent hysteria over the Bobbitts exposed the raw nerve of castration anxiety among men. This is akin to the massive paranoia that gripped white slave-owning communities about the possibility of slave rebellions; it is rooted in guilt and fear, the projection that women (or slaves), having been mutilated and victimized for millennia, will rise up and vengefully turn the tables. ("International" 1994, 1)

There may be reason for men to feel anxious. While the news media and Lorena Bobbitt's defense attorneys described Lorena's deed as if it were a unique occurrence brought on by temporary insanity, information emerging from diverse sources suggests otherwise. On 20 September 1992—nine months before the Bobbitt incident—Aurelia Macias of Los Angeles, California, cut off her husband's testicles with a pair of scissors. The defense argued that her husband had beaten Macías throughout their seventeen-year marriage, that she was about to be raped by him, and that he had threatened to kill her.[20] The Associated Press released a story describing how, in July 1993 (just a month after the Bobbitt event), Cynthia Gillett was charged with malicious maiming after she reportedly doused her sleeping husband's penis with nail polish remover and set him on fire in Waynesville, North Carolina ("Woman" 1994, 29).[21]

Similar incidents were reported around the world, usually in conjunction with media coverage of the Bobbitt cases. In 1992, a German woman, Heidemarie Siebke, cut off her former lover's penis when he demanded they have sex. They argued, and she smashed a chair over his head, fracturing his skull. While he was unconscious, she severed his penis with a carving knife and set the house on fire to cover her crime (Atkinson 1994, C1–2).[22] In Zimbabwe, Shanangurai Tinarwo pleaded guilty to assault charges after slicing off her husband's penis in January 1994, when she found him sleeping with another woman ("How Do You Say" 1994, 20). The practice of women severing men's penises appears to be well-known in Thailand (Gleick et al. 1993, 96), Korea ("How Do You Say" 1994, 20), and the Philippines (Ch'ien 1994, 20), either in abuse cases or when a wife catches a husband having an extramarital affair.[23]

During the Bobbitt trials, women came forward to announce that although they had never actually done so, they often wished they had found the courage to mutilate their own rapists. Evelyn Smith, who was acquitted of killing her husband in 1992—the first successful use of the battered-woman defense in the state of Maryland—was one of the few spectators allowed in the very small courtroom in Manassas, Virginia. Reflecting on her experiences, she told reporters, "No, I didn't cut my husband's penis off, but to be honest with you, I thought about it many times. I've been raped, and I would lay there and cry and wish that it would rot and fall off" (Leiby 1994, B8).[24] Meanwhile, urban legends resurfaced and circulated across the United States about women assaulting men's sexual organs. In October 1995, Nancy Michela shared with me a story she heard from a nurse who works in an emergency room. In this legend, jealousy prompts the woman's act:

> Many years ago, a prominent, married state legislator in New York was known in appropriate circles to have a new girlfriend. She was a cub reporter covering politics for the local television station. They had an affair for a period of time. Reelection time came, and his wife said, "Get rid of the girlfriend, or I'll sue you for divorce and you'll lose the election" (the politician was a Catholic). The legislator continued to see the reporter. One night, the legislator was rushed by ambulance to the hospital emergency room. His penis had been glued to the toilet seat by his wife (no one established how this was done). The ER staff removed the penis from the seat, treated his injury, and sent the man home. Within days, the legislator's lover moved to New York City in order to accept a news-anchor position. And the legislator was photographed arm-in-arm with his beloved wife at his reelection celebration in November.

Renegotiating Gender Politics and Decrying Violence against Women

Even though there was little formal support for Lorena from nationally recognized feminist leaders, many women across the country sent letters, postcards, bouquets of flowers, and stuffed animals to "Lorena Bobbitt, Manassas, VA" (Miller and Tousignant 1994a, A9), and they proliferated Bobbitt-lore critical of male dominance. One genre satirized men's obsession about penis size and sexual performance:

> Q: Did you hear about the new hot dog they're offering on Coney Island?
> A: Yeah, it's called the John Wayne Bobbitt: it's a little short and rather unsatisfying. (Electronic mail, 28 Jan. 1994)

> Noting that the Bobbitt incident took place in Virginia, not far from the location where Disney hoped to build a new theme park, feminist comedian Kate Clinton joked that perhaps "it *is* a small world after all." (Leiby 1994a, B8)

Bobbitt-lore of this kind inverted phallocentric discourse by trivializing or negating the primacy of the penis. Stand-up comedian Margo Gómez, for example, included a little Bobbitt humor in her routine on "Comic Relief VI." After identifying herself as a Puerto Rican and Cuban lesbian, she commented, "I am a Latin woman, but I would never sever anybody's penis. I wouldn't really know where it is."[25] During Lorena Bobbitt's trial, a series of jokes entitled "101 Uses for a Dead Penis" appeared on the rec

.humor electronic-mail newsgroup. Among the suggestions offered by subscribers on 2 February 1994 were: one could use a dead penis as "a spout warmer for a teapot," "finger puppet (paint a face on it)," "a garden hose spray nozzle," or one could "skin it to make a wallet (rub it and it turns into a suitcase)." Nicole Hollander, creator of *Sylvia* cartoons, suggested that underlying men's anxiety concerning women's jokes about men and penis-related humor lies a more significant concern: "Men are frightened by women's humor because they think that when women are alone, they're making fun of men. This is perfectly true, but they think we're making fun of their equipment when in fact there are so many more interesting things to make fun of—such as their value systems" (qtd. in Barreca 1991, 198). The process of ridiculing penises through Bobbitt jokes and stories provided women an opportunity to contest male privilege and existing gender relations more generally. Such humor sometimes appeared subtly and in the most domesticated places. One woman recounted this story in which the joke was on the father of the family:

> My mother is a wonderful cook. She really goes all out for Christmas, baking cookies and filling the house with a wonderful aroma. One of my gifts was a tin containing a variety of Christmas cookies. I dug down to the third layer. There, resting on a bed of wax paper, were the most perfect little dough-colored cookies. They were elliptical in shape, about an inch-and-a half long, and one end was dipped in chocolate. My mother said in lowered voice, "I call these 'Bobbitts'! But don't you call them that, it bothers your father." They were delicious, with a slight lemon flavor. I hope my mother makes "Bobbitts" next year, too. (Electronic mail, 21 Jan. 1994)

Feminist Bobbitt-lore often focused on the pattern of abuse and degradation experienced by Lorena, using the Bobbitt trials as a way of calling attention to male domination or violence against women more generally.[26] Despite the fact that John Bobbitt denied he had ever hit or sexually abused her, expert witnesses for both the prosecution and the defense testified that he had mentally and physically battered Lorena, that the abuse was escalating, and that by 1993 she lived in constant fear of him.[27]

Concurrent with the Bobbitt trials, editorials appeared in newspapers citing statistics about the gendered dimensions of sexual and domestic violence: 98.9 percent of rape victims are women, and every year in the United States 3,000 men murder their wives or partners ("Million" 1994, A26).[28] Laura X, from the National Clearinghouse on Marital and Date Rape, discussed Lorena's acquittal in the framework of existing marital rape laws and the need for future legislation to protect women (1994, 151–53). Women often objected to the media coverage of the Bobbitt cases, observing that men rape and brutalize women every day but the press rarely publicizes these crimes (Heimel 1994, 58). One woman protested, "What I find interesting about this whole situation is that every year there are thousands of documented cases of women being abused and raped by men. Yet, there is such huge coverage of this *one* case of a woman attacking a man" (electronic mail from Kathy Homer, 24 Jan. 1994). Another noted, "I can't believe people are getting so bent out of shape about this. Rapists are chopping off women's arms and getting out on parole two years later, and maybe it's covered once in the news. But let one woman touch one single penis and the whole country goes ballistic" (Heimel, 1994, 58).

This disparity became evident in August 1995, when Richard Rosenthal was arrested for beating and killing his wife in Framingham, Massachusetts. Rosenthal allegedly attacked her in a fit of rage, sliced open her chest with a butcher knife, then ripped out her heart and lungs and impaled them on a wooden stake. Afterward, he told passersby that he had become angry about an overcooked pasta dish ("Man Held" 1995, A2). The event received scant media attention. A short summary of the incident appeared in local papers, but it generated little national coverage, nor did it make the headlines. Interestingly, there was no discussion of the length of the knife or the ethnicity of the perpetrator, but the Associated Press article stated that people who knew Rosenthal regarded him as a serious, hard-working person.

Reacting to the androcentric Bobbitt-lore that permeated U.S. popular culture and the lack of recognition of the severity or pervasiveness of violence against women, various groups of feminists responded in their own ways. In San Francisco, an organization called the Lesbian Avengers sponsored a celebratory "Wienie Roast" or "Bobbitt-cue" to commemorate Lorena's action (electronic mail from Jym Dyer, 26 Jan. 1994). Feminists also created their own jokes and limericks, such as the following, which described John Bobbitt as a rapist rather than the hapless victim of a jealous woman:

> There once was a rapist named Bobbitt
> Who wouldn't respect his wife's "Stop it!"
> His dick was a weapon
> And so I do reckon
> She was left with no choice but to chop it!
> (Electronic mail from Melodie Frances, 24 Jan. 1994)[29]

When I asked the author of this limerick how she felt about the verdict, she responded:

> To be honest, I think it's about time. Intellectually, I believe that I should not be happy about someone else being assaulted, but so many women I care about have been sexually abused, that a big part of me really has enjoyed a woman fighting back. This may not be very enlightened of me, but it is how I feel. I

was disappointed when he was not convicted, and I was real glad when she wasn't. I'm only sorry that the doctors were able to re-attach his penis. . . . I should also add, as long as I'm being honest, that I have thoroughly enjoyed the jokes that have made men squirm. (Electronic mail from Melodie Frances, 25 Jan. 1994)

Expressions of Women's Refusal and Retribution

Portrayals of women who use violence as retribution have recently become a more acknowledged part of European and American popular culture. In a B movie entitled *I Spit on Your Grave*, for example, a woman who was gang-raped castrates one of her rapists in a scene involving a bloody bubble bath (Leonard 1993, 618). Helen Birch and the contributing authors to the volume *Moving Targets: Women, Murder, and Representation* note that portrayals of women who are revenge-seeking killers have become a new archetype in Hollywood cinema (e.g., *Thelma and Louise, The Hand That Rocks the Cradle, Basic Instinct, Single White Female*). Birch suggests that while male violence is old news, until recently female violence in films has been relatively rare and is gaining popularity with viewers (1994, 1–2).[30]

Images of women who use violence to avenge male violence against them are also becoming more prevalent in contemporary joke cycles. Women, in particular, seemed to enjoy Bobbitt-lore of this type. Noting the therapeutic and subversive aspects of feminist humor, Regina Barreca suggests that

> certain forms of comedy can invert the world not only briefly but permanently; can strip away the dignity and complacency of powerful figures only to *refuse* to hand them back these attributes when the allotted time for "carnival" is finished. Comedy can effectively channel anger and rebellion by first making them appear to be acceptable and temporary phenomena, no doubt to be purged by laughter, and then harnessing the released energies, rather than dispersing them. (1988, 6)

In her investigations of the ways in which women's humor may be shaped by women's anger and refusal to accept the status quo, Barreca notes that for women, humor and aggression can work together in at least three ways. They can be (1) directed at women, (2) deflected by women, or (3) directed by women (or any other subordinate group) at their oppressors as a way of questioning authority (1991, 72). Much of the Bobbitt humor created by women was of the third type, specifically targeting men and questioning their authority through comedic reversals and metaphors of women's aggression against men who have violated them.[31] Barreca contends that one of the central characteristics of feminist humor is the temporary loss of certainty about men's unquestioned ability to define and control social relations:

> A male friend suggested to me that the real reason many men are worried by funny women isn't even the most obvious one: it's not, he explained, that men are afraid that women will laugh at them. It's not even that men are afraid that women will laugh at them during sex or guffaw at the size of their sexual apparatus. Rather, it's that a man can't *really* laugh and maintain an erection at the same time. . . .
>
> Joking is a reaction that allows the joker to feel in control, however briefly. When someone in a powerless position laughs at the one holding the reins, the figure of authority is sometimes shocked into an awareness of the tenuous nature of any form of control. (1991, 19, 58)

Recognizing that the portrayal of abused women as passive, sick, mentally impaired, or helpless may have the unfortunate side effect of reinforcing existing stereotypes, feminists often told jokes about Lorena and John Bobbitt that depicted Lorena as active, decisive, and aggressive, and John as passive, ignorant, and powerless.[32] Women across the country conveyed a militant and threatening stance when they made V signs for victory by raising two fingers and bringing them together in a snipping motion as a sign of support for Lorena (Ehrenreich 1994a, 74). They also created a new vernacular expression, "We're having a Bobbitt sort of day," to describe times when having to contend with male chauvinism was more likely to meet with their rage than their sympathy (Sameh 1994, 14). These were women who celebrated the woman-warrior images in popular films like *Thelma and Louise*,[33] *Alien,* and *Terminator II*, women who sported bumper stickers identifying themselves as "Beyond Bitch" and who laughed at unflattering comparisons between cucumbers and men. This population of women celebrated "in-your-face" humor that depicted Lorena Bobbitt as a feminist icon. Unconcerned with social propriety and expectations, they attended the daily vigil at the Manassas courthouse wearing T-shirts emblazoned with slogans such as "Revenge—How Sweet It Is" to salute Lorena's actions. For this group, Lorena Bobbitt became a symbol for women who are keenly aware of men's abuse in their daily lives, and who are expressing their anger in unexpected ways.

There was an entire genre of "what I would have done with it" jokes, in which women commented that they would have tossed the severed penis down the garbage disposal or backed the car over it. Women joked that Lorena simply acted on the unspoken social adage "Dress for success—wear a white penis" or laughed heartily when they heard that as a result of his injury, John Bobbitt would now have to sit down to pee (Heimel 1994, 59). A female professor in Indiana who just finished a research project about sexual harassment told the following joke to a small group of students and colleagues: "Did you know that Lorena actually *asked* her husband if he wanted his penis cut off? She did. The problem was that he said 'no,' but she knew he really meant yes" (electronic mail from Heather Walden, 27 Jan. 1994).

In the guise of humor or entertainment, Bobbitt-lore with revenge as its theme sometimes offered thinly veiled warnings to men. One example was a conflated version of two classic urban legends that circulated in early 1994: A man woke up one morning to find a red ribbon tied around his penis. Attached to the ribbon was a note from his wife that simply said, "It could have been you" (Achenbach and Lieby 1994, D7). The message of these jokes, stories, and urban legends was that men, both individually and collectively, were finally going to pay the price for their abusive and violent treatment of women.[34] One especially ominous example was reported in New York City during Lorena's trial, when posters suddenly appeared with images of male genitals being sliced off by a shiny dagger. Underneath the illustration were the threatening words "Rape—A national sport. Well, now it's a whole new ball game, boys!" (Udovitch 1993, 16). Public displays like this one intimated that women were in revolt, threatening that Lorena's actions provided the impetus for other women to follow her lead.

Women's expressions of anger through the castration or penile amputation of abusive men is a theme that also arises in various forms of contemporary feminist humor and art.[35] Some of the best examples appear in Diane DiMassa's cartoons about Hothead Paisan, who is, by DiMassa's own description, a "homicidal lesbian terrorist." Hothead Paisan is a woman who refuses to conform to patriarchal notions of female identity. She constantly encounters, confronts, and often executes obnoxious men. In one cartoon, Hothead uses an axe to sever the penis of a homophobic flasher and then experiments with the penis in different ways: she plays football with it, pretends that it is a microphone, tries to feed it to the dog, makes it into a lamp base, and finally puts it down the garbage disposal (DiMassa 1993, 21–22). In another strip, she takes her revenge by castrating a group of male doctors who have performed unnecessary surgical procedures on women (72–73). At the end of the *Hothead* collection, DiMassa delivers her own metanarrative on the violent images in her cartoons, noting satirically that "a lot of women need to vent their rage and this works for them. . . . Look!" she continues, "we're dealing with fantasy here! Haven't you ever been *so pissed-off* at someone that you fantasized about killing them?" (84).

Newsweek writer Cynthia Heimel suggested that Lorena's actions exemplified the anger felt by many women. They typified the

> rage against guys like the fabulously named John Wayne Bobbitt for attacking, abusing and raping members of our sex. Rage that mutilation of women's bodies and souls are daily fodder for primetime TV, whereas this one instance

of table-turning has caused such a huge hissy-fit. Rage that ritualistic sexual mutilation of girls in Africa is a ho-hum matter of course whereas this [severing John Bobbitt's penis] is Big News. (1994, 58)

Indeed, questions about the recognition and legitimation of women's rage became a strong subtext at Lorena Bobbitt's trial. When the prosecution argued, "This is a case about anger, it is a case about revenge, and it is a case about retribution" (Margolick 1994a, A13), they knew that Lorena would be found guilty if the jury interpreted her actions as retaliation rather than as an irresistible impulse. In turn, the defense built their case on the contention that Lorena's actions were a hybrid of insanity and self-defense, not rage. In order to convince the jury that she responded to an irresistible impulse, it was vital that Lorena's attorneys portray her *not* as angry but rather as temporarily insane—so impaired by the abuse that she was completely unable to control or restrain her actions.[36] Hence, the defense stressed Lorena's fear of John and his abusive behavior. Forensic psychologist Henry Gwaltney testified, for example, that Lorena believed and was immobilized by John's threat, "I will find you, whether we're divorced or separated. And wherever I find you, I'll have sex with you whenever I want to."

Defense attorneys also emphasized Lorena's confused mental state during the time of the incident and glossed over her earlier comments that she would cut off John's penis if she ever caught him sleeping with another woman (Margolick 1994b, A12)[37] and her statement to police just after the incident, "He always have [sic] [an] orgasm and he doesn't wait for me to have [an] orgasm. He's selfish. I don't think it's fair, so I pulled back the sheets then and I did it" (Margolick 1994e, A10). In their 1994 volume entitled *Female Rage: Unlocking Its Secrets, Claiming Its Power*, literary scholars Mary Valentis and Anne Devane explore the ways in which the Medusa myth is relevant to the lives of contemporary women. In interviewing a range of women in the United States, they found that many felt enormous rage at the gender-related limitations and expectations imposed on them, anger so intense that women feared what they might do if they let it explode (Valentis and Devane 1994, 8). Interpreting Lorena's actions as an effort to appropriate the phallus and use it against her rapist, they cite Lorena Bobbitt as an exemplary case of female rage (2):

> Lorena Bobbitt's bedroom surgery entered popular folklore as a symbolic reinstatement of female power. . . . When Lorena became a vigilante taking up Perseus's sword, there was a dramatic turnabout in the old story. In the patriarchal myth, Medusa is a victim; in Lorena Bobbitt's case, it was the victim who claimed Medusa's terrible powers. . . . By identifying with Lorena, women around the world vicariously released their personal fury at husbands, lovers, bosses, and boyfriends. (174–75)

Upon hearing the verdict in Lorena Bobbitt's trial, journalist Catherine Sameh observed that the underlying reason people were shocked by the incident was not only because it involved severing a penis but also because, finally, a woman turned her fury outward rather than inward (1994, 14). Despite the official discourse, some women used Bobbitt-lore to claim and celebrate the idea that it was rage, rather than insanity, that motivated Lorena to strike back at her abuser.

Clearly, Lorena Bobbitt and John Bobbitt became signifiers of many different things to different people, and Bobbitt-lore offered a chorus of discordant voices. People appropriated specific aspects of Lorena's and John's lives, imbuing them with significance in order to symbolize larger social and political issues. Various interpretations were related to ethnic, class, and gender identity. For some people, the Bobbitts became representative of social and political issues extending far beyond the specific circumstances of the two court cases. At the time of Lorena Bobbitt's trial, *Esquire* magazine published the results of a survey of one thousand women, ages eighteen to twenty-five—a group that would have included Lorena (Reimer 1994, A11). The majority responded that they would rather have bigger paychecks than bigger breasts, rather be brilliant but plain-looking than sexy but dumb, and if they could choose, they would rather be Hillary Rodham Clinton than Princess Diana. They were concerned about financial survival and equity, and about being respected for their work and for their contributions to society. Meanwhile, a story in *Gentleman's Quarterly* magazine—designed for a male readership— asked the tired question "What do women want?" and wondered why women are so damn angry (Reimer 1994, A11). The reactions to the Bobbitt trials—and the expressive culture that arose in response—were emblematic of unresolved issues arising from current battles over identity politics. For different groups of people, Lorena Bobbitt and her acquittal became markers of ethnic pride, class differences, male-bashing, or women's rage.

Acknowledgments

My thanks to Dale Chatham, Jean Dickson, Jim Foley, Allison Fraiberg, Joseph Goodwin, Alan Hall, Sandee and Robert Piculell, Glenna Spitze, Margaret Yocom, and all the other people who shared Bobbitt-lore with me. Thanks also to Amadeo Meana for translating the Spanish texts.

Notes

1. Steven Zeitlin of Hastings, New York, reported that his nine-year-old daughter, Eliza Zeitlin, came home from school one day singing the following song to the tune of "In the Jungle, the Mighty Jungle, the Lion Sleeps Tonight":

   In the bedroom, the mighty bedroom,
   John Bobbitt sleeps tonight.
   In the kitchen, the mighty kitchen,
   Lorena grabs a knife.
   A wienie-wack, a wienie-wack.
   A wienie-wack, a wienie-wack.
   A wienie-wack, a wienie-wack.
   A wienie-wack, a wienie-wack. (Personal communication, 21 Oct. 1994)

2. Unless otherwise cited, all information about the events of 23 June 1993 and subsequent legal proceedings and testimony are quoted from live television coverage of Lorena Bobbitt's trial on the Court TV Network and CNN.

3. In March 1996, two years after her acquittal, officials released Lorena Bobbitt from court-ordered therapy and supervision ("Lorena Bobbitt Is Released" 1995, A2). See Speziale for a discussion of the inequities between the verdicts in the cases against Lorena Bobbitt and John Bobbitt. Speziale notes (1994, 312–13) that while John was acquitted and set free, Lorena's acquittal included the condition that she be sent to a mental institution to undergo psychiatric observation and counseling.

4. Bobbitt jokes appeared in the Top Ten lists on 17 Nov. 1993, and 12, 13, and 18 Jan. 1994.

5. In January 1994, people in nearly fifteen million homes subscribed to the Courtroom Television Network (Cash 1994, 17). Because Lorena Bobbitt was charged with malicious wounding, her case was televised, but John Bobbitt's trial was not broadcast, because Virginia state law prohibits televising sex-crime trials (Tousignant and Miller 1994a, A6).

6. See Gleick et al. 1993; Goldstein 1994; Junod 1995; Leonard 1993; and "Unkindest Cut 1994."

7. Jean Dickson, for example, reported that she had heard a biblical parody: "If thine organ offend thee, bobbitt" (electronic mail, 24 Jan. 1994). In a letter to Dear Abby, Luis Campos from North Hollywood, California, mentioned that he almost "Bobbittized" his finger with a knife (*Times Union* [Albany] 2 June 1994: C2). Robert Piculell from Guilderland, New York, reported that while working at his office, he heard someone use the term "Bobbitt" to describe a crimping tool for cutting wire (personal communication, 26 Jan.

1994). In reporting an incident in which another woman severed the penis of a man who abused her, *Filipinas* magazine stated that she "did a Lorena Bobbitt" on him ("Transitions" 1994, 12).

8. When I posted electronic-mail messages requesting examples of Bobbitt jokes, several people wrote back telling me that the topic was not funny or appropriate for scholarly research. One man from Washington, D.C., said: "I don't think the Bobbitt case is worth making jokes about, let alone writing about the jokes. I think cutting off a penis is about as funny as mutilating a vagina" (electronic mail, 27 Jan. 1994). A woman subscriber to WMST-L, the Women's Studies electronic mail discussion group, objected to the idea of posting Bobbitt jokes to the list:

> Far be it for me to tell anyone what their research interests should include, or what they should or shouldn't find funny or laugh at, etc., etc., etc. But I do not think humor about gender-based violence belongs on a women's studies academic information exchange. . . . I am afraid that humor about racial and gender violence is most welcomed (and also most laughed at) by those who would like to believe that it is not all that serious a concern in the first place. (Electronic mail, 16 Jan. 1994)

9. The following message, posted on the alt.feminism electronic mail newsgroup on 21 Jan. 1994, articulated this position:

> Jeez. What 'n' hell is the U.S. justice system coming to? Mitigating factors are supposed to affect the SENTENCE, not the VERDICT. So the guilty person goes free because of publicity. . . . Yes, I'm bitter. And I'm even more bitter because I imagine that some clueless snot will say, "And all the feminists are delighted at this verdict." If any such person reads this group, . . . I want to notify him or her that all the feminists-I-know think Lorena Bobbitt is a sick woman. I think she belongs in a mental institution; (I think her husband probably does, too, but that's a separate issue). . . .
>
> I'm disgusted with the courts for their verdict; with the media for their gleeful coverage; with anyone who tries to make the Bobbitt psychopaths into political symbols.

A brief debate about media perceptions of feminists who supported Lorena Bobbitt appeared on the WMST-L electronic-mail discussion list in Nov. 1994. On 8 Nov. 1994, one subscriber described the following incident:

> At a WS conference we hosted here last year, one woman came to the conference wearing a jacket she had painted with the words "Lorena Bobbitt Fan Club" and a knife dripping blood. (I'm not kidding.) OK, so there, it seems to me, is an example of "grand-standing" that is pretty hard to defend. But it is hardly a representative of "feminism" either, at least of any other feminists I know.
>
> In comes the media: the local paper chose one photograph to illustrate the story on the conference (which was, by and large, an awfully tame

conference by anyone's standards) and it was—you guessed it—a photograph of that jacket.

Now is this "our"/feminism's fault or the media? I blame both; certainly I blame the media more, but then, again, in our desire to create a "safe-space" where everyone can voice their views, do we neglect to offer constructive self-criticism? Do we neglect to "call" other feminists on positions that seem more destructive than helpful? I think so. I can certainly say that I didn't say a word to the woman about her jacket—even though I was angered by it.

10. Nor did this group of feminists comment on the repeating pattern of John's violent behavior. Just months after Lorena's trial, the media reported John Bobbitt's subsequent abuse of another woman. He was arrested and convicted twice of beating his new fiancée, twenty-one-year-old Kristina Elliott, who called police after John hit her, twisted her arm against her back, and slammed her against a wall. See "Bobbitt Convicted" 1994, A2; "Jail" 1994, B11; Romano 1994, A4.

11. See Berns 1994, 26; Duhart 1994, A3; Kaplan 1994, 52; Khanna 1994, 3; Masters 1994, 170; Morrow 1994, 54; and Nemeth 1994, 43.

12. For commentary on the sudden popularity and social acceptability of the word "penis," see Algeo and Algeo 1994; "Rise" 1994; and Safire 1994.

13. Goldberg made this comment as cohost of "Comic Relief VI," January 1994. Robert K. Dornan, a U.S. representative from California, made a similar observation during his 28 Jan. 1994 appearance on the television show "Politically Incorrect." As he made jokes about Lorena Bobbitt, Pee-wee Herman, Woody Allen, and Michael Jackson, he commented, "Think of this not as the year of the dog, but of the penis" (Senior 1994, I1).

14. My thanks to the work of Susan Bordo (1993, 697–98) for calling Sheets-Johnstone to my attention. Bordo offers an excellent discussion of the implications of phallic imagery and cultural interpretations of the male body. It is worth noting that with all of the media attention devoted to penises during the Bobbitt trials, none of the major newspapers in the nation included a photo of the severed penis, even though photos were available through the Associated Press ("Rise" 1994, 8). In television coverage of the trial, cameras briefly focused on a large photograph of John Bobbitt's severed penis that was displayed in the courtroom before panning away to an expert witness ("Bits" 1994, 28).

15. It is significant that the word "castration" (the removal of the testicles), although not technically accurate, was frequently conflated with John Bobbitt's injury. During the Bobbitt trials, the word "castration" was often used to indicate what would happen to other men if women began to seek restitution for male sexual assaults against them. Two months after Lorena's trial,

legislators and journalists named a Florida law mandating the castration of rapists the "Bobbitt Bill" ("'Bobbitt Bill'" 1994, D1).

16. Despite the fact that attorneys use the insanity defense in only 1 percent of all felony trials and that three states have eliminated insanity defenses altogether, some men complained that Lorena's acquittal was a sure sign that the legal system had run amok (Goldberg 1994, 42). Foremost among them was attorney Alan M. Dershowitz, whose writing, lectures, and talk show appearances have made him the best-known critic of what he calls the "abuse excuse" used to defend Lorena Bobbitt (whom he dubbed a "feminist Dirty Harry") and other victims of violent crimes who have struck back at their abusers. Arguing that "most women who are mistreated by their husbands do not resort to the kitchen knife," Dershowitz contended that Lorena Bobbitt "was an angry, vengeful woman who chose to exact revenge rather than exercise the option of leaving her abusive husband" (1994b, 27). Her victimization, he asserted, "must not be allowed to become a moral or legal license to engage in vigilantism" (Dershowitz 1994, A6). Responses like this one were based on a series of unspoken assumptions, including the belief that the U.S. legal system has offered all residents an equitable playing field, a failure to recognize the historic inequalities on which the nation has been based, and obfuscation of the multitudinous ways in which laws have often been written to benefit some people and not others.

17. The following are other examples of this genre:

Did you hear about the new mixed drink called the Tonya Bobbitt? It's a club soda with a slice. (Electronic mail from Joseph Goodwin, 2 Mar. 1994)

Question: What do you get when you cross Lorena Bobbitt and Tonya Harding? Answer: I don't know, but I wouldn't date it if I were you! (Electronic mail from Dale J. Chatham, 11 Feb. 1994)

A cable television special entitled "National Lampoon's Attack of the 5 Ft. 2 Women" aired on Showtime TV on 21 Aug. 1994. Written by Julie Brown and Charlie Coffey, the show featured parodies of Tonya Harding ("Tonya Hardly: The Battle of Wounded Knee") and Lorena Bobbitt ("He Never Gave Me Orgasm: The Lenora Babbitt Story").

During a White House staff meeting, Vice President Al Gore asked the president whether "the operation" would be covered in the new health plan.
"What?" the leader of the free world asked.
"You know, the, ah, penile reattachment," the man who is just a heartbeat from the presidency answered.
"I'll check," Clinton told him, picking up the phone. A quick call to the first lady brought a ruling: Having a penis is a preexisting condition, she assured the two men, and is therefore covered by the plan as corrective— rather than cosmetic—surgery. (Electronic mail from Tony New, 22 Jan. 1994)

18. "Assault on the Male," directed by Deborah Cadbury, 4 Sept. 1994, Discovery Channel television. See also Walter Goodman's (1994) article "Something Is Attacking Male Fetus Sex Organs."

19. Men expressed this concern in rhymes such as the following:

> A Bobbitt's Prayer
>
> Now I lay me down to sleep,
> I pray my penis I will keep,
> And if I wake and it is gone,
> I hope to find it on my lawn.
>
> I hope the dog that's running free
> Does not find that part of me.
> A little precaution I must take
> To keep this part I love to shake.
>
> Much attention I must pay
> To ensure I put that knife away,
> The mower, chainsaw, hatchet, too,
> There's just no telling what she'll do
> To relieve me of my manly charm,
> And I must keep it safe from harm.
>
> I cross my fingers as I close my eyes,
> And I cross my legs to avoid surprise.
> And if my penis takes a whack,
> I pray the doctors can sew it back! (Photocopy circulated anonymously, 1995)

20. On 19 Mar. 1994, Macías was acquitted of charges of mayhem and assault with a deadly weapon, by reason of temporary insanity. Prosecutors complained that Macías's defense attorneys watched Lorena Bobbitt's trial and used similar arguments to present their case ("L.A. Woman" 1994, A2). However, on 19 Apr. 1994, California Superior Court Judge Robert O'Neil ruled that Macías should be retried ("Judge" 1994, A5).

21. Electronic mail from Barbara Mikkelson, 23 Jan. 1994, reporting on a story that appeared in the *Ottawa Citizen* on 22 Jan. 1994.

22. Siebke was found guilty of attempted murder, aggravated assault, and arson, but on 16 Feb. 1994, Judge Jutta Hecht imposed only a three-year jail term on the grounds that Siebke acted in self-defense.

23. According to *Filipinas* magazine, Avelina Rule of Cebu City in the Philippines cut off her husband's penis and chopped it into pieces (Viana 1995, 60), and Gine Espina, also a Filipina, was charged with "mutilation of a reproductive organ" for a similar crime ("Transitions" 1994, 12). Filipina activist Ninotchka Rosca commented that she was surprised by all the fuss about

the Bobbitt cases because "it's a standard thing in the Philippines! If you have someone who's fooling around, you cut off his penis" (Ch'ien 1994, 20). See also Agnihotri (1994, 53) for a discussion of a 1994 film entitled *Purush*, the story of a young woman in India who severed the penis of a lecherous politician. In addition to the above-mentioned incidents, other similar cases were reported by various individuals, newspapers, and magazines. See, for example, "How Do You Say" (1994, 20) for incidents in four countries, and Caher (1995a, 1995b) concerning the case of Vicki-Crystal A. Wright from Albany, New York, who was charged with second-degree assault for a Feb. 1990 incident in which she severed the penis of a man who allegedly attempted to rape her. See also Lewis (1994, 2) and Nemeth (1994a, 66) for discussions of the 1992 acquittal of a battered woman in Canada who allegedly cut off her husband's penis. On 22 Jan. 1994, Jiri Severa posted this notice about related incidents on the alt.feminism electronic mail newsgroup:

> In Canada we have had "a spate" of three castrations in the last two years . . . , none of which resulted in the perpetrator ending up in jail. One of the cases was [only] an attempt, which resulted in minor injuries to both parties. The charges were dropped. In another, a substitute teacher nearly cut off all of her lover's penis (this was an extramarital affair). She was charged with attempted murder, as she had tied him down and left him to bleed to death. She is a fugitive from justice, eluding arrest since last April. Finally, in a scenario almost identical to that of the Bobbitts, a Mississauga woman in 1992 completely severed her husband's penis. It was reattached, and she was later acquitted. The jury accepted her act as self-defense (!) against an abusive husband, even though . . . she actually planned the assault and drugged him before cutting him up.

24. Another woman wrote the following letter to Dear Abby, expressing her sympathy and understanding:

> Dear Abby: About the Lorena Bobbitt case: I am a 60-year-old woman, and her story is nothing new to me. I have been married for nearly 40 years to a man who is well-thought-of in the community and who has provided well for me and our family, but if he was ever denied anything in bed, it was a different story. He would throw things, slam doors, take off in the car; then come back still angry and tell me I didn't understand a man's needs.
>
> Rather than risk being embarrassed if the neighbors heard us, or risk upsetting the children, I would give in. I never refused him. He was far from gentle. He thought it was manly to take whatever he wanted. That's the way he got full enjoyment. It was more like rape. If I complained, he would start all over again even though I was worn out and exhausted.
>
> He kept saying I was stupid and didn't understand a man's "needs." The problem was, he didn't understand mine. And he didn't care. I can understand Mrs. Bobbitt's feelings. If I had the courage, I might have done what she did. I assure you, I'm not the only woman who has had

such thoughts. I have always wanted to tell someone this, but I was too ashamed.

Thanks, Abby. I feel better for having gotten this out of my system.

Signed, Georgia (my state, not my name) (Van Buren 1994, 12)

25. Gómez's joke was the only one I heard that overtly addressed heterosexism or challenged heterosexuality as the cultural norm.

26. Friends and family members described the way John repeatedly threatened and hit this five-foot-two-inch, ninety-two-pound woman (John was five feet eleven inches tall and weighed 190 pounds). During her testimony, Lorena Bobbitt related more than a dozen times when her husband had kicked, punched, choked, or raped her (Margolick 1994c, A12) and said that she was afraid of contracting HIV from John because of his sexual relations with other women (Masters 1993, 210). She contended that in 1990, John had coerced her into having an abortion. She wanted the baby, but John convinced her that the child would be ugly and she would be a bad mother. She testified that after the abortion, she "felt like nothing, like my life was over, like I was falling apart. It lasted a long time." Both John's and Lorena's friends testified that they had seen him belittle and strike her for trivial matters, such as how she cooked and dressed. Others stated that they had seen bruises on her face and arms from the beatings she received (Margolick 1994b, 1994c, 1994e). Some of John's male friends testified that they had heard him brag about how he liked to force Lorena to have sex, and how he controlled and dominated her (Margolick 1994b, A10; Miller and Tousignant 1994b).

27. Court-appointed clinical psychologist Henry Gwaltney, who was supposed to be a witness for the prosecution, testified during Lorena's trial that the defendant was in a state of "clinical depression" and that she exhibited symptoms of disorientation, distraction, and sleeplessness; showed no interest in life; and suffered from hyperventilation, anxiety attacks, shaking, cramping, and exhaustion.

28. See also Gelles (1994, A13), who noted in the context of the Bobbitt trials that between two and four million women (and about one hundred thousand men) are battered each year in the United States and that nearly 90 percent of the victims of violence between male and female partners are women.

29. Another similar limerick by a woman follows:

There once was a fellow named Bobbitt.
Rough sex was his forte. She sobbed, "It's
not mine," and objected.
Her pleas he rejected.
So, his wife took a knife and she bobbed it. (Electronic mail from Mary E. Gaiser, 21 Jan. 1994)

30. For additional insight into media images of violent women, see Holmlund's essay, "A Decade of Deadly Dolls: Hollywood and the Woman Killer."

31. According to Barreca, the comic is inherently rooted in cultural particulars. She noted:

> Why not see comedy as the last frontier of the universal, humor as that glorious patch of hallowed ground where we all meet and laugh with equal joy? A charming thought, but dangerous in its attempt to seduce the reader into a belief that we all laugh at the same things, even when we happen to laugh at the same time, that we all see the same thing when we stand next to one another. Comedy, out of all the textual territories explored, is the least universal. It is rigidly mapped and marked by subjectivity. It is most liable to be filtered by history . . . , social class . . . , race and ethnicity . . . , and gender. (1992, 2–3)

> For feminist studies of humor see Barreca (1988, 1991, 1992); Cantor (1976); Collier and Beckett (1980); Coser (1960); Finney (1994); Green (1977); Kaufman and Blake (1980); Klein (1984); Mitchell (1977, 1978); L. Morris (1994); Neitz (1980); Sheppard (1986); Sochen (1991); Stillman and Beatts (1976); Walker (1988); and Weisstein (1973).

32. See Radford for a discussion of the battered woman's syndrome legal defense developed by Lenore Walker in the late 1970s, which takes into account the effects of violence upon women as well as the social constraints that keep them in violent relationships. Radford expresses her concerns that this argument is a "gender-specific, double-edged defense with a tendency to fuel images of abused women as sick or passive, mentally impaired and unable to help themselves" (1994, 190).

33. See Signe Wilkinson's (1993) political cartoon, in which Thelma and Louise drive by Lorena Bobbitt as she walks down the road and ask her, "Want a lift?" Wilkinson, one of few women political cartoonists whose work is nationally syndicated, celebrates the rebellious nature of all three women. For insightful analyses of the image of the avenging or rampaging female in films and the mass media, see Birch (1994) and Holmlund (1994).

34. During her stand-up routine on the January 1994 television special "Comic Relief VI," Whoopi Goldberg offered her own similar commentary on the Bobbitts:

> From my perspective, as a woman, I was so glad to see that someone finally evened up the odds. You know what I mean? It's like [she gestures as if she has sliced off a penis using one hand and is holding it up in the other], mother fuckers are panicking all across the country! Men don't know what to do! Do you realize what a cachet this is? You see, women live with the knowledge that weird shit could happen at any point. You go down a dark alley, and whoop, somebody grabs [attacks] you. And *now*,

men actually have to think about this shit! It's 1994, and the shit is hitting the fan! Women are pissed!

35. For a description of feminist performance artist Karen Finley's use of castration humor and women's retaliatory violence against men, see Pramaggiore (1992).

36. During the trial, clinical psychologist Evan Nelson defined for the court the conditions that must occur under the legal rubric of "irresistible impulse": (1) the accused is able to understand the nature and consequences of her/his act and knows it is wrong, but (2) the thinking of the accused is so impaired by disease or trauma that she/he is totally deprived of the mental power to control or restrain her/his actions. A guilty verdict would have meant that the jury had to find that (1) Lorena wounded John Bobbitt; (2) she did so with the intent to maim, disfigure, disable, or kill him; and (3) she acted with malice (intentionally and without legal justification). In legal terms, malice can result from anger, hatred, or a desire for revenge. The rationale behind the irresistible-impulse defense is that people should not be punished when mental illness precludes them from refraining from the criminal act or prevents them from understanding the nature of their actions (Garcia 1994, 39).

37. Connie James, manager of the nail salon where Lorena Bobbitt worked, testified that Lorena once told her she would cut off John's penis if she ever found him having an extramarital affair (Miller and Tousignant, "Lorena" B3). During Lorena's trial, the defense entered as evidence a list that John kept, naming women with whom he supposedly had sex; Lorena testified that he used it to taunt her (Tousignant and Miller 1994d, A16).

References

Achenbach, Joel, and Rich Lieby. 1994. "We Find the Defendant . . . : The Bobbitt Verdict from the Court of Public Opinion." *Washington Post*, 22 Jan., D1, D7.

Agnihotri, Emily. "Ashwini Bhave Plays Lorena Bobbitt." *News-India Times* 24.12 (1994): 53.

Algeo, John, and Adele Algeo. 1994. "Among the New Words." *American Speech* 69.3: 294–305.

"ASA Upholds Complaint against 'Offensive' Bobbitt Advert." 1995. *New Statesman and Society* 8.377: 8.

Atkinson, Rick. 1994. "The Lorena Bobbitt of Germany." *Washington Post* 17 Feb., C1–2.

"The Ballad of John and Lorena." 1994. *New York Times*, 13 Jan., A20.

Barreca, Regina. 1991. *They Used to Call Me Snow White . . . but I Drifted: Women's Strategic Use of Humor*. New York: Viking.

———, ed. 1988. *Last Laughs: New Perspectives on Women and Comedy*. New York: Gordon and Breach.

———, ed. 1992. *New Perspectives on Women and Comedy.* Philadelphia: Gordon and Breach.

Berger, Arion. 1994. "Class, Not Sex." *New Republic* 210.7: 12–13.

Berns, Walter. 1994. "Getting Away with Murder." *Commentary* 97.4: 25–29.

Birch, Helen. 1994. *Moving Targets: Women, Murder, and Representation.* Berkeley: U of California P.

"Bits and Bobbitts." 1994. *Economist* 330.7846: 28.

" 'Bobbitt Bill' to Chemically Castrate Rapists." 1994. *Detroit News* 2 Mar., D1.

"Bobbitt Convicted of Battery." 1994. *Times Union* [Albany] 28 Sept., A2.

Bordo, Susan. 1993. "Reading the Male Body." *Michigan Quarterly Review* 32.4: 696–737.

Buchwald, Art. "Husbands and Knives." 1994. *Washington Post* 18 Jan., B1.

Caher, John. 1995a. "Slashing Charges Dropped." *Times Union* [Albany] 12 Dec., B4.

———. 1995b. "Top Court Gets Case of Penis-Slasher." *Times Union* [Albany] 11 Nov., B6.

Cantor, Joanne R. 1976. "What Is Funny to Whom? The Role of Gender." *Journal of Communication* 26.3: 164–72.

Cash, William. 1994. " 'Her Visa Was Running Out.' " *Spectator* 272.8637: 16–17.

Ch'ien, Evelyn. 1994. "Asian Americans and the 'New Feminism.' " *A. Magazine* (spec. iss.): 20.

"Clinton Steals the Bobbitts' Spotlight, Briefly." 1994. *Washington Post* 13 Jan., C4.

Collier, Denise, and Kathleen Beckett. 1980. *Spare Ribs: Women in the Humor Biz.* New York: St. Martin's.

Coser, Rose Laub. 1960. "Laughter among Colleagues: A Study of the Social Functions of Humor among the Staff of a Mental Hospital." *Psychiatry* 23.1: 81–95.

Crawford, Mary. 1992. "Just Kidding: Gender and Conversational Humor." In Barreca, 1992, 23–37.

Daly, Mary, with Jane Caputi. 1987. *Webster's First New Intergalactic Wickedary of the English Language.* Boston: Beacon.

Dershowitz, Alan M. 1994a. "The Abuse Excuse." *Times Union* [Albany] 17 Jan., A6.

———. 1994b. *The Abuse Excuse and Other Cop-Outs: Sob Stories and Evasions of Responsibility.* Boston: Little.

———. 1994c. "Provocation Is No Excuse." *Times Union* [Albany] 7 Mar., A6.

DiMassa, Diane. 1993. *Hothead Paisan, Homicidal Lesbian Terrorist.* Pittsburgh: Cleis P.

Douglas, Mary. 1966. *Purity and Danger: An Analysis of the Concepts of Pollution and Taboo.* London: Routlege.

———. 1970. *Natural Symbols: Explorations in Cosmology.* New York: Pantheon.

Duhart, Bill. 1994. "Lorena Bobbitt Case Raised Questions about Domestic Abuse." *Philadelphia Tribune* 11 Feb., A3.

Ehrenreich, Barbara. 1994a. "Feminism Confronts Bobbittry." *Time* 143.4: 74.

———. "Oh, *Those* Family Values." 1994b. *Time* 142.3: 62.

Estrich, Susan. 1994. "Abuse of Victim Defense Puts the Rule of Law on Trial." *Times Union* [Albany] 23 Jan., E1, E3.

Finney, Gail, ed. 1994. *Look Who's Laughing: Gender and Comedy.* Philadelphia: Gordon and Breach.

Fotheringham, Allan. 1994. "The Sweet Mystery of Manhood." *Maclean's* 107.4: 72.

Garcia, Sandra. 1994. "Verdict: Understanding Lorena Bobbitt." *Black Issues in Higher Education* 10.26: 39.

Gelles, Richard T. 1994. "Men, Too, Can Be Victims of Intimate Violence." *Times Union* [Albany] 4 Mar. A13.

Gleick, Elizabeth, et al., 1993. "Severance Pay." *People Weekly* 40.24: 92–96.

Goldberg, Stephanie B. 1994. "Fault Lines." *American Barristers' Association Journal* 80: 40–44.

Goldstein, Richard. 1994. "Grin and Bobbitt." *Village Voice* 39.5: 8.

Goodman, Walter. 1994. "Something Is Attacking Male Fetus Sex Organs." *New York Times* 2 Sept., D17.

Green, Rayna. 1977. "Magnolias Grow in Dirt." *Southern Folklore* 4.4: 29–33.

Heimel, Cynthia. 1994. "Sure, Women Are Angry." *Newsweek* 123.4: 58–59.

Holmlund, Christine. 1994. "A Decade of Deadly Dolls: Hollywood and the Woman Killer." In Birch 1994, 127–51.

"How Do You Say 'Reattach' in Korean?" 1994. *Time* 143 (28 Mar.): 20.

"International Women's Day." 1994. *Turning the Tide: Journal of Anti-Racist Activism, Research and Education* 7.2: 4.

J. 1995. "Memoirs of a Home Wrecker: Why I Love Married Women." *New Woman* 25.1: 78–81.

"Jail for John Bobbitt." 1994. *New York Times* 1 Sept., B11.

"Judge Wants Retrial in Testicle Attack." 1994. *Times Union* [Albany] 20 Apr., A5.

Junod, Tom. 1995. "Forrest Stump." *Gentleman's Quarterly* 65.3: 230–37.

Kaplan, David A. 1994. "Bobbitt Fever: Why America Can't Seem to Get Enough." *Newsweek* 123.4: 52–55.

Kaufman, Gloria, and Mary Kay Blake, eds. 1980. *Pulling Our Own Strings: Feminist Humor and Satire.* Bloomington: Indiana UP.

Khanna, Anisha. 1994. "Mixed Reactions to Bobbitt Case Verdict." *News-India Times* 28 Jan., 3.

Kissling, Elizabeth. 1994. "Skating on Thin Ice: Why Tonya Harding Could Never Be America's Ice Princess." *Undercurrent: An Online Journal for the Analysis of the Present*, 3.

Klein, Julia. 1984. "The New Stand-Up Comics: Can You Be a Funny Woman without Making Fun of Women?" *Ms.* 13.4: 116–26.

"L.A. Woman Acquitted in Husband's Castration." 1994. *Times Union* [Albany] 19 Mar., A2.

Leiby, Richard. 1994. "Bobbitt: A Slice of America." *Washington Post* 11 Jan., B1, B8.

Leonard, John. 1993. "Phallus Interruptus." *Nation* 257.17: 617–19.

Lewis, Robert. 1994. "From the Editor: Tabloid Journalism?" *Maclean's* 107.4: 2.

"Lorena Bobbitt Is Released from Therapy." 1995. *Times Union* [Albany] 3 Apr., A2.

"Lorena Bobbitt no es ninguna heroina." 1994. *El Mundo* 2 Feb., 8.

Lowther, William. 1993. "Battle of the Bobbitts, Round 2: The Case of the Severed Penis." *Maclean's* 106.47 (22 Nov.): 35.

Luckovich, Mike. 1993. "Thanksgiving at the Bobbitts." Editorial cartoon. *Newsweek* 122.21: 25.

"Man Held in Wife's Brutal Slaying." 1995. *Times Union* [Albany] 30 Aug., A2.

Mann, Judy. 1994. "The Lessons of Lorena." *Washington Post* 21 Jan., E3.

Margolick, David. 1994a. "Jury Begins Deliberating Bobbitt Mutilation Case." *New York Times* 21 Jan., A13.

———. 1994b. "Wife Says She Does Not Recall Cutting." *New York Times* 15 Jan., A7.

———. 1994c. "Wife Tells Jury of Love Story, Then 'Torture.'" *New York Times* 13 Jan., A12.

———. 1994d. "Witness Says Lorena Bobbitt Earlier Threatened to Maim Husband." *New York Times* 20 Jan., A12.

———. 1994e. "Witnesses Say Mutilated Man Often Hit Wife." *New York Times* 12 Jan., A10.

Martínez, Javier. 1994. "Cortar por lo Sano." *El Diario/La Prensa* 18 Jan., 21.

Masters, Kim. 1993. "Sex, Lies, and an 8-Inch Carving Knife." *Vanity Fair* 56.11: 168–72, 207–12.

Miller, Bill, and Marylou Tousignant. 1994a. "Bobbitt Acquitted in Attack on Husband." *Washington Post* 22 Jan., A1, A9.

———. 1994b. "Bobbitt Liked Rough Sex, Jury Told." *Washington Post* 12 Jan., A1, A12.

———. 1994c. "'Just So Many Pictures in My Head.'" *Washington Post* 15 Jan., A1, A12.

———. 1994d. "Lorena Bobbitt Said She Would Cut Husband, Ex-Colleague Testifies." *Washington Post* 20 Jan., B3.

"A Million Mrs. Bobbitts." 1994. *New York Times* 28 Jan., A26.

Mitchell, Carol. 1977. "The Sexual Perspective in the Appreciation and Interpretation of Jokes." *Western Folklore* 36: 303–29.

———. 1978. "Hostility and Aggression toward Males in Female Joke Telling." *Frontiers* 3.3: 19–23.

Morris, Linda A., ed. 1994. *American Women Humorists*. New York: Garland.

Morris, Stephanie. 1994. Letter to the Editor. *New York Times* 19 Jan., A20.

Morrow, Lance. 1994. "Men: Are They Really That Bad?" *Time* 143.7: 53–59.

"Most Intriguing People of 1993." 1993. *People Weekly* 40.26: 110–11.

Neitz, Mary Jo. 1980. "Humor, Hierarchy, and the Changing Status of Women." *Psychiatry* 43: 211–23.

Nemeth, Mary. 1994a. "Hot off the Presses." *Maclean's* 107.4: 66–67.

———. 1994. "Judgment Day." *Maclean's* 107.5: 43.

Paglia, Camille. 1994. *Vamps and Tramps: New Essays*. New York: Vintage.

Pollitt, Katha. 1994. "Lorena's Army." *Reasonable Creatures: Essays on Women and Feminism*. New York: Knopf, 145–48.

Pramaggiore, Maria. 1992. "Belly Laughs and Naked Rage: Resisting Humor in Karen Finley's Performance Art." In Barreca 1992, 127–51.

Radford, Lorraine. 1994. "Pleading for Time: Justice for Battered Women Who Kill." In Birch 1994, 172–97.

Reimer, Susan. 1994. "What Exactly Does the 21st-century Woman Want?" *Times Union* [Albany] 27 Jan., A11.

"Rise of the Penis: Fall of Inhibitions?" 1994. *Columbia Journalism Review* 32.6: 7–8.

Roman, Ivan. 1994. "Ventura viene que corta en neuvo merengue." *El Nuevo Herald* 9 Feb., B1.

Romano, Lois. 1994. "Spokesman Gives Verdict on Bobbitt, Says Client Will Need Legal Guardian." *Buffalo News* 27 Mar., A4.

Safire, William. 1994. "On Language: The Horny Dilemma." *New York Times* 6 Feb., F10.

Sameh, Catherine. 1994. "The Rebel Girl: Having a Bobbitt Sort of Day?" *Against the Current* 8.6: 14.

Sanchez, Carlos. 1994. "Neither Icy Roads nor Cold Deters Hispanic Supporters of Lorena Bobbitt." *Washington Post* 20 Jan., B3.

Santana, Maydel. 1994. "Espertos: condena contra Lorena Bobbitt sería golpe para victimas domesticas." *El Nuevo Herald* 21 Jan., B1.

Senior, Jennifer. 1994. "When Politicians Get Silly." *New York Times* 6 Mar., 1–1.

Shales, Tom. 1994. "To Bobbitt or Not to Bobbitt?" *Washington Post* 14 Jan., G1, G7.

Sheets-Johnstone, Maxine. 1992. "Corporeal Archetypes and Power." *Hypatia* 7.3, 39–76.

Sheppard, Alice. 1986. "From Kate Sanborn to Feminist Psychology: The Social Context of Women's Humor, 1885–1985." *Psychology of Women Quarterly* 10: 155–70.

Simon, Rita J., and Cathy Young. 1994. Letter to the Editor. *New York Times* 4 Feb., A22.

Sochen, June, ed. 1991. *Women's Comic Visions.* Detroit: Wayne State UP.

Solinger, Rickie. 1984. "Unsafe for Women." *New York Times* 20 Mar., G17.

Speziale, Bette A. 1994. "Crime, Violence, and the Saga of Lorena Bobbitt." *Affilia* 9.3: 308–11.

Stephanos, Dale. 1994. "And Now, a Bobbitt Update." Editorial cartoon. *Capital Comic Connection* 27 Jan., 5.

Stillman, Deanne, and Anne Beatts, eds. 1976. *Titters: The First Collection of Humor by Women.* New York: Collier.

Tousignant, Marylou, and Bill Miller. "Bobbitt Trial Starts with Details." 1994a. *Washington Post* 11 Jan., A1, A6.

———. 1994b. "Lorena Bobbitt Details Demise of Marriage." *Washington Post* 13 Jan., A1, A16.

"Transitions." 1994. *Filipinas Magazine* 3.30: 12.

Udovitch, Mim. 1993. "The Cutting Edge." *Village Voice* 38.48: 16.

"The Unkindest Cut of All: Enough Already." 1994. *U.S. News and World Report* 116.4: 14.

Valentis, Mary, and Anne Devane. 1994. *Female Rage: Unlocking Its Secrets, Claiming Its Power.* New York: Carol Southern Books.

Van Buren, Abigail [Dear Abby]. 1994. "Bobbitt's Story Not New to Too Many Women." *Times Union* [Albany] 6 Mar., 12.

Viana, France. 1995. "Brown Bag." *Filipinas Magazine* 2.23: 60.

Walker, Nancy. 1988. *A Very Serious Thing: Women's Humor and American Culture.* Minneapolis: U of Minnesota P.

Weisstein, Naomi. 1973. "Why We Aren't Laughing Anymore." *Ms.* 2.2: 49–51, 88–90.

Wilkinson, Signe. 1993. "Want a Lift?" Editorial cartoon. *Capital Comic Connection* 2 Dec. 5.

"Woman Admits Setting Husband On Fire." 1994. *Ottawa Citizen* 22 Jan. 29.

X, Laura, 1994. "A Brief Series of Anecdotes about the Backlash Experienced by Those of Us Working on Marital and Date Rape." *Journal of Sex Research* 31.2: 151–53.

CHAPTER TWELVE

Representing Domestic Violence
Ambivalence and Difference in *What's Love Got to Do with It*

DIANE SHOOS

> Does it seem late in the day to be writing about abused women? Hasn't the subject
> filled our newspapers and magazines and talk shows? Haven't we seen enough
> battered women, enough psychologists, enough lawyers, on "Donahue" and
> "Oprah" and "Sally"? Haven't we watched those terrible stories dramatized often
> enough on the TV Movie of the Week?
> —Ann Jones (1994, 5–6)

One of the most disturbing scenes in director Brian Gibson's 1993 biopic, *What's Love Got to Do with It,* occurs more than halfway through the film when for the first time we see Tina Turner (Angela Bassett) assaulted by her husband Ike Turner (Laurence Fishburne). Knocked off-balance by the force of Ike's slap, Tina lands on a nearby couch and falls behind it in a frantic attempt to escape. In the next shot, Ike, arm flexed and fist balled up, bends over Tina, and pausing between hits, punches her twice in the face. As he does, however, the camera remains fixed in front of the couch in a low-angle medium shot, thereby obscuring the sight of Ike's fist coming into contact with his wife's body.

The moment is an unusual one for Hollywood cinema, renowned for its ongoing love affair with jaw-breaking, eye-popping, gut-spilling violence. Within the context of an otherwise graphic depiction of the brutality of wife abuse as experienced by one of its real-life victims, this literal if momentary "punch pulling" has the quality of an unconscious lapse or omission. For film and media critics, such a textual lapse evokes questions of the visual as evidence ("seeing is believing") and intersects with ongoing debates about the representation of, especially, the violated female body. Viewed within a larger context, this omission is an uncanny metaphor for what battered women advocates like Ann Jones have argued is the continued invisibility of battering in the United States. Following on this claim, in this paper I interrogate the problem of visibility/invisibility as it relates to our ways of "seeing" domestic abuse. I re-view the film *What's Love Got to Do with It* in order to consider how the complexities of gender, race, and class construct popular representations of abusive relationships and how these popular representations can offer us comfortable positions from which to see what we already assume about men as abusers, women as victims, and the racial and class politics of violence.

Considering the events of the past decade, it may seem paradoxical to argue that we still do not see abuse. Certainly this is a social problem that, following the broadcast of the O. J. Simpson double murder trial in 1995, has received increasing attention from the U.S. media and appears to be widely condemned. Yet the trial's controversial verdict and the racial and class tensions that it evoked are manifestations of the complexity of domestic violence as well as our reactions to it. Jones herself comments in her powerful book *Next Time She'll Be Dead*, published the year before the Simpson trial:

> A great many people now agree that men who beat up their wives or girl-friends do a bad thing. Many understand that children who witness such violence against their mothers can only be harmed by the experience. Many sympathize with battered women, and hardly anyone any more—apart from religious fundamentalists—seems to think that women should put up with abuse. . . . But no matter how you interpret the numbers it's clear that male violence is not going *down*. . . . Why, when things seem to have changed so much for the better, do they seem so much the same? Why, when we actually keep score, do they seem *worse*? (1994, 6–7)

Part of the answer, Jones suggests, is the simple but still compelling point that awareness is not always the same as understanding: the ubiquity and visibility of battering has not fundamentally changed our attitudes or altered our denial about certain aspects of abuse. Having heard the voices of battered women and seen their photos, many people—including many feminists—still have only a superficial knowledge of the emotional labyrinth of the lived experience of domestic violence. We thus fail to comprehend the scope and depth of the abuser's control, which may assert itself through physical, psychological, social, and financial means; the variety of strategies through which this control is maintained; or the loving behavior that is part and parcel of the cycle of abuse. Our sympathy notwithstanding, we may underestimate the terrible dilemmas that a battered woman faces, the serious risks she takes, and the price she pays no matter what choices she makes—even those that seem to be for her ultimate good. As a result, we may minimize or discount (if no longer label masochistic) the victim's powerful emotional attachment to the abuser, which researchers note exists "not because of the violence, but in spite of it" (Jacobson and Gottman 1998, 51). As private individuals who witness or suspect battering, we may still succumb to the temptation to remain silent out of embarrassment or respect for privacy. As public citizens—police officers, judges, and jury members—we may still lean toward treating abuse as a family matter rather than a criminal act and thus fail to pursue and prosecute abusers to the full extent of the law.

As Jones argues, above the veneer of awareness and *zero tolerance* hover the ghosts of old attitudes about abuse. They haunt us especially in the form of latent ambivalence about battered women, embodied in the persistent question that we know we shouldn't ask but that revisits us nonetheless, if only in our minds: "Why does she stay?" On some level we may continue to condemn abused women, if not for the battering itself, for their bad choices or their failure to terminate abusive relationships.[1] Speaking about what she calls our "pernicious habits of mind," Jones comments:

> Whether we blame battered women or pity them for their plight, we tend to think of them as a kind of pariah group, rather like prostitutes, who apparently choose to live "abnormal" and dangerous lives because of some peculiar kinks of background and personality. (After all, we think, she *could* leave.) (1994, 14)

As Jones notes, even more pernicious is the fact that it is these very attitudes that often cause abused women to keep silent, "out of shame and a fear of being blamed, thereby appearing to acquiesce to violence" (14).

Other ghosts inhabit our attitudes toward batterers. In her pioneering 1979 work *The Battered Woman*, Lenore Walker enumerated not only myths about abused women but those surrounding the motivations and characteristics of the abuser, such as "batterers are unsuccessful and lack resources to cope with the world," "batterers are psychopathic personalities," "the batterer is not a loving partner," "batterers are violent in all their relationships" (24–28). Although Walker's study is twenty-three years old at this writing, only within the last eight years have there been any significant challenges to these myths in the form of sustained research on the methods, motives, and psychology of batterers.[2] Indeed, some of our most harmful habits of mind have manifested themselves not in what we think about batterers but in our failure to think about them. In popular as well as clinical discourses on domestic violence, the place of the batterer has been virtually empty, causing two male researchers to remark: "It is sometimes forgotten that men's violence is men's behavior. . . . What is surprising is the enormous effort to explain male behavior by examining characteristics of women" (quoted in Jones 1994, 153). Statements like the one from an American Medical Association report issued in the mid-1990s—"Each year, 4 million women are battered in the United States" (quoted in Felder and Victor 1996, 69)—point to the continued tendency to treat abuse as something that happens to women rather than something that a current or former intimate partner does to them.[3]

In sum, if some of our previous habits of mind seem to have changed, others have simply gone underground or, to use the term Stuart Hall has applied to a kind of invisible or naturalized racism, become "inferential": that is, they have "premises and propositions inscribed in them as a set of unquestioned assumptions," making them more difficult to identify and address (1981, 36). Current ideas about domestic violence have also been complicated and ambivalence compounded by often competing contemporary discourses on victims and victimization, sexual politics in/after feminism, theories of female subjectivity and agency, and the meaning and politics of difference. As a result, responses to domestic violence in the new millennium are at once reformed and recidivist, outwardly resolute yet internally conflicted, more open yet just as frequently displaced and/or repressed.

A case in point is the representation of abuse in popular culture, specifically popular visual media. No longer relegated to daytime talk television and self-proclaimed women's channels like Lifetime and Oxygen, or social documentaries shown primarily on public broadcasting channels or in art cinemas, the topic of abuse has been embraced by primetime television and the Hollywood movie industry. In 2002, for instance, domestic violence was featured on multiple episodes of the perennially popular television dramas *ER* and *NYPD Blue* and the much-lauded HBO series *Six Feet Under* and *The Sopranos*. The same year it was one of the subjects of the Academy Award-nominated film *In the Bedroom* (Field 2002), starring Sissy Spacek and Marisa Tomei, as well as the Jennifer Lopez vehicle *Enough* (Apted 2002). These productions followed in the footsteps of earlier films such as *Sleeping with the Enemy* (Ruben 1991), *What's Love Got to Do with It* (Gibson 1993), and *Dolores Claiborne* (Hackford 1995) in positioning abuse at the center rather than the periphery of the narrative.

This list suggests that representations of domestic violence, like women directors and producers, seem to have finally broken through the celluloid ceiling. Yet, as I propose in the pages that follow, despite their increased number and accessibility, there are nonetheless modes of invisibility at work in many of these representations. These modes include the tacit denial of the many complexities and contradictions of abuse, to which there are no easy Hollywood solutions; the continued if continually disavowed construction of abused women and abusive men as the Other; and, most significantly, the linking of this Otherness to particular categories of race and class.

What's Love Got to Do with It is one of the best-known and most commercially successful of the "new wave" of Hollywood films on domestic violence, owing perhaps to Turner's status as a black female star who survived an abusive relationship and went on to become a solo Grammy Award-winning rock and roll artist. *What's Love* sets itself apart from other recent film representations of abuse by offering audiences a powerful, nuanced portrait not only of a battered woman but of the complex psychology and tactics of a male batterer. Most importantly, the film's focus on a black man and woman whose musical success became their ticket out of poor, working-class families provides the opportunity for an analysis of the ways in which larger ambivalences about race and class become caught up with and support those that circulate within discursive formulations of abuse.

The primary goal of this discussion, then, is to re-view Gibson's film through a variety of intersecting discursive lenses, including that of the growing literature by both researchers and victims of abuse.[4] Admittedly, it has become almost a critical cliché to argue that representations not only reflect but help to shape social experience. Yet, particularly in the case of domestic violence, it bears repeating, as Joan Scott reminds us, that experience itself is not a natural or transparent category and that simply bringing hitherto invisible experiences to light is not a productive end in itself:

> Making visible the experience of a different group exposes the existence of repressive mechanisms, but not their inner workings or logic. . . . For that we need to attend to the historical processes that, through discourse, position subjects and produce their experiences. It is not individuals who have experience, but subjects who are constituted through experience. (1992, 26)

For my purposes here, then, experience is defined not in opposition to discourse or representation, but as Teresa de Lauretis has proposed as "a complex of habits resulting from the semiotic interaction of 'outer world' and 'inner world,' the continuous engagement of a self or subject in social reality," a reality that increasingly includes visual texts (1984, 182).

At the same time, the material and social consequences of experience mean that it cannot be reduced to mere discourse. Indeed, I want to suggest that examining the complex of discourses that constitute subjectivity may be particularly crucial in the case of a form of violence whose victims are psychologically and often physically isolated from society and which, as one of the most underreported crimes in the United States, is less likely to be the subject of open discussion. In other words, what we see in the widely available popular culture representations of domestic violence may have serious implications for our ability to recognize and intervene in abuse.

Domestic Violence and Difference

> No one has to "provoke" a wife-beater. He will strike out when he's ready and for whatever reason he has at the moment. I may be his excuse, but I have never been the reason.
> —Letter excerpt from an abused woman (quoted in Martin 1981, 3)

The first I heard of women's lib was when *Time* magazine ran this picture of some
women waving their bras in the air. Great picture, but I didn't really get it. . . .
They were talking about "liberation"—but liberation from, like, housework. That
was the least of my problems. My problem was simply survival.

—Tina Turner (1986, 170)

As I have noted, the concept of difference/Otherness is mobilized in multiple ways in discourses on domestic violence. Canadian psychologist
and researcher Donald Dutton comments, for instance:

A woman returning to an abusive relationship represents a salient example of
what, to common sense, is unusual or counter-normative behavior. In other
words, outside observers, be they male or female, believe that they and others would act differently than does the assaulted woman. Furthermore, from
their perspective, there do not appear to be tangible impediments to her leaving: she is not physically confined, imprisoned, under constant surveillance.
When we observe behavior that appears unusual and is not externally determined, we tend to attribute it to a trait indigenous to the person who performs the behavior and overlook the impact of subtle situational forces on
his/her behavior. (1995, 169)

Such reasoning allows us to retain our conviction that, despite its apparent ubiquity, domestic violence is an aberration. Most importantly, it erects
a mental wall around abuse, marking both batterers and victims as Other
and reassuring us that we could never be them. Jacobson and Gottman
pinpoint this often hidden anxiety:

When we first started our research one question we heard frequently was,
Why do battered women stay in these abusive relationships? This question implies an accusation, namely, what is wrong with these crazy women for staying
with these awful men? Often what the questioner really means is, "They are
not like me. I would never stay. It's their own fault, and don't ask me to care
about them. Serves them right for not getting out." (1998, 136)

Similarly, referring to the deep divide among feminists in the 1980s
about the Hedda Nussbaum case,[5] Gloria Steinem observed, "Either you
allow yourself to realize that it could have happened to you or you're so
invested in making sure it couldn't have been you that you reject the
victim" (quoted in Jones 1994, 176). Yet for those who assume the latter
stance some of the research on trauma is less than reassuring. Judith
Lewis Herman, for example, has noted that survivors of trauma attribute
their survival primarily to good luck rather than any particular mental
or emotional strength (quoted in Jones 1994, 174). Such a perspective flies
in the face of our collective idea that we would not succumb to abusive
behavior or tolerate its continuation.

The need to see ourselves as above and beyond the reach of domestic
violence also resonates in our definitions of abuse. It is well established

among researchers that physical battering is a very small part of an abuser's tactics and that, correspondingly, emotional or psychological abuse is the primary form of domestic violence. Jacobson and Gottman observe, "Emotional abuse is so common in batterers that, in the majority of instances, emotional abuse is *not* followed by physical abuse" (1998, 62). They go on to note that this form of abuse persists after physical abuse subsides and that it is often the most important factor in a woman's decision to leave (148). Commenting on the persistence in popular imagination of the notion that only physical battering merits the designation abuse, Felder and Victor remark, "There are very few individuals who are immune to or exempt from becoming either a victim or a batterer, and those who claim that they have never been in an abusive relationship might change their minds if they were to learn all the different forms that kind of relationship can take" (1996, 204).

This reluctance to accept broader, more complex definitions of domestic violence may be even more acute for feminists in the new millennium. Acknowledging that even in a Western democratic country like the United States women are still subjected to such a heinous form of sexism may seem to call into question the very achievements of feminism and undermine conviction about the possibility of female agency within patriarchy. So-called anti-victim feminists such as Katie Roiphe, Naomi Wolf, and Camille Paglia may be especially resistant to calling attention to abused women as an oppressed group with special needs, since from this perspective doing so seems to define these women as passive or weak and thus may encourage them to abdicate responsibility for their own welfare and independence. Yet, as Alyson Cole points out in her excellent article on the rhetoric of anti-victim feminism:

> Women's liberation can be neither properly conceived nor actualized if women are considered nothing more than victims. But as formidable as this problem is, it is unlikely to be resolved by ignoring women's oppression. Women have been and continue to be discriminated against as women, despite their great advancement over the course of the last quarter of a century. (1999, 90)

Popular and clinical discourses about abused women have also been structured, often in conflicting ways, by issues related to racial and class differences. On the one hand, beginning with Lenore Walker and Del Martin in the 1970s, battered women researchers have struggled to counter the myth that abuse occurs only in relationships between low-income, working-class men and women of color, pointing to evidence that neither race, education, nor financial or professional status guarantees women immunity from domestic violence. Indeed, testimonies and exposés of abuse in middle-class, professional households suggest that humiliation and fear of exposure—which compound the problem of underreporting—

may be especially acute for these women, who believe that they should be *above* the abuse or able to control it and whose careers and professional reputations may also be at risk.[6] On the other hand, just as mainstream feminism's emphasis on commonality and unity long suppressed crucial discussions of the diversity of female experience (a diversity evident in the citation from *I, Tina* [1986] that describes Tina Turner's reaction to "women's lib"), focus on the widespread occurrence of abuse has contributed to a tendency to theorize domestic violence outside of social categories or to underplay its significance. Recently, however, advocates and researchers have underlined the importance of balancing an under-standing of the ways in which abuse cuts across lines of difference with analysis of the particular social, racial, and economic contexts in which it occurs. Felder and Victor comment, "While economic or social status does not eliminate certain men from becoming batterers, the techniques they use to control their partners can reflect their level of education or sophistication. In all cases, however, without exception, the batterer uses whatever means are within his social, financial, and emotional power to control his partner" (1996, 205).

The lived social experience of race and class and the racist and classist meanings all too frequently assigned to them are central to an analysis of the politics and representation of violence against women, including domestic violence. Susan Bordo's (1997) observations about the decision in the O.J. Simpson case foreground this point. Bordo suggests that the verdict of the Simpson jury points to an "intellectual failure to *think* race and gender at the same time, let alone to analyze the interrelations between the two," a failure that she describes, in language that recalls that of Ann Jones, as "more indicative of contemporary habits of thought than unique" (103). She goes on to comment, "Popular culture provides virtually no models of such multidimensional, analytic thinking but instead continually encourages us to take sides, assign villains and victims, come to the 'bottom line' and so forth" (103). Given Bordo's claim, it seems particularly important to closely examine popular culture texts such as *What's Love Got to Do with It* that mobilize and condense the multiple meanings of difference.

Representing Domestic Violence

> It was like a horror movie. That's what my life had become: a horror movie, with no intermissions.
>
> —Tina Turner (1986, 138)

Based on a screenplay by Kate Lanier, *What's Love Got to Do with It* has many of the characteristics of other performance musical bio-pics, whose codes and conventions consequently structure the experience of domestic violence as it takes place on screen. The film's narrative, for instance, has a rise-fall-rise line that alternates between private moments that reveal Ike's increasingly abusive treatment of Tina and performances and interviews that portray an apparently happy, successful professional couple. This counterpoint between public *niceness* and private *roughness* is ironically echoed in Tina's stage introduction to the song "Proud Mary," where she tells the audience: "We never ever do nothin' nice and easy; we always do it nice and rough." *What's Love*, however, ultimately reveals the destructiveness of this cycle even as it effectively demonstrates that violence and coercion are completely compatible with the abuser's conception of love. Furthermore, by foregrounding the socio-cultural and ideological contexts in which Ike's abuse of Tina takes place, including the tacit acceptance of his behavior by her family and most of her friends and colleagues, the film not only avoids the temptation to blame the victim but also reveals the many subtle but powerful pressures and deterrents that work to keep women imprisoned in abusive relationships.

In his introduction to the collection *Mythologies of Violence in Postmodern Media*, Christopher Sharrett remarks, "The belief in violence as an aberration is a prominent aspect of American ideology" (1999, 12). The narrative of domestic violence in *What's Love* presents an important challenge to this ideology through its emphasis on battering, not as an involuntary or aberrant reaction to stress or anger, but as one point along an extended continuum of male dominance. Similarly, the film does not focus solely on instances of physical violence but situates these along an ever-escalating trajectory of abuse that includes a broad range of controlling behaviors that exert their own psychological damage. The beginning of *What's Love*, for instance, chronicles more subtle forms of manipulation in the form of Ike's comments to young Anna Mae (Tina Turner's birth name) about her behavior and personal appearance. In one early scene he asks Anna Mae to open her mouth; when she obeys, anticipating a kiss, he inspects her teeth as if inspecting a horse and promptly orders her to go to the dentist. In the film, Ike's attentiveness carries with it the threat of disapproval and rejection that itself can function as a form of control: when he comments that Anna Mae is "putting on some pounds," she nervously begins to apologize until he expresses his approval.

As the film's narrative progresses, such controlling tactics, camouflaged as affection and concern, evolve into more overt instances of dominance that prioritize Ike's welfare and needs over Anna Mae's. After the birth of their first child, Ike kidnaps an anemic Anna Mae from the hospital in order to avoid canceling a series of important concert dates that will further his career. When she objects that she is seriously ill, Ike plays on her sense of guilt and loyalty and asks whether she is going to listen to the doctor or to her "man." Saying that he wants to take her to Mexico to marry her because he "can't wait any longer," Ike skillfully transforms abduction into seduction through song: leaning toward Anna Mae and holding out a wedding ring as a bribe, he croons "You're just a fool, you know you're in love." A reverse shot of Anna Mae shows her face softening as she then responds with the rest of the musical phrase.

The abduction scene is framed on either end by home movie footage, two in a series of such scenes that serve as temporal transitions in the first half of the film. The first home movie shows Ike filming his new-born son in the nursery and then Anna Mae in her hospital bed, sur-rounded by her mother and sister and a disapproving doctor who tells Ike that Anna Mae is too sick to be discharged. The grainy black and white images of the wailing baby and Anna Mae's wan, exhausted face stand in sharp contrast to the ostensibly happy occasion. Similarly, the home movie of the Mexican wedding scene, accompanied on the soundtrack by Ike and Tina singing "It's Gonna Work Out Fine," concludes with a mock fight in a limousine, foreshadowing the later ride to the Hilton where, sub-jected once more to Ike's beatings, Anna Mae fights back in self-defense and shortly thereafter makes her escape. The home movies function, then, as an inadvertent visual record of the violent underside of marital bliss.

The music that punctuates the film's narrative also serves to decon-struct Ike and Tina's relationship. Many of the song lyrics suggest that certain controlling behaviors are not only socially acceptable but desir-able, the mark of true passion. The title and words of the first number that the young Anna Mae rehearses with Ike's band, "I Wanna Be Made Over," make explicit both the power that Ike already exerts over her and her own vulnerability to his obsessive attention. A sequence of her per-forming "A Fool in Love," with the lines "You know you love him, you can't understand / Why he treat you like he do when he's such a good man," follows immediately on a scene of verbal and psychological abuse. Shortly after Ike beats Anna Mae and she blames herself for criticizing him and then pledges to take responsibility for getting the relationship "back on track," we see her in the studio recording "River Deep," whose second verse compares the woman in love to a "faithful puppy" who al-ways follows her lover around. Such musical cues are reinforced at strate-gic moments by the film's visuals. During the "faithful puppy" line, for instance, the camera cuts pointedly to a shot of a stony-faced Ike, angered by Anna Mae's first solo venture.

What's Love counters the myth that domestic violence is an individ-ual pathology and identifies it instead as the product of a set of culturally sanctioned attitudes about men and women, attitudes supported on mul-tiple levels by a range of institutions, including popular culture. The point here is not to condemn popular culture as a *bad object* but to understand how it functions and participates in the particular ideological climate that the film delineates. In this context, scenes like the "I Wanna Be Made Over" sequence, while seemingly unremarkable in the larger flow of the story, are in fact narratively overdetermined. The montage of Anna Mae's physical transformation from innocent girl into sexual seductress operates most obviously to connect the film with other star and "overnight success" narratives: the specifics of Anna Mae's transformation—we see her modeling outfits for Ike's approval and later dying her hair blond at his request—recall other male-orchestrated makeovers such as Kim Novak's transformation in *Vertigo* (Hitchcock 1958). *What's Love*, however, explicitly links male obsession to a media-perpetuated female ideal. In the scene where Ike tells Anna Mae to get a bleach job, he first states that he wants her to look like Marilyn Monroe and then, gesturing to a large billboard featuring a blond woman, commands, "Make her look like that." Perhaps most striking is the racial specificity of this ideal, its coding of femininity as necessarily white. Significantly, Ike later gives Anna Mae the stage name "Tina" because of its resemblance to "Sheena" and the names of other white jungle goddesses from the Saturday matinee movie serials.

By the time Ike's control finally explodes into the physical assault supposedly provoked by Anna Mae's comment that his songs "all sound the same," the beating, although shocking, seems not an exception to but a logical extension of his already abusive behavior. Anna Mae's plea during the attack ("You promised you wouldn't hit me.") and a later comment by her friend and back-up singer Jackie ("You can't keep hiding those black eyes from us.") indicate that this is not the first instance of physical violence but a pattern of mounting tension, followed by abuse, apology, and increased attention, one that echoes the by now well-documented cycle of violence first identified by Lenore Walker in *The Battered Woman* (1979). Tellingly, after the first scene of physical abuse we see Ike leave a gift on Tina's bed. Immediately following the vicious verbal battering that ends with Ike calling Tina a "sorry mother-fucker," he makes a show of delaying the opening number of their concert in order to move downstage and gently kiss Tina's tear-stained cheek. The staging of this scene in particular brings home the pain of emotional abuse as well as the covert dynamics of domestic violence, in the context of which even apparently loving behavior can be abusive. Jones reminds us, "Those seductive periods of male contrition . . . are not respites from battering, as they appear, but part of the coercive process, pressuring women to forgive and forget, to minimize and deny, to *submit*, and thus to appear complicitous: they *are* battering" (1994, 93).

The sequence where Anna Mae records her song "Nutbush City Limits" and Ike brutally rapes her serves as the turning point in the narrative, a moment of horrific violence after which she tries to commit suicide and then decides to leave the relationship. The scene is set in Ike and Tina's home recording studio, suggesting, as Yvonne Tasker remarks, that work and marriage function together to maintain the image of Ike and Tina (1998, 190). The strong association of "Nutbush" with Anna Mae/Tina—the song is her solo composition about her hometown—gives the scene its centrality in terms of the real motivation for Ike's battering. Tasker notes, "The violence of their fight over this song, that she has written, comes to signify their struggle over creativity, popularity and her independence" (190). Thus, rather than a momentary loss of control, Ike's battering is symptomatic of his need to manipulate all aspects of Anna Mae's life, from her emotions and her personal life to her work and professional achievements. This need in turn stems from Ike's fear of abandonment, suggested in the film through his repeated comment to Tina, "I suppose you gonna leave me now," which itself becomes a self-fulfilling prophecy and has its parallel in Tina's own abandonment by her mother.

What's Love Got to Do with It challenges some of the most common misconceptions, prejudices, and myths surrounding domestic violence. Like *Sleeping with the Enemy* (Ruben 1991) and *Enough* (Apted 2002), which portray abused women who terminate abusive relationships only to be stalked and threatened by their abusers, *What's Love* makes the important point that the story isn't over and women aren't safe just because they leave. At the point when Anna Mae escapes from Ike in their hotel room and runs to a nearby Ramada Inn, it would have been narratively convenient to abandon the domestic violence plot for the more upbeat rock star success story. Instead, in tacit response to the question "Why doesn't she just leave?" the film relates the experience of not only Tina Turner, but many abused women who find themselves more rather than less endangered when they finally break away from their abusers (Jacobson and Gottman 1998, 239; Jones 1994, 149–50). Significantly, in the final scene of *What's Love*, as Tina is about to go on stage for her comeback solo concert, Ike sneaks past security and enters her dressing room, brandishing a gun and threatening her life.

Yet there are, equally, tensions and splits in this text that are emblematic of those found in discourses on domestic violence more broadly. Indeed, this scene sends another, dangerous message. When Ike threatens her, Anna Mae dares him to shoot her, recalling the earlier limousine scene where she beats him back. Such moments seem to imply that the ultimate solution to domestic violence—rather than to seek help or to make a plan to achieve safety—is to simply stand up to the abuser, a tactic that may put women at increased risk (Jacobson and Gottman 1998, 252–53).

Furthermore, in spite of the fact that, through the character of Jackie, the film acknowledges the importance of informal support systems for abused women, it fails to address the role that institutions such as the police and the legal system play in either intervening in or, in some cases, facilitating and perpetuating domestic violence. Thus, just as its star narrative and performance numbers foreground Turner's phenomenal talent and her superstar potential, the film's portrayal of Turner as a fighter, who through her newfound religious faith succeeds in saving herself, comes perilously close to suggesting that the responsibility for the abused woman's fate begins and ends with her. To put it another way, although *What's Love* doesn't blame the victim for the abuse itself, it continues to place the burden of change solely on her shoulders. In this way, the film conforms to Hollywood's much-analyzed penchant for narratives of individual triumph over those that chronicle collective action or the possibility of social intervention or systemic change. In a similar way, the film's focus on a celebrity figure obscures the problems of material resources, childcare, and custody that confront many victims of abuse and serve as powerful obstacles to leaving.

Other tensions in this film relate specifically to interrelated issues of performance and spectacle, stardom, and race. Yvonne Tasker notes that performance as a cinematic mode has allowed black women, in particular, movement, however limited, into films. She goes on to comment on the double edge of this mode: "Performance has long been a Hollywood staple, allowing the production of both female flesh and women's work as sexual spectacle, whilst simultaneously evoking women's strength through the very power of the performance" (1998, 184). Such a tension is evident in Turner's representation in *What's Love*. There is no doubt that in many ways Turner's image in and out of the film intersects with stereotypical representations of woman as fetishized sexual object (her ad campaign for Hanes stockings is a striking example). However, the power of her voice on the soundtrack and the incredible energy of the musical performances in the narrative in many ways make it difficult to come away from *What's Love* with anything other than an impression of strength and independence. The disjunction between sound and image in the performance sequences of the film—the use of the real Tina Turner's voice over Angela Bassett's body—may unconsciously enhance this effect.

Along with Tina Turner's career as a successful black vocal artist, her previous film appearance as the matriarch Auntie Entity in George Miller's 1995 film *Mad Max 3: Beyond the Thunderdome* and her ongoing construction as a star are of course important as contexts for *What's Love*. Many critics and theorists have observed that a star's image is never homogeneous or complete, but dynamic, incorporating diverse and conflicting elements. Tasker's comments about the complex layering that characterizes the construction of the star are relevant here:

The star's body, worked out/on, transformed or preserved by surgery as it is, both offers and undermines a guarantee of authenticity, that of the "natural-ness" of the star herself (whether this is in terms of natural talent or natural beauty). Ultimately the body itself, the supposed ground of what it is to be sexed and raced, for example, a body which is only ever experienced by an audience as an image in any case, provides just one more layer to the star image, operating as another component that is worked over. (1998, 180)

Clearly, *What's Love*'s final sequence, consisting of a direct cut from Bassett to a shot from behind of Turner performing, is meant to mend the film's voice/body split and authenticate what we have just seen as *real*. Yet Tasker's analysis of the paradoxical way in which the changeability of the star's body undermines as well as supports authenticity—contributes to an awareness of the body *as* (mere) image—seems particularly significant for a film whose audience may be, first, mentally resistant or unprepared to confront the reality of domestic violence and, second, conscious of the performance/artifice that structures the film's diegesis. Although I do not wish to push this analysis too far by suggesting that these factors completely discredit the abuse we see on screen, it is nonetheless possible that for some viewers they may work subconsciously to undermine the portrayal of Turner's victimization, making the abused body in effect just another layer or role.

Turner's identity as not only a female performer but a black female performer is of prime importance here. In *Cinema and Spectatorship* Judith Mayne argues that "for white audiences, one of the most stereotypical and therefore comforting relationships between black and white is that of performer and onlooker" (1993, 154). Her comments suggest that the very fact of Turner's race may potentially distance as well as engage the audience. Such a possibility leads to larger questions about spectatorship and difference as crucial components of the representation of domestic violence.

Domestic Violence, Spectatorship, and Difference

At the beginning of this discussion I suggested, perhaps rather naively, that the question of how domestic violence is portrayed in film and television might be particularly important because of the ubiquity of these media and their potential access by a large number of viewers, including abused women, many of whom are physically and psychologically isolated by their abusers and for whom external validation is one of the most important factors in deciding to leave the abusive relationship (Jacobson and Gottman 1998, 140). Certainly, however, as cultural critics of all kinds have noted, identification or even what is more mundanely termed "viewer response" is a many-layered and dynamic process rather than a static, unified position, and one constructed by gender, race, class, age, ethnicity, and a multiplicity of factors.[7] In some ways *What's Love Got to Do with It* goes out of its way to point out that abuse cuts across these lines—for example, by noting that Anna Mae, like the real-life Turner, had nothing but a Mobil card and 36 cents when she escaped. Yet these issues are much more complex and intertwined than the flat, one-dimensional treatment that the narrative gives them: for example, despite Ike's control of her finances and the fact that she has only 36 cents in her pocket, Turner's position is not equivalent to, for instance, that of working-class women; certainly the white Ramada Inn manager who takes Turner in, for instance, recognizes her not simply as an abused woman, but as a (presumably wealthy) celebrity.

In a similar and equally intricate way, Tina Turner's position as a black woman from a Southern working-class background is undoubtedly a central factor in the film's reception as well as its production and marketing. As the shots of the horrified white mother and children who see Ike abuse Tina in a restaurant or those of the white clientele who witness the couple's bloody entrance into the Hilton lobby suggest, many spectators will associate the abuse in the film with particular class and racial stereotypes like those Tina Turner herself confronted when she sought help. In an interview in *Vanity Fair,* she comments, "In those days, believe me, a doctor asked you what happened and you say, 'I had a fight with my husband,' that was it. Black people fight. They didn't care about black people" (Orth 1993, 172). Similarly, scenes of Ike's drug use and womanizing may allow spectators to attribute his behavior to his cocaine habit or see it as a natural part of the degenerate lifestyle of sixties (especially black) R & B musicians. And, while the graphic sounds and images accompanying Ike's rape of Tina in the sound studio convey the inhumanity and degradation of domestic violence, they are also consistent with the racial stereotype of the black man as savage animal. On this level, what the film tells us is what we already assume about the volatility and violence of black heterosexual relationships. Perhaps it is not surprising, then, that the predominantly white viewers who made up the audience when I saw the film laughed during the scene where Tina returns Ike's blows as the limousine speeds past their names on the marquee.

Black feminist critic bell hooks's reaction to *What's Love* brings home the fact that spectator response is based on a complex of elements and does not divide neatly along, for example, gender or racial lines (1994). Speaking of the film in the course of an interview, hooks remarks, "What I kept thinking about was why this culture can't see a serious film that's not just about a black female tragedy, but about a black female triumph. It's so interesting how the film stops with Ike's brutality, as though it is Tina Turner's life ending. Why is it that her success is less interesting than the period of her life when she's a victim" (41)? In this way, hooks rightfully insists that the narrative's portrayal of abuse be considered not in isolation, but rather in the historical context of the representation of black women within Hollywood cinema. In the same way, a full analysis of *What's Love* would need to consider the often contradictory Hollywood film representations of black men.

hooks's comments suggest that the fact that abuse does indeed occur across lines of difference makes its representation and corresponding issues of spectatorship more rather than less complex, the need for a diversity of representations and spectators more and not less urgent. In addition, it calls for divergent critical methods and perspectives that attempt to identify, confront, and analyze rather than dismiss or reconcile the contradictions of difference. As hooks states, it demands a focus on, precisely, "the question of representation, what function it serves, whose interests" (1990, 71). In the case of *What's Love Got to Do with It*, it entails open acknowledgement of the functioning of gender with and through race and class and rigorous dialogue about the ways in which a film that condemns domestic abuse in the black community can at the same time perpetuate racist ideas about both black men and black women. Ultimately, an examination of the intersections of abuse and difference requires a radical reconceptualization of both terms, a rewriting of difference itself, as Linda Gordon (1991) has so eloquently argued, not as separation or immobilizing pluralism, but as a series of relationships of power that have repercussions for all subjects.

Like the moment in the film where Anna Mae confronts her own bruised and bleeding face in the hotel mirror, the release of *What's Love Got to Do with It* marks a shift in cinematic representations of domestic violence. In its foregrounding of abuse as a spectrum of controlling behaviors bolstered by popular culture's image of passionate love, this film deconstructs many of the habits of mind that have functioned to keep abuse invisible. Nevertheless, another moment from the film sticks in the mind: that of the look of desperation on Tina Turner's face as she is raped by her husband inside the transparent walls of the recording studio. Through its lack of acknowledgment of the need for systemic support and fundamental institutional change for battered women, along with its failure to directly confront the racism and classism that inform our attitudes about domestic violence, *What's Love* also serves as a barometer of our denial and ambivalence, our failure to contend with the continued invisibility of abuse.

Acknowledgments

I would like to thank Marilyn Cooper, Judith Mayne, and Cindy Selfe for their insightful comments on early drafts of this article and Vicky Bergvall,

Heidi Bostic, Elizabeth Flynn, Diana George, Stephen Pluhacek, and Patty Sotirin for their generous intellectual and moral support during the later stages of revision.

Notes

1. Deborah Sontag notes in her cover story in the 17 November 2002 *New York Times Magazine* that "abused women often make calculated decisions to stay with their partners. Sometimes a woman really has no choice; she's scared that leaving would make him more dangerous, or she doesn't think she can survive financially on her own. But other times she stays for the same reasons that people in other kinds of imperfect relationships do: because of the kids, because of her religion, because she doesn't want to be alone or simply because she loves him" (54).

2. See the work of Donald Dutton (1995) and Neil Jacobson and John Gottman (1998).

3. As Jones has remarked, the term *domestic violence* is itself a euphemism, since all available data indicate that men are overwhelmingly the major perpetrators of this crime. I have retained this term in my discussion because of its common usage, along with *abuse* and *battering*. Although my focus here is exclusively on domestic violence in heterosexual relationships, I wish to emphasize the importance of acknowledgment and analysis of abuse that occurs in same-sex relationships.

4. These categories often literally overlap. The first chapter of Ann Jones's *Next Time She'll Be Dead*, for instance, recounts the author's own abuse at the hands of her father (1994).

5. Nussbaum was a battered woman who testified against her partner Joel Steinberg after he beat to death their six-year-old illegally adopted daughter Lisa. For a detailed account of the controversy surrounding Nussbaum, see Jones's articulate analysis in chap. 6 of *Next Time She'll Be Dead: Battering and How to Stop It* (1994).

6. See, for instance, Hillary Johnson's article "The Truth about White Collar Domestic Violence" (1995), part I of Ann Goetting's book *Getting Out: Life Stories of Women Who Left Abusive Men* (1999), and Susan Weitzman's *"Not to People Like Us": Hidden Abuse in Upscale Marriages* (2000).

7. For a critical discussion of cinematic theories of spectatorship see Mayne (1993).

References

Apted, Michael, dir. 2002. *Enough*. New York: Sony Pictures. Motion picture.

Bordo, Susan. 1997. *Twilight Zones: The Hidden Life of Cultural Images from Plato to O.J.* Berkeley: University of California Press.

Cole, Alyson M. 1999. " 'There Are No Victims in This Class': On Female Suffering and Anti-'Victim Feminism.' " *NWSA Journal* 11(1):72–96.

de Lauretis, Teresa. 1984. *Alice Doesn't: Feminism, Semiotics, Cinema*. Bloomington: Indiana University Press.

Dutton, Donald G. 1995. *The Domestic Assault of Women*. Vancouver: UBC Press.

Evans, Patricia. 1992. *The Verbally Abusive Relationship*. Holbrook, Mass.: Bob Adams.

Felder, Raoul, and Barbara Victor. 1996. *Getting Away with Murder: Weapons for the War against Domestic Violence*. New York: Simon and Schuster.

Field, Todd, dir. 2002. *In the Bedroom*. New York: Miramax Films. Motion picture.

Gibson, Brian, dir. 1993. *What's Love Got to Do with It*. Burbank, CA: Touchstone Pictures. Motion picture.

Goetting, Ann. 1999. *Getting Out: Life Stories of Women Who Left Abusive Men*. New York: Columbia University Press.

Gordon, Linda. 1991. "On Difference." *Genders* 10(1):91–111.

Hackford, Taylor, dir. 1995. *Dolores Claiborne*. New York: Castle Rock Entertainment. Motion picture.

Hall, Stuart. 1981. "The Whites of Their Eyes: Racist Ideologies and the Media." In *Silver Linings: Some Strategies for the 80's*, ed. George Bridges and Rosalind Brunt, 28–52. London: Lawrence and Wishart.

Hitchcock, Alfred, dir. 1958. *Vertigo*. Universal City, Calif.: Universal Studios. Motion picture.

hooks, bell. 1990. *Yearning: Race, Gender and Cultural Politics*. Boston: South End Press.

———. 1994. *Outlaw Culture: Resisting Representations*. New York: Routledge.

Jacobson, Neil, and John Gottman. 1998. *When Men Batter Women: New Insights into Ending Abusive Relationships*. New York: Simon and Schuster.

Johnson, Hillary. 1995. "The Truth about White Collar Domestic Violence." *Working Woman* March:54–57; 92–96.

Jones, Ann. 1994. *Next Time She'll Be Dead: Battering and How to Stop It*. Boston: Beacon Press.

Martin, Del. 1981. *Battered Wives*. Volcano, Calif.: Volcano Press.

Mayne, Judith. 1993. *Cinema and Spectatorship*. New York: Routledge.

Miller, George, dir. 1985. *Mad Max 3: Beyond Thunderdome*. Burbank, Calif.: Warner Brothers. Motion picture.

Orth, Maureen. 1993. "The Lady Has Legs." *Vanity Fair* 56(May):114–21, 166–77.

Ruben, Joseph, dir. 1991. *Sleeping with the Enemy*. Los Angeles: Twentieth Century Fox. Motion picture.

Scott, Joan W. 1992. "Experience." In *Feminists Theorize the Political*, ed. Judith Butler and Joan W. Scott, 22–40. New York: Routledge.

Sharrett, Christopher. 1999. *Mythologies of Violence in Postmodern Media*. Detroit: Wayne State University Press.

Sontag, Deborah. 2002. "Fierce Entanglements." *New York Times Magazine*, 17
    November:52–57, 62, 84.
Tasker, Yvonne. 1998. *Working Girls: Gender and Sexuality in Popular Cinema.*
    New York: Routledge.
Turner, Tina, with Kurt Loder. 1986. *I, Tina.* New York: Avon Books.
Walker, Lenore E. 1979. *The Battered Woman.* New York: Harper Perennial.
Weitzman, Susan. 2000. *"Not to People Like Us": Hidden Abuse in Upscale
    Marriages.* New York: Basic Books.

CHAPTER THIRTEEN

"Non-Combatant's Shell-Shock"
Trauma and Gender in F. Scott Fitzgerald's
Tender Is the Night

TIFFANY JOSEPH

The era between the wars is marked by an intensified attention to gender issues that, in the eyes of many, worked to overturn repressive gender identities. After all, during World War I, suffragists lobbied for political agency while other women donned overalls to join the war effort as factory workers, and still others traveled to Europe to serve as nurses. With so many men away at the front, women assumed roles previously denied them and made household and economic decisions usually reserved for the "men of the house." It appeared that the ideology of gender was changing. And, after the Great War, the situation *had* changed; the twenties bore witness to rising hemlines, increasing sexual openness, and voting rights for women. Despite these changes, however, American gender relations in the 1920s and 1930s weren't completely harmonious. As often as not, change was met with backlash, freedom with restriction, enthusiasm with fear. Thus, although the era between the wars did produce an opportunity for gender liberation, it also produced conditions that abetted a traumatization of gender.

War, because of its disruption of traditional familial and social roles and authority, is one of the reasons for this gender upheaval. War is a "gendering activity, one that ritually marks the gender of all members of a society, whether or not they are combatants" (Higgonet qtd. in Berg 1993, 441). The time after any war, therefore, is often spent reorganizing domestic and economic spheres to conform to gender ideals, but the situation after World War I was especially volatile. By the time war broke out, gender identities were already undergoing a process of change and interrogation. In the newly modern era of the early twentieth century, Victorian notions of manhood and womanhood were destabilized and challenged. Or, perhaps it is more accurate to say that these Victorian notions persisted but were becoming increasingly difficult to recognize, accept, or fulfill. On one hand, suffragists and other feminists challenged the contention that a woman's rightful place was in the home: "For many women, moreover . . . the war facilitated not just a liberation from the constricting trivia of parlors and petticoats but an unprecedented transcendence of the profounder constraints imposed by traditional sex roles" (Gilbert and Gubar 1989, 299). Despite these gains, however, women still struggled against resentment and resistance during and after the war. Many men—and some women as well—rejected the wisdom of a female migration into public, economic, and political spheres.

Men, on the other hand, struggled with an elusive ideal of manliness. While Victorian mores dictated that middle-class men be independent breadwinners who claimed heroism and respect in the world of business, modern reality instead presented a series of numbing, repetitive, white-collar jobs that required neither heroics nor initiative (Filene 1998). At first, the Great War seemed the ideal opportunity for American men to reestablish their masculinity. Here, perhaps, was the chance to reclaim manliness on the battlefield. However, instead of becoming heroes, soldiers often found themselves reduced to anonymous bodies in trenches, where life and death seemed the result of dumb luck rather than bravery, skill, or cunning. Sandra Gilbert and Susan Gubar write,

> World War I virtually completed the Industrial Revolution's construction of anonymous, dehumanized man, that impotent cypher who is frequently thought to be the twentieth century's most characteristic citizen. . . . Whether he shot off his own hands in an attempt to escape the front or had his hands or feet or worse shot off by the enemy, his manhood was fearfully assaulted: by a deadly bureaucracy on one side, and a deadly technocracy on the other. (1989, 259)

Meanwhile, at home, women often occupied the jobs vacated by soldiers sent to the front. In 1918 England, for instance, 700,000 of the 1.3 million employed women were in jobs previously filled by men; a similar situation undoubtedly existed for American women as well. Certainly such a change in power and position would have been threatening to men and, accordingly, when the war ended, men struggled to redraw the lines of access and power, and women, despite new experiences of employment and political agency, found themselves expected to resume their places in the domestic sphere. Describing the state of gender relations after the passage of the Nineteenth Amendment, Peter Filene argues, "[o]utside of the familiar female havens, it remained a man's world, and most men wanted to keep it that way" (1998, 129).

Thus, while change was happening, it was also contested, and traditional ideas of gender did not disappear; rather, these gender ideals frequently surfaced in traumatic ways in an atmosphere of heightened gender anxiety. Gains in gender equality met with all-too-frequent backlash as individuals and groups struggled to hold their ground. Penny Summerfield writes,

> [c]ontemporary responses suggest that neither men nor women perceived what was happening as the maintenance of the gender divide, let alone the further polarization of the sexes. Nowhere is this clearer than in the evidence, from across national boundaries, of men's hostile and suspicious reactions to what they perceived as encroachment on their territory. (1997, 5)

This hostility, uncertainty, and insecurity ignited tensions already present within conceptions of gender. Not only was it becoming increasingly difficult to perform gender ideals, it was becoming increasingly unclear what that performance should look like.

In this paper, then, I would like to explore the implications of gender performance from the context of war and postwar trauma in order to examine the intersections of gender and trauma. Judith Butler's (1993) work on gender performativity and Cathy Caruth's (1997) work on trauma offer starting places to interrogate the ways that gender is traumatic and the ways that trauma is gendered. Specifically, I will be examining this relationship vis-à-vis F. Scott Fitzgerald's 1934 novel *Tender Is the Night*.[1] Much of Fitzgerald's work concerns itself with gender, and more than a few critics have pointed out Fitzgerald's own gender anxieties, especially in response to the avowed masculinity of the high modernists whom he admired. As Frances Kerr writes, "Asserting masculinity but confessing femininity is a thread that runs through several of Fitzgerald's private declarations" (1996, 409).

Tender Is the Night brings the gender concerns described above to the foreground, and the novel's preoccupation with mental illness, psychological decline, and performance provides an ideal starting ground for my questions about the relationships between gender and trauma, trauma and performative gender, and trauma and the body. To attempt to answer these questions I will begin by looking at the nature of trauma and post-traumatic stress disorder as illustrated in the novel. Then, I will discuss how these traumas are gendered and how such trauma relates to gender performativity in the era between the wars.

In many ways *Tender Is the Night* is a book that is difficult to summarize. More sprawling and perhaps more flawed than Fitzgerald's *The Great Gatsby* (1925), *Tender* is nonetheless a visceral and effective novel. It is also, because of its nonlinear narrative and change of perspective, aligned more closely with the narrative experimentation that characterizes much modernist writing.[2] Although the novel traces the fates of several American expatriates living or working in several parts of Europe, the main protagonist is the aptly and unfortunately named Dick Diver[3] and, primarily, the novel is about Dick's decline. Dick is an intelligent, promising psychiatrist who, after the publication of some pamphlets and a text, serves as an American military psychiatrist in World War I. Through a friend and fellow doctor, Dick meets the young psychiatric patient Nicole Warren who was institutionalized for schizophrenia following the incestuous advances of her wealthy father, Devereux Warren. Ultimately, the two fall in love and marry. After scandals and affairs, Nicole and Dick eventually divorce, and by the end of the novel Dick has become a drunken, anonymous figure, the former promise of his career disintegrated and forgotten.

Although I will be discussing several other characters and events in the novel, Dick and Nicole's relationship is the obvious place to begin looking at the relationship between gender and trauma. Nicole's schizophrenia, explicitly connected by Fitzgerald to the specific event of incest, offers an example of one of many types of trauma in the text. One central characteristic of trauma and posttraumatic stress disorder is repetition, a characteristic frequently demonstrated by Nicole. Cathy Caruth (1997) writes that such repetition is the victim's attempt to claim his or her survival; it is a cycle brought about by the victim's inability to assimilate or understand the original traumatic event. This traumatic repetition, or reenactment, certainly describes Nicole's relationship and marriage to Dick. As a doctor, Dick assumes a paternal role; he is both father figure and lover to Nicole. Through Dick's embodiment of the paternal/protective father/lover position, Dick and Nicole reenact the incestuous relationship that instigated Nicole's illness. And later, Nicole reenacts the original event once more in her affair and later marriage to Tommy Barban, a career soldier and friend of the Divers: "In layman's terms, she is not cured, has not worked out the original neurosis, but simply switched doctors, under the pretext that the new man is a more forceful father figure than the man she has used up" (Burton 1985, 138). Fitzgerald symbolically illustrates Tommy's assumption of Dick's role when Tommy wears Dick's clothes after staying the night at the Divers' villa in France. Fitzgerald, then, shows the way that trauma, although it may be based on one original event, is cyclical and self-replicating. Trauma is something that is relived, reenacted—a fact that becomes evident with several other traumatized characters in the novel.

Nicole's story also allows us to begin to address the ways that trauma is gendered. Nicole's history is one of passivity and victimization, and, as Michael Nowlin (1998) asserts, *Tender Is the Night* is essentially about patriarchal violence. Nicole's trauma seems to level an accusing finger at fathers and father figures, at those who are trusted to heal and nurture but instead abuse and misuse their power and authority. Of course, not all men or all fathers in *Tender Is the Night* are molesters, but Fitzgerald's text nonetheless seems to critique patriarchal power even as it often seems to lament the loss or challenge to such power in the wake of the war. Certainly Nicole's life is lived under the direction of men; decisions about her life tend to be made by the men she is with—her doctors, her lovers, her friends. When she becomes Tommy's lover, Fitzgerald writes, "[f]or the first time in ten years she was under the sway of a personality other than her husband's. Everything that Tommy said became part of her forever" (293). The men in her life define Nicole's very existence—frequently with tragic results.

Although the postwar world was one where women were widely gaining voices in the political and economic spheres, *Tender Is the Night* reveals a certain ambivalence regarding the voices of its female characters. For instance, when Nicole communicates, she must imagine herself as masculine: "Talk is men. When I talk I say to myself that I am probably Dick. Already I have been my own son, remembering how wise and slow he is. Sometimes I am Doctor Dohmler and one time I may even be an aspect of you, Tommy Barban" (162). In some ways, Nicole seems to perceive the way that gender is fluid, the way it can be unhinged or unfixed; she can assume a male persona when the situation seems to call for it. But "talk" still cannot be imagined as a female pursuit, as something acceptable within femininity. Furthermore, by imitating men, Nicole also sometimes recalls those father figures who have participated in her trauma. Thus, while Nicole's gender fluidity seems an improvement over the rigid gender roles that bind many of *Tender*'s characters, her performance of masculinity remains neither liberatory nor playful.

Power and communication rarely exist for women in *Tender Is the Night*, but one notable exception is Baby Warren, Nicole's sister. Wealth gives Baby access to power (as it might have given Nicole power had Nicole not been rendered a victim), and her interactions with Dick illustrate how gender roles and gender identities were contested during this period. Baby intends to buy Nicole a doctor—a medical man who can "look after" Nicole. Dick Diver, because of his middle-class origins, is not the type of aristocratic man Baby imagines, but he nonetheless ends up playing the role. And, despite his initial resistance to the lure of the Warren empire's fortunes, Dick eventually allows Baby to buy him a clinic. Fitzgerald writes, "[t]he idea attracted him. He decided to let Baby speak for him, as one often lets women raise their voices over issues that are not in their hands. Baby became suddenly her grandfather, cool and experimental" (176). Baby's power is described in terms of the masculine—she "became" her grandfather, and Dick imagines himself as "letting" Baby speak for him. Although Dick seems to be almost humoring Baby, his lack of financial power is problematic in terms of Victorian notions of manhood that still influenced postwar ideas of gender. If to be a man is to be the breadwinner, then Dick's masculinity is slighted by Baby's offer. In fact, Dick's image of Baby as her grandfather allows him to imagine a deal between two businessmen and so play down his loss of power to a woman. Still, Dick is frequently "suspicious and hostile," protecting the territory of manhood in the way that Penny Summerfield describes in the citation I referred to earlier (1997, 5); he can only conceive of feminine strength in terms of the masculine, a rhetorical device Fitzgerald uses frequently in the novel.

Near the end of the book, Dick finds himself once more under Baby's power. Dick, now a declining figure in the novel, is arrested and beaten by Italian police, and Baby negotiates his release from jail: "It had been a hard night but now she had the satisfaction of feeling that, whatever Dick's previous record was, they now possessed a moral superiority over him for as long as he proved of any use" (235). Dick, despite his beliefs to the contrary, never had any real power over Baby. His decline represents, on one level, the corresponding decline in masculine power perceived by many men after the Great War. Ultimately, he must depend on Baby for his salvation. Thus, while in many ways *Tender Is the Night* asserts traditional gender hierarchies (by figuring feminine power as masculine, for instance); the novel also usurps them.

While Nicole Diver's situation corresponds with traditional notions of trauma, Dick's fate seems less straightforward and complicates and expands our understanding of trauma. In fact, the cause of Dick Diver's decline has been the subject of considerable interpretive debate. Interpretations range from Dick's failure to withstand the corrupting influence of the Warren money, to his depletion of emotional capital, to his moral degeneration beginning with his extramarital affair with the young actress Rosemary Hoyt. The novel provides no explicit reason for Dick's downfall, but one place to begin thinking about Dick's traumatic decline and its relation to gender is in the novel's frequent references to war.

War-related trauma is most commonly associated with the shell-shocked soldier who is emotionally and psychically devastated by the violence of warfare. Thus, shell shock is a disease of the trenches. From this viewpoint, it would seem that Dick Diver, who served in the war as a doctor, not a combatant, would be spared the horrors of modern warfare and its potentially debilitating consequences. Fitzgerald, however, implies otherwise: "Even in war-time days, it was a fine age for Dick who was already too valuable, too much of a capital investment to be shot off in a gun. Years later, it seemed to him that even in this sanctuary, he did not escape lightly, but about that, he never fully made up his mind" (115). It appears, in fact, that Dick did not escape. Later in the novel, years removed from the war, he wakes up after a nightmare:

> His dream had begun in sombre majesty; navy blue uniforms crossed a dark plaza behind bands playing the second movement of Prokofieff's "Love of Three Oranges." Presently there were fire engines, symbols of disaster, and a ghastly uprising of the wounded in a dressing station. He turned on his bed lamp and made a thorough note of it ending with the half-ironic phrase: "Non-combatant's shell-shock." (179–80)

Nightmares like Dick's are examples of the kinds of traumatic reenactments typical among shell shock sufferers (Niles 1991; Talbott 1997). Furthermore, a common theme in such reenactments is a sense of helplessness in the face of others' destruction. Dick's passivity as he watches the "ghastly uprising" of the wounded is consistent with his non-combative role in the war. Additionally, as a psychiatrist whose job is to make men psychologically able to return to the front, Dick is complicit in their suffering. Although Dick's self-diagnosis may be half-ironic, it is more than half-true. According to Joanna Bourke, a social historian, a sample of

British soldiers suffering from combat trauma revealed that only 20 percent had actually been under fire (1999, 236). Furthermore, she writes, "Major Marvin F. Grieber found that non-combatants within the military suffered the highest level of psychological breakdown because the pacific nature of their jobs brought them little satisfaction" (237). As a war psychiatrist, Dick is certainly at risk for trauma.

Tender Is the Night, however, is also concerned with the ways that trauma is tied to gender and gender expectations. Furthermore, the text suggests why shell-shock or combat records include so many non-combatants. Shell shock is a gendered trauma that is closely linked to ideas of masculinity and femininity, and men who suffered from shell shock were frequently stigmatized as unmanly (Bourke 1999; Harris 1998; Summerfield 1998). Such a charge would be doubly effective—or doubly devastating—in an era in which men were trying to reclaim what they thought was a lost masculine ideal. Joanna Bourke writes that "psychiatrists never tired of implying that the man who collapsed under the strain of combat was 'feminine'" (1999, 241). Dick, a psychiatrist himself, would have been well versed in these condemnations, and when he half-ironically diagnoses himself with non-combatant's shell shock, he is also identifying himself as womanish.

Even Dick's survival of the war is damaging in a sense. First, survivor's guilt is one common aspect of trauma. Additionally, however, it was widely, if romantically, believed that the men who died in World War I were among the best of their generation. Such an assumption would have had a great effect on survivors of the war, since, as Samuel Hynes notes, "if one had survived, one must have been less than those who died" (1991, 371). Thus, Dick's very survival and his later inability to reestablish himself as heroic would have compounded his trauma.

We might think of Dick, then, as not just shell-shocked, but shocked—shocked by his own fading career, shocked by the suddenly untenable ideal of masculinity, shocked by the postwar world itself. And, perhaps he is most shocked to find that he, Dick Diver, once the "only" American man with "repose," once a brilliant and promising doctor, is now emasculated. Dick's feminization might begin with shell shock, but it is also indicated in several other ways throughout the novel, further highlighting how trauma is gendered. Dick's status as non-combatant, for instance, becomes a slight on his masculinity. World War I recruitment posters proclaimed, "Join the Regular Army—It's a Man's Life!" (Woodward 1998, 277), while war itself was "regarded as a true test of manliness" (Mosse 1990, 102). Denied this opportunity (albeit a false one) to demonstrate or prove his manhood, Dick must turn to other outlets. John Haegert argues: "To the degree therefore that Dick abandons or represses his earlier ideas of romantic destiny, he also displaces them onto Nicole, recreating in their marriage an opportunity for 'heroic' action denied him in the war"

(1994, 97). Dick's marriage to Nicole, then, might be seen as an attempt to replace what he has lost by not being a combatant in the war, a way of reasserting his masculinity by reclaiming his status as manly hero: "Masculinity in 1918 was manifested in two ways—in heterosexuality, and in war" (Hynes qtd. in Harris 1998, 292). What is ironic, however, is that while masculinity was still equated with the image of the warrior, World War I offered few chances for such manly demonstrations. The technology of the war itself—gas warfare, aerial bombardment, machine guns—meant that soldiers' fates were often determined by mere chance, or, in the case of gas attacks, on some external factor such as wind direction. In such a situation of passivity and helplessness, it is no wonder that Allison Berg, for instance, describes the Great War as "emasculating" and the World War I soldier as "sexually-deflated" (1993, 442). Dick, then, might be read as an analogue to other men of his time, even those who made it to the front. Whether through combat trauma, anonymity, or perceived social change, World War I veterans and their non-combatant brothers found the ideal of manhood receding, even while they clung to it:

> Most middle-class men of the 1920s were trying to retrieve a time gone by, because only in the frame of the Victorian past did they know who they were and how to act. It had been hard enough then, in the waning years of Victorianism, to "be a man." After the Great War, the task became even more baffling and frenzied. (Filene 1998, 147)

Dick could not reshape his masculinity into the Victorian ideal of strenuous manhood. His attempt to reclaim heroism and therefore manliness in love and work fails. In love, his relationship with Nicole is tainted by his assumption of a paternal role. And, Dick constructs a similar dynamic during his affair with teenage actress Rosemary Hoyt. Shortly before he kisses Rosemary for the first time, for instance, Dick looks at her and says "gravely, . . . Such a lovely child" (63). Dick's career likewise fails to provide a sense of unquestionable masculinity, and may, according to Michael Nowlin, be counterproductive: "Dick's desire to perform the 'world's rarest work' [psychiatry] has uncannily left him performing the world's most common—namely, mothering" (1998, 73). This association with mothering is underscored when Nicole finally leaves Dick near the end of the novel and thus "cut[s] the cord forever" (302). Dick unwittingly substitutes femininity for masculinity and is simultaneously the incestuous father and the incestuous mother, an assertion repeated when, after an argument, Rosemary tells him that she feels like she had "quarreled with Mother" (219). Dick's emasculation is further highlighted by Fitzgerald's description of him as he leaves the clinic that Baby had purchased: "He had lost himself—he could not tell the hour when, or the day of the week, the month or the year. . . . Between the time he had found Nicole flowering under a stone on the Zurichsee and the moment of his meeting with Rosemary the spear had been blunted" (201). Similar to Ernest Hemingway's Jake Barnes in *The Sun Also Rises* (1926), who is literally emasculated by war, Dick Diver has psychologically lost his phallus, a symbol of power that "in Dick's hands, becomes simply grotesque" (Nowlin 1998, 76).

Thus, despite his efforts to the contrary, Dick Diver is repeatedly feminized. Like Nicole, Dick is stuck in a traumatic cycle, replaying the role of the doomed, perverted father, first as a father figure/lover to the actress Rosemary Hoyt, star of the appropriately named film *Daddy's Girl*, and second as a failed psychiatrist whose career fades into minor scandal and anonymity. Dick Diver's traumatic origin seems to stem from his repeated failure to achieve the contemporary masculine ideal. In other words, considering Judith Butler's concept of the performative, we can see that Dick inadequately enacts traditional masculinity. This can be read not so much as a cultural failure, but a biological one:

> The performativity required in fulfilling gender expectation is so ingrained it becomes unconscious, as one perceives his or her gender not as a cultural allocation but rather, as a biological condition. Hence, when the gendering becomes unraveled, it seems to the gendered subject that she or he is becoming undone, somehow ill-functioning, unnatural, and out of sync with his or her inherent sexual nature. (Harris 1998, 301)

Dick's trauma is the social made personal, the trauma of failing to live up to a socially dictated gender ideal. What is interesting is the way that Dick's experiences expose the methods by which cultural constructions become biological imperatives—I must be such and such a way because I am a man, because I am a woman—thus resulting in a gendered type of trauma born of an inability to recognize (or recognizing too late) the performativity of gender. Dick's story informs our understanding of gender ideals during this period and the potential of such ideals to cause trauma or psychic pain. Writing about the connection between trauma and gender, Lynne Layton explains the ubiquity of gendered trauma: "The tomboy and the effeminate male are only the most obvious sufferers of gender identity development" (1995, 113). Dick and Nicole are seen as symbols of a larger concern with gender in the postwar era; they represent both the trauma and the potential violence of gender expectations.

If Dick is the novel's central feminized male, then Tommy Barban, the Divers' militant friend and Nicole's eventual lover and second husband, is *Tender*'s hypermasculine representative, the apparent embodiment of social expectations of manhood. Comparing Dick and Tommy highlights the novel's concern with gender and gender-based trauma and provides an illustration of what happens when gender codes and expectations are actually fulfilled. A career soldier, Tommy is everything Dick is not and comes to replace him as Nicole's lover, husband, and protector. Tommy, as a tried and true veteran of many wars and military escapades, already seems to have achieved the masculine ideal. Describing himself, Tommy says, "Well, I'm a soldier. . . . My business is to kill people" (35). Furthermore, Tommy is the successful suitor, the experienced lover. He is consistent with Joanna Bourke's description of the perception of "normal" men of the period who "were psychologically capable of killing because they were tough, did not mind seeing animals slaughtered, and were actively heterosexual" (1999, 242).

It would be simple, it seems, to read Tommy Barban as the novel's paragon of masculinity, the undamaged male, Fitzgerald's answer to the impending threat of feminization in the postwar world. It becomes increasingly clear, however, that Tommy actually undermines expectations of the masculine and reveals these gender ideals to be hollow and absurd. Tommy's brusque, matter-of-fact violence presents a poor solution to the postwar malaise and anxiety of *Tender Is the Night*. His relationship to the modern world is incongruous; although some parts of the novel idealize the past, Tommy clings to history's most ridiculous heirlooms, such as the antique dueling pistols he always carries. And, his duel with the bumbling, drunk Albert McKisco is no throwback to a lost heroic ideal where "real" men settled their scores in hand-to-hand combat, but is instead merely comic. Later in the novel, Tommy's toughness is exposed as empty bravado. In Munich, while Tommy is drinking with some comrades and laughing his "martial laugh," Fitzgerald notes that Tommy's companions are "always a little afraid of him. [Yet] recently, an eighth of an area of his skull had been removed by a Warsaw surgeon and was knitting under his hair, and the weakest person in the café could have killed him with a flip of a knotted napkin" (196). Hemingway's Jake Barnes may have lost his phallus, but Fitzgerald's Tommy has lost his head. Clearly, this is no solution. Tommy is an anachronism; his methods no longer apply. Furthermore, his invincibility is an illusion, his machismo a performative gesture designed to align himself with social expectations and ideals. Is his gender identity also, as it is for Dick Diver, traumatic?

Fitzgerald does not provide the reader direct access to Tommy's thoughts as he does for Dick, but it is clear that Tommy's character does not provide a suitable alternative to Dick's fate. By the end of the novel, Tommy assumes the role Dick abdicated and becomes part of Nicole's traumatic cycle. Tommy's desperate soldiering also alludes to the trauma of fixed gender ideals. In order to realize the expectation of the warrior-hero denied in modern warfare, Tommy must involve himself in outlandish plots to save kidnapped aristocrats, carry pistols with the hope of reviving the glory possible in hand-to-hand combat, and wear "the uniforms of eight countries" (30). And Tommy, who swears allegiance to no country, inhabits instead the sort of no man's land described by Sandra Gilbert and Susan Gubar: "having traveled literally or figuratively through no man's land, all [modernist anti-heroes] have become not just no-men, nobodies, but *not* men, *un*men" (1989, 260). Thus, Tommy's obsessive return to battle is a sort of traumatic reenactment, a constant battle against feminization.

The connection between trauma and gender coalesces in two short episodes in the novel. The first involves a character referred to as the Iron Maiden, a woman at Dick's clinic who suffers from a skin disorder: "On her admittance she had been exceptionally pretty—now she was a living, agonizing sore. All blood tests had failed to give a positive reaction and the trouble was unsatisfactorily catalogued as nervous eczema" (183). The Iron Maiden is an excellent example of the way that the psychological becomes physical; trauma of the mind becomes trauma of the body. Furthermore, the Iron Maiden illustrates Cathy Caruth's idea of the "speaking wound." Caruth writes that trauma is the "story of a wound that cries out, that addresses us in the attempt to tell us of a reality or truth" (1997, 4). The Iron Maiden's "truth," as well as her trauma, is clearly gendered. She tells Dick, "I'm sharing the fate of women of my time who challenged men to battle" (184). The Iron Maiden seems to be refusing or attempting to refuse the gender expectations of femininity; rather than live through men, she hopes to live through her art by exploring "frontiers of consciousness" that Dick thinks are "not for her, ever" (185). Her refusal has grave consequences, and the trauma caused by fighting against gender ideals has marked her body and her health. "I am here as a symbol of something" (185), she tells Dick, and certainly she symbolizes the difficult "battle" of gender identity. Like other women of her time, she is scarred by her attempt to negotiate the breadth of the feminine sphere. Her wounds bear testimony to the link between mind and body; trauma in one becomes trauma in the other, intertwined and inseparable. Physical symptoms arise from the cultural and social conditions of gender, and the trauma of the mind is the trauma of the body—simultaneously. Trauma, then, is also social, born of external expectations and demands that cannot be fully realized and also, paradoxically, cannot be fully refused.

Another short event at the end of the novel highlights the continuous negotiation of gender and sexual identity. Dick is called to bail two women out of jail, Mary North and Caroline Sibley-Biers. He finds them waiting outside a cell, dressed as French sailors. Explaining their predicament, Caroline remarks, "It was merely a lark. . . . We were pretending to be sailors on leave, and we picked up two silly girls. They got the wind up and made a rotten scene in a lodging house" (303). Dick manages to bribe the police with help from a friend of his, a hotel owner named Gausse. After the women are released, Gausse says to Dick, "I have never seen women like this sort of women. I have known many of the great courtesans of the world, and for them I have much respect often, but women like these women I have never seen before" (306). Gausse has no context for understanding Lady Caroline and Mary North; by dressing as men, they have upset his understanding of women, an understanding that can encompass prostitution, but not cross-dressing or homosexuality.[4]

This incident in the novel reveals a larger concern over the blurring of sexual and gender identity: how do you account for "this sort of women"? Caroline and Mary's actions are merely exaggerations of a more widespread type of cross-dressing during the era: the masculine lines of some flapper styles as well as the uniforms of military women, factory workers, and nurses. The presence of these "uniformed" women before, during, and after the war could easily aggravate men already fearing the slip of masculine power and authority:

> As nurses, as mistresses, as munitions workers, bus drivers, or soldiers in the "land army," even as wives and mothers, these formerly subservient creatures began to loom malevolently larger, until it was possible for a visitor to London to observe in 1918 that "England was a world of women—women in uniforms." (Gilbert and Gubar 1989, 236)

Dress signals gender, and when dress changes, gender is performed differently:

> A woman who dressed as a man was sending a lot of signals. She could be titillating men by inviting them to reveal the truth about her body and therefore her sexual identity. . . . Her apparent claim to be equal to a man could challenge men to prove their superior masculinity by dominating her physically and sexually. Her manly appearance might mean that she would develop manly characteristics and male patterns of behaviour: drinking, swearing, spending her earnings, and making sexual advances. (Summerfield 1997, 7)

After Lady Caroline refuses to pay Gausse for his help in the affair, Gausse kicks her "in the most celebrated of targets" and Lady Caroline's "sailor-clad form sprawled forward on the sidewalk" (306). Gausse asserts his masculinity here, his actions demonstrating both his frustration and confusion, and his desire, perhaps, to "dominate" the male imposter. Lady Caroline and Mary North, by performing masculinity, not femininity, seem to suggest that gender identity can be donned as easily as a sailor suit, a suggestion that is as unsettling to Gausse as it might be for other men who fear their territory is threatened. Here, for Mary and Caroline, gender and sexuality can be enacted playfully; the world around them, however, is still ill prepared for the ramifications of such gender fluidity and playfulness.

In Fitzgerald's novel, the social expectations of gender are too ingrained and omnipresent to deny completely. Yet, accepting these expectations can also be damning. The character of Rosemary Hoyt occupies something of a middle ground between these positions, and she allows for a slightly different means of examining these issues. The importance of gender performativity in *Tender Is the Night* is underscored by the overall prevalence of role-playing and performance in the novel that is best characterized by Rosemary who, as a movie actress, represents the socially constructed ideals to which many of the characters aspire. In fact, the novel opens from Rosemary's point of view, as if to emphasize her particular perspective. At the beginning of the novel, Rosemary is seventeen years old and has just finished her highly successful film, *Daddy's Girl*. Fitzgerald presents Rosemary as both naïve and worldly; on one hand she is young and inexperienced, but on the other hand she is a successful actress who understands the performativity of gender and sexuality. For instance, early in her relationship with Dick, Rosemary fashions herself as would-be lover: "She was astonished at herself—she had never imagined she could talk like that. She was calling on things she had read, seen, dreamed through a decade of convent hours. Suddenly she knew too that it was one of her greatest roles and she flung herself into it more passionately" (64). Rosemary's very understanding of performativity appears to insulate her. Dick sees her as naïve and immature, but by the end of the novel, Rosemary is more intact, more aware, and less damaged than he is. She says to him, "Oh, we're such actors—you and I," and she comprehends the truth of that statement. In fact, it is the "most sincere" thing she says to Dick (105).

Rosemary, who is "Daddy's girl" in the movies, emerges from the novel relatively unscathed, certainly more than Nicole Diver.[5] One reason is that she seems to recognize and utilize performativity to her advantage. Professionally and publicly she is the socially defined feminine; her body is "calculated to a millimeter," defined and constructed by Hollywood (104). She is exploited, perhaps, but she also exploits her exploiters in turn. Michael Nowlin (1998) argues that women, more practiced in the art of masquerade, are in a better position to use the knowledge that both masculinity and femininity are charades. Certainly this is doubly true for Rosemary, who "masquerades" for a living. For instance, when meeting with a director, she muses, "[i]f her person was property she could exercise whatever advantage was inherent in its ownership" (23).

Rosemary, in some ways, does challenge social expectations, partly through the tutelage of her mother, Elsie Speers, who had brought her up on the "idea of work" (40). Before Rosemary embarks on an amorous pursuit of Dick, Mrs. Speers tells her daughter,

[y]ou were brought up to work—not especially to marry. Now you've found your first nut to crack and it's a good nut—go ahead and put whatever happens down to experience. Wound yourself or him—whatever happens, it can't spoil you because economically you're a boy, not a girl. (40)

Like her daughter, Elsie Speers understands that gender ideals are constructs; there is no reason why Rosemary can't move into the economic sphere, a realm typically reserved for men. Rosemary's public femininity is performative and at odds with her "economic" gender. In fact, she uses the performative feminine to enable a masculine independence.

Throughout the novel, Rosemary maintains this independence, and while everyone else declines around her, her character remains fairly stable. By recognizing and using the performative, Rosemary seems to have made gender less traumatic. Certainly she is in better shape than Nicole Diver, the character with whom she can most readily be compared. Yet, like Tommy Barban, Rosemary does not provide a true solution to the problem of traumatic gender. First of all, she cannot live completely on her own terms; she is still subject to the rules and expectations imposed upon her by a patriarchal society. Therefore, Rosemary is always required to maintain the correct image: "Her contract was contingent upon an obligation to continue rigidly and unexceptionally as 'Daddy's Girl'" (110). Fitzgerald, in fact, aligns her with female characters who often submitted to masculine dominance: "Their point of resemblance to each other and their difference from so many American women lay in the fact that they were all happy to exist in a man's world—they preserved their individuality through men and not by opposition to them" (53). The "man's world" of *Tender Is the Night*, however, is neither stable nor supporting and many of the female characters suffer at the hands of a paternal figure.[6] Furthermore, while Rosemary's life isn't especially tragic, it also isn't entirely autonomous, especially at the beginning of the novel. For instance, Fitzgerald writes, "[l]ike most women [Rosemary] liked to be told how she should feel, and she liked Dick's telling her which things were ludicrous and which things were sad" (58). Although Rosemary may be a "boy" economically, she nonetheless seems to internalize social expectations of femininity, thus depriving herself of any shot at real power beyond a sort of economic imitation of masculinity. This imitation can be compared to Nicole's imitation of men when she talks, relying on preexisting masculine assumptions and desires in order to participate in the world. Rosemary's whole career, in fact, is founded on a male gaze and the objectification of women. Describing a screening of *Daddy's Girl*, Fitzgerald writes,

[t]here she was—the school girl of a year ago, hair down her back and rippling out stiffly like the solid hair of a tanagra figure; there she was—so young and innocent—the product of her mother's loving care; there she was—embodying

all the immaturity of the race, cutting a new cardboard paper doll to pass before its empty harlot's mind. . . .
Daddy's girl. Wasn't it a "itty-bitty bravekins and did it suffer? Ooo-ooo-tweet, de tweetest thing, wasn't she dest too tweet?" Before her tiny fist the forces of lust and corruption rolled away; nay, the very march of destiny stopped; inevitable became evitable, syllogism, dialectic, all rationality fell away. Women would forget the dirty dishes at home and weep, even within the picture one woman wept so long that she almost stole the film away from Rosemary. (68–69)

Rosemary's film presents a stereotypical femininity: childish, naïve, pure, sentimental, and irrational. This, too, is the image Rosemary must maintain, the image of the "true woman," the keeper of moral codes, the dainty bulwark that keeps "lust and corruption" at bay—rather than a "modern woman" who might smoke, drink, work, and expect sexual pleasure. The figure of Daddy's girl is, of course, a cardboard paper doll, but it is nonetheless an ideal many of the characters cling to, and the image on which Rosemary bases her career. And, certainly, it could be argued that no other image of woman—one, perhaps that is strong without "tiny fists," one that isn't an "itty-bitty bravekins"—would be so successful. Despite the gains made by women in the 1920s, then, Daddy's girl is still the dominant icon.

Recognizing performativity does not seem to be enough to overcome gender's traumatic potential. By the end of the novel, Dick, for instance, has reached a nadir. His marriage is falling apart, his love affair with Rosemary is over, his career is stalled, and his health is threatened by alcoholism. The man who once claimed widespread adoration from other characters now tells Rosemary that he has gone into a "process of deterioration." He says, "The change came a long way back—but at first it didn't show. The manner remains intact for some time after the morale cracks" (285). Dick is bitter, ruined, but also, apparently, self-aware. With his world crumbling around him, he delivers a speech on acting that strangely parallels Rosemary's earlier comments: "What do you do in life? What does anyone do? They act—face, voice, words—the face shows sorrow, the voice shows shock, the words show sympathy. . . . But in the theatre, No. In the theatre all the best comediennes have built up their reputations by burlesquing the correct emotional responses—fear, love, and sympathy" (288). Dick comments on Rosemary's performance—on everyone's performance—on the ability to play a role, produce the "correct" emotion. He implies that Rosemary has succeeded by exaggerating the proper responses, overplaying just enough, maneuvering "out of character" just enough to regain attention until she can slip back into character again and thus make the lapse part of her attraction. Dick realizes what Rosemary seems to have already grasped on some level—the fact that social expectation can be used—but for Dick, the knowledge is worthless. Not even exploiting the performative insulates Dick from trauma. Eventually, all that seems left in *Tender Is the Night* is performance, and recognizing it as such only robs Dick of his illusions of authenticity.

The world of *Tender Is the Night* is characterized by an upheaval of gender ideology, and its thematic concerns mirror those of the postwar world. Fitzgerald's treatment of gender is ambiguous and contradictory; sometimes, his characters mourn the loss of old, fading ideals, as when Dick, visiting a World War I battlefield, muses sadly, "All my beautiful lovely safe world blew itself up here with a great gust of high explosive love" (57). At other times in the novel the text seems to rebel against strict gender binaries, challenging the wisdom of gender ideals that doom its characters. This is a world in flux, and even as progress is made—a woman can have a career—the status quo and deeply embedded ideas of gender check that progress: a woman's career can only exist through the agency of male desire.

The years after World War I were marked by its effects on gender, but these effects were by no means uncomplicated. As Allison Berg notes, "[i]f war inevitably inscribes gender, it often does so in unexpected and contradictory ways" (1993, 441). Fitzgerald provides no answers, no solutions to the traumatic potential of gender identity except perhaps a call for more flexibility in understanding and characterizing gender. But, his novel does expose the way that gender defined the lives of both his characters and the men and women living in the period between the wars. In *Tender Is the Night*, gender performativity presents a traumatic fact: trauma is not just personal, but social, and often, those social roots are gendered.

Notes

1. Some other novels of the era that explore gender and/or trauma in World War I include Ford Maddox Ford's *Parade's End* (1924), Ernest Hemingway's *The Sun Also Rises* (1926), Helen Zenna Smith's *Not So Quiet . . . Stepdaughters of War* (1930), Edith Wharton's *A Son at the Front* (1923), Virginia Woolf's *Mrs. Dalloway* (1925), and Rebecca West's *The Return of the Soldier* (1918).

2. I refer here to the text as it was originally published, despite Fitzgerald's later complaints that the novel might have sold better if it were arranged chronologically. In 1951, Malcolm Cowley released a version of the novel that rearranges the text in chronological order.

3. Dick's name isn't the only symbolic one in the novel. Others include: Elsie Speers (a phallic name for an influential woman), Tommy Barban (the novel's "barbarian" warrior), Campion (a homosexual character), and Abe North (who finds himself in a racial riot).

4. *Tender Is the Night* contains other references to homosexuality. The attitude of the text is both sympathetic and deprecating. For instance, Dick is sent to interview a young homosexual man for possible admission to the clinic. During his visit, he learns that the young man's father, in an attempt to cure his son, sends him on trips to bordellos and "lashed him with a whip" (244). The obvious cruelty of the father (another example of perverse paternity) is paired with the young man's "abnormality." Nonetheless, Dick thinks of the young man as having a "courageous grace" (245). These episodes, which have little to do with the plot, suggest instead the exploration and re-exploration of a question that is never resolved in the text.

5. At one point in the novel, one of Rosemary's friend's remarks, "You'd never know Mama's little girl" (208). In the world of *Tender Is the Night*, being Mama's girl is quite a bit safer than being Daddy's girl.

6. In fact, the novel's only positive father figure is Dick's father, his "moral guide" (203). Dick's father, however, dies during the course of the novel and exists in the text only as a figure in Dick's memories.

References

Berg, Allison. 1993. "The Great War and the War at Home: Gender Battles in *Flags in the Dust* and *The Unvanquished.*" *Women's Studies* 22(4):441–52.

Bourke, Joanna. 1999. *An Intimate History of Killing: Face-to-Face Killing in Twentieth Century Warfare.* New York: Basic Books.

Burton, Mary. 1985. "The Counter-Transference of Dick Diver." In *F. Scott Fitzgerald*, ed. Harold Bloom, 129–39. New York: Chelsea House Publishers.

Butler, Judith. 1993. *Gender Trouble: Feminism and the Subversion of Identity.* New York: Routledge.

Caruth, Cathy. 1997. *Unclaimed Experience: Trauma, Narrative, and History.* Baltimore: Johns Hopkins University Press.

Filene, Peter G. 1998. *Him/Her/Self.* Baltimore: Johns Hopkins University Press.

Fitzgerald, F. Scott. 1925. *The Great Gatsby.* New York: Scribners.

———. 1934. *Tender Is the Night.* New York: Scribners.

Ford, Ford Maddox. (1924) 1950. *Parade's End.* New York: Knopf.

Gilbert, Sandra M., and Susan Gubar. 1989. *No Man's Land: The Place of the Woman Writer in the Twentieth Century.* Vol. 2. New Haven, CT: Yale University Press.

Haegert, John. 1994. "Repression and Counter-Memory in F. Scott Fitzgerald's *Tender Is the Night.*" *Essays in Literature* 21(1):97–116.

Harris, Greg. 1998. "Compulsory Masculinity, Britain, and the Great War: The Literary-Historical Work of Pat Barker." *Critique* 39(4):290–304.

Hemingway, Ernest. 1926. *The Sun Also Rises.* New York: Scribners.

Hynes, Samuel. 1991. *A War Imagined: The First World War and English Culture.* New York: Atheneum.

Kerr, Frances. 1996. "Feeling Half-Feminine: Modernism and the Politics of Emotion in *The Great Gatsby.*" *American Literature* 68(2):405–31.

Layton, Lynne. 1995. "Trauma, Gender Identity and Sexuality: Discourse of Fragmentation." *American Imago* 52(1):107–25.

Mosse, George. 1990. *Fallen Soldiers: Reshaping the Memory of the World Wars.*
New York: Oxford University Press.

Niles, David P. 1991. "War Trauma and Posttraumatic Stress Disorder." *American Family Physician* 44(5):1663–70.

Nowlin, Michael. 1998. "The World's Rarest Work: Modernism and Masculinity
in F. Scott Fitzgerald's *Tender Is the Night.*" *College Literature* 25(2):58–77.

Smith, Helen Zenna. 1930. *Not So Quiet . . . Stepdaughters of War.* London: Albert E. Marriott Ltd.

Summerfield, Derek. 1998. "Shell-Shock Patients: From Cowards to Victims."
British Medical Journal 317(7169):1394.

Summerfield, Penny. 1997. "Gender and War in the Twentieth Century." *International History Review* 19(1):3–15.

Talbott, John E. 1997. "Soldiers, Psychiatrists, and Combat Trauma." *Journal of
Interdisciplinary History* 27(3):437 55.

West, Rebecca. 1918. *The Return of the Soldier.* New York: The Century Co.

Wharton, Edith. 1923. *A Son at the Front.* New York: Scribners.

Woodward, Rachel. 1998. " 'It's a Man's Life!': Soldiers, Masculinity and the Coun-
tryside." *Gender, Place, and Culture* 5(3):277–300.

Woolf, Virginia. 1925. *Mrs. Dalloway.* New York: Harcourt, Brace, and Co.

CHAPTER FOURTEEN

Microcredit, Men, and Masculinity

FAUZIA ERFAN AHMED

The impact of masculinity on poverty alleviation has been little studied in gender and development studies. The literature on the Nobel Prize–winning Grameen Bank (a bank that gives small loans to women), a paradigm that has emerged as the cornerstone of the global poverty reduction agenda, is vast. However, it does not explore male relatives of the loanee households, their attitudes, or practices. Indeed, changing gender roles have been extensively researched in Bangladesh; the focus, however, has been exclusively on women.

Voices of low-income women are the impetus for this field study. Sharecropper women repeatedly told me that they cannot reach their full potential and help their families climb out of poverty unless their male relatives also transform their attitudes and practices. The everyday existence of poor women is embedded in multiple spheres of extended family and village community; it is inextricably interwoven with that of their male kin. Women want these different contexts to be included in the formulation and implementation of microcredit and poverty alleviation strategies.

By asking gender and development experts to include their male relatives as a solution, these sharecropper women contest the male and female universals that frame the basis of gender and development programs. The concept of "universal man" that is implemented in these programs falsely assumes that men are all alike and inimical to women's rights.[1] On the other hand, this framework also assumes that once the woman starts earning, her husband, as the "universal man," will inevitably start to value her and things will improve in the household.

But this imposition of sameness on the male relatives of Grameen Bank loanees is a belief as yet unsupported by any evidence. Concerns that masculinity is undertheorized in gender and development (Baden and Goetz 1998) and that male violence is not addressed in Grameen Bank training (Schuler, Hashemi, and Badal 1998) have been raised. But there has been no comprehensive investigation of male relatives of microcredit loanees and how different masculinities impact poverty alleviation and gender empowerment programs. Women loanees also have profound questions for the gender and development academics and microcredit practitioners: How can their male relatives be "put right?" How can low-income men become stakeholders in gender empowerment programs? I chose to live with sharecropper families in a village in Bangladesh during 2001 to explore their concerns.[2]

The women's questions are based on the problems they face as they try to become successful entrepreneurs: increased domestic violence

(Bates et al. 2004; Rahman 1999) and little decision-making power over loan use (Goetz and Sen Gupta 1996). Even though their earnings increase household living standards (Pitt and Khandker 1998) and other family members benefit, evaluations of microcredit and gender empowerment show mixed results. I argue, as do sharecropper women, that the answers to these questions are not solved by changes in Grameen Bank program strategy alone; aspects of gender and development theory, on which this program is based, need to evolve. As Johnson and Wilson (2000) indicate, the assumption that women can increase agency as they earn more money, without specific strategies for dealing with gender subordination, needs to be questioned. On the basis of my findings, I argue that manhood can be an analytical category in gender and development theory. If patriarchy as monolithic male dominance has been challenged (Kandiyoti 1987), then masculinity as uniform also needs to be disputed. If, as Wiegman (2002) writes, men have used a subordinate view of universal woman to create solidarity, then a research agenda that explores how the presumed unity of men and women breaks down across religion, race, class, and gender is important.

As part of the larger feminist theoretical project, I argue that it is the way in which microcredit impacts the gendered social relations among and between men and women in the household and how this dynamic affects the multiple dimensions of female agency that needs to be examined. Much of the current debate and polemic focus on attempts to answer a complex question in a simple manner: Have women been empowered or not? In essence, experts look for a zero-sum answer. But it is entirely possible that microcredit has empowered some groups of women in certain ways while disempowering others. Similarly, male relatives can also react in varying ways depending on who they are and what is happening in the household and in the community at a certain point in time. Difficult to measure, gender empowerment is not static; a process as well as a goal, it is subtle and nuanced across time and place. Legitimate concerns have been raised by activists that plural interpretations of contexts and identities can be an impediment to getting things done. But I argue that the "congealed opposition" (Pearson and Jackson 1998, 6) between a liberal feminist agenda that views women's problems as universal and a postmodern feminist approach that analyzes gender as a category in flux is not, in fact, congealed. It can be overcome. This article illustrates how an acknowledgement of the subtlety and complexity of household gender patterns does not have to lead to a state of political and strategic paralysis in microcredit programs.

This perspective of gender and development, then, is the framework for my study of microcredit, masculinities, and poverty alleviation. In this article, I focus on two aspects of what is clearly an overarching indigenous feminist vision: a description and analysis of four different

masculinities in rural Bangladesh and how the Grameen Bank can identify, support, and reward high-minded men to stop domestic violence.

To guide my analysis, I ask the following questions. First, which masculinities support patriarchy in Bangladesh and which masculinities
rebel against it? Second, how can a spectrum of masculinities be used by
microcredit practitioners to empower low-income women and men? Specifically, what kinds of field-based interventions should the Grameen
Bank undertake?

Accordingly, I present vignettes of abusive (*beshi mare*), high-minded
(*udaar*), "mixed," and *habla* (lacking in common sense) husbands, who
exemplify four different masculinities contrasting the following categories of gender empowerment: notions of an ideal wife, domestic violence,
loan decisions, and fatherhood. (With the exception of "mixed," these
terms are indigenous and are used by men and women to describe different masculinities.) I explore two specific questions:

1. What are the different masculinities that these men represent?
2. How can the Grameen Bank include high-minded men in its
   programs so that they can act as social change agents to stop
   domestic violence?

The *Methods* section, which emphasizes the need for ethnography to
inform public policy, is followed by an examination of Grameen Bank
philosophy and a critique of the studies that have had a direct impact on
its program. This segment is then linked to the theoretical confluence of
feminism, men's studies, and domestic violence prevention, a nexus I consider essential for the evolution of gender and development theory. In
conclusion, this multidisciplinary prism is then used to make specific
recommendations for the Grameen Bank program on how to include low-
income male relatives as stakeholders so that domestic violence in loanee households can be prevented.

Methods

The findings of this field-based multimethod study are based on three
ethnographic techniques: participant observation, five videotaped focus
groups consisting of approximately thirty villagers each (total 150) in
four different neighborhoods, and seventy-three interviews. The subset
of seventy-three male and female interviews was chosen from three Hindu,
Muslim, and untouchable villages that were within a five-mile radius of
each other.

Based on geographic proximity, to eliminate possible environmental
confounding factors, this subset was drawn from a larger sample of two
hundred villagers throughout the union. The sample was chosen through

snowballing, a standard anthropological technique, in which conversations with key informants leads to other interviews, and theoretical sampling, the basis of grounded theory in qualitative sociological research methods. I developed, challenged, and reframed hypotheses in the field as I collected data. It is important to note that my sample, unlike Kabeer's (2001), which focuses on male loanees, comprised women who are microcredit loanees of the Grameen Bank and their relatives: husbands, brothers-in-law, fathers-in-law, sisters-in-law, and mothers-in-law.

Trust and access are key in ethnographic research. I chose to work in the villages of Satkhira district because that was where I knew village families, having worked there periodically for the past ten years; my ancestral home is situated in a neighboring union. The investigation lasted from 1999 to 2001. The pilot study was carried out in 1999, primarily to include participants' views on empowerment in the questionnaire; the full-scale investigation followed in 2001. The research team consisted of myself and a Bangladeshi male interviewer, whom I had trained.

Grounded theory and theoretical sampling helped me integrate anthropological and sociological methods. Rural proverbs and songs were part of the grounded theory technique to explore indigenous meanings of empowerment and gender roles and practices. Specifically I developed twelve domains, both indigenous and inductive, ranging from investment in fatherhood to gender wage equity, which were used to investigate the objectives of field study.

Ways of knowing influence what one comes to know. I found that living with the villagers and sharing their everyday concerns, as much as possible, was invaluable. It is also true that the multiple disparities between myself and the villagers as well as the nature of my research raised ethical concerns. Although beyond the scope of this article, these issues occupied a great deal of my everyday existence as a researcher and were incorporated into the research design.

Grameen Bank Gender Strategy: Implementation Without Context

I use a conversation between the local Grameen Bank loan manager and a loanee as a springboard for my analysis of Grameen Bank program strategy. This scenario depicts Mehrun, a long-term borrower for ten years, trying to explain to Habib, the manager, why her husband has forced her to leave. A description of the Grameen Bank, its history, and philosophy is followed by a critique of the salient gender and development studies. I conclude this section by presenting indigenous definitions of empowerment, purdah, domestic violence, and masculinity based on my findings.

A Conversation in the Field

MEHRUN, GRAMEEN BANK LOANEE (IN TEARS): I have to withdraw my savings and to stop being a Grameen Bank loanee. It is not my wish, but this is what my husband wants.

HABIB, GRAMEEN BANK MANAGER: Please don't withdraw. You have been a loanee for ten years. You will qualify for an educational loan for your son's college expenses. You should convince your husband. Everything is in your hands. After all you are the loanee.

MEHRUN (ASIDE TO ME): I cannot displease my husband. I do not wish to lie to him nor do I wish to hide anything from him. After all he is my husband.

As a participant observer, I was both witness to and part of this revealing exchange between Mehrun, a sharecropper female loanee, and the manager of the local Grameen Bank branch. The following week, I visited her home and talked with her husband, Ibrahim, and her son. There was an enormous skills and awareness gap between Ibrahim and Mehrun, who had been both treasurer and chair of her local Grameen Bank committee. Resentful of Mehrun's growing entrepreneurial skills and status, Ibrahim wanted her to quit being a Grameen Bank loanee. Mehrun, as a rural Bangladeshi woman, knew better than anyone else the risks of directly confronting patriarchy. She had to obey his wishes.

On the other hand, Habib told her in no uncertain terms that she was now head of the household, especially since microcredit has given her economic independence. The Grameen Bank manager asked Mehrun to confront her husband and the patriarchal system in which the household is embedded. By so doing, he also asked her (unwittingly) to expose herself to domestic violence. When I later told him that no rural Bangladeshi woman, no matter how much she earned, could defy her husband to this extent and declare herself the head of the household, Habib agreed. He said that he used this argument, illusory as it was, as a last resort. He advised her to challenge her husband out of sheer desperation. As a long-term borrower, Mehrun was eligible for an educational loan for her son's college education. Habib did not want her to lose the benefits (educational, latrine, and home-building loans) Grameen Bank gives to its excellent (long-term) borrowers. An intelligent, committed, and hard-working manager, Habib was also a kind man. But it was clear that he had not been trained to help female loanees deal with the complex and often dangerous situations that arise in the households whenever women challenge traditional gender roles. Habib simply did not know what to do.

Mehrun was compelled to quit the Grameen Bank without being able to enjoy the rewards of ten years of hard work, thrift, discipline, and entrepreneurial development. Her inability to continue was not only a blow to her and the dreams that she had for her household, but it is also a serious obstacle to the Grameen Bank poverty alleviation agenda, which aims to

move poor women out of poverty to sustainable levels of income and assets through a program strategy of graduated loans. (I found it difficult to
get figures on the dropout rates of mature borrowers from the Grameen
Bank, despite several visits and phone calls.) This scenario is not uncom-
mon: A quantitative study of 2,074 households of 104 villages in rural
Bangladesh indicated that 56% of the women said that their husbands
had compelled them not to work outside the household and 78% reported
that they had been forced to give the money to their husbands (Pitt,
Khandker, and Cartwight 2006). Why is this happening? An examination of the history and philosophy of this remarkable organization does
not yield simple answers.

The Grameen Bank: History and Philosophy

The Grameen Bank began in 1976 with the general purpose of providing
banking facilities to the poor. It also aimed to replace the exploitative
money lenders, provide self-employment, and include women so that
they could learn how to manage credit and develop organizational skills.
It was based on the theory that people without collateral can be loanees,
a paradigm shift that has revolutionized banking and poverty alleviation
strategies. As of May 2008, Grameen Bank had 7.5 million borrowers, 97
percent of whom were women. A vast organization, it works in over 82,000
villages in Bangladesh and has over 24,000 employees.[3]

Well known for its management systems, innovativeness, and flexibility, the Grameen Bank does not just lend money. A loanee is also taught
how to manage a business through a series of excellent workshops, which
range from market appraisal to accounting procedures. (However, personnel changes make it unclear whether the excellent management principles on which the organization was founded continue to be sustained;
the workshops program may have been discontinued.) The Grameen Bank
also encourages asset building through mandatory savings and pension
schemes. A loanee who has participated for a certain number of years can
also take out a low-interest loan for her children's education. The Grameen
Bank is more than a bank; it is a paradigm shift. This much-needed innovation continues to provide microloans to the middle and better-off poor
(Wood and Sharif, 1997).[4]

Initially, the Grameen Bank did not focus on women loanees. But Dr.
Mohammed Yunus, the founder, quickly realized that women had to become a priority in order to fulfill the poverty alleviation goals of his bank.
They were also the poorest group in Bangladesh society and at that time
received less than 1 percent of all the credit in Bangladesh (Yunus 1999,
71). Angered by the apathy and discrimination of government officials, senior management felt that development efforts would be enhanced if
women received the money because they would spend it on household
welfare. Yunus declared that 50 percent of all experimental projects would

focus on women. Female borrowership climbed from 25 percent in 1978 to 40 percent in 1983 (Bornstein 1996, 140).

The ability of the Grameen Bank to critique its own programs and then to reinvent itself is perhaps its signal achievement. In their revealing and informative book, Dowla and Barua (2006) describe how the Grameen Bank changed its philosophy after they lost 20 percent of their borrowers in the aftermath of the floods of 1998. Some flood victims had fallen too far below the poverty line to be loanees. The Grameen Bank II model, introduced in 2002, is an attempt to recognize the precariousness of the existence of those who live below the poverty line. Critiquing their original model as rigid, senior management proposed a new vision of open-access savings, flexible loans, self-reliance, and higher education loans to better meet the needs of the rural poor. The Grameen Bank then proceeded to the more difficult task of convincing its staff to transform themselves and to adopt an entirely new banking system.

I argue that this new program design conflates financial and empowerment goals. It does not include what empowerment means to rural women and the obstacles that they face in the household as they try to increase their incomes. An economist himself, Yunus believed that women's income could be the single powerful vector that would change women's self-perception and male attitudes toward women. At the same time, he had to build an efficient and trustworthy credit delivery and recovery system.

Clearly, this meant that there were two very different performance indicators: women's empowerment and credit disbursement and repayment. But neither the Grameen Bank program strategy nor training was based on gender analysis; as a result, the indicators were conflated. Repayment rates became the proxy for women's agency. As the bank grew, area managers who supervised branch managers like Habib, and zonal managers who in turn supervised area managers, ignored qualitative input from the field, focusing solely on what could be numerically measured—namely credit. This reward and training system, which excluded the gendered contexts of women's lives, meant that Habib could not rely on his superiors for any advice or guidance when confronted with the intransigence of Mehrun's husband and the complex impact of microcredit on gender patterns in her household. Despite Goetz and Sen Gupta's (1996) brilliant gender analysis of loanee households, Grameen II also conflates income with agency, quantitative with qualitative, and tangible with intangible. This reinvention, laudable as it is, excludes the realities of the everyday existence of its loanees. I argue that it is not simply Mehrun's "difficult" husband but this lack of sophistication in Grameen Bank program strategy about how gender works in rural Bangladesh that forced Mehrun to leave.

Men, Empowerment, and Spousal Violence

It would be a mistake to think that the philosophy of the Grameen Bank is shaped by Muhammad Yunus alone. Development experts, funded by either the Grameen Bank or the various international development agencies, also influence how the organization thinks about gender. The literature on men, microcredit, and spousal violence is replete with conflicting accounts. Kabeer (2001) cogently argues that mixed evaluations and confusion exist because the women themselves have not been asked. Based on my findings, I present indigenous definitions of empowerment, purdah, and domestic violence, and then distinctions between men, masculinity, and masculine regimes. Against this backdrop, I then critique the literature on microcredit.

Toward Indigenous Definitions

Empowerment. Low-income men and women know what a good life means to them. They want financial security, peace within the household (*shanghare shanti*), to walk with dignity (*shonman rekhe chola*), and voice in village institutions. Financial security, a key to a good life for the villager, requires not only microcredit but a multidimensional package consisting of female property ownership and control, gender wage equity, and salaried jobs. Village men and women both agree that peace at home is paramount; I have accordingly listed it as an empowerment outcome. Living with dignity is central to all villagers, but it means different things to men and women. Gender equity in the legal and political institutions is critical because the presence of women jurors encourages other women to bring their grievances to court. When women realize their leadership potential and hold public office, they enable widespread social change to take place.

There is no question that the Grameen Bank has empowered Mehrun in terms of financial security and social mobility: she gained entrepreneurial and leadership skills and has savings in the bank, which contributed to the household economy. As one of the first loanees in her village, she defied the oppressive form of *purdah* (veil), a social system that segregates space and occupation by gender denying women access to, *inter alia*, business opportunity. Mehrun defied *purdah* by redefining it. As she said, "What I think of my actions is most important. Whether I think that I am going against *purdah* or not is key. I do not think that I am doing anything wrong by joining the Grameen Bank." But increased mobility and asset building are not the only things that villagers value. Peace at home is all important; Mehrun quit the bank because she did not want to jeopardize it.

Domestic Violence: A Gendered Definition of Poverty. If the Grameen Bank has recognized that poverty means vulnerability, then it also must recognize that vulnerability means different things for women than it does for men. The phenomenon of gender-related violence is complex; it ranges from rape and female feticide to pornography and child abuse (El-Bushra and Lopez 1993). Violence exists at four levels: household, community, nation, and international. Each level can then be divided into categories. Several studies give an excellent textured description of violence in rural Bangladesh (Bates et al. 2004; Schuler et al. 1996; Schuler, Hashemi, and Badal 1998). This article focuses on physical and verbal violence at the household level between husband and wife. I do not include violence between other household members.

As Kabeer (2001) notes, village women distinguish between extreme and mild forms of violence. The extreme form, to them, is characterized by frequent—if not daily—beating without reason. This form is defined as "cruelty" by both female *and* male villagers. The mild form of violence means a slap or two on occasion and is dismissed by the wife and the community at large. As one woman said, "My husband has only beaten me 11 times in the 10 years we have been married. I think that's pretty good." In fact, she does not consider him an abusive husband and said that she was happy in her marriage. Village women focus on physical abuse, but they know that words can wound. Sharecropper women cried when they described verbal abuse, even though the incident may have happened years ago. Vivid and haunting, the memory of insult itself is enough to humiliate a victim over and over again.

Men, Masculinity, and Masculine Regime. Men are not a homogenous group, nor is masculinity uniform. Analyzing men is not the same thing as analyzing masculinities. In fact, there are different kinds of masculinities. Individual men conform in their attitudes and practices to a certain kind of masculinity. Masculinities are characterized by certain ideals and social structures in the extended family, but women also can support a masculinity type while some men choose to rebel against it. I build on Nye's distinction (2005) between men and masculinity as two separate but analytically connected categories. But I expand his definition of a masculine regime as ideals and practice to include larger structures. Masculine regimes comprise legal, socioeconomic, cultural, and religious structures that sustain various masculinities. It is important to think of masculinity and masculine regimes as part of gender relations and gender regimes.

Conflicting Studies

Defining Empowerment. Perhaps the earliest definition of empowerment was presented by Hashemi, Schuler, and Riley (1996). It was useful not so much because of its indicators—which ranged from mobility to knowing who the head of state was—but because it compelled gender and development experts to define the concept. Though the authors acknowledge difficulties in creating measures of women's empowerment, it is unclear to what extent their empowerment indicators reflect what empowerment means to the women themselves and in their own words. Loanees like Mehrun have not been asked whether they find knowing the name of the prime minister to be empowering. Goetz and Sen Gupta (1996) challenged this definition and included safety, access to reproductive health, and control over loan usage as components of female agency. At first glance, Pitt, Khandker, and Cartwight (2006), who defined empowerment as an unobserved latent variable, appear to take a more sophisticated approach. Indeed, their literature review is excellent. They rightly stated that bargaining power can change over the duration of the marriage and that traditional sources of female agency should be acknowledged. They also try to correct for the selection bias that may exist in the study by Hashemi et al. (1996). But Pitt et al. (2006) do not emphasize dignity or peace at home, (*shanghare shanti*)—key indigenous empowerment goals that, at the very least, mean no domestic violence.

Men as Loanees or Relatives of Loanees? The debate reverberates around whether Grameen Bank should lend to men as well as women. Clearly, this framework also influences sample selection and analysis. Though they lie in two opposing camps, both Hashemi et al. (1996) and Goetz and Sen Gupta (1996) base their findings on a predominantly female sample. (In fact, the former's sample is exclusively female.) Goetz and Sen Gupta include twenty-two male borrowers, but unlike my study they are not male relatives of women loanees. They also suggest that men should also be included as loanees as a way of changing negative male attitudes, a recommendation with which I strongly *disagree*.

In contrast, Pitt et al. (2006) analyze in great detail why female credit increases the latent empowerment factor. Although they included male borrowers and male relatives, their findings suggest that men not be included as loanees. However, they did not analyze why 68 percent of husbands interviewed believed that their wives were less intelligent than they were, nor why the remaining 32 percent (a surprisingly large number) think that their wives are as intelligent (or more) than they are. Such an investigation would have inevitably led to the analysis of masculinities. Goetz and Sen Gupta (1996) stated that when there is a good relationship between the borrower and her male relative, the loanee finds it easier to make the weekly installments. None of these studies, however, focus on the distinction between individual men and masculinity. In short, there is no explanation of how different masculinities might lead to different gender patterns in outcomes.

Microcredit and Violence. At first, Schuler et al. (1996) stated that micro-credit empowers women by reducing violence, but they later acknowl-edged (1998), using the same data set, that violence increased. They found that it is not microcredit per se that reduces violence among mem-bers, but a selection process whereby only those women whose husbands are agreeable allow them to join such programs. Mahmud (2000) argued the opposite: Women who are in abusive relationships are pressured to join microcredit and violence continues despite her membership. Other studies indicate that the link between female credit and a change in hus-band's attitudes and conduct (Pitt et al. 2006) and violence (Schuler et al. 1996) was not significant.

Bates et al. (2004) summarized the various debates about microcredit and violence in their excellent article on socioeconomic factors associ-ated with domestic violence in Bangladesh. They concluded with an un-ambiguous statement: Once a woman starts earning income in larger amounts and becomes a major contributor to the household, then there is an increased risk of violence because this undermines male authority. Confusing as they are, these studies do lead to a single conclusion: If husbands are the pivotal factor, the theoretical and program emphasis should also be on how to transform husbands as well as on empowering the loanees.

Yet, theoretical distinctions between men, masculinities, and mascu-line regimes are not made and as a result the underlying philosophy of the Grameen Bank strategy is not questioned. Goetz and Sen Gupta (1996) did not provide concrete suggestions for the Grameen Bank program to work toward these goals. Pitt et al. (2006) also found that participation in a mi-crocredit program increases female agency. But even as they admit that "drawing conclusions from a large number of regressions is problematic" (Pitt et al. 2006, 799), the investigators proceed to do just that. It is not surprising, therefore, that neither the Grameen Bank leadership nor Habib know what to do with the results of these studies. Schuler et al. (1998) gave some excellent practical suggestions: separate sessions for men and discus-sions of domestic violence with couples. However, they did not explore dif-ferent indigenous definitions, the analysis of masculinities, and how high-minded men can be used as social innovators, which are the pur-poses of this article.

I want to emphasize that the presentation of indigenous definitions should *not* mean that practitioners have to agree with them. But it is im-perative that they seek to understand how their clients perceive things. These indigenous perceptions can help managers to view the loanee and her entrepreneurial activities in the context of systems of male domi-nance and to understand the ways in which a woman's contexts impinge on her efforts to be a successful entrepreneur. The construction of the universal woman loanee and her husband as inflexible categories is also contested by emerging scholarship in the broader feminist arenas.

Masculinity and Gender Development Theory

The Grameen Bank manager's depiction of Mehrun as the universal woman and her husband as the universal man has been challenged by three different groups of scholars. First, feminist scholars (Cain, Khanam, and Nahar 1979; Kandiyoti 1987) claim that it is risky for women to directly confront patriarchy, based on a more contextual and variegated view of women's lives in South Asia. Second, masculinity studies, a more recent development, disputes sameness in men. Scholars (Connell 1995; Donaldson 1993; Nye 2005) focus on deconstructing the masculine/feminine binary and present a range of masculinities. Third, extensive research on domestic violence has produced the gender politic model (Stark and Flitcraft, 1991), which highlights the ways in which abusive men are supported by larger social structures of gender inequality. Researchers argue that individual batterers will only transform if the legal, social, and economic institutions that sustain gender inequality are also modified.

Feminist Theories of Patriarchy

Had Kandiyoti (1987) been present during the conversation, she would have had much to say to Habib, the Grameen Bank manager. She would have argued that Mehrun's decision to withdraw from the Grameen Bank represents a breakdown of the precarious patriarchal bargain that Mehrun has struck with her husband in Bangladesh, a country that conforms to the classic model of patriarchy.

Challenging the definition of patriarchy as monolithic male dominance, Kandiyoti (1987) contrasts sub-Saharan patriarchy, in which women can openly resist domination, to classic patriarchy prevalent in South Asia and other countries, where women have to both accommodate and manage patriarchy. A convincing argument for a nuanced picture of gender relations is made by Cain et al. (1979), who argue that the focus on the household as an entity ignores differences between men and women within the household. They describe kinship, political systems, and religion as various contexts of patriarchy that prevent women from openly opposing patriarchy. Direct confrontation in Bangladesh is risky, as Cain et al. (1979) also point out. These feminist scholars also dismantle binarism by analyzing age and patrilocality as gendered contexts. Patriarchy is internalized; older women strive to keep their sons loyal while young daughters-in-law try to circumvent mothers-in-law. Young women endure this inequity in the hope that they will eventually become insiders (nijer lok) and gain seniority (Lamb 2000).

But even as Cain et al. (1979) deconstruct "universal" woman as a concept, they do not similarly deconstruct "universal" man as a framework. They analyze how some women support patriarchy, but they fail to investigate how some men resist it. Class and age hierarchies among men are mentioned but not explored. They state that older men dominate younger men, but do not question whether all older men are dominant in the same way. Poor men are seen as disadvantaged as compared to rich men, but the possibility that a spectrum of masculinities may exist among a low-income male population is not raised. Third-world scholars (Kabeer 1994; Mohanty 1991; Siddiki 1998) challenge Boserup's (1970) depiction of rural women in developing countries as passive and subordinate, but neither Siddiki (1998) nor Kabeer (1994) have shifted the locus of the debate to explore notions of manhood—specifically, male relatives of the Grameen Bank loanees. In fact, Cain et al. (1979) argue that even though low-income men's lives may improve if their wives find more employment, they will not join the women's movement because they are financially dependent on rich men—an argument that is not supported by any empirical evidence and which this article challenges.

Implicit in their argument is the belief that the basis of authority is ultimately material, an approach that resonates with Yunus's original philosophy and finds practical expression in microcredit programs. If women earn income, they will be empowered—a belief echoed by the manager of the Grameen Bank, but disputed by the increased domestic violence in loanee households. Other scholars challenge these generalized classifications (Feldman 2001; Harding 1986; Shehabuddin 1999); Abu-Lughod (1990) cautions against the application of universal categories to specific contexts. But unlike Cain et al. (1979), these scholars do not give specific policy recommendations. In fact, little theoretical work has been done on the nexus between masculinity and gender and development studies and how this exploration can inform policy makers and practitioners.

Masculinity Studies

Theories of masculinity explain how and why there are different types of men. Particularly relevant is the distinction between masculinity and men as discrete but analytically connected categories (Nye 2005). Students of masculinity seek to deconstruct the feminine/masculine binary and scholars explore the nexus between masculinity and social change. They would ask the Grameen Bank manager to find out more about Mehrun's husband and to analyze whether his attitudes and practices conform to or defy the prevailing dominant (hegemonic) masculinity.

Patriarchal Dividend. Connell (1995) suggests that men have not changed even as women have taken great strides because of the "patriarchal dividend"—most men gain by the way society is organized. This concept would help the Grameen Bank manager understand the dynamic between loanee Mehrun and her husband Ibrahim. Mehrun's entrepreneurial success and her presumed "liberation" from a traditional role have not resulted in a similar transformation in her husband, nor in the village structures—a belief popular to both doctrinaire Marxist and Women in Development feminists. Ibrahim, like some other men whom I interviewed, felt that men have been forced to take a backseat and compelled to suffer a "loss" (of masculinity) by the microcredit activities. Not surprisingly, he is resentful.

Masculinities are performed in various ways in different cultures, but the concept of hegemonic (dominant) masculinity is universal. Although some men may not conform to it in real life, it is the dominant cultural lexicon, an expression of the prevailing hegemonic masculine regime. Donaldson (1993) defines hegemonic masculinity as the control of power by men through the process of subordinating women. As much a cultural ideal as actual experience, hegemonic masculinity is socially sustained; it is created and perpetuated by those who regulate and manage gender regimes in society. Nye (2005) describes hegemonic masculinity as in flux (if not in crisis), constantly reinventing itself to retain and secure advantage.

Social Change. The social change agenda in masculinity studies is less well developed. Donaldson (1993) argues that some men—namely working class, gay, and black men—are excluded from the patriarchal benefit provided by social structures that support the hegemonic masculinity. This theoretical framework suggests that it is the exclusion from privilege that differentiates men and masculinities from each other, and it is those men who are deprived who will be agents for social change. Hooks (2003), however, disputes the imposition of sameness on black men and identifies four different types of black masculinities.

Based on evidence that men who invest in fatherhood change their ideas about children, childcare, and women and come to see their wives as equal partners and to respect women's work, Donaldson (1993) suggests that active fathering and men's counter sexist groups are the solution. But it can be legitimately argued that these "new" men do not change the dominant masculinity in the absence of a movement to change larger structures. To understand why changing women has not automatically resulted in changing men and why changing men as individuals will not automatically lead to changing masculinity, we must understand the connection between masculinity and masculine regimes—namely the economic, social, and religious structures. Men as individuals can (and do) contest dominant masculinity in their attitudes and household practices, but social change can only be effected when altering a masculine regime becomes a matter of large-scale social policy.

In the West, policy debates center around two models: father-as-breadwinner and father-as-hands-on parent. The breadwinner model, which means tax and financial incentives to help fathers provide economically, has proponents in the United States. On the other hand, Sweden follows the hands-on-parent model, providing maternity and paternity leave to ensure that fathers participate in bonding and raising children as much as possible. In Bangladesh, the successful government family planning program, which reduced fertility from 6.3 in 1971 (BDHS 1997) to 2.9 in 2001 (Jahan and Germain 2004), altered the dominant masculine regime. A major social change, it has contested the son preference and has given women control over their bodies. But ways in which the program transformed men, masculinity, and masculine regimes have yet to be analyzed.

Domestic Violence Prevention

The gender politics model of domestic violence prevention (Stark and Flitcraft 1991) explains why Mehrun's increased income and entrepreneurial skill made her more vulnerable at home. Based on the theory that domestic violence is but one aspect of a larger societal phenomenon, this model has mounted the most effective counterargument to acontextuality. It is the way in which gender is structured in the economy and the society that explains patterns of domestic violence, not a particular subset of families and individuals. Intrafamilial violence is simply an expression of the way in which gender relations are structured; the society, not the family, is the setting. This perspective then explains patterns of violence that extend from dating relationships through parenting and marriage. Social, cultural, and economic inequities combine to give men more power than women. Violence then becomes an implicitly sanctioned way for some men to either get resources (sex or money) or establish control when their privilege is threatened by female independence.

Status Inconsistency. Recent quantitative studies about microcredit, decision making, and violence in Bangladesh reveal disturbing trends (Bhuiya, Ahmed, and Hanifi 2003; Khan et al. 1998; Rahman 1999). A study of 2,038 married women indicated that violence peaked when credit was introduced but tapered off when other inputs, which remain undescribed, were introduced (Khan et al. 1998). Goetz and Sen Gupta's (1996) groundbreaking study of 253 loanees showed that 63 percent of interviewees had no direct control over how to use the loan. Women's profits have benefited the entire family, but have their contributions put them at greater risk? The household is better off, but the loanee is more vulnerable to violence. These findings continue to puzzle the gender and development community, which believed that microcredit increased female status within the home and reduced violence (Schuler et al. 1996).

Theories of status inconsistency help explain this nightmare. Described as a situation where the husband is threatened by the wife's perceived higher status (Stark and Flitcraft 1991), status inconsistency means that domestic violence can increase even as the woman's economic status increases. Women whose education or income is higher than their partners (status inconsistent) are at greater risk, particularly since most conflicts "involve making it clear who is in charge" (Stark and Flitcraft 1991, 133). Men also resort to violence when they feel that their wives have failed to fulfill domestic responsibility. My research illustrates that other inputs, such as business workshops, did not reduce violence. Rather peace at home, something that also has religious overtones in rural culture, was obtained at a cost of *resubordination*. Faced with violence (and the possibility of being beaten to death), the wife struck a patriarchal bargain and was eventually forced to hand over the loan to her husband. Allowing male relatives to control the loan is a woman's way of managing a status imbalance in the household that could otherwise result in domestic violence. In extreme cases, resubordination helps her stay alive.

Divorce Is Not an Option. Why doesn't Mehrun leave her husband? Why do women often stay in abusive relationships? The gender politics model explains this harsh irony by stating that cultural norms of victim-blaming and lack of support, in addition to lack of financial resources and economic dependency, combine to make staying in an abusive marriage "more practical than escape" (Stark and Flitcraft 1991, 133). Mehrun and other low-income women like her do not want divorce. They feel that divorce benefits the man. As they say, "He can always marry some young thing." In a country where female sharecroppers get 60 taka to every 100 taka the man gets, a divorcee will be out on the street (Ahmed 2003). Here the women point to gender wage inequity, a larger aspect of the dominant masculine regime, as sustaining domestic violence. As Jennings (1990, 53) said, "Ending violence is not the only change needed." Men must learn to see women as equals and to value their work. The reason that men view any attempt by women to be independent as threatening—and therefore a precursor to violence—is because society is structured around hierarchical gender relations.

Solutions that are based on this model include political change and female empowerment. Those who espouse this model insist on the identification and punishment of batterers and support for a community-based shelter movement. The gender politics model views social change as a solution, but it is limited. There is no theoretical space for men who want to change; although it dismantles hegemonic masculinity, this approach does not support high-minded men or reward high-minded masculinity. In fact, implicit in this a model is a binary notion of sameness in men and masculinity. To include men in gender empowerment programs, we have to first concede that not all men are alike.

Different Men, Different Masculinities

I discovered four distinct masculinities in rural Bangladesh: high-minded (*udaar*), batterer (*beshi mare*), *habla* (lacking in common sense), and "mixed." The definitions of the "abusive" (*beshi mare*) and "high-minded" (*udaar*) are indigenous.[5] In this section, I contrast the attitudes and practices of Shafiqul, a high-minded husband; Nurul, an abusive husband; Robi, a "mixed" husband; and Kamal, a *habla* husband, across four categories: notions of an ideal wife, decisions on household finances, domestic violence, and fatherhood. Although the vignettes focus on these men as the husbands, I also include ways in which their wives view them.

On the surface, Shafiqul and Nurul had much in common: both were rickshaw pullers, Muslim, young, and illiterate. Robi had actively participated in men's groups organized by a women's nongovernmental organization (NGO). Kamal was older and his wife was no longer a microcredit loanee, having found a salaried job. These four Muslim men lived in the same neighborhood, but each exemplified masculinities in rural Bangladesh that were markedly distinct.

High-Minded Husband, Loving Household

Shafiqul and Shefali were a high-minded family. This young couple described their marriage as happy. They had two daughters, Vicky and Nicky, and lived in the Muslim neighborhood of Kunjpukhi with Shefali's mother and younger brother in a three-room mud hut. A rickshaw puller who was dependent on a daily wage, Shafiqul's day started around 6 A.M. and often ended at 10 P.M. Shefali and her mother, Amina, were both microcredit loanees. Shefali raised and sold livestock with the loans from the Grameen Bank; she managed all the household finances. Shefali's mother also tended livestock and helped with the household chores. Shefali and Shafiqul did not have a *pukka* (brick) home, unlike some of their better-off neighbors, but there was a glow about them.

Wife as Team Member. Shafiqul was proud of Shefali. When I visited their home, he brought her embroidery to show me how talented she was. As far as he was concerned, Shefali was the ideal wife. When I asked him what this meant, he said:

> She gets along so well with everyone. She manages the household so well. She is a great money manager. Yes, it is important that she is pretty, but other things also count.

By village standards, Shefali was not fair-skinned and therefore not considered attractive. But to Shafiqul she was beautiful; he was in love with her. When I interviewed them, she was wearing a blue sari with a matching blue blouse; an iridescent blue bangle sparkled against the deep sun-brown skin of her arm. When I asked her if the bangle was a gift from Shafiqul, she smiled and nodded shyly. He was always buying her little gifts, with money saved from his meager income, to show his appreciation. Early on in the marriage, Shefali said that she tried to make her husband understand that a mutually affirming marriage was key to raising children. As she said, "I have a husband who listens to me . . . there is no sin in his heart." Wise beyond her years, this young woman was highly capable and had a great deal of common sense—a quality much appreciated by her husband and valued in village culture.

Joint Financial Decisions. The trust and faith that Shafiqul has in Shefali also extends to financial matters and loan activities. He gave her all his earnings because he realized that she managed finances much better than he did. He supported all the household entrepreneurial activities that she had undertaken with the loan from the Grameen Bank.

> If she wants to sell her chickens, I never stopped her. Ducks, chickens, whatever she can sell. My wife also makes crafts. I never stopped her. Let her make as much money as she can . . . She took out a loan (for taka 5000) and leased some land for taka 2000. This left 2000–3000 takas for the household. I never asked her to account for this money . . . but before I do anything with the money I earn, I ask her.

Shafiqul acknowledged that women needed their husbands' help in paying back the loan. He said that "trouble in the household" (a euphemism for domestic violence) resulted when husbands were irresponsible and squandered the loan in unproductive activities. He felt that women have a right to "talk back" if men are selfish and "don't think of how all in the household" will benefit. Shefali described Shafiqul as "reasonable." At the same time, she was not blind to his shortcomings. He had a tendency to waste money (which he acknowledged); she helped him to realize that such habits would be an obstacle to the life they wanted for their children.

No Complaints about Violence. Shefali had no complaints about domestic violence.

> There are some husbands who beat their wives even if they don't do wrong. They have sin in their hearts. But there is no sin in my husband's heart. I don't have to get his permission before I leave the house. But other husbands want reasons, and if their wives leave, they will not take them back. Some husbands are just not open to reason.

But later in the conversation, Shafiqul admitted to slapping her once or twice during the early years of their married life because she hit Vicky, the eldest daughter, who was being naughty. However, neither men nor women consider an occasional slap for "a good reason" to be domestic violence. As Kabeer (2001) notes, what abuse means to village women is key; they make the distinction between extreme violence as part of every-day existence and a yearly outburst. Shafiqul felt strongly that violence is wrong. As this quote indicates, he saw a clear connection between domestic violence and well being:

> Domestic violence takes place because of certain behaviors (of the man). Why should I beat her (my wife)? I listen to what she says; she also listens to me, that is why there is no bad behavior . . . If our family is destroyed (due to my bad behavior), then who will take care of my children?

Fatherhood Is Rewarding. Family gives meaning and purpose to this low-income, illiterate, rickshaw driver. The very first day that I met Shafiqul, he told me all about how well his oldest daughter, Vicky, was doing in school. He was very interested in and kept track of her academic prowess. He wanted his girls to study as much as they wanted to; if this meant all the way to a master's degree, Shafiqul was committed to saving for it. They did not want any more children, but the fact that they did not have any sons did not bother Shafiqul. "The truth is, whether you have a son or a daughter, in today's world they have to be treated equally." Shefali also said that, at first, he had really wanted a son, but she persuaded him that it would be very expensive to have more than two children.

"Mixed" Husband, Caring but Shadowed Household

Robi and Salma had one daughter and two sons. When I first met them ten years ago, they had joined a local women's NGO, which focused on easing the double burden that women faced when they worked outside and inside the home and changing gender roles. Loans were given to cooperatives. Salma had joined a women's rice mill cooperative and Robi had belonged to a fishermen's joint venture. These cooperatives also functioned as consciousness raising groups for men and women. Although he was once one of the most violent men in the neighborhood, Robi stopped beating Salma as a result of these interventions. They were doing well financially. The household economy had stabilized; they had savings in the bank; they ate three meals everyday; their children were in school. But poor management within the NGO compelled them to leave and join the Grameen Bank. Robi had run, unsuccessfully, for public office. He also tried a three-wheeler auto taxi business, which had failed.

Wife's Position Ambivalent. Ambivalence, rather than persistent inequity, characterized this household. When Salma applied for a high-paying security guard position during the elections, Robi supported her over the objections of his male peers. But this support did not extend to property matters. Robi made it clear that he would not allow Salma to own property in her name, even if it was bought with her earnings, because this might give her enough economic independence to leave him—a common male nightmare in rural Bangladesh. His objections made it difficult for her to access the Grameen Bank housing loan, targeted exclusively for women loanees. But Salma was able to refute him publicly. When she told him that his refusal to let her own property meant that he had "sin in his heart," Robi laughed shamefacedly.

Intimacy did not necessarily mean that Robi saw his wife as a partner in all respects. It certainly did not mean that he was willing to help her rise to her full potential. Sometimes he spoke disparagingly about Salma. "I only studied up to class five because my father did not have the means to educate me further. Had it been otherwise, I would have been an educated man and would have been able to get an educated wife. Not like the one I have now."

Some Joint Decisions. As her husband, Robi wanted to make sure that Salma did not "rise above" him. This meant, among other things, that in principle, she had to account to him for her activities outside the household. But Salma did not always do so. Robi also acknowledged that she made good financial decisions. Robi wanted Salma to keep her place. But he was not always successful because of his own ambivalence about gender roles and Salma's *boodhi* (ability to argue), which was bolstered by her women's solidarity group.

Shadows of Violence Remain. Easily the most abusive man in the neighborhood, Robi used to beat his wife frequently and at whim. As a result of joining a men's group and through the intervention of his older sisters (who also belonged to a women's group), Robi stopped. But shadows remained in this marriage. "It has been five years since I stopped beating my wife, which is why she no longer gives my words any importance. So I threaten her from time to time. Then she gets scared and shuts up. Of course, I do not believe that it is right to batter one's wife, and those men, who are aware, have learned from my example and have also stopped beating their wives."

Fatherhood Is Rewarding. Robi loved his children unabashedly. He was always talking about them and would often discuss his plans for their future with me. Especially close to his daughter Meena, he did not appear to distinguish between his aspirations for her and his sons. In fact, he said that it was unfair to make her help in the cooking and other household chores when she had the same amount of homework that her brothers had. According to Robi, this extra work would contribute to a gender gap among the siblings.

Habla Husband, Household with Woman Decision-Maker

An older couple, Kamal and Alveera had three grown-up children. The older daughter and son were married and had left home; their youngest was studying for his college examinations. Competent and intelligent, Alveera had a highly coveted salaried job as a field worker in the local NGO. However, Kamal was *habla*. It was unclear what he did to contribute financially to the household. *Habla* is a colloquial word that means lacking common sense; the *habla* male characteristic defined gender dynamics in this household. They had a *pukka* (brick) home, a status symbol in rural Bangladesh—built, no doubt, with Alveera's earnings.

Wife as Sole Decision-Maker. Alveera made all the decisions. Alveera always gave her husband the *macher matha* (fish head) at meals, a sign of respect in rural Bangladesh. But Kamal was, at best, a figurehead. Everyone came directly to Alveera; Kamal always deferred to her, as this response to a question asked in a male focus group indicates:

> QUESTION: Do you think that your wife should vote as you wish?
> KAMAL: I vote for whoever my wife tells me to vote for.

There were no joint decisions. Alveera often felt lonely in the marriage and complained that everything—raising the children, managing the household, getting them married—was all up to her. Although kind and loving, Kamal was, at best, an absent-minded father. It was Alveera who had to keep track of how her children were doing in school. She could not turn to him for advice on major household decisions.

Alveerah also had a great deal of power in the public and the private arenas. Witty to the point of being ascerbic, Alveera was a force to be reckoned with and everyone in the neighborhood knew that. Younger women looked up to her as a role model. As a leader in the community, Alveera's concerns extended beyond the narrow confines of her own household. She would often enlighten me with sophisticated analyses of how women could achieve gender equality.

No Violence. Alveera told me that, early in the marriage, Kamal would fly into a temper and beat her. Resentful of her prowess, male neighbors instigated the violence, hoping to ensure that Kamal would keep her "in her place." But after she joined the women's group and started earning money, Alveera was able to confront the men and the beating stopped. When I met Kamal and Alveera, there was no physical or verbal violence in their marriage. But Alveera also was careful not to taunt him, even though she felt frustrated at times. She always made sure that, as her husband, she gave Kamal the respect that society felt that he should be accorded. This created peace in the household.

Abusive Husband, Fractured Household

Nurul, Nasima, and their seven-year-old son, Karim, lived in the same neighborhood as the other couples, but their household was completely different. It was characterized by extreme violence. In fact, Nurul had tried to poison his wife a few years ago. Unlike Shafiqul, Nurul lived in his parents' village. Nasima's family lived nearby. She was on especially good terms with her older sister-in-law. Generally unhappy with his lot in life, Nurul did not like being a rickshaw puller and wanted to go into

the entertainment business. He wanted me to make the appropriate connections for him. Both said that they wanted their son to go on to college,
but it was unclear whether Karim was doing well in school.

Wife as Subordinate. Nurul was very clear about what he thought a good
wife should be:

> NURUL: An ideal wife is someone who says her prayers. She carries herself
> well. She doesn't leave the home, and she doesn't talk back.
> QUESTION: What causes trouble in the household?
> NURUL: It has been seven years since our son was born. My wife has put on
> weight; well, she's just not that attractive anymore. She gets upset when
> she sees me talking to the young girls in the village. This causes trouble in
> the household. But she has to understand, I am a man, and I am still young.

Clearly, Nurul felt that a wife, by definition, is subordinate. It is crucial
that she obey him and keep quiet. The focus on regular prayers was an
injunction that he did not follow himself. Nurul wanted Nasima to stay
home, but as a Grameen Bank loanee, Nasima had to leave the household
to go to the local bank office. He allowed her to go because they needed
the money, but on one condition: he had to have complete control over
the loan. Nasima had no choice but to comply.

Attractiveness ranked high on Nurul's list. He did not describe any of
Nasima's other qualities. I wondered if he knew what she was really like.
Her growing entrepreneurial skills were seen as a threat, not an asset. I
do not think that her "increasing unattractiveness" was why he tried to
poison her. Nurul found the responsibilities of marriage—and of the
householder stage[6]—burdensome. He did admit, however reluctantly,
that his immaturity also caused trouble in the household. As he said, "It
is not good to get married too young."

Conflictual Financial Decisions. Financial decisions were not made
jointly. Nasima did not complain about her husband's flirtations (perhaps
they were too painful to talk about). But she was upset that he was secre-
tive about his earnings, and that they did not work as a team to plan for
their son's education.

> I want my son to be educated at least to the intermediate [college] level. But
> we are poor, and I need my husband to sit down with me and to make a finan-
> cial plan together. He doesn't share his earnings with me. Raising our child is
> all up to me. I feel as if I am a single mother.

Nurul did not like the idea of his wife having a separate savings account. He wanted to have access to it:

> Yes, women also have a right to save. But now we don't have enough money
> for a savings account for her. If wives give their earnings to their husbands,
> then the husbands gain—they can put the money in their own accounts.

But the Grameen Bank is adamant (and rightly so) that the bank account should be in the loanee's name alone. Only Nasima can withdraw money. Loanees are required to save on a weekly basis and, in general, they are not allowed to take out more than 50 percent of the savings. It was up to Nasima to manage his ego, which was threatened by her savings account and their need for microcredit earnings.

Violence Is Extreme. Not surprisingly, Nurul felt that violence was needed if his wife did not listen to him.

> It was necessary to beat her. It is necessary to beat her if she doesn't listen to me. In that case, a slap or two is entirely appropriate.

Nasima handed over every penny to him in order to keep peace in the household. But despite this, Nurul had tried to poison her.

> One day, I noticed that he was especially nice to me. He cooked the rice himself and brought it to me to eat. I thought, "He has changed." He then left the room. When I started eating it, I noticed blood on my tongue. He had ground up a light bulb and mixed it into the rice. I told my sister-in-law immediately.

Nasima did not want me to take action against Nurul; she repeatedly told me that she did not want me to tell her brothers, who lived in the neighboring village. A certain degree of illusion and denial were an essential feature of this abusive household. Nurul doesn't want Nasima to leave the home, but she has to go out to the Grameen Bank office—an all-male space. Nurul doesn't want her to have her own savings account, but as a Grameen Bank loanee she is required to have one. He has no choice but to allow her to continue because the household needs the money. To rationalize this, Nasima has to pretend that it is his money. She does what he orders her to do with the loan, but he still has to ask her to withdraw from her savings account. It is difficult to maintain this façade, especially in a relationship as intimate as marriage, and violence results when it inevitably cracks.

Little Investment in Fatherhood. Even though Nurul wanted his son to go to college, he was unwilling to plan for it. He did not show any interest in how his son was doing in school or spend much time with him. Faced with domestic violence and attempted murder, Nasima found it difficult to be a good mother—yet another source of anxiety. Nurul found the responsibilities of being a father and husband burdensome. Unable to enjoy family life, Nurul was bitter and unhappy.

Different Masculinities

It would be a mistake to view these four men as isolated from the contexts that shape them. Indeed, to see Shafiqul as a saint and Nurul as a villain would be to fall into the same binary trap that I described in an earlier section. Instead, we need to analyze how the attitudes, beliefs, and practices of these men are shaped by the different masculinities that arise from the dominant masculine regime, either by conforming to or by defying it.

High-Minded Masculinity. Characterized, in essence, by its repudiation of gender convention, this masculinity defies patrilocality, the penultimate symbol of manliness in rural Bangladesh. Men and women who support this type of masculinity rely on broader analyses of how society is organized to shape their attitudes and conduct. Such women speak out publicly, especially if they are older, using feminist interpretations of Islam to refute abusive men and the masculinity that they represent.

High-minded masculinity is sustained by a supportive extended family. The wife has more status and mobility in the neighborhood in which she was raised. An equal partner, she participates in all decisions in this type of masculinity, which sees marriage as a "matching of minds" (*moner mil*). Disagreements are resolved through active listening: the emphasis is on how the husband and wife create a reflective space within the marriage. In a culture where domestic violence is a norm, this masculinity is striking in its condemnation of abuse. The wife's microcredit earnings do not lead to violence; her contributions to the household are valued and recognized. Considered at best uncivilized, violence is seen as a threat to good fatherhood, yet another central value of this masculinity. As important as mothering, fathering is critical to the successful adjustment of children in school and to peace at home. High-minded masculinity considers being a good husband and caring father as central to its vision of poverty alleviation.

Abusive Masculinity. If violation of gender convention is a major characteristic of the high-minded masculinity, then conforming to gender norms distinguishes the abusive masculine regime. Extreme violence consisting of physical and verbal abuse is part of daily existence. Women, particularly mothers-in-law and older sisters, also play a role: not only do they support violence, but often they instigate it. This masculinity is based on the wife and daughter-in-law as an outsider. Convention requires that she has to prove herself in various ways before she becomes an insider (*nijer lok*). Most striking is the absence of investment in fatherhood, based as it is on a marital relationship characterized by mutual hostility. Not surprisingly, in this context, the wife's earnings do not increase her status. They are appropriated by her husband, who views the profits from her Grameen Bank loans as his money. Patriarchal notions of Islam are the lexicon of abusive masculinity. The Grameen Bank activity is seen as a violation of Islam because it allows women to leave the home and encourages them "to talk back." Typically, men who conform to this masculinity force their wives to quit once they feel that the household economy has stabilized. This masculinity is characterized by rigidity; it requires conformity in all aspects.

"Mixed" Masculinity. Perhaps the most interesting of all the masculinities, the "mixed" type is not devoid of caring, nor does it repudiate all aspects of women's empowerment. Similar to high-minded masculinity, there is a high degree of investment in fatherhood and girls are encouraged to study. But unlike high-minded men, mixed men will interrupt daughters' studies if there is a good marriage proposal in the offing. Investment decisions on the loans are made together—up to a point. Such husbands do not want their wives to own property. They have no objection to women earning income, as long as the women do not rise above the men. Physical violence is not a daily facet of mixed masculinity, but the threat is always there. It is entirely possible that verbal abuse increases even as physical violence stops, as a study in the United States illustrated (Jennings 1990). Most striking is the contrast between public performance and private conduct. Such men joined in the chest-thumping displays of hegemonic masculinity in the focus groups, but in private, they said that the abusive men were cruel.

Habla Masculinity. Characterized by subordination to women, this masculinity has always existed in rural Bangladesh. Its existence in society is predicated on the woman's ability to show respect for her husband. In fact, parents, who have *habla* boys make sure to marry them to unusually competent women. Clearly, the household would not run if two *hablas* were married to each other. Wives of such men emerge as leaders and frequently want to run for public office. Male peers do not taunt such men, even though they are disturbed by how powerful the wives are.

Masculinity and Patriarchal Risk

I noticed that Shafiqul, who was present at the focus group during the above discussion, did not speak out. He chose to leave an abusive family to live with his wife's parents and become a *ghar jamai* (house son-in-law), which is very low status for a male villager. Considered effeminate by the other men, Shafiqul is an outsider in the brotherhood of male peers. Few male villagers follow this risky path because it poses a direct challenge to male culture.

It is worth asking what made Shafiqul take this societal risk in the first place. Love, expressed as a high degree of investment in fatherhood, empowers such men to act as agents of social change, however indirectly. These house son-in-laws were indirect change agents because their pathway made them outsiders in kin relations of the *para* (neighborhood). Unwilling to verbally confront older insider men, they were reluctant to publicly support progressive women. Challenging the dominant masculine regime in a direct way involves considerable patriarchal risk, including the threat of violence. Given their low status in the male hierarchy, these men find it prudent to confront abusive men indirectly. They follow a "yes, dear" strategy, in which they publicly agree with the male elders but then go ahead and do exactly what they want to do—an approach that many women have always used. Centuries of tradition support the viability of this strategy, which means keeping quiet in public and doing exactly what you want in private. Indeed, Shafiqul's household practices were very different. He saw his wife as a teammate and gave her all his earnings because she was better at household finances. "Yes, dear" endures precisely because it does not directly flout male privilege and the benefit for the household is high.

On the other hand, abusive men do not need to use the "yes, dear" strategy. Given that the dominant masculine regime supports abusive masculinity, such men can use direct confrontation to silence women who speak out. In the focus groups, this often meant drowning out women as they tried to speak, using vituperative language, and simply saying, "Shut up." As sociolinguistic studies (Nye 2005) have shown, men enact masculinity through speech. Verbal assault increases patriarchal risk for those women *and* men who dispute abusive masculinity. Abusive men can afford to behave in this manner because they are supported by the dominant masculine regime.

Transforming Men and Masculinities

Men like Nurul will not change over time and men like Shafiqul may not remain high-minded forever. To reward Shafiqul, gender and development experts and microcredit practitioners need to support the high-minded masculinity that he represents. Similarly, we need to transform the dominant masculine regime and the abusive masculinity that have made Nurul an oppressive husband, in order to transform him.

I argue that the transformation of men, masculinity, and masculine regimes can only be achieved and sustained when we simultaneously exalt high-minded masculinity and change the abusive masculine regimes that it challenges. As Donaldson (1993) rightly argues, movements to change patriarchy have failed because they have concentrated on dismantling hegemonic masculinity rather than building gender equality. Examining masculine regimes means examining the cultural, legal, religious, and economic bases of notions of manhood at the societal, national, and global levels. Institutions such as patrilocality (which requires women to leave their natal home) the village court with its all-male jury, and gender wage inequity in the agricultural labor market (which pays women only sixty percent of what men earn) are among the many aspects of a masculine regime that sustains abusive masculinity.

Recommendations for the Grameen Bank

The Grameen Bank, government, and women's movement sector each has a different role to play in this antipoverty strategy. The government with its mass programs and the women's movement with its national advocacy programs can focus on masculine regimes. The decentralized nature of the Grameen Bank and other such field-based organizations enables them to target individual men and the different masculinities at the village level.

The field-based strategy that I propose for the Grameen Bank is conceptually simple: use men to change men. But implementation requires an understanding of the dynamic between men and masculinity at the household and in the community. Transforming gender regimes at the national level is beyond the scope of this article.

Household Interventions: Use High-Minded Men as Social Change Agents. It is at the household level that the field-based organizations like the Grameen Bank can be most effective in the transformation of masculinity. The Grameen Bank can create peace at home. As it embarks on its strategic planning exercise, the Grameen Bank needs to include male relatives in its overall scheme not as loanees but as partners in the poverty alleviation effort. The organization needs to seek out high-minded men and use them to convince other men. The staff also needs to be aware of trigger points, as illustrated by Shafiqul's case, and intervene to identify, support, and reward high-minded men. This can be done through the excellent system of mutually reinforcing home visits, workshops, and town meetings that already exists.

Identify High-Minded Men. What made Shafiqul high-minded? He lived in a way that was strikingly different from most men in rural Bangladesh. In a patrilocal society, women move in with their in-laws after marriage. Shafiqul was a *ghar jamai* or the son-in-law who stays with his wife's parents—a position of low status for men (Lamb 2000; Todd 1996). The *ghar jamai* phenomenon is rare and generally involuntary because villagers show scant respect for the house son-in-law as the proverb indicates: "*Jamaier hate chati, ghar jamiaer pechone lathi* (The *jamai* deserves an umbrella, but the *ghar jamai* gets a kick)."

Shafiqul volunteered his biography, which helped me trace the pattern of change. At first, he and Shefali—like everyone else in a patrilocal culture—lived with his parents. His father kept borrowing money from him to live a lifestyle that they, as poor people, could not afford. Shafiqul realized that if he continued to live with his parents he would not be able to educate his girls. So as a solution to problems with his parents, he chose to leave. Why did he decide to break with tradition? Predictably, when he and Shefali moved in with her parents, they faced *katha* (gossip) and taunts. Opposition is inevitable when there is a violation of accepted gender-related norms. As a result, they decided to go back to Shafiqul's parents.

Shefali had applied for a job as a cook in the office of an NGO—a salaried job, which would have assured her family of financial security. He went back to live with his parents only to face a worsened situation: this time they physically threatened him. They had to go back again to her parents, but the job vacancy at the NGO had been filled. Shafiqul realized that the family had paid a very high price for following convention. This strengthened his resolve to live permanently as a *ghar jamai*, thereby creating a new gender role.

To say that men who are *ghar jamai* are high-minded is too simple a conclusion. In fact, all the high-minded men in my sample were *ghar jamai*, which complements Todd's (1996) findings that wives of such men had more power. Yet, deeper analysis helps us identify high-minded men: those who have violated a gender convention may be more amenable to progressive attitudes and practices.

Support and Reward High-Minded Men. It is neither easy nor simple for a sharecropper male in rural Bangladesh to choose to be a high-minded man. The Grameen Bank needs to understand that this choice is far from equivocal; it is fraught with doubt, especially because such men are taunted by their peers. High-minded men need support at key intervention points during the trajectory of the decision-making process.

Shafiqul had to make all these decisions on his own without any outside intervention. The Grameen Bank staff who are required to visit loanee homes at least twice a week should use this time to support such men who actually need counseling when they decide to defy convention. Had he received assistance before the decision to return to his parents' home and to follow convention, his wife would not have withdrawn her application for the salaried job and the family would have been in a better position. Finally, high-minded men need to be rewarded in their decision to create new gender norms so that they can act as social change agents.

If high-minded masculinity is to become the norm, it needs to be rewarded. Grameen Bank staff can recognize their tangible and intangible contributions in a variety of ways. Such families may have more savings in the bank. Also, a woman who has a high-minded husband will be a long-term loanee and therefore can take advantage of house building and educational loans. The Grameen Bank can use these families as examples in a workshop specifically designed for male relatives.

Community Intervention: Use Cost-Effective Domestic Violence Prevention. The Grameen Bank needs to realize that the unidimensional focus on the female loanee leads to disempowerment. Women are embedded in larger family and community structures and can only go so far without the support and understanding of their male relatives. In general, men feel neglected by Grameen Bank officials who focus on their wives, the loanees. This neglect has led to a credibility gap: men feel that all jobs, all opportunities, and all development efforts are going (and unfairly so) to women. Abusive men, like Nurul, express their feelings of marginalization by thwarting their wives. In addition to increased domestic violence, these men force their wives to quit the Grameen Bank after the household economy has stabilized, something that is an obstacle to the organizational mission of poverty alleviation.

It is too much to expect the Grameen Bank to work on all aspects of gender empowerment, but it can and should work on domestic violence, an unintended social consequence of the loan. There are preventative as well as curative aspects; high-minded men can play this dual role in changing abusive men. The one-step strategy based on the inclusion of high-minded men should be added to the current three-step domestic violence prevention strategy.

Three-Step Strategy. The current domestic violence prevention strategy used by NGOs all over Bangladesh is, at best, only partially effective. It almost exclusively focuses on women, who are also the targets of domestic violence, as the agents of change. First, women have to try to find a sympathetic in-law. In this case, Nasima established an affectionate relationship with her husband's older sister-in-law, which actually saved her life. But Nasima was lucky because this strategy does not always work. As the family violence model indicates (Stark and Flitcraft 1991) and as my research findings confirmed, abusive men are the product of an abusive family in which oppressive masculinity prevails. In-laws, especially the mother-in-law, instigate violence against the daughter-in-law, who is seen as the outsider. A pattern of violence persists. In many cases, the daughter-in-law, especially if she has little support from her natal home, has no choice but to bear the violence.

Also, if the violence is extreme and if the woman has NGO support, she takes the case to the *shalish* (the village court). Reports of the *shalish* are mixed, but sometimes the case can be decided in her favor. The final step is to take the case to the civil court. Very few women, however, take this route because it is costly and results in the dissolution of the marriage, something that village women do not want.

One-Step Strategy. Based on my research findings, I argue that including high-minded men is a one-step strategy that should be added to the current three-step strategy. In Bangladeshi rural culture, men listen to older men. Men are also influenced by their male peers much more so than by older women. If a father or any other older man in the neighborhood tells his son to stop beating his wife, then the husband has no option but to cease and to do so immediately. I do not argue that the current three-step strategy be eliminated; indeed, women have the right to speak out. But the one-step strategy exposes the false unity of patriarchal brotherhood.

High-minded male relatives of the Grameen Bank loanees can be used as social change agents to stop domestic violence on Grameen Bank loanee households. The Grameen Bank has a number of workshops for women on various aspects of credit management, but nothing for their male relatives. I do not suggest that men be included as loanees, but sessions with men on issues of masculinity and microcredit are needed. Instead of ten workshops exclusively for women, there could be one workshop to help male relatives understand how women's entrepreneurial activities contribute to the family. Such sessions can help men to understand how women's earnings and increased social mobility help the entire household. These male-only workshops should focus on violence and why it is wrong. High-minded men can play a catalytic role in these discussions. The higher savings and standard of living of high-minded families and good school attendance rate of the children should be exemplified as the rewards of peace at home.

Use Women Staff. Gossip (*katha*) arises when village male elders, the leaders of village society (*samaj*), decide that the *purdah* has been violated. A form of patriarchal control, the very anticipation of gossip is enough to prevent deviance, often causing women to self-restrict their activities. Female loanees are accused of going to the all-male local Grameen Bank office to have affairs. This kind of gossip increases patriarchal risk for the loanees and her husband if he is high-minded. Abusive men use gossip to get their wives to drop out of the Grameen Bank.

This obstacle could be overcome if the Grameen Bank hired more women staff to work at the village level. Despite repeated visits, I was unable to get official statistics from the Grameen Bank. However, female staff at the Grameen Bank are scarce: less than 10 percent of its staff are women (a figure based on an informal conversation with a staff member). This is surprising because women constitute 97 percent of the loanees. In fact, villagers have told me that they would like to see more women working in the Grameen Bank office. Female staff would also serve as role models for the loanees and raise the consciousness of Grameen Bank male staff. Recurrent workshops need to take place within the organization to ensure that discrimination is eliminated and that women (and minority staff) are not tokenized.

Conclusion

Low-income village women told me that they want their male relatives to change. They believe that a redefinition of masculinity is essential to gender empowerment and poverty alleviation. Indeed, such conversations are the inspiration for this study, its purposes, and its inductive methods.

I have presented four different men and masculinities that they exemplify in the hope that this analysis may represent a first step in advancing the framework of inquiry in gender and development studies. Theories of patriarchy must include theories of masculinity. This allows us to create the analytic nexus of men, masculinity, and patriarchal risk and to see how it is essential to gender and development theory. But the distinction between men and masculinity is also important for practice. These definitions also lead to specific recommendations for practitioners and policymakers. At the household level, the Grameen Bank can use high-minded men as social agents; at the community level, it can introduce a new one-step domestic violence strategy.

Sharecropper women told me that they have redefined what it means to be a woman to empower themselves, their families, and to change society. Arguing that men are equally responsible, these women say that they need specific strategies to overcome gender subordination as they gain economic power in the household. It is now time to listen to them, and to use men to change men.

Notes

1. Conversations with NGO leaders and gender experts in Bangladesh.

2. The sample consisted of loanees of the Grameen Bank and a women's NGO. Here, I focus on the Grameen Bank.

3. From the Grameen Bank website (http://www.grameen-info.org).

4. Wood and Sharif (1997) describe the poor as a varied group and analyze how microcredit can help the middle-off and better-off poor, but cannot help the extreme poor.

5. The "mixed" masculinity type is inductively derived, although villagers had no name for it.

6. There are four stages in the Hindu religion: celibate student, householder, forest dwellers *(vanaprasth)*, and renouncer *(sannyasi)*.

Acknowledgments

I am indebted to the villagers for sharing their lives with me. This research was funded by a grant from the American Institute for Bangladesh Studies (AIBS).

References

Abu-Lughod, Lila. 1990. "The Romance of Resistance: Tracing Transformations of Power through Bedouin Women." *American Ethnologist* 17(1):41–55.

Ahmed, Fauzia Erfan. 2003. "Low Income Progressive Men: Microcredit, Gender Empowerment, and the Redefinition of Manhood in Rural Bangladesh." PhD dissertation, Brandeis University.

Baden, Sally, and Anne Marie Goetz. 1998. "Who Needs (Sex) When You Can Have (Gender): Conflicting Discourses on Gender at Beijing." In *Feminist Visions of Development: Gender Analysis and Policy*, ed. Ruth Pearson and Cecile Jackson. London: Routledge.

Bangladesh Demographic and Health Survey (BDHS). 1997. Preliminary Report. Calverton, MD: Macro International.

Bates, Lisa M., Sidney Ruth Schuler, Farzana Islam, and Md. Khairul Islam. 2004. "Socioeconomic Factors and Processes Associated with Domestic Violence in Rural Bangladesh." *International Family Planning Perspectives* 30(4):190–99.

Bhuiya, Abbasuddin, Tamanna Sharmin Ahmed, and S.M. Manzoor Hanifi. 2003. "Nature of Domestic Violence against Women in a Rural Area of Bangladesh: Implication for Preventive Interventions." *Journal of Health Population and Nutrition* 21(1):48–54.

Bornstein, David. 1996. *The Price of a Dream*. New York: Simon and Schuster.

Boserup, Ester. 1970. *Women's Role in Economic Development*. London: Allen and Unwin.

Cain, Mead, Rokeya Khanam, and Shamsun Nahar. 1979. "Class, Patriarchy, and Women's Work in Rural Bangladesh." *Population and Development Review* 5(4):405–38.

Connell, Robert.W. 1995. "Politics of Changing Men." *Socialist Review* 25:135–59.

Donaldson, Mike. 1993. "What is Hegemonic Masculinity?" *Theory and Society* 22:643–65.

Dowla, Asif, and Dipal Barua. 2006. *The Poor Always Pay Back: The Grameen II Story*. Bloomfield, CT: Kumarian Press.

El-Bushra, Judy, and Eugenia Piza Lopez. 1993. "Gender-Related Violence: Its Scope and Relevance." *Focus on Gender* 1(2).

Feldman, Shelley. 2001. "Exploring Theories of Patriarchy: A Perspective from Contemporary Bangladesh." *Signs* 26.4:1097–1127.

Goetz, Anne Marie, and Rina Sen Gupta. 1996. "Who Takes Credit? Gender, Power, and Control over Loan Use in Rural Credit Programmes in Bangladesh." *World Development* 24(1).

Harding, Sandra. 1986. "The Instability of the Analytical Categories of Feminist Theory." *Signs: A Journal of Women in Culture and Society* 11(4):283–302.

Hashemi, Syed M., Sidney Ruth Schuler, and Ann P. Riley. 1996. "Rural Credit Programmes and Women's Empowerment in Bangladesh." *World Development* 24(4).

hooks, bell. 2003. "Reconstructing Black Masculinity." In *Masculinites Interdisciplinary Reading*, ed. Mark Hussey. New Jersey: Prentice Hall.

Jahan, Rounaq, and Adrienne Germain. 2004. "Mobilizing Support to Sustain Political Will Is the Key to Progress in Reproductive Health." *Lancet* 364:742–44.

Jennings, J.L. 1990. "Preventing Relapse Versus 'Stopping' Domestic Violence: Do We Expect Too Much Too Soon from Battering Men?" *Journal of Family Violence* 5:43–69.

Johnson, Hazel, and Gordon Wilson. 2000. "Biting the Bullet: Civil Society, Social Learning and the Transformation of Local Governance." *World Development.* 28(11):1891–1906.

Kabeer, Naila. 1994. *Reverse Realities.* London: Verso.

———. 2001. "Conflict over Credit: Re-evaluating the Empowerment Potential of Loans to Women in Rural Bangladesh." *World Development* 29(1):63–84.

Kandiyoti, Deniz. 1987. "Bargaining with Patriarchy." *Gender and Society* 2(3):274–90.

Kahn, M. R., et al. 1998. "Domestic Violence against Women: Does Development Intervention Matter?" Joint Project Working paper no. 28. Dhaka: BRAC, ICDDR, B.

Lamb, Sarah. 2000. *White Saris and Sweet Mangoes: Aging, Gender, and Body in North India.* Berkeley: University of California Press.

Mahmud. S. 2000. "The Gender Discrimination of Programme Participation: Who Joins a Microcredit Programme and Why?" *Bangladesh Development Studies* 26(2–3):79–101.

Mohanty, Chandra. 1991. "Under Western Eyes: Feminist Scholarship and Colonial Discourse." In *Third World Women and the Politics of Feminism*, ed. Chandra Mohanty, Ann Russo, and Lourdes Torres. Bloomingdale: Indiana University Press.

Nye, Robert A. 2005. "Locating Masculinity: Some Recent Work on Men." *Signs: A Journal of Women in Culture and Society* 30(31):1937–62.

Pearson, Ruth, and Cecile Jackson. 1998. "Introduction: Interrogating Development: Feminism, Gender and Policy." In *Feminist Visions of Development: Gender Analysis and Policy*, ed. Ruth Pearson and Cecile Jackson. London: Routledge.

Pitt, Mark, and Shahidur R. Khandker. 1998. "The Impact of Group-Based Credit Programs on Poor Households in Bangladesh: Does the Gender of Participants Matter?" *Journal of Political Economy* 106:958–96.

Pitt, Mark, Shahidur R. Khandker, and Jennifer Cartwight. 2006. "Empowering Women with Microfinance: Evidence from Bangladesh." *Economic Development and Cultural Change* 54(4):791–831.

Rahman, Aminur. 1999. *Women and Microcredit in Rural Bangladesh: An Anthropological Study of the Rhetoric and Realities of Grameen Bank Lending.* Boulder, CO: Westview Press.

Schuler, Sidney Ruth, Syed M. Hashemi, and Shamshul Huda Badal. 1998. "Men's Violence against Women in Rural Bangladesh: Undermined or Exacerbated by Microcredit Programmes?" *Development in Practice* 8(2):1–9.

Schuler, Sidney Ruth, Syed M. Hashemi, and Ann P. Riley. 1996. "Credit Programs, Patriarchy, and Men's Violence against Women in Rural Bangladesh." *Social Science and Medicine* 43(12):1729–42.

Sen, Amartya. 1990. "Gender and Cooperative Conflict." In *Persistent Inequalities: Women and World Development*, ed. Irene Tinker. New York: Oxford University Press.

Shehabuddin, Elora. 1999. "Contesting the Illicit: Gender and the Politics of Fatwas in Bangladesh." *Signs: A Journal of Women in Culture and Society* 24(4), 1011–44.

Siddiki, Dina. 1998. "Taslima Nasreen and Others: The Contest over Gender in Bangladesh." In *Women in Muslim Societies: Diversity within Unity*. Boulder, CO: Rienner Publishers.

Stark, E., and A.H. Flitcraft. 1991. "Spouse Abuse." In *Violence in America: A Public Health Approach*, ed. M.L. Rosenberg and M.A. Fenley, 123–57. New York: Oxford University Press.

Todd, Helen. 1996. *Women at the Center: Grameen Bank Borrowers after One Decade*. Bangladesh: University Press Limited.

Wiegman, Robyn. 2002. "Unmaking: Men and Masculinity in Feminist Theory." In *Masculinity Studies and Feminist Theory: New Directions*, ed. Judith Kegan Gardiner. New York: Columbia University Press

Wood, Goeffrey D., and Iffath A. Sharif. 1997. *Who Needs Credit? Poverty and Finance in Bangladesh*. Bangladesh: University Press Limited.

Yunus, Muhammad. 1999. *Banker to the Poor*. New York: Public Affairs.

PART IV   **Performing Social Expectations:
The Public Stage**

CHAPTER FIFTEEN

The Hillbilly Defense
Culturally Mediating U.S. Terror
at Home and Abroad

CAROL MASON

Two of the spurious reasons for invading Afghanistan and Iraq have been liberating women from repressive fundamentalism and keeping women free from barbaric terrorism. In the midst of such gendered rationale, images and stories of Appalachian women have reflected profound ambivalence about the fundamentalism of Iraqi resistance and American responses to it. This essay examines the way U.S. media and government officials deflect criticism by deploying a hillbilly defense against accusations of American terror and military extremism. Somewhat like the dubious Twinkie defense, in which criminals try to "avoid responsibility for their action by claiming some external force beyond their control had caused them to act the way they had" (Mikkelson and Mikkelson 2003; Pogash 2003), the hillbilly defense is an effort to deflect criticism of lethal American force and to deny that American extremism is systemic by directing public attention to hillbillies, those mountain folks who are beyond the control of authorities because they are presumably beyond the reach of modernity's civilizing influence. In other words, the hillbilly defense is a defense of the United States of America as a civilized nation—a defense in which hillbillies are the scapegoats for any behavior deemed uncivilized. But unlike the courtroom Twinkie defense, the hillbilly defense is deployed in the cultural arena. Three cases in particular—two involving Appalachian women and a third featuring an Appalachian man—demonstrate how recent representations of hillbillies have helped to culturally mediate the "war on terror," providing a defense of American actions in the domain of the popular, which is as much a battleground as any militarized terrain (Barkawi 2004, 115).

The narrative of Jessica Lynch, the West Virginia soldier famously rescued from an Iraqi hospital in 2003, provides the first case study. Her story was widely publicized, beginning with the greenish videotaped account of her rescue, which was distributed in May 2003, when U.S. plans for swift success in Iraq were beginning to prove untenable. Details of her capture entailed descriptions of her upbringing in West Virginia and her courageous combat skills in Iraq—these references to her heroic fighting, she later stated, were untrue. A made-for-television movie was broadcast nationally nearly a year after her rescue from the hospital. A biographical account of her ordeal, *I Am a Soldier, Too: The Jessica Lynch Story*, was written by erstwhile *New York Times* journalist Rick Bragg and published by Knopf in 2003. Jessica Lynch thus became more than an army supply clerk; she became a story about a country girl who fought bravely and then was saved from barbaric Iraqis—a story to win the hearts and minds of an American public that was becoming more and more disturbed over the absence of weapons of mass destruction in Iraq, as Iraqi and American casualties multiplied, and as rebellion against the American invasion increased. The hillbilly story of Jessica Lynch gave hope that the preemptive war in Iraq was right and good, not a matter of rash military extremism.

Public outrage peaked a year later when images of American soldiers degrading and torturing Iraqi inmates of Abu Ghraib prison were published and broadcast. The second example of the hillbilly defense I will explore involves a second female soldier, Lynndie England, who became another West Virginia poster child used to deflect criticism of U.S. actions in Iraq. Although other soldiers were photographed amid naked bodies chained and posed in sexually humiliating positions, England's picture was most widely publicized, becoming synonymous with torture in Abu Ghraib. Responding to serious allegations of breaking international codes prohibiting the torture of prisoners of war, U.S. officials were reported to say that what happened at Abu Ghraib was the work of "recycled hillbillies" (Hersh 2004b, 41). The phrase resonated on television, radio, and throughout the Internet; discussions of Lynndie England as a gender-bending hillbilly pervert proliferated. Like a photographic negative of the good Jessica Lynch, the evil Lynndie England appeared as another hillbilly gal to deflect criticism of systemic U.S. extremism, in this case the extremism of torture and terrorist humiliation in prisons. By blaming the so-called hillbillies in Abu Ghraib prison, official statements sought to restore the idea that the vast majority of U.S. military personnel (and by extension, the whole of America) are—contrary to the photographs of torture—civilized.

The third case of deploying the hillbilly defense against accusations of terror and systemic extremism is that of Eric Rudolph, the elusive mountaineer "soldier" in the "Army of God," who confessed in 2005 to bombing the 1996 Olympic celebration, a lesbian nightclub, and two abortion clinics. Like convicted "pro-life" bombers and "anti-abortion terrorists," Rudolph has been depicted as a hillbilly (Mason 2004, 808). Reported to be hiding out in the dense forests of Appalachia, Rudolph was arrested in 2003 after five years on the lam and after the events of September 11, 2001, made his actions easily recognizable as domestic terrorism. Along with other cases of anti-abortion extremism, Rudolph's case brought into question the terrorist aspects of "pro-life" bombings, anthrax scares, and snipers. Depicting Rudolph as a loner mountain man compelled by uncivilized ideologies and predilections helped to deny that there is any connection between pro-life militants (those uncivilized people who "kill for life") and mainstream pro-life organizations (comprised of civilized people who "defend life" through legislation or legal protest).

Illuminating how the hillbilly defense has been deployed in these cases will necessarily entail a feminist contribution to theorizing the hillbilly—that liminal, primitive white icon of ambivalence about modernity's "progress" and its American discontents. Feminist insights about the roles that violence, race, reproduction, and sexuality play in the war on terror help explain the "semantic and ideological malleableness" of the hillbilly, who is variously portrayed as noble in poverty, pure in intentions, innately violent, and sexually wild (Harkins 2004, 220). Especially as representative of Appalachia[1]—that geographic imaginary where resistance to modernity is both romantically applauded as devotion to tradition *and* scornfully disdained as a refusal of civilized ways—the hillbilly appears as a transgressor of gender and sexual boundaries, sometimes even as a hybrid he/she, a blending (for better or worse) of characteristics that modern America sees as distinctly male and female. A brief examination of the hillbilly in this liminal capacity serves as a prelude to the discussion of the three cases of deploying a hillbilly defense vis á vis the war on terror.

The Liminal Hillbilly

Beginning with William Byrd's 1728 portrait of white settlers in North Carolina, which "introduced many of the standard tropes" and reflected "the ambiguity that would thereafter always characterize hillbilly imagery," Appalachians have been portrayed as people who do not conform to gender roles considered to constitute a natural order (Harkins 2004, 15). Byrd described Appalachian women as too physical, often taking on the manual labor that their male counterparts appear too lazy to do (15). In the 1800s, writers portrayed Appalachian women as transgressors of gender roles by lampooning the essentialist notions of purity and femininity that constituted the "Cult of True Womanhood" in urban centers of the eastern United States (Smith-Rosenberg 1985, 104). Similarly, stories of Appalachian men—most notably and quintessentially Davy Crockett— also represented a challenge to bourgeois gender roles, "invert[ing] absolutely the values and admonitions of the male moral reformers" of the time (Smith-Rosenberg 1985, 93). Thus by the time the word "hillbilly" first appeared in print in 1899 (Harkins 2004, 49), Appalachian men and women were well established as transgressors of modern, middle-class gender roles.

Moreover, as sexual beings, hillbillies such as Crockett defied categories produced by sexologists, physicians, and moral reformers of the nineteenth century. Tall tales of Crockett's polymorphous perversity included episodes with animals, men, and women that suggested a kind of "liminality," according to scholar Carroll Smith-Rosenberg. She defines liminality as "the stage of being between categories and the power inherent in that process" (1985, 98). Like an adolescent who is neither child nor adult, the hillbilly is a liminal figure in American culture and letters, exuding a sexuality that can be construed as comically or dangerously crossing the bounds of proper sexuality, often inverting "repressive bourgeois heterosexuality, the bourgeois family, and bourgeois social order" (107).

Especially in this capacity to offend middle-class sensibilities, "hillbilly" in the twentieth century emerged as a derogatory term for poor people. As the poster population for the mid-century "War on Poverty," images of Appalachian whites in particular were used to upset the bourgeois myth of American classlessness.[2] But manufacturing paternalistic empathy for Appalachians also produced a byproduct of fear and hatred of "rednecks" and "white trash."[3] As a stereotype of impoverished living, "hillbilly" is akin to "white trash," a term that "calls our attention to the way that discourses of class and racial difference tend to bleed into one another, especially in the way that they pathologize and lay waste to their 'others'" (Newitz and Wray 1997, 169). Depicting Appalachians as trash or as hillbillies thus inextricably conjoins matters of poverty with matters of race. Moreover, "stereotypes of white trash and 'hillbillies' are replete with references to dangerous and excessive sexuality [such as] rape (both heterosexual and homosexual), incest, and sexual abuse," even though "such abuse occurs in all segments of the population" (171). In this way, the hillbilly serves as a foil for middle-class social mores, defining modern norms against the perceived abnormality of a liminal subject whose sexuality, gender, class, and race are distinctly "other."

As a white "other," the hillbilly has a particular racial status defined by premodern "nobility" or "backwardness."

> Despite their poverty, ignorance, primitiveness, and isolation, "hillbillies" were "one hundred percent" Protestant Americans of supposedly pure Anglo-Saxon or at least Scotch-Irish lineage, which countless commentators of the late-nineteenth- and early-twentieth centuries, greatly concerned by waves of Southern and Eastern European immigrants, took pains to prove. Thus, middle-class white Americans could see these people as a fascinating and exotic "other" akin to Native Americans or Blacks, while at the same time sympathize with them as poorer and less modern versions of themselves. (Harkins 2004, 7)

This racialization implied in any representation of the hillbilly can be maligned or championed but is nonetheless part of its appeal and function. In this way the hillbilly's ambiguous liminality is matched by America's ambivalence toward those labeled hillbillies. Female Appalachians, for example, are idealized or demonized not only in terms of racial purity or inbreeding, but also as all natural "hillbilly gals" or unnatural "mannish misfits" (Williamson 1995, 225–63).

As representatives of mountain, country life, hillbillies can thus reflect either heroism—bravery and loyalty to traditional ways—or a deviance, sadism, and primitivism that is said to fly in the face of modern progress. In other words, the hillbilly

> served the dual and seemingly contradictory purposes of allowing the "mainstream," or generally non-rural, middle-class white, American audience to imagine a romanticized past, while simultaneously enabling the same audience to recommit itself to modernity by caricaturing the negative aspects of pre-modern, uncivilized society. (Harkins 2004, 7)

And of course, since modernity and "civilization" are racialized as Western and white, the dual function of the hillbilly is as much a matter of race as it is a marker of primitivism and poverty—and as much a matter of race as of gender and sexual transgression.

Therefore, during a time when various fundamentalisms worldwide are so intent on imposing rigid gender distinctions, it is no wonder that now the hillbilly would emerge powerfully to contain in one embodiment the monstrous or heroic deeds of the war on terror that seem to blur "male" and "female" characteristics. In relation to modern distinctions of masculinity and femininity, the hillbilly—as someone who balefully or wonderfully resists modernity—occupies that liminal space between such modern bifurcations.

Of course, it is important to keep in mind that in discussing the hillbilly, we analyze a representation, a fabrication, a personification, and embodiment of the narrative of mountain living in which resistance to modernity is a basic element. I am less concerned about actual persons or communities that "the hillbilly" might reference and more interested in its function as a trope that deflects criticism of America's uncivilized behavior.

The Ballad of Jessica Lynch

Traditionally, ballads are tales of romantic tragedy, but when George Bruns and Tom Blackburn spent about twenty minutes penning the words to a song for Walt Disney's new television program in 1954, there was nothing tragic about "The Ballad of Davy Crockett" (Bender n.d.). It was a hit, launching the Crockett craze that garnered plenty of revenue for the Walt Disney Company and rearticulating for millions of baby boomers the heroic myth of "the king of the wild frontier" (Bruns and Blackburn 1954). Disney's version of Crockett extended the well-established view of

Crockett as "the heroic frontiersman and Indian fighter" who nonethe-less was a "comical hick" with a "backward ignorance" that often hu-morously proved wiser than the more cosmopolitan legislators he worked with in the U.S. House of Representatives (Harkins 2004, 21–23). In this way, representations of Crockett reflected the ambivalent attitude toward Appalachia as full of liminal hillbillies whose loyalty to nature, God, and country was ultimately their tragic flaw. So it is not surprising that Davy Crockett's ballad was revitalized to honor another Appalachian soldier whose loyalty to God and country also reached mythic propor-tions of heroism.

Featured on a website devoted to Scotch-Irish solidarity, the "Ballad of Jessica Lynch" (2004) replaces Crockett with the 19-year-old army supply clerk who served in the current war in Iraq. Instead of hearing how Crockett "give his word an' he give his hand / that his Injun friends could keep their land" (Bruns and Blackburn 1954), "The Ballad of Jessica Lynch" tells of how "President Bush give his word and he give his hand / that our Iraqi friends could keep their land." So even though she is ex-alted as the "Queen of the Iraqi Campaign," Jessica Lynch is only an aux-iliary of President Bush, not quite the lone frontiersman to whom she is compared. Also, instead of "Born on a mountain top in Tennessee / Green-est state in the land of the free" (Bruns and Blackburn 1954), Jessica's bal-lad opens with "Born on a mountain top in West Virginia / Poorest state in the land of the free" ("Ballad of Jessica Lynch" 2004). Portraying Lynch as hailing from "the poorest state" is in keeping with the way "mountain women have been portrayed on film as poverty goddesses, making *hill-billy* synonymous with *poor* when poor is meant to be noble" (William-son 1995, 247). Lynch's presumed nobility lay not in the ownership of land but in her presumed *lack* of ownership of anything but her county-fair-pageant-winning looks and her fighting mountaineer spirit.

In addition, as a product of the place that some read as a monument to antimodernism (Whisnant 1980), Lynch symbolizes more than poverty-as-nobility; she is the rugged antidote to urban modernization. As one conservative commentator wrote, "Rural West Virginia can still produce a Jessica Lynch. The foot soldiers still exist in the forgotten corners of the culture where the infection of the effete elites have not yet penetrated" (Reynolds 2003). This quotation perpetuates the idea of West Virginia, in particular, and Appalachia in general, as a forgotten corner where moder-nity, here maligned in populist and misogynist terms, has not yet cor-rupted the natural order. This nostalgia for a pre-modern culture often meshes with the fantasy of an all-white culture, a forgotten corner where racial purity has not yet been "penetrated" by "other" cultures or races. Perhaps this explains why the "Ballad of Jessica Lynch" is featured on a Scotch-Irish website whose readers, according to Chip Berlet, an expert on right-wing movements, "quickly fall through the thin ice of ethnic pride into a racialized subtext of white racial nationalism" (2005).

In the service of a perhaps more subtly racialized nationalism, Jessica Lynch's story reproduced the idea of the liminal hillbilly woman. In the spring of 2003, 19-year-old Jessica Lynch from Palestine, West Virginia, was presented first as the mannishly tough soldier whose primitive fighting spirit was ignited under the pressure of war, and then as the frail white hillbilly gal whose violation was worthy of rescue and revenge. In May, she was injured and captured from her overturned Humvee during an assault on American forces in Iraq. She thus became a prisoner of war sent to a hospital because of her injuries. A combat camera team videotaped the nighttime rescue operation, which entailed soldiers dramatically kicking down a door, rushing up stairs as if there were enemies to elude or encounter, and transporting the petite woman from the hospital. "On television, the army's grainy footage of Lynch being carried out of the Iraqi hospital on a stretcher and whisked into a waiting Black Hawk helicopter was played over and over, and became an enduring image of the war" (Eviatar 2003). The story that circulated with the videotape was that, before being captured, Lynch had fired relentlessly at her enemies. There were also allegations that her Iraqi captors had abused her physically and sexually. Such stories were circulated as breaking news once the video was released.

Controversies ensued over why the video was taken, how it got circulated, and what the military said about it. Some said the actions seen on the video seemed staged like a movie or a publicity stunt. Also, the story seemed fishy. "It didn't pass the smell test," said a journalist for *Newsday*. "She's a 19-year-old supply clerk, and they made her sound like Rambo" (Eviatar 2003). Referring to a trilogy of movies featuring John Rambo, a veteran of the U.S. war in Vietnam, the journalist could as easily have said that Lynch was made to resemble Granny Clampett, Calamity Jane, Ruby Thewes, or any number of gun-toting hillbilly gals who defend their land and honor to the teeth (Creadick 2005; Williamson 1995). The image of Lynch shooting round after round in combat recirculated the old idea that Appalachian women are mannishly physical and aggressive.

In addition to the rumor that Lynch had fired her weapon repeatedly, the media suggested that she had been sexually violated in the Iraqi hospital, arousing a whole host of old, nationalistic fears about white women's vulnerability. The "daring rescue," as it was called, started to sound not like *Rambo* but like *The Birth of a Nation*, D. W. Griffith's 1915 film based on Thomas Dixon's novel about the rise of the Ku Klux Klan. According to author Minnie Bruce Pratt, "The U.S. media has saturated us with the image of a frail, helpless, blonde-haired white girl being saved from captors who are people of color, the old racist lie of the South replayed on an international screen" (2004, 22). The "old racist lie" Pratt speaks of involves not only the myth of the black rapist (Davis 1981) but also the related notion of whiteness as purity (Dyer 1997). Whiteness as purity, in the sense of racial integrity, was the presumption that made the thought of black rapists and captors of color so sinister. As in *The Birth of a Nation*, the reason to fear the ravishing of white women by dark-skinned men was the physical abuse itself *and* the result of mulatto offspring, the dilution of the white race, which was tantamount to the death of the nation. Mentioning the "old racist lie," Pratt makes explicit the implicit logic underlying the horror of blonde Jessica Lynch in the hands of dark-skinned men: what is at stake is not only her individual safety but the safety of the whole body politic and its ability to reproduce a pure victory, a white future for America, and a Western civilization for the world.

Moreover, Pratt claims that "none of what was reported was accurate, including the supposed violence against Private Lynch at the hands of the Iraqis. It turns out that the doctors had been trying to get her to U.S. troops only to have their ambulance fired upon repeatedly" (2004, 22). This assertion parallels the contention that the stories about Lynch's combat skills and abuse in the Iraqi hospital were bogus. Such contentions were confirmed when Jessica Lynch herself denied that she fired her weapon during her capture *and* that she was mistreated at the hospital. She refused to go along with the social script that was written for her, a script in which a poor country girl from West Virginia was saved from the brutality and barbarism of the Iraqis.

According to various scholars, the Jessica Lynch story was popular because it reflected themes that entertainment media have made recognizable in tales about U.S. soldiers in Vietnam. Key among the themes are a small group or single American soldier pitted against "hordes of non-Europeans" who intend to punish "oppressed," "indigenous" "natives" in "peasant villages" (Barkawi 2004, 134–36). Tarak Barkawi successfully uses these observations to make the point that "the rewriting of the Vietnam War was crucial to politically enabling the conquest and occupation of Iraq for purposes of liberating the oppressed Iraqi people" (136). But Barkawi never considers how Lynch is narrated as liminally occupying both subject positions: she represents the U.S. soldier pitted against hordes of dark non-Europeans *and* the oppressed person from the supposed "peasant village" of Palestine, West Virginia. Moreover, in discussing Lynch as the real-life soldier in the type of rescue story and propaganda stunt satirized in Barry Levinson's film *Wag the Dog*, John Carlos Rowe avoids the obvious observation that instead of a male soldier being rescued, it is a woman. In this sense, the "carefully constructed narrative" of Jessica Lynch not only "undoes the irony" of Levinson's critical film, but one-ups it by locating in a single person all the characters of the narrative (Rowe 2004, 586). Who but a woman from Appalachia, long thought to be America's internal colony with its third-world economic conditions, its "backward" cultural isolation, and its resistance to modernity, could better achieve what Barkawi says this narrative attempts: to reproduce the tropes of civilization and barbarism upon which Western and American identity rely?

Thus the appeal of Jessica Lynch may also be the sheer economy of her story: one body represents both the Rambo-esque heroism of the American underdog fighting to the teeth *and* the noble savage who waits for salvation from the West. This is accurate in two ways. First, the army is said to be salvation for Lynch, her ticket out of what Lynch's biographer Rick Bragg calls the "isolated," "inert" culture of West Virginia and its always presumed poverty (2003, 8). Second, the Special Forces unit that takes her from the hospital is Lynch's salvation from Iraqi culture (or a lack thereof). Lynch embodies the feminine vulnerability usually represented by the feminized non-European civilians whose survival is made to depend on Western soldiers in war movies. Thus one woman's body contains both aspects of the narratives Barkawi says have been prevalent in discourses of "small wars": the one who saves, bringing Western-defined liberation and civilization, and the one who must be saved from the uncivilized ways, including (in this case) those of Appalachia as well as the Persian Gulf.

Moreover, another layer of references that makes Lynch's story so resonant involves the threats—both real and imagined—to her bodily and sexual integrity. One threat is the aforementioned idea, dramatized by the army rescue video, of white Western soldiers saving Lynch from dark non-Europeans. Another is the media and medical report that "she was the victim of anal sexual assault" (Bragg 2003, 96). Lynch does not remember any such assault and her memoirs do not include any complaints about that kind of violation. While she gives plenty of details of excruciating pain in her arms, legs, feet, back, and neck in *I Am a Soldier, Too,* she never refers to her anus (2003). So there is some doubt whether this, like the allegation that she was slapped in the hospital by interrogators and mistreated by doctors, which she flatly has denied in statements to various media, was a fabrication for the sake of instilling a sense of injustice and vengeance among American civilians and soldiers. *I Am a Soldier, Too* details how one soldier in particular heard of the "blonde captive" prisoner of war suffering and abused in the hospital and was motivated to kill more (Bragg 2003, 121–22). If the anal assault was a lie circulated with that purpose in mind, it was an effective one, according to Lynch's book. The fear of sodomy, even more than vaginal rape, might profoundly resonate with male soldiers, causing them to fear for their own anal safety and to regard more fully the Iraqis as a "backward" enemy, meaning that they are so uncivilized that they would rather take a woman from behind.

Jessica Lynch's hillbilly story, replete with fears of maintaining bodily integrity against a non-European "other," defended the war in Iraq as a civilizing mission and deflected allegations that Americans were barbaric invaders by directing public attention to an Appalachian woman whose fighting spirit and safety became the popular reason for war in Iraq. As the months of wartime progressed, Lynch's disavowing tales of her abuse *by* Iraqis lent a peculiar symmetry to Lynndie England's picture-perfect evidence of abuse *of* Iraqis. That picture-perfect evidence of abuse is also picture-perfect evidence that the media and the government have relied on opposite images of Appalachian women to deflect criticisms of the war. Although seven soldiers have been undergoing court martials for their abuse of Iraqi prisoners, the images of one woman, Lynndie England, have been circulated most often and most widely.

Delivering Lynndie England

If Lynch was made to represent, alternately, the Davy Crockett/Rambo of the Iraqi campaign and then the good-hearted "hillbilly gal" whose sexual (and implicitly racial) purity warranted rescue, England's image followed more precisely the hillbilly stereotype of the "mannish misfit" (Williamson 1995, 225, 242). "What more gender-bending icon have Americans seen this year than Private First Class Lynndie England with a naked Iraqi prisoner on a leash?" (Goodman 2004, A15). Featuring short, dark hair, combat boots, flaccid cigarette dangling from a smirking mouth, England's images are a conglomeration of stereotypes of she-male sexual deviance. Too man-like, she appears as a khaki dominatrix presiding over her whipped subordinates, kinky leash in hand.

The facts of England's Appalachian heritage and, specifically, her residence in a mobile home in Fort Ashby, West Virginia, were reported in the media. She was the "trailer trash torturer," not a goddess of poverty like Jessica Lynch but an *ignoble* savage (Jennings 2005). Moreover, some suggested that the racism involved in terrifying Arabs was endemic to her regional upbringing. Thus the very images and stories most circulated from the Abu Ghraib scandal not only raised awareness of the truly despicable behavior of U.S. military police but also located that behavior very neatly in the liminal, even androgynous, person of Lynndie England.

With pictures of England first and foremost, reports of the Abu Ghraib scenes maligned the Military Police Company that recruited and trained her. Based in rural Maryland, the 372nd Company recruits heavily and primarily in West Virginia and rural Pennsylvania, where jobs are scarce and money is tight. Without a doubt, the 372nd Military Police Company did, intolerably and inexcusably, humiliate and torture inmates in most dehumanizing ways. But the 372nd was also maligned on the *less* legitimate grounds that those soldiers, by virtue of their Appalachian-ness, were inherently incapable of humanity. Journalist Seymour Hersh reported that a former intelligence officer blamed recycled hillbillies for not knowing the boundary between humane and inhumane treatment.

> The military-police prison guards, the former official said, included "recycled hillbillies from Cumberland, Maryland." He was referring to members of the 372nd Military Police Company. Seven members of the company are now facing charges for their role in the abuse at Abu Ghraib. "How are these guys from Cumberland going to know anything? The Army Reserve doesn't know what it's doing." (Hersh 2004b, 41)

The recycled reservists from hillbilly country were not only criminally torturous; they were too stupid to know any better.

This reported claim of recycled hillbillies from an intelligence official spawned less official, more hostile claims on internet blogs and chat rooms. "The abuse in Iraq was solely the work of a few cretinous [sic] hillbillies," according to one; it was "the work of a few sadistic hillbillies and miscreants," agreed another. Most demeaning, the photographs were said to show "mating rituals of wild hillbillies."[4] The fact that Lynndie England became pregnant during her stay in Iraq lent salacious evidence of this last demonizing claim. Out-of-control female sexuality was not only a sign of liminal, "wild hillbillies." According to some, it was also a sign of feminism.

Famous career conservative Phyllis Schlafly claimed that Lynndie England's behavior was the logical extension of feminism and women's striving for equality in the military. She asked, "Why were female GIs assigned to guard male prisoners anyway?" (Schlafly 2004). But in fact, they were not assigned that job; England had a desk job (Duke 2004, D1). Schlafly also predicted that the famous picture of England holding a leashed man would "soon show up on the bulletin boards of women's studies centers and feminist college professors" because "that picture is the radical feminists' ultimate fantasy of how they dream of treating men" (Schlafly 2004). For Schlafly, England's picture was a sign of feminism. But what kind of feminism? Schlafly's commentary begs the question that those who value feminism felt compelled to ask as England's image circulated.

For example, in a commencement speech to Barnard students Barbara Ehrenreich, the author most recently of *Nickel and Dimed* (2001), claimed she lost a naïve sense of feminism in which women are presumed to be morally superior to men and less capable of violence, cruelty, or conquest (2004). According to Ehrenreich, this kind of feminism shaped discussions of Bosnian rape camps as "an instrument of war and even war as an extension of rape" in the early 1990s (2004). Ehrenreich's point is that because some feminists retained the idea that women have an innate moral superiority, the pictures from Abu Ghraib caused them to "wrestle with that assumption today" (2004). In this way, Ehrenreich, like Schlafly, saw the Abu Ghraib photos as an opportunity to scrutinize feminism, or at least particular variations of it. Also like Schlafly, Ehrenreich's critique of (a particular kind of) feminism did not extend to the deployment of the images themselves.

Focusing only on the three women soldiers who were charged with abusing prisoners at Abu Ghraib (Lynndie England, Sabra Harmon, and Megan Ambuhl), Ehrenreich suggests that their lower-class status and desire to move beyond it demanded conformity. "They are working class women who wanted to go to college and knew the military as the quickest way in that direction. Once they got in, they wanted to fit in" (2004). Later, Ehrenreich tells the new Ivy League graduates, "we need a kind of woman who doesn't want to be one of the boys when the boys are acting like sadists or fools" (2004). This message utterly ignores the fact that, among the reportedly hundreds of photographs, the American public saw the three women's faces—and mostly the butchest of them all, England— more than those of the four men who were charged along with them. Ehrenreich's discussion thereby accepts the portrayal of abuse at Abu Ghraib as the result of poor, desperate, and uneducated Appalachian women. Moreover, couching her discussion of Abu Ghraib in the context of Bosnia, Ehrenreich situates England and the other Appalachian women in the politics of rape, a specific form of sexual violence that usually is attributed to men.

This "mannish misfit" stereotype is of course the flipside of the innocuous hillbilly gal represented by images of Jessica Lynch. Countless other commentators have noted the rather obvious and dichotomous way that Lynndie England was represented as a whore while Jessica Lynch was represented as an angel. Or, to translate the old angel/whore stereotype in Appalachian terms, if Jessica was the female Davy Crockett, Lynndie was the female version of the hillbilly rapist.

This degrading stereotype of the hillbilly rapist was made popular during the war in Vietnam by a 1972 movie called *Deliverance*, which was based on James Dickey's 1970 novel (Harkins 2004, 205–10; Williamson 1995, 155–67). Understanding how scapegoating England deflected accusations that the abuse at Abu Ghraib was something systemic entails learning how the hillbilly rapist stereotype has been perpetuated for an audience too young to remember *Deliverance*. Twenty-two years after *Deliverance*, the enormously popular film *Pulp Fiction* showcased a significant episode that featured hillbillies. The episode begins as Marcellus, a black man, and Butch, a white man, enter the "Mason-Dixon" pawn shop fighting, only to become victimized by Maynard, the shop owner, and Zed, two "hillbillies [who] are obviously brothers," according to the screenplay written by Quentin Tarantino (1994, 124). With a confederate flag and Tennessee license plates on the wall, Maynard and Zed take sadistic pleasure in torturing people in the basement. They tie up and gag Marcellus and Butch and they have locked up a third man dressed in leather bondage wear. When Zed proceeds to sodomize Marcellus, *Pulp Fiction* reinvigorates the image of the barbaric hillbilly rapist for a new generation.

Like the rapists of *Deliverance*, the rapists of *Pulp Fiction* die an especially violent death with specifically chosen weapons. In *Deliverance* it was a hunting bow; the hillbilly is penetrated through the chest by an arrow. In *Pulp Fiction*, Maynard is similarly penetrated by an exotic Japanese sword. In both cases, the fatal penetration obviously refers to the agonizing rape; the punishment symbolically fits the crime. But also, both these weapons symbolize a nonWestern, ancient method of killing. In *Deliverance*, the white male protagonist appropriates the bow and arrow from American Indian culture; in *Pulp Fiction*, the white male protagonist appropriates the ceremonial sword from the Japanese samurai. In doing so, both men justify their killing as morally right because, presumably, it takes a primitive to kill a primitive.

When it is Marcellus's turn to kill his rapist, he does not take the sword from Butch to attack Zed. Rejecting the ceremonial, choreographed, artistic sword fight of ancient cultures, Marcellus shoots Zed in the groin with the more modern technology of Zed's own shotgun, at first providing swift justice at the root of his pain, namely the white man's penis. The character and actions of Marcellus thus present a reversal of lynching, which historically had white men castrating black men before hanging and/or burning them. But instead of saying I'm going to lynch you now, Marcellus famously declares, "Hear me talkin', hillbilly boy? I ain't through with you by a damn sight. I'm gonna get Medieval on your ass" (Tarantino 1994, 131). This appeal to pre-Enlightenment torture follows the film's established logic that the punishment fit the crime, especially as it involves the "ass." Moreover, it indicts Zed, the hillbilly rapist, as a thing from the Middle Ages, a creature not evolved to modern ways and, therefore, deserving of barbaric retribution (Dinshaw 1999, 182–91).

Such vengeance is particularly warranted, according to Hollywood logic, when the sexual assault of a man is perpetrated by a man. Homophobic portrayals of gay sadists, rapists, and murderers are peppered throughout the history of the silver screen. Popular culture has thereby perpetuated stereotypes of gay men and women as predators who deserve excruciating death or shameful suicide (Russo 1987). The myth of the hillbilly rapist intersects with this homophobic discursive tradition because in relation to modern distinctions of gender, both "the hillbilly" and "the homosexual" are liminally queer. Both blur the lines between female and male; both are therefore deviating from "civilized" sexuality.

Be that as it may, rape and sodomy are common practices. And there are Americans who practice sadism in terms of bonding rituals (such as gang bangs) or as erotic role play (as commercial sadomasochistic enterprises across the country attest). But, as the filmmakers who produced *Deliverance* and *Pulp Fiction* know, Appalachia is one of the "backward" places to invoke if you want to depict sadism and coerced sex as inevitable and inherent. Sexual deviance is portrayed as endemic to the region and its people.

So when officials who were trying to explain the abuse of inmates at Abu Ghraib prison circulated the idea that a few recycled hillbillies were the only bad apples in the whole U.S. military bunch, it resonated with this longstanding image of Appalachia as sadistic and sexually deviant. In this way, some Pentagon officials, who had been notified of the abuse by the Red Cross months before the scandal broke, deflected blame for the very fact of the inflicted abuse in the first place, for knowing about it prior to its publicity in the second instance, and, third, for any criminal neglect of international laws against torture. Lest we consider the Abu Ghraib violations connected to prisoner abuse at Guantanamo Bay or within our own domestic correctional facilities, officials and media attempted to channel our ire toward a particular poster girl. Circulated widely and repeatedly was the image of Lynndie England, representative not simply of bad prison management, but of West Virginia womanhood gone wrong. The legacy of deviant hillbillies, popularized by *Deliverance* during the Vietnam era and later by *Pulp Fiction,* has successfully been recycled in the image of Lynndie England to contain and explain away some of the most disturbing images of our nation's military.

This analysis in no way undermines the claims that the acts of sexual degradation at Abu Ghraib had a more localized political purpose. According to journalist Seymour Hersh, these pictures were taken for the purpose of blackmailing prisoners (Hersh 2004a, 38–39). If they refused to comply with every command, U.S. forces could show these pictures to prisoners' friends and families whose religious beliefs would be so offended the prisoner would be ostracized. Hersh's political explanation meshes with a more psychological explanation for torture formulated by Klaus Theweleit. He explains that "like a lover," a torturer

> needs another person for his own growth; but where a lover makes the other person grow, the torturer tries to annex this other: he transforms the other person into a part of his own body; a part of his body he wants to get rid of. The tortured thus are treated as parts of the body of the torturer: parts of his body the torturer doesn't have under control; parts of his body the torturer hates; parts of his body the torturer feels himself forced to kill. (1993, 300)

According to this view, the torture at Abu Ghraib could be seen as a matter of abjection more than punishment or "intelligence" tactics, a way to expel from the world the parts of the body politic that U.S. forces deemed out of control and hated.

In *Powers of Horror*, feminist Julia Kristeva has theorized abjection as that which delineates the difference between a person and the external world, between the subject and object (1982). In so doing she moves from abjection as a concern for the individual, whose expelled bodily wastes (such as feces, semen, menses, mucus, milk) determine the boundaries of a single body, to abjection as a concern for society, in which expelled bodies—that is, corpses—serve as a visible border that reminds us who is to be considered a subject and who an object in this world.

> These bodily fluids, this defilement, this shit are what life withstands, hardly and with difficulty, on the part of death. There, I am at the border of my condition as a living being. My body extricates itself, as being alive, from that border. Such wastes drop so that I might live, until, from loss to loss, nothing remains in me and my entire body falls beyond the limit—*cadere*, cadaver. If dung signifies the other side of the border, the place where I am not and which permits me to be, the corpse, the most sickening of wastes, is a border that has encroached upon everything. (71)

Thus, images of tortured bodies enact the powers of horror, in which objectifying one body is the requirement for establishing the subjectivity—hence the political supremacy—of another. Or, as scholar Norma Claire Moruzzi explains, "historically, the nation-state establishes itself through the convulsions of a body politic which rejects those parts of itself, defined as other or excess, whose rejected alterity then engenders the consolidation of a national identity" (1993, 143).

It is this process of consolidating a national identity and thereby becoming supremely dominant that elicits a smile, according to Theweleit. "This moment of happiness and laughter, that is to be found at the very center of so many torturings, is no accident at all. It's the boyish way of feeling like 'a man' all over the world, it seems" (1993, 303). Theweleit's interpretative logic seems validated by the reactions to seeing Lynndie England—a woman—smile over the stacked, tangled bodies of inmates. She appears to behave and show feelings that, presumably, only a man could or should be able to do and emote in such circumstances.

Especially since it is Lynndie England's smiling face, more than any other, that is circulated, we are hard pressed to "realize that there is an element of stage management involved in the release of the few photos seen so far, out of what are reported to be thousands of pictures (not unlike the staging of the rescue of Private Jessica Lynch)" (Marshall 2004). In both cases, the image of a West Virginia woman serves as much—if not more—a military function as the women themselves serve in their capacity as army personnel. Their function is the cultural mediation of the war on terror, in which stereotypes of Appalachian women as either mannish and heroic or as mannish and deviant help articulate what there is to be terrified of: the violation of bodily boundaries (Lynch's "anal sexual assault"; the various sexualized degradations and torturing of prisoners at Abu Ghraib); and, relatedly, the liminal lack of boundaries (within singular bodies and within societies at large) between men and women, male and female. Lynndie England's gender-bending appearance became all the more saturated with mixed meanings when she appeared pregnant in army fatigues for her court martial trial; as a mother and a torturer, England embodied some of the worst misogynist fears of women without boundaries.[5]

According to Kristeva, there is no greater fear of violating bodily boundaries than the fear of the maternal body and the idea of pregnancy, a tremendous event in which one body becomes two. Aborting pregnancy entails much of what people find "monstrous" about pregnancy and giving birth—the abjection of flesh and blood, the splitting into two what was one, and the demonstration of women's innate power to give or deny "life" (1982). Anti-abortion imagery reflects these so-called monstrosities; lately it has served to equate abortion with the kind of horror we see in the Abu Ghraib pictures. In recent depictions of abortion, it is the re-contextualization—rather than the decontextualization of "the fetus" from "the mother"—that is so remarkable. Comparing fetuses with victims of disaster, war, torture, and terrorism, "pro-life" propaganda engages the powers of horror, presenting women's extracted fetal/vaginal flesh first as fetal "bodies" and further representing that womanly flesh as fetal "corpses." As the "most sickening of wastes," the fetal "corpse" is bodily abjection thrown back in women's faces, sometimes literally (Vinzant 1993). Like American torturers in Iraq who oversee prisoners smeared with feces, "pro-life" protesters who fling fetuses and otherwise force women to face their bodily abjection attempt to achieve what was achieved at Abu Ghraib: establishing the subjectivity and political identity of those who would determine what and who is American.

While there are limits and dangers to Kristeva's kind of psychosexual analysis that supposedly bridges cultures and eras, I have found it useful for making sense of the seemingly contradictory case of anti-abortion murders of clinic personnel. As I have examined in depth elsewhere, the case of "pro-life" murders—that is, of killing for life—is situated profoundly in what Susan Jeffords (1989) has called the remasculinization of America after the Vietnam War. In *Killing for Life: The Apocalyptic Narrative of Pro-life Politics*, I argue that anti-abortion violence was another aspect of that remasculinization, that cultural mediation of U.S. failure in Vietnam that produced the New Warriors of the militia movement, the Christian men's movement, the New Right, and Rambo Reaganomics

(Mason 2002). Like the *Rambo* movies that helped to culturally mediate "small wars" and the preemptive war in Iraq, stories of abortion warriors (along with stories of militia and organized white supremacists) have helped prepare the U.S. public for terrorism committed by Americans. None have culturally mediated the war on terror more than the story of Eric Rudolph, another deployment of the hillbilly defense.

In the Cave with Eric Rudolph

Eric Robert Rudolph was one of several domestic terrorists who wreaked havoc on the reproductive rights community in the United States during the 1990s. He was the suspect sought for bombings in 1996, 1997, and 1998 that were, like other acts of "pro-life" terrorism, accompanied by letters signed by the Army of God. Rudolph detonated bombs at Centennial Park during the Olympics, at a lesbian bar near Atlanta, and at two abortion clinics, one in Georgia and one in Alabama. These bombings injured more than a hundred, killed two, seriously maimed a third, and terrorized innumerable people. Rudolph was first suspected of these acts in 1998. When he was caught in 2003, after the terrorist attacks of September 11, 2001, Rudolph was not taken to Guantanamo Bay like other people suspected of terrorism. On the contrary, in accounts of his eventual capture, reporting the locals' romance with Rudolph was just as prevalent as reporting his white supremacist ideas and murderous anti-abortion and anti-gay attacks.

As a representative of the Army of God, Rudolph became a sort of folk hero said to be eluding police in the dense terrain of North Carolina (Horwitz 1999). Moreover, as a fugitive supposedly hiding out in the caves of Nantahala forest, Rudolph was the American version of fugitives supposedly hiding out in the caves and spider-holes of Iraq and Afghanistan. In each case, these fugitives were portrayed as anti- or pre-modern hillbillies or fundamentalists who were acting out of "childish rebellion, a confirmation of the 'underdeveloped' features of those 'backward cultures'" (Rowe 2004, 592). Rudolph was thus demonized by the pro-choice community as a throwback to fundamentalism and anti-modernism, refusing the enlightened view of sexuality that includes reproductive freedom. But some locals saw his anti-abortion, anti-gay, anti-miscegenation, and anti-Semitic stances as a matter of standing up for traditional mountaineer values. In the media Rudolph was represented as a mountaineer survivalist outwitting the big city leaders of a high-tech manhunt that lasted for more than five years. Even the sketch released by the FBI depicted a scruffy, longhaired mountaineer, despite the fact that when captured Rudolph was clean shaven and closely shorn, causing one incredulous commentator to consider wryly "how Davy Crockett got his hair cut" (Buchanan 2003). By examining a particularly literary defense of Rudolph offered by a respected novelist, we can see how Rudolph's terrorism was explainable, if not dismissible, by his Crockett-like hillbilly ways and, hence, by his underdevelopment, his backwardness, his childish rebellion. Ultimately, the violence Rudolph confessed to is framed not as terrorism at all, but as a quaint relic of the nineteenth century.

Allan Gurganus, author of *Oldest Living Confederate Widow Tells All*, penned an elaborate defense not only of Rudolph but also of the people who may have aided him and thereby harbored a suspected terrorist. Gurganus's *New York Times* essay is titled "Why We Fed the Bomber" and explains the support for Rudolph not in terms of anti-abortion sentiment but by situating him in the literary tradition of the "cantankerous outlaw protester" (2003, 13). Gurganus traces this character through canonical fiction by Cooper, Twain, Wolf, O'Connor, Williams, Fitzgerald, and Faulkner, arguing that Rudolph's "tale seems a green boomerang hurled forward from the 19th century" (2003, 13).

Rudolph's terroristic violence therefore was not, according to Gurganus, part of the reinvigorated white supremacy of the 1980s and 1990s, or of the paramilitary culture that seeped into the mainstream after the Vietnam War, or even of the backlash against women whose reproductive freedom was being whittled away with punitive and regulatory legislation that undermined the 1973 decision in *Roe v. Wade* (Mason 2002). No, Gurganus explains the violence as part of Rudolph's folksy upbringing in Appalachia, that retarded culture of poverty so intricately linked to violence. Rudolph is one of those "people who, accustomed to failure, make that their merit. Folks who'll find reasons, foes, religions, races to bear the brunt of such vast generational disappointment. Violence, for them so personalized and omnipresent, comes to seem their bully pulpit of achievement" (Gurganus 2003, 13). For Gurganus, Appalachians only know "vast generational disappointment" and, as white trash are wont to do, turn to violence for a sense of achievement (13).

But in Rudolph's case this violence seems mitigated by another "achievement," namely his outsmarting government officials and bounty hunters. In this regard, Rudolph is a populist hero, a hillbilly who, like his third-world counterparts, makes a mockery of modernity. "The feds literally asked locals which cave Eric Rudolph might like best, as soldiers would later grill amused Afghan tribesmen" (13). This comparison suggests that both Afghans and North Carolinians are remnant populations holding out against the corruptions of modern, Western, "big city" life. Like Afghan tribesmen, hillbillies are depicted as something more primitive and savage, but also more noble and pure than the urbanized federal agents who, for all their technology, cannot (amusingly enough) find a "cantankerous outlaw protester" whose closeness to nature is his salvation (13).

Gurganus is not the only one who sees a comic conflation between fugitives presumed to be hiding out in Appalachia and Afghanistan or Iraq. Consider a digital depiction, titled "Jihad Clampett," of Osama bin Laden as the patriarch of the television family the Beverly Hillbillies, Jed Clampett.[6] This image simultaneously renders bin Laden as an anti-modern, backward mountain man and renders Jed Clampett as a racial-ized "other" no better than the so-called "sand nigger" who arranged to topple the World Trade Center and kill thousands of people in the pro-cess. Furthermore, replacing Clampett's first name "Jed" with "Jihad" is not only a mockery of the Islamic call to sacred duty and bin Laden's power, but also an assertion that backward buffoons (like the Buddy Eb-sen character) in America have their own version of spiritual warfare, which is, presumably, no less comical. Indeed, the HBO film *Soldiers in the Army of God* is edited precisely to this effect: militant "pro-lifers" are portrayed as holy-war hillbillies who are as funny as they are fright-ening (Mason 2004, 807–8).

But to those who are the targets of America's homegrown religious ret-ribution, domestic terrorism is no laughing matter. Several books have delineated the scope, frequency, and impact of domestic terrorism com-mitted in the name of "pro-life" activism, including bombings, butyric acid spills, arson, death threats, and snipers that have resulted in the death of seven clinic workers and terrorism of countless people for more than a decade (Baird-Windle and Bader 2001; Mason 2002; Risen and Thomas 1998). No one has argued that such acts of terrorism are equal to the vast political, legal, and humanitarian injustice of the attacks on September 11 or the abuse at Abu Ghraib prison, although several have argued convincingly that similar psychological dynamics, guerrilla tac-tics, and apocalyptic ideologies undergird both anti-abortion and anti-American attacks (Juergensmeyer 2000; Mason 2002; Stern 2003). Put-ting anti-abortion violence in the global context of religious warfare helps make sense of the "pro-life" Army of God or the "Embryonic Jihad"—a name copyrighted beneath an illustration for the Pensacola Pro-life Hunt Club, which is an in-joke for those who defend Florida "pro-life" murder-ers Paul Hill and Michael Griffin.[7] It was not until after the attacks of September 11 that the U.S. government publicly and officially acknowl-edged the systemic attacks on abortion personnel—specifically the hun-dreds of anthrax scares delivered to clinics—as domestic terrorism (Ma-son 2004, 804–6).

But the flipside of such long-awaited acknowledgment from the gov-ernment is the idea that, next to 9/11, anti-abortion terrorism is not so bad. Looking back on Rudolph's bombings from the post-9/11 perspec-tive, Allan Gurganus asks, "have five years' terrors numbed us to Eric Rudolph's demonstrations of his wild faith in the fetus, the family, the flag?" (Gurganus 2003, 13). In effect, Gurganus is suggesting that maybe what Rudolph did does not seem so extreme now. We can read this as Gurganus's indictment of our becoming desensitized to terrorism. But following his narrative logic of Rudolph as a cantankerous outlaw protester, we can also read the comparison as apologia. Maybe compared to Al Qaeda and Osama bin Laden, Rudolph can be seen as just a noble savage, a hillbilly who was too loyal to God and country for his own good. He was following his profound religious convictions; he was just following orders as a soldier in the Army of God. The same could be said of Lynndie England; she was just following orders. If such logic does not hold for Lynndie England—and it should not and has not—why should it hold for Eric Rudolph?

Gurganus's essay is important because it rearticulates established cultural assumptions about Appalachia in order to explain (if not excuse) "why we fed the bomber," why Americans support homegrown extremism like bombing abortion clinics, lesbian bars, and multicultural events. Certainly hypocrisy abounds in such support of domestic terrorism during a war on terror. But the larger point is that by invoking Appalachia, Gurganus's essay culturally mediates the domestic front of the war on terror in the same way that the stories of Lynch and England deploy the hillbilly to mediate the war in Iraq.

This becomes clearer as we realize that in Rudolph's story Appalachia itself becomes the site of liminality that is embodied by Lynch and England in their stories. According to historian Douglas Powell, discussions of Rudolph reflect and promote a "right-wing vision of the Appalachian landscape," presenting it as "a gap, an occlusion, a cavern in a broader, global multicultural landscape, wherein the order of nature itself might still sustain some idealized, pre-lapsarian version of white, Christian culture" (2003, 9). It is in this gap, this space within multicultural modernity that is not modern, this stage of being between the categories of civilized and uncivilized, that Rudolph presumably lived. Media and right-wing supporters of Rudolph have romanticized the caves of Nantahala forest and, metonymically, all of Appalachia as precisely that liminal space where one might reverse the modern notions of what is and is not civilized. In this way not only Rudolph but all of Appalachia and the hillbillies said to inhabit this liminal state stand for transgression of modern, bourgeois, civilized ways.

In the war on terror, those hillbillies are called up again and again to steer the public away from thinking that any such transgressions or negotiations between civilized and uncivilized, humane and inhumane behavior are systemic. Most recently, a U.S. soldier in Iraq asked Secretary of Defense Donald Rumsfeld why army vehicles are not adequately equipped to withstand roadside bombs, only to be discredited as a Tennessean who was coached by journalists to ask such a question. News media referred to the exchange as a discussion about "hillbilly armor."

To those of us who study Appalachia, the ongoing war in Iraq has demonstrated how effectively representations of hillbillies are deployed to define America in times of doubt about government motives and national character. Alternately demonizing and romanticizing Appalachians have made it possible for the "pro-life," pro-war Bush administration to deny systemic U.S. terror in both domestic and foreign contexts. But blaming recycled hillbillies for the torture at Abu Ghraib or excusing anti-abortion terrorists as Appalachian survivalists opposing the corruptions of modern life—these recent deployments of the hillbilly defense—are not only a matter of perpetuating stereotypes. Defending America as a civilized nation by scapegoating Appalachians for "uncivilized" behaviors or events—the hillbilly defense—is a redeployment of the embodied narrative of Appalachian life, in which resistance to modern ways is alternately applauded and disdained.

Acknowledgments

Thanks to the following for their assistance: Crystal Jackson, Rachel Jennings, Anna Creadick, Matt Wray, Barb Brents, Kate Hausbeck, Robert Futrell, Tony Harkins, Jane Olmsted, Eric Patterson, colleagues from the 2004 National Endowment for the Humanities Summer Institute at Ferrum College, and the fabulously helpful editors and anonymous readers for this volume.

Notes

1. "The hillbilly" does not signify Appalachia alone, but I link them explicitly for the purposes of examining the stories of Lynch, England, and Rudolph, in which Appalachia (rather than the Ozarks or places like Detroit, where hillbillies are also said to reside) figures prominently.

2. For more on Appalachia and the War on Poverty, see Batteau (1990 Chapter 8), and Williams (2002, 348–50).

3. For a discussion on the distinctions between these terms, see Hartigan (2003, 95–112).

4. I obtained these statements from an electronic submission to Google, which yielded about 800 hits for the phrase "Abu Ghraib hillbillies" on 25 May 2004. The first statement appeared on www.maxlogan.com/margolis~0509. htm. The second statement appeared on www.redress.btinternet.co.uk/ pjballes24.htm. The third statement appeared on www.the-hamster.com/ mtype/archives/001111.html.

5. See the image of a pregnant, fatigues-clad England at http://www.sdimc.org/en/2004/90/105611.shtml.

6. The "Jihad Clampett" image can be found at www.almostaproverb.com.

7. The Pensacola Pro-life Hunt Club image can be found at www.christiangallery.com/aogpics.html.

References

Baird-Windle, Patricia, and Eleanor J. Bader. 2001. *Targets of Hatred: Anti-abortion Terrorism.* New York: Palgrave.

"Ballad of Jessica Lynch." 2004. Retrieved 2 April 2005, from http://www.scotchirish.net/Jessica%20Lynch.php4.

Barkawi, Tarak. 2004 "Globalization, Culture, and War: On the Popular Mediation of 'Small Wars.'" *Cultural Critique* 58:115- 17.

Batteau, Allen. 1990. *The Invention of Appalachia.* Tuscon: University of Arizona Press.

Bender, Howard. n.d. Davy Crockett Craze Home Page. Retrieved 31 March 2005, from http://www.geocities.com/toppsgreen/03Song.html.

Berlet, Chip. 2005. Electronic mail correspondence with author. 4 January.

The Birth of a Nation. 1915. D.W. Griffith, director.

Bragg, Rick. 2003. *I Am a Soldier, Too: The Jessica Lynch Story.* New York: Knopf.

Bruns, George, and Tom Blackburn. 1954. "The Ballad of Davy Crockett." Song lyrics. Burbank, CA: Walt Disney Company.

Buchanan, Jim. 2003. "Let's Raise the Bar for 'Survivors.'" *Citizen-Times.* Asheville, NC. 7 June.

Creadick, Anna. 2005. "A Message to Ruby: On Being a Homefront Hillbilly Heroine." Paper presented at NWSA conference. Orlando, FL.

Davis, Angela Y. 1981. *Women, Race, and Class.* New York: Vintage.

Deliverance. 1972. John Boorman, director.

Dickey, James. 1970. *Deliverance.* Boston: Houghton Mifflin.

Dinshaw, Carolyn. 1999. *Getting Medieval: Sexualities and Communities, Pre- and Postmodern.* Durham, NC: Duke University Press.

Duke, Lynn. 2004. "A Woman Apart; For Fellow Soldiers, Lynndie England's Role at Abu Ghraib Is Best Viewed From a Distance." *Washington Post,* 19 September, D1.

Dyer, Richard. 1997. *White.* New York: Routledge.

Ehrenreich, Barbara. 2001. *Nickel and Dimed: On (Not) Getting By in America.* New York: Henry Holt.

———. 2004. "Barbara Ehrenreich's Commencement Address at Barnard College." The Rockridge Institute. Retrieved 31 March 2005, from http://www.rockridgeinstitute.org/perspectives/ becommencement.

Eviatar, Daphne. 2003. "The Press and Private Lynch." *The Nation.* 7 July. Retrieved 31 March 2005, from http://www.thenation.com/docprint.mhtml?i=20030707&s=eviatar.

Goodman, Ellen. 2004. "Tender Terrorists?" *Boston Globe.* 23 September, A15.
Gurganus, Allan. 2001. *Oldest Living Confederate Widow Tells All.* New York: Vintage.
———. 2003. "Why We Fed the Bomber." *New York Times.* 8 June, 13.
Harkins, Anthony. 2004. *Hillbilly: A Cultural History of an American Icon.* Oxford and New York: Oxford University Press.
Hartigan, John. 2003. "Who Are These People?: 'Rednecks,' 'Hillbillies,' and 'White Trash' as Marked Racial Subjects." In *White Out: The Continuing Significance of Racism,* ed. Ashley W. Doane and Eduardo Bonilla-Silva, 95–112. New York: Routledge.
Hersh, Seymour M. 2004a. *Chain of Command: The Road from 9/11 to Abu Ghraib.* New York: Harper Collins.
———. 2004b. "The Gray Zone: How a Secret Pentagon Program Came to Abu Ghraib." *The New Yorker.* 24 May, 38–44.
Horwitz, Tony. 1999. "Letter from Nantahala: Run, Rudolph, Run: How the Fugitive Became a Folk Hero." *New Yorker.* 15 March, 46–52.
Jeffords, Susan. 1989. *The Remasculinization of America: Gender and the Vietnam War.* Bloomington: Indiana University Press.
Jennings, Rachel A. 2005. "From Frontier Kings to 'Smirking Jezebels': Appalachians in the Iraq War." Paper delivered at NWSA conference. Orlando, FL.
Juergensmeyer, Mark. 2000. *Terror in the Mind of God: The Global Rise of Religious Violence.* Berkeley: University of California Press.
Kristeva, Julia. 1982. *Powers of Horror: An Essay on Abjection,* trans. Leon S. Roudiez. New York: Columbia University Press.
Marshall, Lucinda. 2004. "The Misogynist Undercurrents of Abu-Ghraib." *Off Our Backs: A Woman's Newsjournal.* 34(5/6). May/June:10–11.
Mason, Carol. 2002. *Killing for Life: The Apocalyptic Narrative of Pro-life Politics.* Ithaca: Cornell University Press.
———. 2004. "Who's Afraid of Virginia Dare? Confronting Anti-abortion Terrorism after 9/11." *Journal of Constitutional Law* 6(4):796–817.
Mikkelson, Barbara, and David P. Mikkelson 2003. "The Twinkie Defense." Urban Legends Reference Page. Retrieved 23 May 2005, from www.snopes.com/legal/twinkie.htm.
Moruzzi, Norma Claire. 1993. "National Abjects: Julia Kristeva on the Process of Political Self-Identification." In *Ethics, Politics, and Difference in Julia Kristeva's Writing,* ed. Kelly Oliver, 135–49. New York: Routledge.
Newitz, Annalee, and Matt Wray. 1997. "What Is 'White Trash'? Stereotypes and Economic Conditions of Poor Whites in the United States." In *Whiteness: A Critical Reader,* ed. Mike Hill, 168–84. New York: New York University Press.
Pogash, Carol. 2003. "Myth of the 'Twinkie Defense.'" *San Francisco Chronicle.* 23 November, 23.
Powell, Douglas Reichart. 2003. "Eric Rudolph and the Appalachian Geographical Imaginary: Regionalism and Contemporary Cultural Critique." Paper presented at Association of American Geographers. New Orleans.
Pratt, Minnie Bruce. 2004. "Taking the Horizon Path: Keynote at the NWSA in New Orleans, Louisiana." *NWSA Journal* 16(2):15–33.
Rambo: First Blood. 1982. Ted Kotcheff, director.

Reynolds, John Mark. 2003. "Finding the Good Men: The Courage of Our Regular Troops and the Challenge to the Rest of Us." *California Republic: A Minority Report of Rational Opinion* Thursday, September 26. Retrieved 31 March 2005, from http://www.californiarepublic.org/archives/Columns/ReynoldsJ/20030926ReynoldsJGoodMen.html.

Risen, James, and Judy L. Thomas. 1998. *Wrath of Angels: The American Abortion War.* New York: Basic Books.

Rowe, John Carlos. 2004. "Culture, U.S. Imperialism, and Globalization." *American Literary History* 16(4):575–95.

Russo, Vito. 1987. *Celluloid Closet: Homosexuality in the Movies.* New York: Perennial.

Schlafly, Phyllis. 2004. "Equality for Women in Our Army." *Eagle Forum* (May 19). Retrieved 2 April 2005, from http://www.eagleforum.org/column/2004/may04/04-05-19.html.

Smith-Rosenberg, Carroll. 1985. *Disorderly Conduct: Visions of Gender in Victorian America.* New York: Knopf.

Soldiers in the Army of God. 2000. Home Box Office Undercover Series. Marc Levin and Daphne Pinkerson, directors.

Stern, Jessica. 2003. *Terror in the Name of God.* New York: HarperCollins.

Tarantino, Quentin. 1994. *Pulp Fiction: A Quentin Tarantino Screenplay.* New York: Hyperion.

Theweleit, Klaus. 1993. "The Bomb's Womb and the Genders of War (War Goes on Preventing Women from Becoming the Mothers of Invention)." In *Gendering War Talk*, ed. Miriam Cooke and Angela Woollacott, 283–316. Princeton: Princeton University Press.

Vinzant, Carol. 1993. "Fetus Frenzy." *Spy Magazine.* May: 58–65.

Wag the Dog. 1997. Barry Levinson, director.

Whisnant, David. 1980. *Modernizing the Mountaineer: People, Power, and Planning in Appalachia.* Boone, NC: Appalachian Consortium Press.

Williams, John Alexander. 2002. *Appalachia: A History.* Chapel Hill: University of North Carolina Press.

Williamson, J. W. 1995. *Hillbillyland: What the Movies Did to the Mountains and What the Mountains Did to the Movies.* Chapel Hill: University of North Carolina Press.

CHAPTER SIXTEEN

The Sexual Politics of Abu Ghraib
Hegemony, Spectacle, and the Global War on Terror

MARY ANN TÉTREAULT

News of abusive treatment, torture, and murder of detainees by U.S. military and intelligence personnel at Abu Ghraib prison in Iraq shocked the world. Bursting into public view in May 2004, on CBS's *60 Minutes II* and in a series of articles by Seymour Hersh in the *New Yorker*, the stories were accompanied by sensational photographs of naked prisoners, some engaged in simulated sexual acts. Prominent conservatives sought to minimize the significance of the photos by saying that the actions they document are merely horseplay by soldiers trying to blow off steam in a tense situation and, all in all, no worse than fraternity hazing (People for the American Way 2004).

However, the pictures tell of something more sinister. The few images of corpses convey a mix of triumph and relief: my enemy is dead (and I am still alive). They resemble snapshots taken by soldiers in other wars, for example, pictures of enemy corpses taken by soldiers on the Western Front during World War I, some sporting jaunty epitaphs and sent as postcards to the Allied troops' families and friends (Ferguson 1998, n.p.). But most of the Abu Ghraib photographs belong to a genre that veterans rarely publish. Like the video of the execution of six Muslim prisoners at Srebrenica that was shown at the Miloševic trial in The Hague and rerun interminably on television in the Balkans during the summer of 2005, or images from the Vietnam War of U.S. soldiers posed next to piled-up bodies of dead peasants, of interrogations that ended in the shooting and burial of detainees,[1] or of enemy corpses mutilated after death, these are "trophies" intended for limited distribution only. Author Douglas Kahn wrote

> I grew up in a military town where, during high school in the late 1960s, I saw numerous snapshots of necromutilations, of Vietcong beheaded with their cocks coming out of their mouths, brought back by older brothers of students. These were secretly passed from one person to the next in the same manner as pornographic playing cards and other taboo photos. (Douglas Kahn, quoted in Sturken 1997, 92)

From this perspective, viewers might be tempted to see the Abu Ghraib photos as depicting "normal," if extreme, reprehensible, behavior. Yet there are many elements in the ensemble of images that call for a more disturbing explanation. With a few exceptions, the subjects of these photos are not corpses. They are living persons in the thrall of powerful and sadistic captors. We see them terrified, abject, forced to perform humiliating acts, and subjected to physical torture. Their images are not harmless war souvenirs; like the Šrebrenica video, they are evidence. They document the crimes as well as the impunity with which they were committed.

I would call all these photographs pornographic, if we define pornography as a record of the violation of a subject's physical and psychic integrity. However, many Abu Ghraib images also are pornographic in the conventional sense. Their subjects are naked and lewdly posed, some with clothed American women playing dominatrix roles. These photos—some depicting corpses and brutal interrogation practices—are like stills from snuff films, statements of the utter worthlessness of the prisoners and the life-and-death power over them exercised by their captors. And, like conventional pornography, these images convey complex messages about the persons who produced them (Kuhn 1985).

In this essay, I situate the politics of Abu Ghraib in a tradition of orientalism that fetishizes and feminizes the sexuality of subject peoples as part of a strategy of domination. The photographs record rituals of violence affirming power relations between occupier and occupied (Amnesty International 2005b; Danner 2004a). Sexuality, coded according to complex cultural norms of feminine subjection to masculine power, infuses the language and acts of members of dominant groups against those they seek to subjugate. The pornography of Abu Ghraib constitutes a field report on the production and reproduction of U.S. global dominance.

Hegemony and Spectacle

Hierarchies of international power are outcomes of war, but war is not required to maintain a hierarchy once it is established. Maintenance of the hierarchy depends on prestige—the reputation for power (Gilpin 1981). Because prestige is the bedrock of the authority, war is always a risk for a dominant power, not simply because it uses up valuable resources but, more significantly, because war can weaken a hegemon and even bring about its defeat. Moreover, as Hannah Arendt tells us, violence negates power (1969). An unambiguously powerful actor doesn't have to inflict violence in order to rule. Subordinates may go along out of fear, but successful leaders enjoy deference because others believe in the rightness of their authority.

Policy in the Bush administration is shaped by people who are concerned to orchestrate their "messages" to convince watchers and hearers to share their vision of reality (Lemann 2003). Their pursuit of power runs on two tracks. One is ideological, signified by terms like "neoconservative," and expressed in the policies neoconservatives devise and support, like high levels of defense spending and a willingness to intervene abroad (Mann 2004, 90–91). The other track is theatrical, motivated by the desire to ensure that the United States will remain the most powerful country in the world for generations to come—perhaps forever. The people managing this track believe that perceptions are as important as material resources in the projection of political power: *what you see is what is*. Political analyst Ron Suskind reports,

> In the summer of 2002, after I had written an article in *Esquire* that the White House didn't like . . . I had a meeting with a senior adviser to Bush. He expressed the White House's displeasure, and then he told me something that at the time I didn't fully comprehend—but which I now believe gets to the very heart of the Bush presidency.
>
> The aide said that guys like me were "in what we call the reality-based community," which he defined as people who "believe that solutions emerge from your judicious study of discernible reality." I nodded and murmured something about enlightenment principles and empiricism. He cut me off. "That's not the way the world really works anymore," he continued. "We're an empire now, and when we act, we create our own reality. And while you're studying that reality—judiciously, as you will—we'll act again, creating other new realities, which you can study too, and that's how things will sort out. We're history's actors . . . and you, all of you, will be left to just study what we do." (2004, 50–51)

The success of Osama bin Laden on 9/11 provoked a massive effort to recreate the perception that U.S. power is both indisputable and unassailable. On 7 October 2001, President Bush launched a military attack on Afghanistan, the presumed haven of the authors of the 9/11 attacks (Woodward 2002). But this response was not enough; the president wanted to assert U.S. power in a spectacular way, to demonstrate dominance once and for all.[2] So shortly after U.S. forces entered Afghanistan, he initiated measures for an invasion of Iraq (Boyer 2003; Hersh 2001; Woodward 2004). While he had expected—and received—support from Americans and others for the attack on Afghanistan, it was not likely that an attack on Iraq would be as easily condoned (Wolfowitz 2003). Thus, the president constructed the ideological basis for what he had in mind by making speeches threatening war as an object lesson, identifying potential targets of U.S. military action, and foreshadowing major changes in U.S. military policy (Bush 2002a, 2002b). In September 2002, the White House produced a formal policy statement laying out a new, multi-pronged national security strategy to maintain U.S. global dominance indefinitely. It included the option of preventive war undertaken without the imprimatur of the United Nations (Bush 2002c). Such a war was launched against Iraq in March 2003.

Great attention was paid to managing the war as a spectacle. The telegenic bombing of Baghdad was advertised in advance as a campaign to "shock and awe" (Kaplan 2003; Mann 2004, 334) while media access to the war zone was carefully restricted. Reporters were forced either to rely on official information grudgingly dispensed in Doha, Qatar, far from the front (Noujaim 2004; Rushing 2005), to "embed" with military units on the ground for a micro-level view of the conflict (Katovsky and Carlson 2003), or to travel to Iraq on their own and face a high likelihood of being injured or killed (Garrels 2003; International Federation of Journalists 2004). U.S. government control of information was not absolute, however, thanks to the reporters who braved the third option.

On 1 May 2003, the president, dressed in a flight suit, emerged from a fighter plane that had landed on the deck of the aircraft carrier *USS Abraham Lincoln*. Against the backdrop of a banner proclaiming "Mission Accomplished," he told the assembled troops—and the viewers watching him on TV—that "major combat operations in Iraq have ended. In the battle of Iraq, the United States and our allies have prevailed" (Bush 2003). As it turned out, however, this proclamation was premature. A combination of neoconservative ideology and belief in the magical power of spectacle had led the Bush administration to underestimate the complexity of the mission (Hirsh 2004; Johnson and Russell 2005). In their minds, the Iraqis without Saddam would gratefully accept a new government made up of U.S.-backed exiles, passively acquiesce to U.S. desires regarding their new political and economic role in the world, and gladly pay for it all themselves out of their oil revenues (Hersh 2001). Despite detailed warnings from the "reality community" (Crane and Terrill 2003; Fallows 2002), the White House advisers and Pentagon planners failed to imagine the prospect of Iraqi agency and thus the need for an informed and attentive "post-conflict" policy.

Orientalist Spectacles

The term "orientalist" went from a descriptive to a pejorative term with the publication of Edward Said's influential account of "the formidable structure of cultural domination" that supported the political and economic domination of "the east" by "the west" (Said 1978, 25). Said found that orientalism permeated Western scholarship, art, and politics, underpinning a perspective from which "orientals" are viewed as exotic, Other, not "people like us." Orientalism, like other ideologies, is a way of seeing *and not seeing*[3] that organizes perceptions around a particular view of reality. The messages of orientalist communication imply, when they do not proclaim, the moral and cultural inferiority of orientals and the entitlement of superior Westerners to resources held by such feckless and wicked people.

According to Leila Ahmed, although the "peculiar practices of Islam with respect to women had always formed part of the Western narrative of the quintessential otherness and inferiority of Islam," the issue of women became the centerpiece of the Western narrative of Islam only in the nineteenth century, in conjunction with the European colonization of Muslim countries.

> [T]he colonial powers . . . developed their theories of races and cultures and of a social evolutionary sequence according to which middle-class Victorian England . . . stood at the culminating point of the evolutionary process. . . . In this scheme Victorian womanhood and mores with respect to women . . . were regarded as the ideal and measure of civilization. . . . The Victorian male establishment devised theories to contest the claims of [an increasingly vocal] feminism . . . [while it] captured the language of feminism and redirected it, in the service of colonialism, toward Other men and the cultures of Other men. It was here . . . that the fusion between the issues of women and culture was created. . . . The idea that Other men, men in colonized societies or societies beyond the borders of the civilized West, oppressed women was to be used, in the rhetoric of colonialism, to render morally justifiable its project of undermining or eradicating the cultures of colonized peoples. (Ahmed 1992, 149–51)

In the nineteenth century, sexualized images of the oriental Other proliferated in popular as well as high culture. "Orientalism provided the ideal excuse to paint nudes, but since Moslem women would not sit for the artists, they . . . usually hired models [and] posed [them] in the studio, with suitable eastern accessories. The rising class of industrialists, throwing aside the pruderies of the capital, found it cheaper and safer to buy works by living artists. These erotic pictures gave them an official excuse to enjoy scenes of odalisques and dancers, chained slaves, public baths and harems, with overtones of rape, brutality and sensuality" (Thornton 1978). Orientalism was not confined to elites. Picture postcards of "harem women" were produced in Algeria and sold to legions of male tourists, colonists, and soldiers. These postcards also featured hired models in fabulous costumes, some peering out from behind bars, while others were shown smoking or in "candid" poses that revealed breasts and bare legs.

> The postcard . . . becomes the poor man's phantasm: for a few pennies, display racks full of dreams. The postcard is everywhere, covering all the colonial space. . . . It produces stereotypes in the manner of great seabirds producing guano. It is the fertilizer of the colonial vision . . . [and] the comic strip of colonial morality. (Alloula 1986, 4)

The Politics of the Gaze

"A cat may look at a king," remarked Alice during her adventures in Wonderland (Carroll 1865, n.p.). This statement attests less to the inability

of humans to control cats than to the gulf between the power of dominant persons who have privacy and authority and others, the subjects of
their proprietary scrutiny, who do not. Both the Abu Ghraib photographs
and narratives and the orientalist high and popular art of the nineteenth
century are examples of "the politics of the gaze" (Betterton 1987, 3–14;
Wilson 1987, 166). To be "looked at" in this way is to be put in a feminine
position as an object of the masculine gaze.

Pornography is the quintessential expression of the politics of the gaze
(Kuhn 1985, 22–23). In the Abu Ghraib photos, Arab male captives are
feminized by showing them in settings that emphasize both their sexuality and their helplessness. Perhaps the best example is the photograph
of Private Lynndie England holding a leash while the other end is wrapped
around the neck of a naked Arab prisoner (Danner 2004b, 219). In this
now-iconic image, the power of Americans over Arabs is symbolized not
only by the leash but also by the fact that the prisoner is naked while his
captor is clothed. The message is enhanced by its inversion of conventional gender expectations: the man is the captive of the woman, a juxtaposition that evokes memories of the famous Vietnamese cartoon showing a very small peasant woman pointing a rifle at a very large male pilot
(Tétreault 1994, 122). Another photo takes this "design for living" (Wolf
1982, 388) to a more explicit level. It shows a clothed—and grinning—
American woman leaning over a pile of naked Arab men while over
them all stands a large, clothed—and smiling—American man (Danner
2004b, 223). The ethnic/gender hierarchy could not be clearer.

The gaze is not reciprocal. As Alice implied, the king may look at anyone but few objects of his gaze may look back. In the Abu Ghraib photos,
Americans are the kings while prisoners are stripped and posed so that
every part of their bodies is available to handling by their tormenters and
inspection by the camera's eye. But the prisoners are hooded, physically
prevented from returning their captors' gaze; hooding literally makes the
prisoners faceless, preventing guards and interrogators from seeing them
as people.

Ritual Violence and the Politics of Torture

It is important to see the events at Abu Ghraib in the context of the
treatment of people who were captured and detained in the course of a
war. The hoods are explained in interrogation manuals as tools to disori-
ent prisoners (U.S. Army Field Manual 1987, 34–52, cited in Bazelon,
Carter, and Lithwick 2005). The prisoners are being "softened up" for
interrogation, a procedure that the testimonies of witnesses questioned
by General Anthony Taguba and his staff during his early 2004 investigation of the Abu Ghraib allegations say was often conducted using ille-

gal means under the Geneva Conventions—that is, torture (Greenberg and Dratel 2005, 472–528). As Elaine Scarry argues, the coupling of torture and interrogation constitutes a ritual of violence, another domain in which the basic propositions describing domination and subjection are inscribed.

> Torture consists of a primary physical act, the infliction of pain, and a primary verbal act, the interrogation. The first rarely occurs without the second. . . . The connection between the physical act and the verbal act, between body and voice, is often misstated or misunderstood. Although the information sought in an interrogation is almost never credited with being a *just* motive for torture, it is repeatedly credited with being the motive for torture. (Scarry 1985, 28, emphasis in the original)

The rituals of interrogation are "repeated acts of display . . . having as its purpose the production of a fantastic illusion of power" (Scarry 1985, 28). That the audience was supposed to be limited to the prison, the "intelligence community," and persons occupying top levels in the Bush administration does not change its character.

The Abu Ghraib pictures also call to mind René Girard's theory that ritual violence built around actual or substitutionary human sacrifice functions to draw a community together, especially when it feels itself to be under threat from outside (1977). Sacrifices break the bodies of victims before the eyes of the community in rituals that remind its members of the core values they share. Ritualized criminality "create[s] a climate in which other [such acts], even when unaccompanied by ritual, seem legitimate" (Brundage 1993, 440). One example from American history was elite-sanctioned and guided "sacrificial lynching" (Patterson 1998), which gave permission for entrepreneurial imitations such as vigilante lynching and the many "normal" acts of domination such as expropriations, beatings, and rapes that members of the community could engage in with impunity as long as the perpetrators were white and the victims were black. Even after slavery was legally abolished, a tacit, *de facto* version of the South's "peculiar institution" and the methods used to reproduce its values and practices persisted throughout much of the twentieth century (Ehrenhaus and Owen 2005; McWhorter 2001).

The Abu Ghraib photographs do not record ritual sacrifice; they show vigilantes imitating the criminal behavior enacted in ritual interrogations.[4] The perpetrators of the acts recorded in the pictures were subalterns who knew that their behavior was "wrong" in some sense but also knew that it was tacitly sanctioned and sometimes openly encouraged as an instrumental contribution to the "success" of interrogations. The photos also show that the way interrogations were—*are!*—conducted was accepted by the prison "community" (CBS News 2004b; Danner 2004a; Dratel 2005; *Frontline* 2005; Greenberg 2005). The full set of uncropped photographs also reveals the public nature of the crimes committed, contradicting assertions that instances of vigilantism and ritual interrogation at Abu Ghraib were the sole responsibility of "a few bad apples." Several include images of spectators and bystanders. Like harem postcards, lynching postcards (Allen 2000; Ehrenhaus and Owen 2005), and the photos of mutilated Vietnamese corpses that circulated furtively among adolescent acquaintances of Douglas Kahn, the Abu Ghraib photos widened the scope of normalization as they circulated among select groups of colleagues and friends. They were "commodities" within the prison walls—one of the computers in Abu Ghraib's office of military intelligence even used the now-famous image of naked detainees arranged in a pyramid as a screen saver (Fay 2004, 514)—and knowledge and stories about the photos were propagated outside Abu Ghraib as personnel cycled in and out and news about the events was shared with e-mail correspondents (Hersh 2004). Insofar as their existence went unreported or, when reported, ignored, the Abu Ghraib photos show that vigilantism and the torture of prisoners during interrogation were accepted if not condoned beyond the individuals involved and also beyond the walls of Abu Ghraib.

The Sexual Politics of Abu Ghraib

At last we arrive at the sexual politics of Abu Ghraib, which has an inside dimension relating to the acts themselves and an outside dimension that has shaped social responses in the United States since the photographs became public. Inside, women were used to humiliate and torment prisoners in the vigilante acts captured by the photos. Narratives and other documents reveal that women were similarly used to extract "information" from prisoners in interrogation settings.[5] Outside, the participation of women domesticated these acts, making them seem trivial rather than criminal. Reporters and commentators fastened their attention on the women, deflecting attention from both those who organized the torture events and those who endured them.

The Abu Ghraib images and documents describe violations of the captives' bodily integrity, masculine self-image, and religious rules about cleanliness. Photos show naked victims arranged in piles, smeared with filth, and forced to simulate sexual acts. Their manhood is disparaged in many ways. Indeed, they are feminized—unmanned—by the gaze of their captors who strip them, scrutinize and manipulate their bodies, taunt them, and create pornography out of their humiliation by taking pictures of them.[6] Documents from and about Abu Ghraib and other U.S. prisons holding Global War on Terrorism (GWOT) captives speak repeatedly of prisoners being stripped and interrogated for long periods of time by women as well as by men; being forced to wear women's panties on their heads; and being physically violated, beaten and sodomized, and subjected to women's intrusions on their bodily privacy. The prisoners' spiritual integrity also is assaulted, by being unable to pray when they are bound, naked, or dirty; by being forced to simulate sinful sexual acts; and by the actions of female guards and interrogators intended to create other near occasions of sin and contamination, all of which evoke religious dread in those who are devout.[7]

Women are even more useful outside, where they focus popular outrage away from the men responsible for the GWOT prison system and from the conduct of U.S. personnel stationed there. The image of Private Lynndie England dressed in her t-shirt, camouflage pants, and Army boots became the logo of the Abu Ghraib scandal (Cagle n.d.). The mainstream press featured her in their stories (CBS News 2004a); cartoonists and commentators speculated on her upbringing, education, intelligence, and morals (Cagle n.d.; San Francisco Bay Area Independent Media Center 2004); when lists of participants were compiled, her name usually appeared at the top (Hirsh and Barry 2005). Private Charles Graner, identified in the narratives and in court martial testimony as the orchestrator of the photographed prisoner abuse, also received his share of criticism, but the image of Lynndie England is one of the two instantly recognizable icons of the scandal.

The psychology of deflection by Lynndie is clearly illustrated in an editorial written by an Oklahoma publisher following the rejection of England's guilty plea at her court martial in May 2005.

> Thank goodness a military court judge had the wisdom and courage to throw out the guilty plea by the U.S. army girl private that she "abused" those murderous Abu Ghraib war criminals. Somebody had convinced PFC Lynndie England she had committed a terrible wrong worth 16 years imprisonment. Sending that young lady to prison for, at worst, humiliating those Saddam soldiers out to kill Americans, would have been one of the worst injustices ever to occur in our military judicial system. . . . There was no torture, no abuse, no physical injury of any kind, no scandal. . . . Actually, our guards and interrogators should have done something that would have scared the hell out of them until they talked and revealed the names and location of ringleaders of current lethal insurgencies. Let's get it straight. There was not one drop of blood lost by any of those prisoners. Not a bone was broken. Not a bruise was inflicted. Not a scratch. (Gourley 2005, n.p.)

The Gourley editorial is an egregious example of seeing and not seeing. Appearing to be solicitous of her welfare in praising the judge for rejecting England's guilty plea, Gourley omits the fact that her lawyers believed it was her "best shot at leniency." He also fails to report that her chances to limit her time in prison were "ruined" by the testimony of the man who had fathered a child with her during her time at Abu Ghraib—

Charles Graner (Zernike 2005).[8] To anyone who had seen the photos of prisoners being squashed, beaten, and mocked after death (Danner 2004b, 217, 221–24; 2004a), Gourley's omissions are heightened by the obvious falseness of his statement that "not one drop of blood [was] lost. . . . Not a bone was broken. . . . Not a bruise [or a] . . . scratch." For Gourley, the sum total of U.S. actions at Abu Ghraib is contained in the photos of Lynndie England, smoking, smirking, and touching, but never wounding the bodies of prisoners.

Lynndie England is the popular face of the scandal. Another woman, General Janis Karpinski, is the official scapegoat:

> Although some 10 Pentagon investigations have highlighted "systemic" problems in the Iraqi operation, they found that higher-level officials issued no policies nor orders that could have led to the prisoner abuses that were aired around the world in a series of graphic photos. Only two senior officers with direct command responsibility for Abu Ghraib—Brig. Gen. Janis Karpinski and Col. Thomas Pappas—have been reprimanded, but not prosecuted, for their oversight of the facility. (Bowers 2005)

Janis Karpinski believed even before the photos became public that she would be saddled with command responsibility for the crimes committed at Abu Ghraib. In her sworn statement to General Antonio Taguba, on 11 February 2004, she said:

> I think that General Sanchez is [pause] I think that his ego will not allow him to accept a Reserve Brigade, a Reserve General Officer and certainly not a female succeeding in a combat environment. And I think he looked at the 800th MP Brigade as the opportunity to find a scapegoat for anything that his active component MI Brigade or his active component MP Brigade was failing at. And if I was not capable, why didn't he tell me? Why didn't somebody tell me sit down and let me give you some suggestions because when DEPSECDEF Wolfowitz came into the theater, the first time he came out to Baghdad Central he stayed an extra hour and forty-five minutes because he was so proud of me and what the MPs were doing. (quoted in Greenberg and Dratel 2005, 542)

Those who chose to focus on the sex of General Karpinski, like those who chose to focus on that of Lynndie England, could reframe the meaning of the torture and humiliation taking place at Abu Ghraib as nothing more than what might have been expected from putting a woman in charge of a group of impressionable young men. As she does on other issues, Ann Coulter takes the prize for the most colorful expressions of such scorn,

> I think the other point that no one is making about the abuse photos is just the disproportionate number of women involved, including a girl general running the entire operation. I mean, this is lesson, you know, one million and 47 on why women shouldn't be in the military. In addition to not being able to

carry even a medium-sized backpack, women are too vicious. (quoted in People for the American Way 2004)

A third woman completed the domestication of Abu Ghraib when she was sent to clean up the diplomatic mess resulting from the scandal. In December 2005, U.S. Secretary of State Condoleezza Rice traveled in Europe where she had to respond at every stop to questions about prisoner interrogation. Despite her repeated insistence that "the United States does not permit, tolerate or condone torture," the U.S. position remained at best ambiguous because Rice failed to respond to queries about what constitutes torture in the eyes of the Bush administration. Even so, after a difficult week, an Associated Press photo published on 9 December 2005 showed Rice at the center of a large group of smiling NATO foreign ministers. The Dutch foreign minister, Ben Bot, reflected some of the thoughts behind those smiles when he told *New York Times* reporter Joel Brinkley, "I think we have gotten . . . all the satisfactory answers we can hope for" (2005, A6).

Making Sense of Abu Ghraib

It is not clear that we can make more sense of Abu Ghraib than the Dutch foreign minister, at least, not yet. As I have tried to show, the scandal is symptomatic of Americans' moral confusion and unwillingness either to confront problems in U.S. leadership and policy or to examine the role of the United States in the world. Those who dismiss the vigilantism at Abu Ghraib as trivial or understandable deny the reality of the ritual interrogation that informs it. Indeed, although most Americans accept the idea that torture and abuse are horrible, a majority believe that torture is part of the price we have to pay to keep ourselves safe (Bowden 2003; Kull et al. 2004; Lelyveld 2005; Pew Research Center 2005). U.S. personnel serving at Abu Ghraib are a microcosm of America. Not all of the individuals witnessing or participating in these activities condoned them, but most did. Whistle-blower, Specialist Joseph Darby was the only one at Abu Ghraib who stood against what he saw as illegal acts, a confirmation of the success of ritual violence as a strategy for normalization. Following the release of Darby's name, Associated Press and Reuters reported that he and his wife had to be placed in protective custody, and that members of his family in the United States had received death threats.

The numbed acceptance of what the photos and narratives reveal is a response to the always-present threat of vigilante action, such as the death threats against the Darbys, and to the denial that emanates from the top level of the U.S. government. Together, they induce moral and political paralysis (see Danner 2005). Despite the wide exposure of the Abu Ghraib scandal in the press, and the streams of supporting documents, testimonies, and reports, American political culture seems to be paralyzed—unable to demand both a full and unbiased account of how prisoners are treated at U.S. detention facilities and a set of transparent procedures for the future. Meanwhile, like the statements by Condoleezza Rice, official responses to the scandal have been either cosmetic or artfully strategic (Amnesty International 2005a). The rules governing interrogation were officially modified on 30 December 2004, prior to U.S. Senate hearings on the appointment of Alberto Gonzalez, the man who had dismissed the Geneva Conventions as "quaint" (U.S. Department of Justice 2004), to the position of attorney general. But news reports since then confirm that prisoner torture continues at Abu Ghraib and elsewhere in the GWOT system. When Gonzalez was confirmed by the U.S. Senate, Mark Danner wrote, "we are all torturers now" (Danner 2005).

Some Americans may prefer to deny the existence of ritual torture and the significance of prisoner abuse because they sense that it is part of the apparatus of what Campbell Craig calls "American imperialism," a policy that promises safety from terrorists, continued cheap oil, and a buy-now-pay-later lifestyle that few expect to be billed for in their lifetimes (Craig 2004, 161, 166). Yet like white citizens at a lynching, Americans contemplating Abu Ghraib may have mixed feelings about the violence committed in their names. Yes, torture is a scandal when news of it penetrates the media and outsiders criticize us by comparing our words to our actions. At the same time, we remain convinced that it is the price we have to pay for that full shopping cart, abundant gasoline, and victory in the global war on terror. However it plays outside the United States or on television sets across the country, the spectacle of Abu Ghraib is an outward sign of the hidden rituals that, since 9/11, distinguish Americans from others. Abu Ghraib has brought us together. And yes, we are all torturers now.

Notes

1. Several photos of stacked bodies in destroyed hamlets were shown by the photographer-veteran to one of my classes in 1987. I own copies of a short series of photos of the interrogation and its aftermath given to me by a relative of another photographer.

2. The president had complained to Condoleezza Rice that responding to individual al-Qaeda attacks, such as the one on the *USS Cole* made shortly before he took office, was like "swatting flies," and that he was tired of it. He told her he preferred to take a "comprehensive" approach (Rice 2004).

3. "Seeing and not-seeing" is analogous to Stanley Cohen's "knowing and not-knowing." Information is "somehow repressed, disavowed, pushed aside or reinterpreted . . . or . . . 'registers' well enough, but its implications—cognitive, emotion or moral—are evaded, neutralized, or rationalized away" (Cohen 2001, 1).

4. The strenuous efforts of the Bush administration to establish counterarguments defending the legality of their interrogation practices shows that these practices were believed to be potentially, if not actually, criminal (Ashcroft 2002/2004; Bush 2001/2004; Bybee 2002/2004; Gonzalez 2002/2004; Yoo 2002/2004).

5. I put "information" in quotes to express my doubts about the instrumental value of what prisoners tell those who torture them. In this, I agree with the interrogators described in Bowden (2003) and Mayer (2005) who believe that skill trumps torture in producing useful information. A pertinent example can be found in the 9 December 2005 story in the *New York Times* by Douglas Jehl that summarizes previous piecemeal and now discredited reports tying Saddam Hussein to al-Qaeda as having come from a prisoner who was tortured and subsequently recanted his story.

6. Many such sessions are described in the statements in Greenberg and Dratel (2005, 471–527). On page 505, you can read testimony about a tormented son forced to watch his father stripped and humiliated. Few sources available when this paper was written—one exception is Hersh (2004)—offered much information about the systematic rape and torture of female prisoners, now seeping into public media thanks to the capture of Jill Carroll, a reporter for the *Christian Science Monitor*, whose captors offered to release her after all female prisoners at Abu Ghraib were freed. At this writing, women remain at Abu Ghraib although Jill Carroll was released unharmed on 30 March 2006.

7. One account from Guantánamo Bay tells of a prisoner who was smeared with a red liquid by a female interrogator who told him it was menstrual blood. The legality of such techniques is questionable under both the Geneva Conventions and the Uniform Code of Military Justice (Bazelon, Carter, and Lithwick 2005; Gebhardt 2005).

8. Two days earlier, Lynndie England had learned that her lover had married another Abu Ghraib vigilante, Megan M. Ambuhl, who had pleaded guilty to the two lesser of four violations and been discharged from the Army (Zernike 2005). On 26 September 2005, England received a three-year sentence for her participation in the Abu Ghraib vigilantism. Graner is serving ten years for his part in these crimes.

References

Ahmed, Leila. 1992. *Women and Gender in Islam.* New Haven: Yale University Press.

Allen, James. 2000. *Without Sanctuary: Lynching Photography in America.* Santa Fe: Twin Palms.

Alloula, Malek. 1986. *The Colonial Harem.* Trans. Myrna Godzich and Wlad Godzich. Minneapolis: University of Minnesota Press.

Amnesty International. 2005a. "A.I. Report 2005." Retrieved from http://web .amnesty.org/report2005/index-eng.

———. 2005b. "Guantanamo and Beyond: The Continuing Pursuit of Unchecked Executive Power." Retrieved from http://web.amnesty.org/library/print/ ENGAMR510632005.

Arendt, Hannah. 1969. *On Violence.* New York: Harvest Books.

Ashcroft, John. 2002/2004. "Letter to the President." 1 February. In *Torture and Truth: America, Abu Ghraib, and the War on Terror,* ed. Mark Danner, 92–93. New York: New York Review Books.

Bazelon, Emily, Phillip Carter, and Dahlia Lithwick. 2005. "What Is Torture: An Interactive Primer on American Interrogation." *Slate.* 26 May. Retrieved from http://www.slate.com/id/2119122/.

Betterton, Rosemary. 1987. "Introduction." In *Looking On: Images of Feminity in the Visual Arts and Media,* ed. Rosemary Betterton, 1–17. London: Pandora.

Bowden, Mark. 2003. "The Dark Art of Interrogation." *Atlantic Monthly.* October. Retrieved from http://www.theatlantic.com/doc/200310/bowden.

Bowers, Faye. 2005. "Abu Ghraib's Message for the Rank and File." *Christian Science Monitor.* 6 May. Retrieved from http://www.csmonitor.com/2005/ 0506/p03s01-usju.html.

Boyer, Peter J. 2003. "The New War Machine." *The New Yorker.* 30 June:54–71.

Brinkley, Joel. 2005. "Rice Appears to Reassure Some Europeans on Treatment of Terror Detainees." *New York Times.* 9 December:A6.

Brundage, W. Fitzhugh. 1993. *Lynching in the New South: Georgia and Virginia, 1880–1930.* Urbana: University of Illinois Press.

Bush, George W. 2001/2004. "Detention, Treatment, and Trial of Certain Non-Citizens in the War against Terrorism." Military Order of 13 November. In *Torture and Truth: America, Abu Ghraib, and the War on Terror,* ed. Mark Danner, 78–82. New York: New York Review Books.

———. 2002a. "The President's State of the Union Address, The United States Capitol, Washington, D.C." 29 January. Retrieved from http://www.white house.gov/news/releases/2002/01/20020129-11.html.

———. 2002b. "Remarks by the President at 2002 Graduation Exercise of the United States Military Academy, West Point, New York." 1 June. Retrieved from http://www.whitehouse.gov/news/releases/2002/06/20020601-3.html.

———. 2002c. "The National Security Strategy of the United States of America." 20 September. Retrieved from http://www.whitehouse.gov/nsc/nss.html.

———. 2003. "Full Text: Bush Speech aboard the *USS Abraham Lincoln.*" 1 May. *Washington Post.* Retrieved from http://www.washingtonpost.com/ ac2/wp-dyn/A2627-2003May1.

Bybee, Jay S. 2002/2004. "Re: Status of Taliban Forces under Article 4 of the Third Geneva Convention of 1949." Memorandum for Alberto R. Gonzalez, Counsel to the President. 7 February. In *Torture and Truth: America, Abu Ghraib, and the War on Terror*, ed. Mark Danner, 96–104. New York: New York Review Books.

Cagle, Daryl. n.d. "Professional Cartoonists Index: Lynndie England." *Slate*. Retrieved from http://cagle.slate.msn.com/news/LynndieEngland/main.asp.

Carroll, Lewis. 1865. *Alice's Adventures in Wonderland*. Retrieved from http://www.cs.cmu.edu/~rgs/alice-table.html.

CBS News. 2004a. "The Pictures: Lynndie England." 12 May. Retrieved from http://www.cbsnews.com/stories/2004/05/12/60II/main617121.shtml.

CBS News. 2004b. "60 Minutes II." 28 April. Retrieved from http://www.cbsnews.com/stories/2004/04/27/60II/main614063.shtml.

Cohen, Stanley. 2001. *States of Denial: Knowing about Atrocities and Suffering*. Cambridge, UK: Polity Press.

Craig, Campbell. 2004. "American Realism versus American Imperialism." *World Politics* 57 October:143–71.

Crane, Conrad C., and W. Andrew Terrill. 2003. "Reconstructing Iraq: Insights, Challenges, and Missions for Military Forces in a Post-Conflict Scenario." Carlisle, PA: U.S. Army War College. February. Retrieved from http://www.carlisle.army.mil/ssi/pubs/display.cfm/hurl/PubID=182/.

Danner, Mark. 2004a. "Abu Ghraib: The Hidden Story." *New York Review*. 7 October. Retrieved from http://www.markdanner.com/nyreview/100704_abu.htm.

———. ed. 2004b. *Torture and Truth: America, Abu Ghraib, and the War on Terror*. New York: New York Review Books.

———, "We Are All Torturers Now." *New York Times*. 6 January:27.

Dratel, Joshua L. 2005. "The Legal Narrative." In *The Torture Papers: The Road to Abu Ghraib*, ed. Karen J. Greenberg and Joshua L. Dratel, xxi–xxiii. New York: Cambridge University Press.

Ehrenhaus, Peter, and A. Susan Owen. 2005. "Race Lynching and Christian Evangelicalism: Performances of Faith." *Text and Performance Quarterly* 24(3/4) October:276–301.

Fallows, James. 2002. "The Fifty-First State?" *Atlantic*. November:53–56, 58–64.

Fay, George R. 2004. "AR 15-6 Investigation of the Abu Ghraib Detention Facility and 205th Military Intelligence Brigade (U)." In *Torture and Truth: America, Abu Ghraib, and the War on Terror*, ed. Mark Danner, 437–579. New York: New York Review Books.

Ferguson, Niall. 1998. *The Pity of War: Explaining World War I*. New York: Basic Books.

Frontline. 2005. "The Torture Question." 18 October. Retrieved from http://www.pbs.org/wgbh/pages/frontline/torture/etc/script.html.

Garrels, Anne, with letters by Vint Lawrence. 2003. *Naked in Baghdad*. New York: Farrar, Straus and Giroux.

Gebhardt, James F. 2005. "The Road to Abu Ghraib: U.S. Army Detainee Doctrine and Experience." *Military Review* (January–February):44–50. Retrieved from http://www.au.af.mil/au/awc/awcgate/milreview/gebhardt.pdf.

Gilpin, Robert. 1981. *War and Change in World Politics*. New York: Cambridge University Press.

Girard, René. 1977. *Violence and the Sacred*. Trans. Patrick Gregory. Baltimore: Johns Hopkins University Press.

Gonzalez, Alberto R. 2002/2004. "Memorandum for the President: Decision Re Application of the Geneva Convention on Prisoners of War to the Conflict with al Qaeda and the Taliban." 25 January. In *Torture and Truth: America, Abu Ghraib, and the War on Terror*, ed. Mark Danner, 83–87. New York: New York Review Books.

Gourley, J. Leland. 2005. "Abu Ghraib Prisoners Were Not Tortured!" *Edmond Life and Leisure* 5(51). 19 May. Retrieved from http://www.edmondlifeandle isure.com/detail.php?118765,5,51.

Greenberg, Karen J. 2005. "From Fear to Torture." In *The Torture Papers: The Road to Abu Ghraib*, ed. Karen J. Greenberg and Joshua L. Dratel, xvii–xx. New York: Cambridge University Press.

Greenberg, Karen J., and Joshua L. Dratel, ed. 2005. *The Torture Papers: The Road to Abu Ghraib*. New York: Cambridge University Press.

Hersh, Seymour. 2001. "The Iraq Hawks." *New Yorker*. 24 and 31 December. Retrieved from http://www.newyorker.com/fact/content/?011224fa_FACT.

———. 2004. "Torture at Abu Ghraib." *New Yorker*. 10 May:42–47.

Hirsh, Michael. 2004. "Bernard Lewis Revisited." *Washington Monthly*. 14 November:13–9.

Hirsh, Michael, and John Barry. 2005. "The Abu Ghraib Scandal Cover-Up?" *Newsweek*. 7 June. Retrieved from http://www.msnbc.msn.com/id/5092776/site/newsweek/.

International Federation of Journalists. 2004. "Justice for Journalists Killed in Iraq—April 8th Protest." 20 March. Retrieved from http://www.ifj.org/default.asp?index=2348&Language=EN.

Jehl, Douglas. 2005. "The Reach of War: Intelligence; Qaeda-Iraq Link U.S. Cited Is Tied to Coercion Claim." *New York Times*. 9 December:A1.

Johnson, Thomas H., and James A. Russell. 2005. "A Hard Day's Night? The United States and the Global War on Terrorism." *Comparative Strategy* 24:127–51.

Kaplan, Fred. 2003. "The Flaw in Shock and Awe." *Slate*. 26 March. Retrieved from http://slate.msn.com/id/2080745/#ContinueArticle.

Katovsky, Bill, and Timothy Carlson, eds. 2003. *Embedded: The Media at War in Iraq*. Guilford, CT: Lyons Press.

Kuhn, Annette. 1985. *The Power of the Image: Essays on Representation and Sexuality*. London: Routledge and Kegan Paul.

Kull, Steven, with Clay Ramsay, Stefan Subias, Stephen Weber, and Evan Lewis. 2004. "Americans on Detention, Torture, and the War on Terrorism." Retrieved from http://www.pipa.org/OnlineReports/Terrorism/Torture_Jul04/Torture_Jul04_rpt.pdf.

Lelyveld, Joseph. 2005. "Interrogating Ourselves." *New York Times Magazine*. 12 June. Retrieved from http://select.nytimes.com/search/restricted/article?res=FA0E11FC395C0C718DDDAF0894DD404482.

Lemann, Nicholas. 2003. "The Controller: Karl Rove Is Working to Get George Bush Reelected, But He Has Bigger Plans." *New Yorker*. 12 May. Retrieved from http://bnfp.org/neighborhood/Lemann_Rove_NYM.htm.

Mann, James. 2004. *Rise of the Vulcans: The History of Bush's War Cabinet*. New York: Viking.

Mayer, Jane. 2005. "Outsourcing Terror." *New Yorker.* 14 & 21 February:106–10, 112, 114, 116, 118, 120, 123.

McWhorter, Diane. 2001. *Carry Me Home: Birmingham, Alabama, the Climactic Battle of the Civil Rights Revolution.* New York: Simon and Schuster.

Noujaim, Jehane, director. 2004. *Control Room.* New York: Magnolia Pictures.

Patterson, Orlando. 1998. *Rituals of Blood: Consequences of Slavery in Two American Centuries.* New York: Basic Books.

People for the American Way (PFAW). 2004. "Right-wing Response to the Abu Ghraib Scandal." *Right Wing Watch Online.* Retrieved from http://www.pfaw.org/pfaw/general/default.aspx?oid=15487.

Pew Research Center. 2005. "Opinion Leaders Turn Cautious, Public Looks Homeward: America's Place in the World." Survey Report. 17 November. Retrieved from http://people-press.org/reports/display.php3?ReportID=263.

Rice, Condoleezza. 2004. "Transcript of Rice's 9/11 Commission Statement." CNN. 19 May. Retrieved from http://www.cnn.com/2004/ALLPOLITICS/04/08/rice.transcript.

Rushing, Josh. 2005. Public Lecture on His Role as U.S. Military Liaison with the Press in Doha during the Early Phase of the War in Iraq. Trinity University. San Antonio, TX. 23 March.

Said, Edward. 1978. *Orientalism.* New York: Random House.

San Francisco Bay Area Independent Media Center. 2004. Compilation of Stories about Lynndie England. May. Retrieved from http://www.indybay.org/news/2004/05/1679966.php.

Scarry, Elaine. 1985. *The Body in Pain: The Making and Unmaking of the World.* New York: Oxford University Press.

Sturken, Marita. 1997. *Tangled Memories: The Vietnam War, the AIDS Epidemic, and the Politics of Remembering.* Berkeley: University of California Press.

Suskind, Ron. 2004. "Without a Doubt." *The New York Times Magazine.* 17 October:44–51, 64, 102, 108.

Tétreault, Mary Ann. 1994. "Women and Revolution in Viet Nam." In *Women and Revolution in Africa, Asia, and the New World*, ed. Mary Ann Tétreault, 111–36. Columbia: University of South Carolina Press.

Thornton, Lynn. 1978. "Orientalism in Victorian Paintings." *Eastern Encounters: Orientalist Paintings of the Nineteenth Century.* London: Fine Art Society. Retrieved from http://www.victorianweb.org/painting/orientalist/thornton1.html.

U.S. Department of Justice. 2004. "Memorandum for James B. Comey, Deputy Attorney General." 30 December. Retrieved from http://www.usdoj.gov/olc/dagmemo.pdf.

Wilson, Elizabeth. 1987. "Interview with Andrea Dworkin." In *Looking On: Images of Femininity in the Visual Arts and Media*, ed. Rosemary Betterton, 161–69. London: Pandora.

Wolf, Eric R. 1982. *Europe and the People without History.* Berkeley: University of California Press.

Wolfowitz, Paul. 2003. "News Transcript: Deputy Secretary [of Defense] Wolfowitz Interview with Sam Tannenhaus," *Vanity Fair.* 9 May. Retrieved from http://www.defenselink.mil/transcripts/2003/tr20030509-depsecdef0223.html.

Woodward, Bob. 2002. *Bush at War*. New York: Simon and Schuster.
———. 2004. *Plan of Attack*. New York: Simon and Schuster.
Yoo, John C. 2002/2004. "Letter to Alberto R. Gonzalez, Council to the President." In *Torture and Truth: America, Abu Ghraib, and the War on Terror*, ed. Mark Danner, 108–14. New York: New York Review Books.
Zernike, Kate. 2005. "Behind Failed Abu Ghraib Plea, a Tangle of Bonds and Betrayals." *The New York Times*. 10 May. Retrieved from http://www.nytimes.com/2005/05/10/national/10graner.html?ex=1273377600&en=652512e8d786ae31&ei=5090&partner=rssuserland&emc=rss.

CHAPTER SEVENTEEN

Uncle Sam Wants You to Trade, Invest, and Shop!

Relocating the Battlefield in the Gendered Discourses of the Pre- and Early Post-9/11 Period

STACEY L. MAYHALL

> The global economy has become the primary battlefield of the first war of the 21st century. The first wave of troops deployed in the new war has been business leaders who are racing to mend the country's horribly scarred confidence.
>
> —McNish 2001, A1

As we well know by now, the World Trade Center in New York was attacked more than seven years ago on September 11, 2001. In response to the attack on this prominent symbol of American financial power, the New York markets remained closed for four excruciating days. After the initial shock began to subside, attention on Wall Street turned to the stress and anticipation of the chaos that would inevitably ensue the moment the markets reopened. International markets, like the Toronto Stock Exchange (TSE), which remained open during this time, responded in the immediate aftermath by taking significant losses. Despite and in the face of those losses, commentators anxiously claimed that "nobody's panicking" (Ebner 2001a), and that things were orderly in the markets. But worries about loss of confidence in the market continued to manifest themselves in national stock exchanges days after the attack. Reports by Canadian and American news media implicitly acknowledged the perceived need to steady nerves and reduce panic when they reported on the active role taken by the central banks in Canada, the United States, and elsewhere internationally. In the intervening days, before the reopening of the New York (NYSE) and American Stock Exchanges (ASE), a series of highly politicized responses from a range of stakeholders—government and industry leaders and key individual investors being the most obvious— bear striking witness to the wholesale if sometimes subtle ongoing masculinization of economic discourses in North America.

The importance of an orderly day of market trading in the United States on the Monday following the attack was endlessly emphasized in international media. The message was clear: "Panic is unpatriotic—if you sell the terrorists will have won." The media was awash with money and business reporters; analysts and CEOs; head of the U.S. Federal Reserve (Fed), Alan Greenspan; mayor of New York City, Rudy Giuliani; and the president of the United States, George W. Bush, all anxiously affirming the need for order and restraint. Throughout these responses was also a rallying repetition of phrases like resilience, unity, American strength, and belief in the perpetuation of the "American model" of political and economic neoliberalism, a market-based order, in anticipation of future challenges. This language of "market order" was clearly drawing on the tropes of both gender and nationhood. Hence, actions taken in support of "normal" market operations, by both the financial sector and the general public, were widely expressed and thus interpreted as heroic, patriotic expressions of unity and resilience. Derek DeCloet, a financial analyst for the *National Post*, wrote: "New York's financial district will rebuild and the world's most powerful economy will, in the end, remain so. The terrorists struck at the very heart of capitalism. But they couldn't make the people who manage capital flinch" (DeCloet 2001, C6). The key individuals in the communities of the market and in society played a leading role in constraining, constructing, and reconstructing the security discourses of post-9/11. Thus, the events around 9/11 created a rare situation in which the existing, but typically invisible, connection between gender and the market economy, gender and the "high"[1] politics of war and security, were suddenly rendered all too apparent, all too visible.

This article is a textual exploration of some of the mechanisms of gendering and engendering that characterize international market discourses and thus impact on the management of both national and international relations more generally. It will show that the language of a certain hegemonic, binary construction of masculinity and femininity, which continues to dominate much of the existing gender ordering of society, also infused the financial and even national discourses of post-9/11. Even more concerning, perhaps, is the way in which the post-9/11 security context has been used by conservative stakeholders to reassert rigid and often essentialized visions of sex and gender, thus influencing individual and collective understandings of expected everyday "normal" behavior, and adding considerable fuel to the negative reinterpretation of any behavior that seemed to run counter to those dominant expressions. Post-9/11 Otherness and difference can be seen to be negatively associated with nationalism—unpatriotic at best and treachery at worst.

R. W. Connell (2002) describes the ways in which gender practices (or gender "arrangements") are "powerfully constrained" by existing social structures, which are themselves enduring patterns and practices of everyday life, and by the very construction and reconstruction of those practices, "[g]ender is something actually done; and done in social life, not something that exists prior to social life" (54–55). In the post-9/11 environment, the use of gender-coded images and language provided an important way for those individuals seeking to influence social, political, and economic responses to 9/11 to encourage desired behavior from men and women consistent with the dominant forms of masculinity and femininity. The responses by market operatives, government and industry leaders, and the "average" consumer/investor/worker citizen extended from their locations in the financial markets to participants and observers. This distinction between locations mattered, both politically and economically. While the financial market is generally understood to include the buying and selling of stocks, bonds, and commodities, one aspect of that market concerns the movement of money and the power of money as a reified and fetishized commodity handled by a small number of individual market operatives largely for corporate or individual clients with large portfolios. For the average citizen, however, the "market" is usually understood to be a place where consumers exchange money for products, some of which are simply the products of "everyday life," and for some of those citizens, the products purchased can also include investments (stocks, bonds, commodities). Notwithstanding that money is itself also a commodity, in the post-9/11 period the distinction between a tangible everyday product-based market and an intangible/unknowable financial market contributed to the differentiation of gender codes of behavior that guided expressions of masculinity and femininity. The intangibility and risk inherent in the operations of financial markets encouraged masculinized roles, language, and behavior on the part of traders who made those million dollar "bets," with other people's money, in a market of exchange. Arising out of the apparent social, political, and economic crisis that was initiated by 9/11, the already complexly gendered, classed, and racialized market-security discourses that tended to be socially conservative were powerfully reinforced. The post-9/11 context provided the seemingly perfect occasion for expressions of Othering to be strategically deployed in the service of remaking community on a late 1950s/early 1960s model of nationhood, though rather than focusing on a fear of the great Communist other, this time, attempted restructuring relied on frequent invocation of the danger posed by a cultural or civilizational Other. The financial choices of the average citizen/consumer/investor, therefore, were redefined as the choices and actions of "patriots."

Saving Our "Market Civilization": U.S. versus "Those against Us"

President Bush and others focused on New York, the World Trade Center, and the market as the literal "targets" of the attack, exaggerating the "new" security role for finance and the extent to which national security interests and the interests of actors in finance were shared. In this finance-as-security discourse, the 9/11 attack was not "senseless," but a deliberate strategic attack aimed at destabilizing the U.S. economy, the global

economy, and the existing architecture of financial relations by impact-
ing both infrastructure and symbolic supports. The language of war in
association with the attack and the economy was everywhere in the days
and weeks following the attack. P. J. Lim (2001, 42) referred to the attack
as "a direct hit on the economy." Drawing attention to the importance of
New York in the global market, J. Partridge interviewed Bank of Nova
Scotia chief economist Warren Jestin, who spoke in militarized language
about the coordinated actions and high level of integration, past and
present, of the central banks and other major players in the international
financial system:

> First of all, it struck right at the heart of the financial system. "This is not
> collateral damage to something else." Secondly, [Warren Jestin] said, it is
> "very truly a global hit." Because New York is the dominant player in world
> financial markets and those markets have spent the last 15 years becoming
> almost totally integrated in electronics. (Partridge 2001, B3)

In the 9/11 discourse of international media, the battle against terror
and defense of the neoliberal financial order was to be joined by all free
nations and every free citizen. In response to the attack on the U.S. World
Trade Center, and with the assistance of finance and business leaders,
President Bush, in his role as self-proclaimed "leader of the free world,"
transformed the financial and consumer product markets into battle-
fields in a global "war on terror." The "us and them" rhetoric that came to
define Bush's many addresses to "the nation" were implicitly spun around
an opposition between a civilized West—that is, the United States—and an
uncivilized (or worse, barbaric) Middle East that was closely associated
with Islam. Bush's statement was made in the United States, but through
global media, this statement and many that followed were very much received by all "nations." In the immediate aftermath, Bush rallied New
Yorkers, Americans, North Americans, and others to work together for
order and for the protection of "free" global markets; implicit in this language of unity was a patriotic rallying discourse that forged an indelible
association between the concepts of freedom and democracy and the financial markets, an association which thus became the leitmotif of civilization. On September 20, 2001, George W. Bush addressed a joint session of Congress; even a casual glance at the rhetoric makes evident the
point I have been making about the associations between the global
markets, freedom, democracy, and nationalism:

> We will direct every resource at our command—every means of diplomacy,
> every tool of intelligence, every instrument of law enforcement, every finan-
> cial influence, and every necessary weapon of war—to the destruction and to
> the defeat of the global terror network. . . . This is not, however, just Ameri-
> ca's fight. And what is at stake is not just America's freedom. This is the
> world's fight. *This is civilization's fight. This is the fight of all who believe in*

progress and pluralism, tolerance and freedom. We ask every nation to join us. We will ask and we will need the help of police forces, intelligence services, and banking systems around the world. (Bush 2001, A8; emphasis added)

The media adopted Bush's language of a global conflict of "civilizations" in a way that mirrored political science scholar Samuel Huntington's much-maligned thesis of "the clash of civilizations" (Huntington 1993, 1996). Huntington proposed that major conflicts are now most likely to be cultural, between "civilizations": Western, Latin American, Islamic, Chinese, Hindu, Orthodox, Japanese, and African. His belief was that attempts to resolve conflict must necessarily take into account culture, ethnicity, religion, and identity in order to understand the way in which the present conflicts were likely to continue. In a critique of Huntington's thesis that drew attention to his theory's reliance upon a foundation suggesting conflict was inevitable and constant, Ronnie Lipschutz suggested that "both culture and identity have been invoked in essentialist terms, as facts that are as invariant as the earth on which they stand" (Lipschutz 2000, 107). Stephen Gill (1995) examines the ways in which "capitalist norms and practices" are present down to the level of "everyday life" using the construct neoliberal "market civilisation": "[t]he concept entails, on the one hand, cultural, ideological, and mythic forms understood broadly as an ideology or myth of capitalist progress . . . On the other hand, market civilisation involves patterns of social disintegration and exclusionary and hierarchical patterns of social relations" (399). Bush's use of "civilization's fight" is very much along the lines that Gill identifies.

The post-9/11 battle for the market and "the American model"[2] was expressed in cultural and mythic language, as reflections of Western ordering, of asserting and reasserting the centrality of Western ideology and law principles. John Leo from *U.S. News & World Report* wrote on September 24, 2001, about the war as a "cultural battle" that "pits extremists against modern civilization . . . this is a global cultural war, pitting a pan-Islamic movement of fundamentalist extremists against the modern world and its primary cultural engine, America, 'the Great Satan'" (Leo 2001, 47). Fareed Zakaria, then a writer for *Newsweek*, was quick to affirm and re-present the us-them message to the rest of the world:

The world [that countries in Europe, Latin America, and Asia] have gotten used to will not survive if America is crippled. The United States is the pivot that makes today's globalization go around. If other countries believe in individual liberty, in free enterprise and free trade, in religious freedom, in democracy, then they are eating the fruits of the American order. And this order can be truly secure only when those who benefit from it stand in its defense. (2001, 70)

As I and others have already noted, the construction of the events of 9/11 as a civilizational threat facilitated overt, unapologetic discourses of Othering. This Othering assisted in the creation of enemies, a dehumanization and demonizing dynamic that apparently made vengeance necessary and rational and was grounded in the representational deployment of a feminized "enemy Other" and a masculinized civilizational "us." We were all being asked to be agents/soldiers—rational, militarized, gendered agents in a free market system. This coding of market roles is discussed further in the next section where the particular ways citizens are asked to respond can be seen to further support the maintenance of the existing order.

Rallying the Troops: Investing Warriors, Shopping Consumers, and Faith in the American Model

Gender was coded in the market roles men and women were asked to perform in the post-9/11 battle to protect America and save our market civilization. Through the deployment of concepts of unity and resilience, the outlines of gendered roles took shape. While present in financial discourse in reference to particular corporations, industries, individuals, or even the markets in bad times, in post-9/11, these concepts were deployed with an air of patriotism and nationalism in reference to finance and security.

In many cases, investors and workers were gender coded as male warrior types, whereas consumers, who were urged to shop to save the country, were coded female and asked to do their part for the war effort. Historically during wars women, as "the nation's mothers," have been asked to conserve resources, to forego comforts, to sacrifice consumption, and to contribute precious metals to the war effort. It is important to note, however, that this gendered (and racialized and classed) citizenship at once relies upon and reproduces the long existing structural marginalization of women by states, and the specific control of women in national and international politics—equating men with the state (public) and women with the nation, as cultural carriers that are to be protected.[3] After 9/11, women were asked to spend, to shop, and to use rather than conserve their resources. Yet this request arises from the same man-state/woman-nation binary equation that has long been deployed to maintain existing power structures, and is one element of the expression of sexual difference as a means of maintaining the social, economic, political, spiritual, and civilizational "order." Furthermore, this conserve-spend turnabout meant that resiliency had a double gender coding: the resiliency of the wounded warrior. An example of this is the financial manager who got up and continued to trade (that is, battle) or the working-class firefighter who kept digging. Both were distinctively masculine, and the resiliency of the besieged population in general was held together by women—wives and mothers who continued to do their domestic chores of shopping for their families. The latter was auxiliary to the former.

Expressed in market terms as emotional rather than rational choices, "sentimentality" was at once a threat and also a tool for improving market functionality. Ken Hoover discussed the role of optimism and pessimism in the volatility as well as the volume of trade. "Sentiment works as a contrary indicator. The market often bottoms at such times" (2001, A1). Emotion was acceptable as long as it was patriotic and as long as the overwhelming emphasis was on the reacquisition of order in chaotic times. Too much exuberance and excessive pessimism were judged to be equally problematic. Glenn Flanagan, the "Mutual Fund" columnist for *The Toronto Sun*, repeated the same sentiment and applied it not only to the U.S. context but also to the wider international context:

> You, yes you, can actually do a lot to make sure such outright slaughter never happens again. And it can be done without donning fatigues, grabbing a gun and parachuting into some distant land on a midnight search and-destroy mission against some cowardly little people who sneak from hole to hole. *Let your heart and soul feel for the victims, the thousands of victims, but use your head to do some real damage.* The answer: Consume, spend, invest, and keep the cash moving out there. (Flanagan 2001, 44; emphasis added)

This double gender coding separating "heart" from "head" was effective in reinforcing appropriate, state-sanctioned emotions by soldiers and those on the home front. Dividing acceptable options for the "heart" and "head" suggested the association of the *actions* of consumption, spending, investment, and general economic participation with the head, yet what underlies that agency was feminized—it was the answer to why we acted. This plea for consumer spending and confidence was grounded in a belief in the fundamental soundness of a capitalist system and the association of that system, and its symbols, with belief in personal and political freedoms—"our" market civilization. Use of the language of freedom in association with market behavior carried a powerful message. This message, expressed in an ostensibly neutral language of the market "patriot," relies upon a gender coded profile of who might contribute what to the defense of freedom. Fear and insecurity were coded feminine by some, in an effort to rally market participation. According to Glenn Flanagan from *The Toronto Sun*:

> The buildings were targets because of what they represented—financial, political and military power. . . . The bottom line point of this terrorist attack: It was meant as a message to you, personally, to crawl into a corner in a fetal position and be too afraid to keep fuelling our democratic and capitalistic way

of life . . . you can fight terrorism by keeping the system going, which means keeping your money in mutual funds, stocks and bonds and staying the course. (Flanagan 2001)

By personalizing the attack, Flanagan taps into a key element of the post-9/11 discourse: he identifies people's existing economic insecurities and victimization as unacceptable, instead encouraging citizens to bravely "stay the course." Although women were no longer asked to simply keep the home fires burning, they remained the keepers of the national "heart" and were largely portrayed as consumer contributors to the market.

In the days and weeks following the events of 9/11, a shared masculinized, racialized hero image circulated in print and visual media. From firefighters and rescue workers to the returning workers on Wall Street and the military engaged in Operation Enduring Freedom, the image of hero became bound to each one of the defenders of American freedoms and security. Many reporters and correspondents spoke of the firefighters, the police, port authority, and other rescue workers as, according to Bruce Nussbaum in *Business Week*, "working class heroes" and as the "real Masters of the Universe"[4] (Nussbaum 2001, 55). According to Nussbaum:

> Big, beefy working-class guys became heroes once again, replacing the telegenic financial analysts and techno-billionaires who once had held the nation in thrall. Uniforms and public service became "in." Real sacrifice and real courage were on graphic display. Maybe it was the class reversals that were so revealing. The image of self-sacrifice by civil servants in uniform was simply breathtaking.

Editor Nussbaum later added a particular construct of "sacrificing women" to the patriotic imagery, but the description "big, beefy" was a heterosexual, masculinized construct. The use of "real" in the distinction between market actors and firefighters suggested the importance of both discourse and identity in the gender coding of what *should* count as "real sacrifice and real courage," and what risk-acceptance meant. Nussbaum expected things to return to normal in the future where the Americans were defined as the ultimate capitalists, but in the post-9/11 period, the image of the American economy and its workers as institutional and individual economic heroes was becoming more working-class. Despite Nussbaum's emphasis away from market actors, media widely made little or no distinction between forms of heroes made from this crisis. Work, consumerism, everyday life, and well-timed, "appropriate" profit[5] were all rolled into expressions of patriotism and faithful service to America. In fact, financial agents figure prominently among the "real" heroes of 9/11.

The first line of defense in post-9/11 was to be the financial agents, and their leader was embodied in Fed Chairman Alan Greenspan. These individuals were to be the first heroes in the new war. This trope of heroism, inscribed with masculine codes, was particularly prevalent and effective as finance and militarism became publicly joined, reinforcing and normalizing the militaristic attitude adopted by financial discourses; a militaristic attitude that normalized the masculine qualities of aggressiveness and war-making so often valued in the construction of the ideal public citizen. Masculine militarism normalized the practices and character traits of financial agents—re-valuing the greed and predatory behavior that was often associated with financial agents, particularly traders.

When the devastation to the World Trade Center occurred, it wiped out several firms and certainly depleted the workforce and destroyed the infrastructure of many others. For survivors of the attack, decisions had to be made about continuing to do business, trading, analyzing, and research in finance. Aside from the infrastructural issues, attention of the media turned to these firms and judged their constitution in the wake of the attack. Members of a devastated "close-knit" bond-trading firm Cantor-Fitzgerald, a key player in the high-pressure bond market, began work almost immediately after the attack, having voted to return so that the terrorist intention of disruption/destruction did not "win" the day. Eric Roston of *Time Magazine* quoted Ken Pforr, vice-president of Cantor-Fitzgerald's municipal-bonds unit: "Our plan is to not let those bastards get us down" (Roston 2001, 79). The devastation to the firm of Cantor-Fitzgerald and the determination of its employees were repeated in all media sources over the immediate hours and days following the attack. This courageous desire to get back to work was celebrated in the media and by leaders in government and finance.

Financial heroes were made during that early post-9/11 period. We witnessed the establishment and dominance of the trope of heroism from the top down. Patriotic leadership was gender coded during and after the events of 9/11 in specifically racialized, classed, masculinized, and militarized terms iconically associated with Alan Greenspan and George Bush. Greenspan's focus was on calm and resilience. His aim was to steady the financial community and the nation before the market restart. The financial community's expressed anticipation of the actions to be taken by both Greenspan and Bush in the crisis reflected an expectation of a discourse of calm and confidence.

By the end of the first week of trading after 9/11, industry analyst Barrie McKenna raised doubts about the ability of even those with usual influence, like Greenspan, to prevent herd behavior; the "rogues" of Wall Street were expected to "bolt" (McKenna 2001, B11).[6] According to Jacquie McNish, the "muscle" of central bank "generals" like Greenspan, the top general, was to be used to create unity, to influence the "powerful investors" to "put aside their speculative instincts" and to persuade bond traders not to engage in "unusual bond speculation" (2001, A1). Yet despite these efforts, the uncertainty and frayed nerves of the first week caused people to stop listening to calming attempts. McKenna said: "But in the shock and panic sweeping the country, no one is listening to Mr. Greenspan's muted calls for patience and perspective any more. The world has changed" (2001, B11). This acknowledgment of a "changed" world or a deaf public and financial community did not prevent the unity-influenced, perspective message from being repeated, nor did it disrupt the overwhelming influence of the "we are the market, the market is *US*" message.

The Globe and Mail on October 4, 2001, featured a photo of George Bush, New York City Mayor Rudy Giuliani, and New York Governor George Pataki in front of the NYSE, noting in the caption that these men "assured business leaders yesterday that the U.S. economy will rebound and grow" (Ebner 2001c, B1). Numerous experts and economic and political leaders, as well as firms,[7] used the language of resiliency, especially in relation to consumer confidence. Again we witnessed gender coding reinforcing a message of security directed inward to investors and consumers and outward to the international community.

Images of this rallying role were somewhat confused as the traditional security-as-military and more recent security-as-finance images combined to extend the discourse of heroic resilience to the consumer market. As in past state wars, a familiar patriotic icon of Uncle Sam was used to rally Americans. This time, however, there was a market-based redeployment of the masculinized, traditionally militarized image of Uncle Sam[8] with the caption, "Uncle Sam wants you to shop!" The December 2001 cover of *Smart Money: The Wall Street Journal Magazine of Personal Business* featured an image of Bush with the caption that read "The president wants you to buy this magazine, a car, some airline tickets, a computer, a new home—and invest in America now!" (*Smart Money* 2001).

Actions supporting the functioning of capitalism represented a heroic effort that was equated with patriotism; agency was masculinized and patriotic. Strength was represented as capitalism to the wider population. A nonprofit group called Invest in US, composed of communications professionals, had a Web site and advertised its wider media campaign to encourage investment. Invest in US offered downloadable posters and nostalgic graphics that expressed a theme of strength (see http://www.prwatch.org/node/804). The imagery at once powerfully located the dynamism of the American economy in the hands of masculinized, patriotic investors, while it relied on the image of the racialized other of Osama Bin Laden to provide the impetus for that dynamism (Invest in US 2001). Reuters confirmed this masculinization of economic power, referring to "dollar strength [as] a symbol of U.S. economic might" (Reuters 2001, B2). As a result, Reuters suggested, currency trading became an issue of national security as the location for the commodification of money—a means to produce security through the management of risk. Reuters quoted Paul Podolsky, currency strategist at Fleet Global Markets: " 'I think that the Bush administration would regard—not to overstate the issue—a sharp dollar selloff as a national security issue. At the very least, it would spark quiet intervention' " (September 17, B2). Rhetoric balancing the importance of "strong" leadership with the "determination" of the average masculinized citizen encouraged the association of agency both with predictable market and state leaders and with the general investing and feminized consuming population. Both groups contributed to the reestablishment of security for everyone.

Calls for heroic resilience reinforced messages of unity by President George W. Bush. The central bankers themselves offered reassurance through press releases, interviews, and statements given in many venues. They repeated, in many media forms, their individual and collective efforts aimed to keep the international financial system functioning. While the conversation between market and policy makers occurred in more than one venue, the public resiliency conversation in the daily media was also for the benefit of the public and the wider financial community. Through that same discourse, global financial leaders and individual investors were given new responsibilities, beyond money for money's sake. The reification of market actors as the creators of security and the economics-based redefinition of threat and forms of power were as important to the post-9/11 discourse as the shifting designation of heroes to those who were able to "do what it takes" to maintain Grasso's "American model."

Suddenly, an industry obsessed with individual performance and individual motivations, generally separated to a great degree from association with national identity, found itself featured centrally in calls for patriotism across America and, perhaps more importantly, internationally. While the actions of the personnel of the markets are not regularly thought of as patriotic, their contributions to the functioning of the market and the security of investors have been portrayed in financial literature at times as heroic. In this way, members of the New York financial district played important social roles in the continuing transformation of modern national identity. Unlike Nussbaum's (2001) claim of a shift of heroism to the "real heroes" of the working class from white-collar "techno billionaires," we saw the *expansion* of the identity of American hero from its accepted basis in adventurist sport, military prowess,[9] or courageous firefighters to an all-inclusive definition of hero that also tapped into the role of the everyday investor/consumer/worker citizen as agent in the new post-9/11 world. The key point is that the elements of this expanded identity of American citizen hero did not really change; rather, celebrated elements of national identity were shifted to accommodate the specific post-9/11 needs of national security.

"Real" War—Enter the Gendered State

Post-9/11 usage of the discourse of "real" versus imagined/virtual marks an important reintroduction of the formerly dominant (in academic and policy making circles) language of political realism in relation to international politics and the use of power (as power-over/influence/violence/intimidation) by a hegemonic state in its own defense. This reaffirmation of the dominant realist discourse in American politics and finance influenced the positioning of heroes in American and international discourse. Gendered and racialized, dichotomous language was often used to classify the behavior of some as heroic and others as "barbaric" and "cowardly." The language of resilience and unity quickly morphed into a more direct link between finance and war and, more specifically, finance as war.

In the days immediately following the attack on the World Trade Center, there was a perceived emasculation of the military and a concomitant valorization of business and finance by industry and non-industry observers. Some suggested that there was an emasculation of the United States itself. Citing her interview with Dr. Jeremy Mack, a psychiatrist in Manhattan, Judy Gerstel of *The Toronto Star* calls the events of 9/11:

> [a] castration, "knocking down these two prominent things that were the pride of New York and the country." And the aftermath of castration? "Catastrophic impotence," says the Freudian analyst [Dr. Jeremy Mack] . . . For an individual, "the catastrophe of impotence is not being able to connect with the person you love. For America as a nation, it means we're no longer able to have the crazy, grandiose pride that we've had—which, probably permitted us to get into the bemused state where this could happen." (Gerstel 2001, D7)

Mack's gendered language highlighted the pride of the feminized nation and the castration of the masculinized state—a dichotomy that was often deployed to reinforce the nation-state construct through identity. As Peterson (1992) argues, states are gendered, they are mutually constituted with the state as "protector" and nation as "protected." Once again sexual difference infuses this language. This meant that the militarized language used to describe this restructuring was more significant than Mack portrayed, and it was intertwined with masculinity. There was a double message here of the ineffectiveness of the withered neoliberal state due to the perceived inability of the state to either protect the national population from the initial attack or affect an immediate reprisal given the stateless nature of the enemy. Simultaneously, heroic financial operatives and their actions were elevated as a partial answer to this ineffective state. As Jacquie McNish suggested: "With the military might of the United States standing helpless on the sidelines, it has been left to business leaders to demonstrate that the nation has the resolve to overcome its attackers" (2001).

Once the military and government regained their footing and prepared for retaliation, the imagery of heroism, patriotism, duty, honor and war accommodated both active masculinized citizens of the market and military as hero-warriors on a shared battlefield. Targets and agents were constructed similarly for each realm. These images were specific to the roles reserved for financial market agents and the military, but in the market economy, consumers were patriots too. Although the first battlefield was in finance, there was room for all patriots, male and female, masculine and feminine, in this war.

One pronounced theme in the 9/11 literature combined battle/defense language with that of strength and determination. Going back to work becomes represented as heroic, a defense of family and home, life and capitalism. As David Milberg, a lawyer at Schiff, Hardin & Waite in Chicago, explained: "The most patriotic thing I could do was show up for work today . . . we have to show the cowards that did this, that their war of intimidation will lose" (qtd. in Babad 2001, B15). The firm's determination to get the industry "back on its feet" and functioning linked their regular work with a language of battle. All of the "shell-shocked Wall Street survivors" and leaders rebuilt the infrastructure for that "return to the trenches," and in doing so gained stature in the public media for their bravery, sacrifice, and unity of actions and purpose. " 'We're not going to let this defeat us,' said a burly broker with the Stars and Stripes hoisted on his shoulder like a soldier's rifle" (qtd. in Brethour 2001, B11).

The imagery and language of battle located the activities of workers in finance in a discourse of war and merged the interests of public and private in defense of the state and the market economy. Brian Milner of the *Globe and Mail* asserted a significant shift in language, much like Nussbaum's reflections on the "real" heroes of the working class: "The U.S. government's 'war' on Microsoft will never be called that again. That isn't war. What happened on Tuesday was war" (2001, B2). Like many other correspondents, for Milner, the "barbarians" were the perpetrators of the acts of violence, but the defense of "home" was to be both financial and military. Even though Milner is claiming a change of language and an implied distinction between "real" war and financial war, in fact, the "normal" operations of finance were steeped as well in this language of war and battle in reference to the industry. McNish concluded that the crisis of 9/11 created a situation in which politics and business "shared the limelight" (2001, A1).

The battle discourse blurred the lines of citizen-soldier, as some business leaders became literal military and market generals. Prominent on the cover page of *Fortune* for October 15, 2001, was an image of Ford Corporation's Finance executive Robert Smith in his Army Reserve

General's uniform (*Fortune* 2001). The caption read, "Business Goes to War" with subcaptions: "The Economy Under Siege," "Airlines in Crisis," "Terrorism: Other Threats." Michael Schrage (2001), co-director of MIT Media Lab's e-markets initiative, used another image of "Uncle Sam" and the idea of the merging of the interests of public and private in the protection of the state in a "real" war. In a lengthy passage, Schrage wrote:

> The symmetry makes sense: private industry and public citizens are the first victims of this war. They will now become the first line of defense. "In unconventional wartime, public safety is so precious that it must be protected by the phalanx of private enterprise. If the war against global terrorism is more real than theoretical, then a new alliance must emerge between business and the state. Global enterprise and small-town entrepreneurs alike will become agents of the state for the emerging era of national security socialism. Both tacitly and explicitly, private markets and public servants will be called upon (or pressured, or inspired) to cooperate to preempt terrorist activity." *The argument that global corporations are citizens of the world, not of nations, is revealed as wishful fictions.* (Schrage 2001, 266; emphasis added)

In a "real" war, "real" warriors were state-sponsored, be they market or military combat-trained. These citizens, armed with the hegemonic power and weapons of the American model, engaged the "enemy" in an amorphous "war on terror," on financial and military fronts, everywhere and nowhere.

Conclusions

The events of 9/11 shifted into prominent view the interconnected and gendered discourses of security and finance. Communities of individuals, who located themselves as agents of order and security, created the two-headed discourse that reproduced the existing order and supported the continuation of the American model. According to government and financial market leaders, the key to market and country survival was to combat pervasive fear brought on by the 9/11 crisis by refusing to let the "terrorists win." Order, they suggested, must arise from a masculinized "human mind" making free, rational choices, as well as calm determination and leadership demonstrated by those with experience operating in a market that historically had its ups and downs and *always* survived and grew. In part, this order came from a reinterpretation of panic and fear as simply shifting the basis of *choice* temporarily and understanding that shift as "normal" market volatility. Perpetuating *our* "market civilization," with the United States maintaining its central role, depends upon a reassertion of control and redeployment of a now more securitized hegemonic masculinity that helped to maintain the community of operatives.

We saw the influence of the gender identities of the financial market participants on the *movement* of global financial markets. Historically these patterns had also appeared, but the current form of hegemonic masculinity, featuring an emphasis on boldness, aggressiveness, individualism and risk-taking, collided with and absorbed a familiar secondary, but related discourse around values of resilience, calm, patriotism/heroism, and so forth. Explicitly linked to both discourses, and to the underlying operation of global finance in general, was an undercurrent of neoliberalism that emphasized the value of a free market, and in particular the American model. Hegemonic masculinity worked in conjunction with neoliberalism to ensure our national security through the market.

The social environment of the market was influenced by the behavior and self-interested motivations of its operatives (*choosing* to buy and hold or sell short), and by the discourses of those holding influential positions. It also demonstrated the complexity and fluidity of masculine identities in financial markets. Like McDowell and Court (1994; McDowell 1994) argue, there is no singular representative masculine identity in finance but two, both of which constitute hegemonic masculinity, and both of which were influenced by the undercurrent of nationalism: Senior corporate bankers spoke the same language (of resilience, calm, trust, and so on) in "noncrisis" daily finance as their post-9/11 counterparts; traders spoke in the language of risk and power ordinarily, but they were encouraged to shift to a more patriotic discourse to frame their actions. The literature of finance located young, aggressive, and middle-aged "wise" men in the everyday dealings of finance, but the representation of the faces of finance shifts between these two dimensions, depending on the way the market was going. It was not long before references to "bear market virgins" began to appear once again as they had after the October 1987 crash (Warner 2002). This discourse was very much directed *toward* the younger and more aggressive group (and the general public, one might suggest) *by* the older, wiser men who had, this suggested, seen it all. In any case, the community of finance reestablished the basis of behavior and decision-making, once again reaffirming the operation of the existing dominant conservative order.

On a flag-draped Wall Street people repeated the words of patriotism, freedom, independence, and choice, but it was not long before expressions of market and financial loyalty to the system itself, rather than buy/hold strategies, became patriotic.[10] Simple participation in the formal market was patriotic, trading was the defense of a way of life against outside threats, and in the first few days after the attack, the average investor/consumer/worker was the first to be in a position to demonstrate their resolve. Advertising campaigns for the NYSE running since early in

2002 promoted a flag-waving version of patriotism associated with what was portrayed as daily life in the United States: cops directing traffic, kids playing, and the stock market trading, as it has "always" traded—close in on former Mayor Giuliani, "Let freedom ring." The dominant discourse reinvested meaning in such a way that actions of individuals and corporations were reinterpreted as heroic, "defensive," and patriotic. "Real" men and women were made heroes because of their actions and because of what they represented—they were all citizen-soldiers in the fight for an American-led "market civilization."

The discourses deployed post-9/11 utilized and contributed to the existing free-market society, though they appeared to break new ground in their incorporation of markets and market operatives into the national security discourse. This new ground was not so new; familiar gender and race expectations, predicated on the binary deployment of self/us, other/them, and the existing order, helped to clarify roles and interpret behavior that kept the market operating as explicitly patriotic. While acknowledging the role of the market community in making security, in the end, the post-9/11 discourse denied the relationality of security by focusing on the creation of security and the elimination of vulnerability as something that was up to "us" not "them," and certainly not us all.

Acknowledgments

I thank the *NWSAJ* editorial board for their thoughtful comments and assistance in the editing and publication of this article. I would like to extend special thanks to Sal Renshaw, Marlea Clarke, Andrea Harrington, and Mary Young for their critical comments.

Notes

This paper is a revision of Chapter 7: "Patriotism is profitable": Patriotism and profit in the post-9/11 global financial war in my 2002 dissertation *Riding the Bull, Wrestling the Bear: Sex and Identity in the Discourses of Global Finance.* The revised paper was presented at the International Studies Association Annual Meeting 17–21 March 2004 in Montreal, Canada.

1. The distinction between "high" politics and "low" politics is often made with regard to national security politics and domestic politics. This distinction relies on the same gendered binary ordering dynamic as men/women or reason/emotion, where the first in the pair is privileged over the second. We see the high/low distinction functioning in the money/other commodities binary, where increased risk has contributed to a reification of financial markets and their operatives.

2. NYSE chief Richard Grasso said: "this dream [of the American model] will be up and functioning and no one can interrupt that resolve" (Howlett 2001, B1). This "American model" could be maintained in part in the immediate post-9/11 period by supporting financial market operatives; there was never any question that it should be defended. The basis of the unity rally staged by Bush and others was an assumption and public declaration of the ability of the markets and the "American model" to be resilient.

3. There is extensive feminist international relations scholarship discussing the gendered state, public-private dichotomies citizenship, international politics, and security in terms of identity. In particular, on "gendered states" and states as "protection rackets" see Peterson 1992; on social contract and the nature of the public/private divide in gendered citizenship and the structural exclusion of women see Pateman (1988, 1992) and Enloe (1990); for an overview of the state, security, the economy, and global order see Tickner (1992, 2001).

4. See Wolfe (1988) for the original construction of the icon "Masters of the Universe" in his famous book *The Bonfire of the Vanities* (see also Mayhall 2002; Picker 1990).

5. Not all profit taking immediately after 9/11 was deemed acceptable in the industry. In the first week after the event, the need for caution and not "hardheartedness" was repeated. Brent Jang (2001) of *The Globe and Mail* reported that there were firms who chose not only to profit from the tragedy of 9/11 but to publicize their efforts as well. Jang called the actions of Wi-LAN, a high-speed wireless company, to use the tragedy "to promote itself, no matter its original good intentions," a "corporate gaffe." Coca-Cola pulled its ads for this reason. "Profiting from widespread misery, of course, isn't something that companies or investors want to be connected with—but business and investment decisions need to be made all the same." According to Jang, there was also at least one hedge fund manager who "placed bets against Four Seasons Hotels and Sears Canada prior to last Tuesday's horrific attacks." "That manager made money as a result of the 9/11 events," said Jang, who explained that while it is necessary for fund managers to determine or at least attempt to accurately estimate U.S. actions, to anticipate corporate risk and questions about oil supplies and pricing, there remained several controversial choices made by individual managers that were publicly challenged by some.

6. On the subject of herd or crowd behavior in relation to the markets see especially Friedman (2000), Kindleberger (1978), and Le Bon (1896).

7. On Monday, September 17, 2001, in *The Globe and Mail*, Michael Lynch (2001) published a full-page "message" signed "The Employees of Merrill Lynch Canada, Inc" that assured the public that the firm was "financially strong, and our clients' assets are safe and secure; history has shown the resilience of our financial system in times of crisis. We are confident that—as in the past—

the global financial markets will prevail and go forward with renewed strength. In the face of great tragedy, freedom-loving people in Canada and throughout the world will join Americans to move forward with compassion, courage and strength."

8. The association of "America" with Uncle Sam has occurred in the literature before. The cover of the October 1988 *The Banker* showed a small boat labeled "The Good ship G7" containing six rowers with their oars in the air, all men in business suits with superimposed faces of G7 countries and a figure meant to represent Uncle Sam, with his back to the camera. In the distance is an image of the statue of liberty and a banner reading "Presidential elections" draped across it. The Caption reads "IMF-World Bank: Don't Rock the Boat, Guys." Uncle Sam appeared again on the cover of the December 1990 issue cutting through a "BIS Regulations" net to allow U.S. banks to escape. The caption reads, "US Banks Escape the BIS Net." The representation of America through the figure of Uncle Sam reappeared over time.

9. Like wars and police/peacekeeping actions in years past, imagery of sport and patriotism joined together. Linda Diebel of the *Toronto Star* quotes "Vinnie," a US B-1 bomber: "It's like being a football player at the Super Bowl" (2001). Sport, militarism, and masculinity join as well in a trading card series that had been produced by Topps (2001): "An encyclopedic record of America's war against terrorism. Cards contained biographical information on civilian and military leaders entrusted to guide us through this fight, statistical data and photos of military hardware." All of these images and "heroes" were brought together in a card titled "Wall Street Reopens," which stated: "The attack on the World Trade Center shut down stock trading on Wall Street for nearly four days—the longest such interruption since World War I." The New York Stock Exchange reopened on Monday, September 17, by a New York City firefighter, police officer, and an emergency services worker in a star-studded, patriotic ceremony: "'Today, America goes back to business,' Grasso proclaimed" (card 24).

10. In early July 2005, during the G8 summit in Scotland, London experienced four bomb attacks on its underground and transportation system similar to an attack in Madrid in March of 2004. This attack was not explicitly on the financial district of London, yet there was a perception of the link between way of life, security, the economy, and the attack. As Tom Caldwell of Caldwell Securities argued, "We will adjust to this, we are more acclimatized. The west is not shutting down because of this . . . the bond market is actually stronger" (Taruc, 2005). CBC Business correspondent Marivel Taruc later asked Caldwell if 9/11 was a "standard of scale" that would affect the extent of any market response. Caldwell answered "I imagine you are on to something, that's the benchmark people aspire to." There was a "terror premium built in" that comes from the experience of 9/11. London Mayor Ken Livingstone and Police Commissioner Sir Ian Blair drew links to the Blitz on London during WWII. As Charles Hodson, CNN reporter (and resi-

dent of the affected area of London), suggested, "the phrase 'business as usual' was invented here 60 ears ago as Nazi bombs rained down on the city . . . terrible things have happened here in the 2000 years of this city . . . life goes on, life has to go on" (Hodson, 2005). In both the 9/11 and London "7/7" discourses, war dialogue dominated and the financial markets were seen as a front. The vanguard "warrior" discourse of 9/11 was missing in London, where "carry on" was an image of London patriotism. What this means was a specific understanding of New Yorkers and Americans as warriors uniquely cast to fight the global war on terror, in every way possible, with market operatives as the frontline fighters. This marks a deployment of an image of experience of violence in the streets of London, versus a "new" understanding of that violence in the New York context, even accounting for the previous World Trade Center attacks.

References

Babad, Michael. 2001. "Business Comment." *The Globe and Mail*, September 13: B15.

Banker, The. 1988. "The Good Ship G7." *The Banker*. October, 130 (752): Cover.

———. 1990. "US Banks Escape the BIS Net." *The Banker*. December, 140 (778): Cover.

Brethour, Patrick. 2001. "Wall Street Back to Work 'in a War Zone.'" *The Globe and Mail*, September 18: B11.

Bush, George W. 2001. "Text of U.S. Presidential Address to Joint Session of Congress: September 20th, 2001." *The Toronto Star*, September 21: A8.

Carrick, Rob. 2001a. "Now Is Definitely Not the Time to Panic." *The Globe and Mail*, September 12: B7.

———. 2001b. "Shelter from the Storm." *The Globe and Mail*, September 15: B11.

Colvin, Geoff. 2001. "Reality Doesn't Bite." *Fortune*, October 15: 62.

Connell, Relwyn W. 1995. *Masculinities*. Berkeley, CA: University of California Press.

———. 2002. *Gender*. Malden, MA: Blackwell Publishing.

DeCloet, Derek. 2001. "When the Good Drive Out the Bad." *The National Post/Financial Post*, September 14: C1.

Diebel, Linda. 2001. "War 'Like Being a Football Player at the Super Bowl.'" *The Toronto Star*, October 10: A1.

Ebner, Dave. 2001a. "Nerves Steady as TSE Reopens." *The Globe and Mail*, September 14: B1 and B6.

———. 2001b. "U.S. 'Quite Possibly' in Recession, Cheney Says." *The Globe and Mail*, September 17: B2.

———. 2001c. "White House Blueprint Helps Drive Up Stocks." *The Globe and Mail*, October 4: B1 and B18.

Enloe, Cynthia. 1990. *Bananas, Beaches & Bases: Making Feminist Sense of International Politics*. Berkeley, CA: University of California Press.

Flanagan, G. 2001. "Fight Terror: Keep Our System Going." *The Toronto Sun*, September 23.

Flavelle, Doug. 2001. "Drama to Attend Market Opening." *The Toronto Star*, September 15: C1 and C5.

Fortune. 2001. "Business Goes to War." *Fortune*, October 15, Cover.

Fox, Justin. 2001. "War and Recession." *Fortune*, November: 74–82.

Friedman, Thomas. 2000. *The Lexus and the Olive Tree*. New York: Farrar, Straus, Giroux.

Fukuyama, Francis. 1989. "The End of History." *The National Interest*, Summer 3(18).

Gerstel, Judy 2001. "U.S. Psyche Forever Changed." *The Toronto Star*, September 14: D7.

Gill, Stephen. 1995. "Globalisation, Market Civilisation, and Disciplinary Neo-liberalism." *Millennium: Journal of International Studies*. Winter 24(3).

Hodson, Charles. 2005. "CNN: On-going Coverage of the London Bombings." CNN, aired July 8.

Hoover, Kenneth. 2001. "Investor Fear Tears through Market as Stocks Drop, Recover, and Drop Again." *Investor's Business Daily*, September 24: A1.

Howlett, Karen. 2001 "U.S. Brokers Need Time to Heal." *The Globe and Mail*, September 13: B1 and B10.

Huntington, Samuel P. 1993. The Clash of Civilizations. *Foreign Affairs*, Summer 72(3): 22–49.

———. 1996. *The Clash of Civilizations and the Remaking of World Order*. 1st ed. New York: Simon & Schuster.

Ibbitson, John. 2001a. "Bush Says U.S. Winning 'War to Save Civilization.'" *The Globe and Mail*, November 9: A1.

———. 2001b. "Tearful Bush Makes Pledge." *The Globe and Mail*, September 14.

Invest in US. 2001. "Investment Campaign—Downloadable Posters." http://www.Investinus.org/flash/index.cfm. Accessed December 20, 2001.

Jang, Brent. 2001. "Profiting Seems Unsavoury in Tragic Times Such as These." *The Globe and Mail*, September 17: B10.

Keynes, John M. 1936. *The General Theory of Employment, Interest and Money*. London: Macmillan.

Kindleberger, Charles P. 1978. *Manias, Panics, and Crashes*. New York: Basic Books.

Klee, Kenneth. 1990. "High Anxiety." *Institutional Investor*, December 24: 57–61.

Laise, Eleanor. 2001. "Balance of Power—Not So Long Ago, the Formula Seemed Quite Simple." *Smart Money: The Wall Street Journal Magazine of Personal Business*, 10, December: 84–94.

Le Bon, Gustave. 1896. *The Crowd: A Study of the Popular Mind*. New York: Macmillan Co.

Leo, John. 2001. "A War of Two Worlds." *U.S. News & World Report*, September 24: 47.

Lim, P. J. 2001. "A Direct Hit on the Economy." *U.S. News & World Report*, September 14: 42–43.

Lipschutz, R. D. 2000. *After Authority: War, Peace, and Global Politics in the 21st Century*. Albany: State University of New York.

Lynch, Michael. 2001. "Compassion, Courage and Strength." *The Globe and Mail*, September 17: B7.

Mayhall, Stacey. 2002. *Riding the Bull/Wrestling the Bear: Sex and Identity in the Discourses of Global Finance.* PhD dissertation, York University.

McDowell, Linda. 1994. "Gender Divisions of Labour in the Post-Fordist Economy: The Maintenance of Occupational Sex Segregation in the Financial Services Sector." *Environment & Planning.* 26(9): 1397–1419.

McDowell, Linda, and Gillian Court. 1994. "Missing Subjects: Gender, Power, and Sexuality in Merchant Banking." *Economic Geography.* 70(3).

McKenna, Barrie. 2001. "Even Alan Greenspan Can't Explain What It All Means." *The Globe and Mail*, September 21: B11.

McNish, Jacquie. 2001. "The Battlefield Is the Economy." *The Globe and Mail*, September 14: A1 and A17.

Milner, Brian. 2001. "Resilient New Yorkers, and Their City, Will Rise Again." *The Globe and Mail*, September 15: B2.

Northfield, Stephen. 2001. "Attacks Will Shake Fragile Consumer Confidence." *The Globe and Mail*, September 12: B6.

Nussbaum, Bruce. 2001. "Real Masters of the Universe." *Business Week*, October 1.

NYSE. 2002. "Let Freedom Ring." Advertising campaign aired January 2002.

Partridge, John. 2001. "Central Banks Inject Billions." *The Globe and Mail*, September 13: B3.

Pateman, Carol. 1988. *The Sexual Contract.* Stanford, CA: Stanford University Press.

———. 1992. "Feminist Critiques of the Public/Private Dichotomy. In *Public and Private in Social Life*, ed. S. Benn and G. Gaus. New York: St. Martin's Press.

Peterson, V. Spike. 1992. "Security and Sovereign States: What Is at Stake in Taking Feminism Seriously?" In *Gendered States: Feminist (Re) Visions of International Relations Theory*, ed. V. S. Peterson, Boulder, CO: Lynne Rienner, 31–64.

Picker, Ida. 1990. "Masters of the Universe." *Institutional Investor*, September: 280.

Powell, Bill. 2001. "The Economy Under Siege." *Fortune*, October 15: 86–108.

Reuters. 2001. "Bush Team Seen Changing Stance if Dollar Slumps." *The Globe and Mail*, September 17: B2.

Roston, Eric. 2001. "All His Office Mates Gone." *Time*, September 24: 79.

Safian, Robert. 2001. "Keep the Faith." *Money*, November: 77–80.

Sassen, Saskia. 1998. *Globalization and Its Discontents: Essays on the New Mobility of People and Money.* New York: New Press.

Schrage, Michael. 2001. "Enlisting Corporate America." *Fortune*, October 15: 266.

Smart Money. 2001. "The President Wants You to Buy This Magazine, a Car, Some Airline Tickets, a Computer, a New Home—and Invest in America Now!" *SmartMoney*, December Cover.

Stewart, James B. 2001. "Our Spirit Will Stand." *Smart Money: The Wall Street Journal Magazine of Personal Business*, 10 November: 27–30.

Stinson, Marian. 2001a. "BMO Economist Sees U.S. Recession." *The Globe and Mail*, September 13: B1 and B14.

———. 2001b. "Fed Shores Up European Banks." *The Globe and Mail*, September 14: B3.

Taruc, Marivel. 2005. "Bracing for a Sell-Off? Terror in London." *CBC Business Report* July 7.

Tickner, J. Ann. 1992. *Gender in International Relations: Feminist Perspectives on Achieving Global Security.* New York: Columbia University Press.

———. 2001. *Gendering World Politics.* New York: Columbia University Press.

Topps. 2001. *Enduring Freedom.* Duryea, PA: Topps.

Wall Street Journal. 2001. "The Ultimate Strength of a Free Financial Market." *The National Post* (reprinted from the *Wall Street Journal*), *Financial Post*, September 14.

Warner, Edmond. 2002. "Bear for the Very First Time." *The Guardian*, July 13. Available at http://www.guardian.co.uk/business/2002/jul/13/3. Accessed July 6, 2008.

Wolfe, Tom. 1988. *The Bonfire of the Vanities.* London: Jonathan Cape.

Zakaria, Fareed. 2001. "The End of the End of History." *Newsweek*, September 24: 70.

Contributors

FAUZIA ERFAN AHMED is at work on a book, based on her ethnographic research with Grameen Bank families in rural Bangladesh, entitled *Redefining Manhood: Masculinity, Microcredit, and Gender Empowerment*. Additional research interests include masculinity, empowerment, and microcredit; gender and Islam; and the role of the private sector in poverty alleviation. She is Assistant Professor, Sociology and Women's Studies, Miami University of Ohio.

SHARON BERNSTEIN was affiliated with University of California, Berkeley, at the time of her article's publication.

SUE L. CATALDI is Professor of Philosophy and Women's Studies at Southern Illinois University Edwardsville. She is the author of several articles on feminist and twentieth-century European philosophy and is at work on a book manuscript tentatively titled *Engendering Space*.

DORIS T. CHANG is Associate Professor of Women's Studies at Wichita State University, Kansas. Her areas of expertise include Taiwan studies and gender/women's studies, and her most recent book is *Women's Movements in Twentieth-Century Taiwan*.

JUDITH KEGAN GARDINER is Professor of English and of Gender and Women's Studies at the University of Illinois at Chicago. Her publications center on contemporary and early modern women writers as well as on feminist theories and masculinity studies. She is a member of the editorial collective of the interdisciplinary journal *Feminist Studies* and coeditor of the series *Global Masculinities* (Palgrave). Forthcoming essays concern female masculinity and transmen.

SARAH HANLY is a clinical psychologist at Cardinal Glennon Children's Medical Center in St. Louis, Missouri. Her clinical interests include learning disabilities and mood, anxiety, and eating disorders. She works with children, adolescents, and their families and as the psychology liaison on the Eating and Feeding Disorders teams.

BERNICE L. HAUSMAN is professor of English at Virginia Tech, where she coordinates the undergraduate minor in Medicine and Society. She has authored several books, most recently *Viral Mothers: Breastfeeding in the Age of HIV/AIDS*, as well as several journal articles on breastfeeding, medicine, and public culture.

CRESSIDA J. HEYES is Professor of Philosophy and Canada Research Chair in Philosophy of Gender and Sexuality at the University of Alberta, Canada. She is the author of several books and most recently coedited *Cosmetic Surgery: A Feminist Primer*. Visit www.cressida heyes.com.

TIFFANY JOSEPH is an independent scholar and freelance writer. Her interests include nineteenth- and twentieth-century American literature, culture, and film. Recently, she has been examining both popular and canonical literature within a history of transportation to understand how the railroad functioned as both site and symbol of the contradictions and tensions of modernization, democracy, and (im)mobility. Her latest publication is an article in *Post Script* examining the use of reality and fantasy in Joel and Ethan Coen's films.

An interdisciplinary scholar focusing on the rise of the Right since the 1960s, CAROL MASON is a professor of Gender and Women's Studies at University of Kentucky. She is the author of *Killing for Life: The Apocalyptic Narrative of Pro-life Politics* and *Reading Appalachia from Left to Right: Conservatives and the 1974 Kanawha County Textbook Controversy*, and is the recipient of fellowships from the Rockefeller Foundation for the Humanities and the Bunting Institute.

STACEY L. MAYHALL earned her doctorate in political science in 2003 at York University, Toronto, Canada. Her research and teaching specializations include gender and politics, international political economy, and international relations. Executive director of the AIDS Committee of North Bay and Area in Northern Ontario, Dr. Mayhall teaches in the Gender Equality and Social Justice Department at Nipissing University. An active member of the feminist and LGBT communities, she is a strong supporter of social justice projects that integrate local, regional, national, and global concerns. Send correspondence to stacey. mayhall@gmail.com.

LINDA PERSHING is Professor of Women's Studies at California State University San Marcos and director of a research project on U.S. military violence against women (see http://www.usmvaw.com). Her research focuses on the politics of culture and feminist folklore studies, with a focus on the politics of gender in war and peace, particularly on women's activism in contemporary peace movements.

CELIA ROBERTS is a Senior Lecturer in the Department of Sociology, Lancaster University, United Kingdom. She works on several projects in the area of feminist science studies: one on biomedical, environmental, and popular discourses of early puberty; another on birth-related activism; and a third on new technologies of care for older people living at home. She is the author of *Messengers of Sex: Hormones, Biomedicine and Feminism* and is an editor of *Feminist Theory*.

David Schweickart is Professor of Philosophy at Loyola University Chicago. His research focuses on issues at the intersection of economics and philosophy and on philosophical questions concerning race and gender. An updated, revised edition of his most recent book, *After Capitalism*, is scheduled to appear in 2011.

Jeanne Sevelius, PhD, is an Assistant Professor with the Center for AIDS Prevention Studies (www.caps.ucsf.edu) in the Department of Medicine at University of California, San Francisco, and Co-Principal Investigator of the Center of Excellence for Transgender Health (www .transhealth.ucsf.edu), which promotes increased access to culturally competent health care for transgender people through research, training, and policy advocacy efforts. Dr. Sevelius is the Principal Investigator of an NIH/NIMH-funded project to assess HIV risk behaviors and protective factors among transgender women of color to develop a culturally specific HIV prevention intervention for this high-risk, underserved population.

Diane Shoos is Associate Professor of Visual Studies and French in the Humanities Department at Michigan Technological University. She teaches and publishes on cinema and gender and visual representation. Shoos is completing a book on film representations of domestic violence.

Dr. Jayne E. Stake received her doctorate in Clinical Psychology at Arizona State University in 1974 and served on the faculty of the Department of Psychology at the University of Missouri–St. Louis for 33 years. She has published extensively in the area of Psychology of Women, is a fellow in the Society for the Psychology of Women, and is past editor of the journal *Psychology of Women*. Her research has focused on gender issues in self-concept and achievement, the link between gender roles and well-being, and interventions for the empowerment of women. She is currently professor emeritus at the University of Missouri–St. Louis.

Diane Suter was affiliated with Loyola University Chicago at the time of her article's publication.

Mary Ann Tétreault is Una Chapman Cox Distinguished Professor of International Affairs at Trinity University, San Antonio, Texas. She is the author, editor, and coeditor of many books, most recently *Global Politics as if People Mattered*.

Index

Other Books Available in the Series

Diversity and Women's Health
edited by Sue V. Rosser

Feminist Pedagogy: Looking Back to Move Forward
edited by Robbin D. Crabtree, David Allan Sapp,
and Adela C. Licona

*Being and Becoming Visible: Women, Performance,
and Visual Culture*
edited by Olga M. Mesropova and Stacey Weber-Fève